Introduction
to
Literature

British
American
Canadian

Preface

This anthology is intended primarily to serve the needs of students taking introductory English courses in Canadian universities and colleges. It is the first multi-genre anthology to contain Canadian as well as American and British writing, and, in fact, the perceived need for Canadian material in such an anthology provided the impetus for this text. Although there is no attempt either to compare one national literature with another or to separate Canadian works from other writing in the general arrangement, the Canadian selections can readily be identified by a reference to the index by nationality. Because many students are unlikely to pursue the study of English literature beyond their freshman year, the anthology provides a core of general reading to aid in developing critical faculties and writing skills rather than a representative choice of introductory works for majors in English literature.

We have aimed to be both concise and comprehensive. The modest length of the anthology makes it a handy and unintimidating volume to carry to the classroom, yet the selections from three literary genres — essays, poetry, and short stories — are diverse. An attempt has been made to combine more recent works (Bil Gilbert's "Fast as an Elephant, Strong as an Ant," Gwendolyn MacEwen's "Flight One," and Audrey Thomas' "Initram," for example) with standard anthology pieces. In every case the criteria of our choice have been the needs of students in an introductory course. The essays, for example, are included not only to allow students to examine several forms of composition, but also to give them a sampling of various ways of talking about language. Hence the views of prominent writers on the complexities of their own art. In the selection of poetry, on the other hand, some outstanding writers have been either partially represented or omitted altogether on the grounds that they need to be studied within a broader literary context than is possible in a course that emphasizes the development of general language skills. We have attempted to include works that will stimulate the maximum interest in discussion without detailed recourse to either historical or literary background. Since the length of the anthology necessitates the omission of both drama and novels, teachers may find it convenient to select texts from these genres to supplement the shorter works. Alternatively, the anthology could be used for a one-semester course in English literature.

Recognizing that English teachers differ widely in matters of pedagogy, we have tried to anticipate some of the more common teaching methods in our selection and arrangement of material. The anthology has obviously been heavily influenced by the genre approach, with its diminished use of an historical framework and its increased emphasis on both close reading of individual texts and practical understanding of technical devices and conventions. However, we also recognize that some of the aims of historically oriented courses are highly desirable, and we have retained the option of an historical approach to poetry by a chronological ordering of the poems according to authors' dates of birth. The essays and short stories do not have a sufficiently broad historical sweep to be similarly treated, although for the sake of convenience and consistency the chronological ordering has been kept here as well. We have deliberately avoided the grouping of selections according to theme, a mode favoured by some anthologists. Such an arrangement, we felt, tends to be too narrowly suggestive.

We make no apology for inclusions or exclusions. There is, moreover, no attempt to suggest that any one selection is in any way representative of either its author or its literary period. It would be ludicrous to suggest, for example, that a single sonnet by John Milton could give any indication of Milton's importance as a poet or even be typical of late seventeenth-century poetry; nor does the omission of, say, poems by Dryden indicate a failure on our part to recognize his achievement in this same period. It is impossible, especially in a short anthology, to be exhaustive. Nevertheless, there is enough material in this book to spark excitement, amusement, and interest and to enhance the study of language.

The editors wish to acknowledge the valuable advice and assistance given by members of Saint Mary's University Department of English. In particular we thank Janet Baker for her contributions to the anthology in its formative stages; Kathleen Tudor and Lilian Falk for assistance with proofreading and annotations; and Deborah Maskell for secretarial services.

Gillian Thomas
Richard J.H. Perkyns
Kenneth A. MacKinnon
Wendy R. Katz

Contents

xii *Contents*

Introduction to Short Fiction

General Introduction

At the college and university level, most introductory courses aim to enable students to become better readers and writers. Such courses must inevitably serve the needs of students with varied experiences, abilities, and knowledge: some come to higher education needing quite basic training in language skills, while others come well equipped to read critically and write fluently. Introductory courses attempt both to establish and to refine the essential skills. The study of literature, in particular, helps to develop critical awareness in one's approach to language. The potential benefits of literary analysis as a means of improving one's reading and writing are many. It is virtually impossible, we believe, to acquire a fluency of style, together with a sensitivity towards the use of language, without a wide and critical reading of literary forms.

Literature brings the student into contact with a great many kinds and techniques of writing. Description, exposition, argumentation, narration, humour, satire, irony, dialogue, and invective, for example, are all encountered in literary study, and encountered, moreover, at various levels of difficulty. Literary study alerts students to the presence of these different kinds of writing and, in doing so, promises to increase their consciousness of language in all other disciplines. Studying the use of language in literature also enables students to better understand their own writing. It heightens awareness so that language can be used as a tool to say what one means, and it helps to indicate how difficult it is to say what one means. It demonstrates that language has aesthetic properties as well as utilitarian ones, a voice and texture to be heard and felt. It has, in addition, emotive properties; it has the power to move, inspire, bore, or disgust. It is a mistake to believe that literature and language must be separate subjects to be studied independently. Literature is the written language, and the best literature shows us multiple ways in which the finest writers can achieve the richest and fullest development of the art of language.

The works included in this selection of essays, poems, and stories invite numerous methods of reading. Probably there is nothing in this anthology that will make sense to a reader who uses the same technique for reading them that he or she would use to read a daily newspaper or a personal letter. Unfortunately, many students entering college or university have never considered the act of reading as anything other than a somewhat mechanical way of extracting information from the printed page. They do not generally realize the hazards of adopting similar methods for other than strictly factual texts or the most unreflective works of fiction. Indeed, a reader who uses such methods indiscriminately might also be insensitive to the writer's bias in a text that purports to be factual but is subtly slanted. Such a reader is even more at sea when confronted with a text that makes no pretense of being a factual account. Different kinds of material require radically different reading techniques, and students may run into difficulties if they employ a method of reading inappropriate to the text involved. Some attempt will be made here to discuss the

1

most common problems students have in reading and some of the fallacies with which unpractised readers approach literary texts.

Incautious or unpractised readers commonly resort to one of several fallacious reading methods. One such method is to scan the lines of the story or poem in anxious search for a "message." This approach is based on a mistaken idea of what writers do. If writers simply wanted to convey messages to the reader, they would probably be better advised to equip themselves with cans of spray paint with which to write their slogans on walls or highway bridges. Certainly most of them could be more lucratively employed in trying to send "messages" by writing public relations pieces for government departments urging us to eat the right food, keep fit, or develop a better sense of community spirit. Clearly, if writers produce poems or stories instead, we must assume that their objectives are something other than providing us with a bald message. We do not mean to give the impression that poems and stories do not convey ideas, attitudes, emotions, or political opinion, but rather that they cannot be reduced to any one of these. Such things cannot be extracted from the work as a pure distillation of its essence. The bulk of a text cannot be seen as a dispensable residue.

If readers are mistaken in searching for a message, are they equally mistaken in searching for the "meaning" of a work of literature? This is a more complex question. First of all, good readers do not really "search" for the meaning of a literary text any more than they search for a message. Although a text has an objective reality, and thus an inherent meaning, we prefer to see it as having potential for discovered significance. That is, for the individual, meaning is what occurs in the transaction between the text and the reader. Naturally, this transaction is different for each reader and we might seem to be suggesting that any interpretation arrived at by a particular reader is therefore, for that reader at least, the "right" one. Certainly any complex text can call forth a variety of valid interpretations, but no text contains an unlimited number of interpretative variables. Some interpretations will be wildly mistaken because they are based on careless rather than careful reading. An interpretation is only as valid as the evidence summoned to support it.

What, then, are the techniques that careful readers employ when confronted with materials such as the essays, poems, and stories contained in this anthology? First, rather than looking for a "message," such readers bring to the work as much knowledge and sensitivity as possible. Such readers will read the text, be it essay, poem, or story, as many times as is necessary for meaning to emerge, and they will bring to the work whatever knowledge, in the form of definitions from the dictionary, information on obscure references, and so on, that the text may require. Careful readers acknowledge the existence of, and acquaint themselves as well as they can with, basic literary conventions so as not to go astray among well-marked but unregarded signposts. A story written with a first-person narrator, for example, should not be seen as a piece of autobiographical writing. Most writers, admittedly, draw on their own observations and experiences, but these are usually absorbed in the creation of characters and incidents that then take on their own distinct identity. Besides, the technique of the first-person narrator is usually employed to indicate to the reader something about the relation of the storyteller, or narrator, to what is being told. Careful readers know that a single simple definition of what the text is "about" will not be satisfactory because each reading of the text is a process that takes the reader through a variety of changes of attitude and mood. In this way, literature of any significance is constantly fresh to us. It can stimulate and challenge us though we read it many times. For example, Audrey Thomas' story "Initram" begins with the statement "Writers are terrible liars." Clearly, that is not the "message" of "Initram," but rather it is a deliberate setting up of a state of mind in the reader. If writers are liars, in what sense can we believe the story Thomas has written? By beginning with this version of the old paradox "everything is a lie including this statement," she draws the reader into the process of reading the story swinging back and forth between doubt and belief in the narrator's truthfulness, until, frustrated by our doubts, we are drawn into examining just what the "truth" in a work of fiction might possibly be. Does it refer to a "realistic" world outside the text? Is it the created world of the text itself? Is it possibly patent ideology? Finally, even careful readers bring strongly felt ideas and attitudes, even prejudices, to a reading of a text. Readers must be alert to those influences that sway them to hold one or another interpretation, to favour a particular historical, political, or religious view of a text. Careful readers, in other words, are alert to their own strengths and limitations.

Some students who are reluctant to engage in a demanding reading process suggest that the reader who carefully examines the text is "just pulling it apart." This short-sighted description of literary analysis might seem to be a staunch defence of the integrity of the writer's work, but it is, in fact, so falsely based that it constitutes the kind of protection that most writers are glad to do without. Most often applied to poetry, it implies that the poem is so fragile and delicate that close inspection will destroy it forever. While closer examination may sometimes reveal an initially attractive poem to be sloppily written or disappointing, a close reading usually shows us more rather than less of a poem's richness and strength. The argument for leaving well enough alone also presupposes that the poem or story flashed suddenly into the writer's mind in a moment of vision and immediately appeared as if by magic on the page. However, most writers' original manuscripts show that the work has been painstakingly revised many times before reaching its final version. In the face of this long process of revision, which has produced most of the writings appearing in this anthology, readers who fear that an analytical reading will somehow destroy a poem are shying away from a process that resembles the writer's own.

A final note about literary analysis and its potential benefits to the practitioner. Outside the university, students are exposed to a great variety of written material that is read for private interest and enjoyment. Magazines, books on current affairs, best-selling novels, and the like all reach a wide audience. Usually, serious writers do not command a mass audience. A radical move away from reading altogether may be seen in the rather casual abandonment of literature by some for one or other of the popular electronic media—television, films, records. Most people, however—especially those who reach university level—read. The danger, as we see it, is not that they will abandon reading, but that their experience will be superficial. University work commits students to several years of serious reading. If, through an introductory English course, students are challenged to develop habits of critical reading and a taste for good writing, the likelihood is that not only will their entire university experience be richer, but so will their later life and work.

We do not offer any detailed interpretations because these should develop from individual and classroom experience. Although we hope that these selections can be read privately with much pleasure and profit, their choice has been largely governed by the kind of response we hope they will evoke in discussion. The importance of discussion is that students will become increasingly aware that no single method of approach dominates the study of literature, but that a wealth and variety of ideas emerge about what is being read.

We recommend the separate introductions to the three sections of this book as a guide to the study of each genre. Footnotes, though kept to a minimum, are included for quick reference and to aid ready understanding without recourse to reference books. Notes are provided for dialect or foreign phrases, obscure or difficult place names, mythological allusions, folkloric references, etc. They are intended for information and not for interpretation. Basic vocabulary found in most standard dictionaries is not included. You may wish to use the indexes by author, nationality, and titles and first lines. These supplement the general chronological ordering of the text and serve as a guide to national divisions.

Introduction to Essays

An essay may be defined as a short work of nonfiction that is unified and coherent and develops a single idea; but such a definition is only a point of departure. Even the term "nonfiction," with its disturbingly negative ring, does not do justice to the fine texture, the wit, or the intelligence of a good essay. It surely gives no hint of the pleasures to be found in this particular literary form. Since most university courses demand that students write some form of essay, be it a personal statement, a piece of literary criticism, or a history term paper, students should have the opportunity to examine various approaches to the form and to see, moreover, its intellectual and artistic power as well as its utilitarian purpose. The readings in this section show something of the scope of the form in both subject matter and presentation, and they illustrate something of the skill required to organize material, arrange paragraphs, and express oneself with accuracy, style, and variety of expression. More than anything else, they are enjoyable works of prose that whet the appetite for good writing.

Most of the essays here deal with some aspect of language. Those of Sinclair Lewis and Mordecai Richler deal specifically with the craft of writing. Both, in their different ways, show the difficulties that even experienced authors have when they sit in front of a typewriter with a blank sheet of paper; both demonstrate the self-discipline that is required and the ease with which one begins to make excuses for not getting down to the business of writing. Northrop Frye, in his essay "Culture and the National Will," looks at language in relation to history and nationality. This notable literary critic analyses in particular the dilemma facing Canadian writers in attempting to create an individual Canadian literature. Laura Bohannan's "Shakespeare in the Bush," a quite different piece on language and culture, shows some of the difficulties of telling the story of *Hamlet*, one of the world's greatest tragedies, to a people whose ideas of ghosts, of revenge, and of family relationships are startlingly different from either Bohannan's or Shakespeare's. The tradition of tragedy is examined again, this time in relation to the cultures of differing ages, in Robert Warshow's essay on the modern gangster movie.

Three essays are concerned especially with English language usage. George Orwell's practical, unadorned style in "Politics and the English Language" is one that we could do worse than emulate. At least we should not go too far wrong if we heed all his warnings, near the end of his essay, about the corruption of the language. Alleen Pace Nilsen gives many fascinating examples of linguistic disparities that are related to sex. She shows how difficult it is to establish equality of the sexes when the tradition of language works against women in particular. Bil Gilbert takes the study of language into a different milieu, that of the sports commentator, to show that figurative language often bears little relation to the facts of natural history. And M. H. Scargill looks at some of the special features of Canadian English, illustrating his essay with words derived from native roots as well as ones from British and American sources.

5

Finally we come to two of the major stylists of the English language. Whereas experienced writers may enjoy the freedom of stylistic licence in a specific context (Richler and Gilbert both use a modern, informal style complete with fragmentary sentences), the tradition of the essay is one of precision, grace, and formality. Swift and Wilde are both graceful writers and masterful satirists. "A Modest Proposal," written in a great age of satire, is widely considered one of the most brilliant pieces of ironic prose in our language, more remarkable in that, while it apparently advocates savagery, it is an expression of indignation and compassion. Oscar Wilde's essay is much lighter, but it gives us an amusing glimpse of nineteenth-century society on two continents and is written with a characteristic elegance of style, liberally adorned with the epigrams for which Wilde is celebrated.

Students who read these essays will find, among other things, that the essayist tends to have a more precise sense of a particular audience than the poet or short story writer. It is relatively rare for a poem or a short story to be written specifically for a particular publication. More often, the poem or short story finds a particular audience after publication, while the essay is frequently directed to a particular set of readers from the start. For instance, the tone and much of the substance of Frye's essay arises from its function as a speech at a graduation ceremony. In some respects its tone is formal, but Frye discusses his subject in such a way that the thread of his argument can be followed by listeners without the benefit of a printed text. Similarly, Bil Gilbert's "Fast an an Elephant, Strong as an Ant" adopts a chatty, informal tone appropriate to the popular sports magazine in which it was first published. Students will also find that essayists, like writers of fiction, are often concerned with the creation of character. Sometimes, as in the case of Jonathan Swift, essayists will create characters quite separate from themselves who advance their own distinct arguments. Sometimes they will use fictional techniques and characterize a type (as Oscar Wilde does with the 1880s American woman in London) much as novelists do. Sometimes, despite telling the reader very little about themselves (see Sinclair Lewis with his coffee by the kitchen sink), writers create dramatic interest by seeming to take you into their confidence. Even the most impersonal writers, in essays given over to the presentation of research findings, make effective use of personal asides. Alleen Pace Nilsen does this in a pleasantly unobtrusive way in her allusion to working with her husband. In all of these instances of the use of the personal we may note two important facts: the personal is never alluded to for its own sake, and it does not distract us from the main point being expressed. It is always carefully controlled and is used quite deliberately as a literary device.

The word "essay" comes from the Latin word *exagium*, which refers to the act of weighing something on scales. In one sense, then, writing an essay can be seen as the art of assessment. Certainly the essay reader tends to expect rational discussion of the subject at hand. The reader also expects the discussion to be clear, discerning, and approachable. When, in the eighteenth century, the essay became firmly established as a literary form in English, it was described by Addison as bringing "philosophy out of the closets and libraries, schools and colleges to dwell in clubs and assemblies, at tea tables, and in coffee-houses." In other words, the essay was seen as making ideas available to a popular audience. This aspect of essay writing tradition can be seen in the readings selected here. Despite the diversity of their styles and approaches, the essay writers in this section have made available their estimations, valuations, ruminations — their ideas. They have in common their attempt, through whatever means, to tease or provoke the reader into thought.

JONATHAN SWIFT

A Modest Proposal

**For Preventing the Children of Poor
People in Ireland, from Being a Burden
to Their Parents or Country; and for
Making Them Beneficial to the Public[1]**

It is a melancholy object to those who walk through this great town, or
travel in the country, when they see the streets, the roads, and cabin doors
crowded with beggars of the female sex, followed by three, four or six
children, *all in rags*, and importuning every passenger for an alms. These
mothers, instead of being able to work for their honest livelihood, are
forced to employ all their time in strolling, to beg sustenance for their
helpless infants, who, as they grow up, either turn thieves for want of
work, or leave their dear native country to fight for the Pretender in
Spain,[2] or sell themselves to the Barbados.[3]

I think it is agreed by all parties that this prodigious number of
children in the arms, or on the backs, or at the heels of their mothers, and
frequently of their fathers, is in the present deplorable state of the kingdom a very great additional grievance; and therefore whoever could find
out a fair, cheap, and easy method of making these children sound and
useful members of the commonwealth would deserve so well of the public
as to have his statue set up for a preserver of the nation.

But my intention is very far from being confined to provide only for
the children of professed beggars; it is of a much greater extent, and shall
take in the whole number of infants at a certain age who are born of parents
in effect as little able to support them as those who demand our charity in
the streets.

As to my own part, having turned my thoughts, for many years, upon
this important subject, and maturely weighed the several schemes of other
projectors, I have always found them grossly mistaken in their computa-
tion. It is true a child, just dropped from its dam, may be supported by her
milk for a solar year with little other nourishment, at most not above the
value of two shillings, which the mother may certainly get, or the value in
scraps, by her lawful occupation of begging: and it is exactly at one year old
that I propose to provide for them, in such a manner as, instead of being a
charge upon their parents, or the parish, or wanting food and raiment for
the rest of their lives, they shall, on the contrary, contribute to the feeding
and partly to the clothing of many thousands.

There is likewise another great advantage in my scheme, that it will

---

1. This essay, written in 1729, was inspired by
the Irish crop failure of 1727 and of the following years.
2. James, the Old Pretender (1688–1766), son
of the deposed James II of England, claimant
to the English and Scottish thrones. Irish
Catholics were recruited to fight against England in the French and Spanish armies. Irish

troops were involved in an unsuccessful exped-
ition planned in 1719 by Cardinal Alberoni of
Spain to restore the Pretender to the English
throne.
3. There was an unusually large increase in
Irish emigration 1726–29, especially to the
West Indies.

prevent those voluntary abortions, and that horrid practice of women murdering their bastard children, alas, too frequent among us; sacrificing the poor innocent babes, I doubt, more to avoid the expense than the shame; which would move tears and pity in the most savage and inhuman breast.

The number of souls in Ireland being usually reckoned one million and a half, of these I calculate there may be about two hundred thousand couples whose wives are breeders; from which number I subtract thirty thousand couples who are able to maintain their own children, although I apprehend[4] there cannot be so many under the present distresses of the kingdom; but this being granted, there will remain an hundred and seventy thousand breeders. I again subtract fifty thousand for those women who miscarry, or whose children die by accident or disease within the year. There only remain an hundred and twenty thousand children of poor parents, annually born: The question therefore is, how this number shall be reared, and provided for; which, as I have already said, under the present situation of affairs, is utterly impossible by all the methods hitherto proposed: for we can neither employ them in handicraft, or agriculture; we neither build houses (I mean in the country), nor cultivate land:[5] they can very seldom pick up a livelihood by stealing until they arrive at six years old, except where they are of towardly parts,[6] although, I confess they learn the rudiments much earlier, during which time they can however be properly looked upon only as *probationers;* as I have been informed by a principal gentleman in the County of Cavan,[7] who protested to me that he never knew above one or two instances under the age of six, even in a part of the kingdom so renowned for the quickest proficiency in that art.

I am assured by our merchants that a boy or a girl, before twelve years old, is no saleable commodity, and even when they come to this age, they will not yield above three pounds, or three pounds and half a crown at most on the Exchange;[8] which cannot turn to account either to the parents or kingdom, the charge of nutriment and rags having been at least four times that value.

I shall now therefore humbly propose my own thoughts, which I hope will not be liable to the least objection.

I have been assured by a very knowing American of my acquaintance in London, that a young healthy child well nursed is at a year old a most delicious, nourishing, and wholesome food, whether stewed, roasted, baked, or boiled; and I make no doubt that it will equally serve in a fricassee or a ragout.

I do therefore humbly offer it to public consideration, that of the hundred and twenty thousand children already computed, twenty thousand may be reserved for breed, whereof only one-fourth part to be males; which is more than we allow to sheep, black cattle, or swine; and my reason

---

4. Am apprehensive that, anticipate with fear.
5. English legislation restricted cultivation of land, reducing Ireland's capacity for producing food.

6. Fitting ability.
7. One of three counties of the old province of Ulster, now part of the Irish Republic.
8. Building where merchants assembled to transact business.

is that these children are seldom the fruits of marriage, a circumstance not much regarded by our savages, therefore one male will be sufficient to serve four females. That the remaining hundred thousand may at a year old be offered in sale to the persons of quality, and fortune, through the kingdom; always advising the mother to let them suck plentifully in the last month, so as to render them plump, and fat for a good table. A child will make two dishes at an entertainment for friends; and when the family dines alone, the fore- or hindquarter will make a reasonable dish, and seasoned with a little pepper or salt will be very good boiled on the fourth day, especially in winter.

I have reckoned upon a medium, that a child just born will weigh twelve pounds, and in a solar year if tolerably nursed increases to twenty-eight pounds.

I grant this food will be somewhat dear, and therefore very *proper for landlords*, who, as they have already devoured most of the parents,[9] seem to have the best title to the children.

Infants' flesh will be in season throughout the year, but more plentiful in March, and a little before and after: for we are told by a grave author, an eminent French physician,[10] that fish being a prolific diet, there are more children born in Roman Catholic countries about nine months after Lent than at any other season; therefore reckoning a year after Lent, the markets will be more glutted than usual, because the number of Popish infants is at least three to one in this kingdom; and therefore it will have one other collateral advantage by lessening the number of Papists[11] among us.

I have already computed the charge of nursing a beggar's child (in which list I reckon all cottagers,[12] labourers, and four-fifths of the farmers) to be about two shillings *per annum*, rags included; and I believe no gentleman would repine to give ten shillings for the carcass of a good fat child, which, as I have said, will make four dishes of excellent nutritive meat, when he hath only some particular friend or his own family to dine with him. Thus the squire will learn to be a good landlord, and grow popular among his tenants, the mother will have eight shillings net profit, and be fit for work until she produces another child.

Those who are more thrifty (*as I must confess the times require*) may flay the carcass; the skin of which, artificially dressed, will make admirable gloves for ladies, and summer boots for fine gentlemen.

As to our City of Dublin, shambles[13] may be appointed for this purpose, in the most convenient parts of it; and butchers we may be assured will not be wanting, although I rather recommend buying the children alive, and dressing them hot from the knife, as we do roasting pigs.

A very worthy person, a true lover of his country, and whose virtues I highly esteem, was lately pleased, in discoursing on this matter, to offer a refinement upon my scheme. He said that many gentlemen of this kingdom, having of late destroyed their deer, he conceived that the want of

9. Swift often attacked absentee landlords for oppression of farmers and the poor.
10. Rabelais (1494?–1553), a famous French satirist.
11. As Dean of the Anglican St. Patrick's Cathedral in Dublin, Swift scorned the Roman Catholics.
12. Agricultural labourers who would lease a cottage on or near the land they farmed.
13. Meat markets (sometimes slaughter-houses).

venison might be well supplied by the bodies of young lads and maidens, not exceeding fourteen years of age, nor under twelve; so great a number of both sexes in every country being now ready to starve, for want of work and service: and these to be disposed of by their parents if alive, or otherwise by their nearest relations. But with due deference to so excellent a friend, and so deserving a patriot, I cannot be altogether in his sentiments. For as to the males, my American acquaintance assured me from frequent experience that their flesh was generally tough and lean, like that of our schoolboys, by continual exercise, and their taste disagreeable, and to fatten them would not answer the charge. Then as to the females, it would, I think with humble submission, be a loss to the public, because they soon would become breeders themselves: And besides, it is not improbable that some scrupulous people might be apt to censure such a practice (although indeed very unjustly) as a little bordering upon cruelty; which, I confess, hath always been with me the strongest objection against any project, how well soever intended.

But in order to justify my friend, he confessed that this expedient was put into his head by the famous Psalmanazar,[14] a native of the island Formosa, who came from thence to London, above twenty years ago, and in conversation told my friend that in his country when any young person happened to be put to death, the executioner sold the carcass to persons of quality, as a prime dainty; and that, in his time, the body of a plump girl of fifteen, who was crucified for an attempt to poison the emperor, was sold to his Imperial Majesty's Prime Minister of State, and other great mandarins of the court, in joints from the gibbet, at four hundred crowns. Neither indeed can I deny that if the same use were made of several plump young girls in this town, who, without one single groat[15] to their fortunes, cannot stir abroad without a chair,[16] and appear at a playhouse, and assemblies in foreign fineries, which they never will pay for, the kingdom would not be the worse.

Some persons of a desponding spirit are in great concern about that vast number of poor people, who are aged, diseased, or maimed; and I have been desired to employ my thoughts what course may be taken to ease the nation of so grievous an encumbrance. But I am not in the least pain upon that matter, because it is very well known that they are every day dying, and rotting, by cold, and famine, and filth, and vermin, as fast as can be reasonably expected. And as to the younger labourers they are now in almost as hopeful a condition. They cannot get work, and consequently pine away for want of nourishment, to a degree, that if at any time they are accidentally hired to common labour, they have not strength to perform it; and thus the country and themselves are in a fair way of being soon delivered from the evils to come.

I have too long digressed, and therefore shall return to my subject. I think the advantages by the proposal which I have made are obvious and many, as well as of the highest importance.

14. A literary imposter (1679?-1763), born in southern France, who posed as a Formosan and wrote a description of the island. Later he reformed and became a Hebraic scholar.

15. Small coin, obsolete by Swift's day. Figuratively, very little money.
16. Sedan chair.

For first, as I have already observed, it would greatly lessen the number of Papists, with whom we are yearly overrun, being the principal breeders of the nation, as well as our most dangerous enemies; and who stay at home on purpose with a design to deliver the kingdom to the Pretender; hoping to take their advantage by the absence of so many good Protestants, who have chosen rather to leave their country than stay at home, and pay tithes against their conscience to an idolatrous Episcopal curate.[17]

Secondly, The poorer tenants will have something valuable of their own, which by law may be made liable to distress, and help to pay their landlord's rent, their corn and cattle being already seized, and *money a thing unknown*.

Thirdly, Whereas the maintenance of an hundred thousand children, from two years old, and upwards, cannot be computed at less than ten shillings apiece *per annum*, the nation's stock will be thereby increased fifty thousand pounds *per annum*; besides the profit of a new dish, introduced to the tables of all gentlemen of fortune in the kingdom, who have any refinement in taste; and the money will circulate among ourselves, the goods being entirely of our own growth and manufacture.

Fourthly, The constant breeders, besides the gain of eight shillings sterling *per annum*, by the sale of their children, will be rid of the charge of maintaining them after the first year.

Fifthly, This food would likewise bring great custom to taverns, where the vintners will certainly be so prudent as to procure the best receipts for dressing it to perfection, and consequently have their houses frequented by all the fine gentlemen, who justly value themselves upon their knowledge in good eating; and a skillful cook, who understands how to oblige his guests, will contrive to make it as expensive as they please.

Sixthly, This would be a great inducement to marriage, which all wise nations have either encouraged by rewards, or enforced by laws and penalties. It would increase the care and tenderness of mothers toward their children, when they were sure of a settlement for life, to the poor babes, provided in some sort by the public to their annual profit instead of expense. We should see an honest emulation[18] among the married women, *which of them could bring the fattest child to the market*. Men would become as fond of their wives, during the time of pregnancy, as they are now of their mares in foal, their cows in calf, or sows when they are ready to farrow; nor offer to beat or kick them (as it is too frequent a practice) for fear of a miscarriage.

Many other advantages might be enumerated. For instance, the addition of some thousand carcasses in our exportation of barrelled beef; the propagation of swine's flesh, and improvement in the art of making good bacon, so much wanted among us by the great destruction of pigs, too frequent at our tables, and are no way comparable in taste or magnificence to a well-grown, fat yearling child, which roasted whole will make a considerable figure at a Lord Mayor's feast, or any other public entertainment. But this and many others I omit, being studious of brevity.

17. Nonconformist Protestants, claiming freedom of conscience, often resisted payment of tithes to the Established Anglican Church.
18. Rivalry.

Supposing that one thousand families in this city would be constant customers for infants' flesh, besides others who might have it at merry-meetings, particularly at weddings and christenings, I compute that Dublin would take off annually about twenty thousand carcasses, and the rest of the kingdom (where probably they will be sold somewhat cheaper) the remaining eighty thousand.

I can think of no one objection that will possibly be raised against this proposal, unless it should be urged that the number of people will be thereby much lessened in the kingdom. This I freely own, and it was indeed one principal design in offering it to the world. I desire the reader will observe, that I calculate my remedy *for this one individual Kingdom of Ireland, and for no other that ever was, is, or, I think, ever can be upon earth*. Therefore let no man talk to me of other expedients.[19] *Of taxing our absentees at five shillings a pound: Of using neither clothes, nor household furniture, except what is of our own growth and manufacture: Of utterly rejecting the materials and instruments that promote foreign luxury: Of curing the expensiveness of pride, vanity, idleness, and gaming in our women: Of introducing a vein of parsimony, prudence, and temperance: Of learning to love our Country, wherein we differ even from* LAPLAN-DERS, *and the inhabitants of* TOPINAMBOO:[20] *Of quitting our animosities and factions, nor act any longer like the Jews, who were murdering one another at the very moment their city was taken: Of being a little cautious not to sell our country and consciences for nothing: Of teaching landlords to have at least one degree of mercy toward their tenants*. Lastly, *of putting a spirit of honesty, industry, and skill into our shopkeepers, who, if a resolution could now be taken to buy our native goods, would immediately unite to cheat and exact upon us in the price, the measure, and the goodness; nor could ever yet be brought to make one fair proposal of just dealing, though often and earnestly invited to it*.

Therefore I repeat, let no man talk to me of these and the like expedients; until he hath at least a glimpse of hope that there will ever be some hearty and sincere attempt to put them in practice.

But as to myself, having been wearied out for many years with offering vain, idle, visionary thoughts, and at length utterly despairing of success, I fortunately fell upon this proposal, which as it is wholly new, so it hath something *solid* and *real*, of no expense and little trouble, full in our own power, and whereby we can incur no danger in *disobliging* ENGLAND. For this kind of commodity will not bear exportation, the flesh being of too tender a consistence to admit a long continuance in salt; *although perhaps I could name a country*[21] *which would be glad to eat up our whole nation without it*.

After all I am not so violently bent upon my own opinion as to reject any offer, proposed by wise men, which shall be found equally innocent, cheap, easy, and effectual. But before something of that kind shall be advanced in contradiction to my scheme, and offering a better, I desire the author, or authors, will be pleased maturely to consider two points. First,

19. Swift's own serious suggestions for improving Ireland's economic situation, as proposed in some of his other tracts.

20. An area in Brazil.

21. England.

as things now stand, how they will be able to find food and raiment for an hundred thousand useless mouths and backs. And secondly, there being a round million of creatures in human figure, throughout this kingdom, whose whole subsistence put into a common stock would leave them in debt two millions of pounds sterling; adding those, who are beggars by profession, to the bulk of farmers, cottagers, and labourers with their wives and children, who are beggars in effect; I desire those politicians, who dislike my overture, and may perhaps be so bold to attempt an answer, that they will first ask the parents of these mortals whether they would not at this day think it a great happiness to have been sold for food at a year old, in the manner I prescribe, and thereby have avoided such a perpetual scene of misfortunes as they have since gone through; by the oppression of landlords; the impossibility of paying rent without money or trade; the want of common sustenance, with neither house nor clothes to cover them from the inclemencies of the weather; and the most inevitable prospect of entailing the like, or greater miseries upon their breed forever.

I profess in the sincerity of my heart that I have not the least personal interest in endeavouring to promote this necessary work, having no other motive than the *public good of my country, by advancing our trade, providing for infants, relieving the poor, and giving some pleasure to the rich.* I have no children by which I can propose to get a single penny; the youngest being nine years old, and my wife past childbearing.

OSCAR WILDE

Americans in London

A terrible danger is hanging over the Americans in London. Their future and their reputation this season depend entirely on the success of Buffalo Bill and Mrs. Brown-Potter. The former is certain to draw; for English people are far more interested in American barbarism than they are in American civilisation. When they sight Sandy Hook they look to their rifles and ammunition; and, after dining once at Delmonico's, start off for Colorado or California, for Montana or the Yellow Stone Park. Rocky Mountains charm them more than riotous millionaires; they have been known to prefer buffaloes to Boston. Why should they not? The cities of America are inexpressibly tedious. The Bostonians take their learning too sadly; culture with them is an accomplishment rather than an atmosphere; their 'Hub,' as they call it, is the paradise of prigs. Chicago is a sort of monster-shop, full of bustle and bores. Political life at Washington is like political life in a suburban vestry. Baltimore is amusing for a week, but Philadelphia is dreadfully provincial; and though one can dine in New York one could not dwell there. Better the Far West with its grizzly bears and its untamed cow-boys, its free open-air life and its free open-air manners, its boundless prairie and its boundless mendacity! This is what Buffalo Bill is going to bring to London; and we have no doubt that London will fully appreciate his show.

With regard to Mrs. Brown-Potter, as acting is no longer considered absolutely essential for success on the English stage, there is really no reason why the pretty bright-eyed lady who charmed us all last June by her merry laugh and her nonchalant ways, should not—to borrow an expression from her native language—make a big boom and paint the town red. We sincerely hope she will; for, on the whole, the American invasion has done English society a great deal of good. American women are bright, clever, and wonderfully cosmopolitan. Their patriotic feelings are limited to an admiration for Niagara and a regret for the Elevated Railway; and, unlike the men, they never bore us with Bunkers Hill. They take their dresses from Paris and their manners from Piccadilly, and wear both charmingly. They have a quaint pertness, a delightful conceit, a native self-assertion. They insist on being paid compliments and have almost succeeded in making Englishmen eloquent. For our aristocracy they have an ardent admiration; they adore titles and are a permanent blow to Republican principles. In the art of amusing men they are adepts, both by nature and education, and can actually tell a story without forgetting the point—an accomplishment that is extremely rare among the women of other countries. It is true that they lack repose and that their voices are somewhat harsh and strident when they land first at Liverpool; but after a time one gets to love these pretty whirlwinds in petticoats that sweep so recklessly through society and are so agitating to all duchesses who have daughters. There is something fascinating in their funny, exaggerated gestures and their petulant way of tossing the head. Their eyes have no magic nor mystery in them, but they challenge us for combat; and when we engage we are always worsted. Their lips seem made for laughter and yet they never grimace. As for their voices, they soon get them into tune. Some of them have been known to acquire a fashionable drawl in two seasons; and after they have been presented to Royalty they all roll their R's as vigorously as a young equerry or an old lady-in-waiting. Still, they never really lose their accent; it keeps peeping out here and there, and when they chatter together they are like a bevy of peacocks. Nothing is more amusing than to watch two American girls greeting each other in a drawing-room or in the Row.[1] They are like children with their shrill staccato cries of wonder, their odd little exclamations. Their conversation sounds like a series of exploding crackers; they are exquisitely incoherent and use a sort of primitive, emotional language. After five minutes they are left beautifully breathless and look at each other half in amusement and half in affection. If a stolid young Englishman is fortunate enough to be introduced to them he is amazed at their extraordinary vivacity, their electric quickness of repartee, their inexhaustible store of curious catchwords. He never really understands them, for their thoughts flutter about with the sweet irresponsibility of butterflies; but he is pleased and amused and feels as if he were in an aviary. On the whole, American girls have a wonderful charm and, perhaps, the chief secret of their charm is that they never talk seriously except about amusements. They have, however, one grave fault — their mothers. Dreary as were those old Pilgrim Fathers who left our shores more than two centuries ago to found a New England beyond seas, the Pilgrim Mothers who have returned to us in the nineteenth century are drearier still.

Here and there, of course, there are exceptions, but as a class they are either dull, dowdy or dyspeptic. It is only fair to the rising generation of America to state that they are not to blame for this. Indeed, they spare no pains at all to bring up their parents properly and to give them a suitable, if somewhat late, education. From its earliest years every American child spends most of its time in correcting the faults of its father and mother; and no one who has had the opportunity of watching an American family on the deck of an Atlantic steamer, or in the refined seclusion of a New York boarding-house, can fail to have been struck by this characteristic of their civilisation. In America the young are always ready to give to those who are older than themselves the full benefits of their inexperience. A boy of only eleven or twelve years of age will firmly but kindly point out to his father his defects of manner or temper; will never weary of warning him against extravagance, idleness, late hours, unpunctuality, and the other temptations to which the aged are so particularly exposed; and sometimes, should he fancy that he is monopolising too much of the conversation at dinner, will remind him, across the table, of the new child's adage, 'Parents should be seen, not heard.' Nor does any mistaken idea of kindness prevent the little American girl from censuring her mother whenever it is necessary. Often, indeed, feeling that a rebuke conveyed in the presence of

1. Rotten Row, a track in Hyde Park for
horse-riding exercise, frequented by
nineteenth-century London society.

others is more truly efficacious than one merely whispered in the quiet of the nursery, she will call the attention of perfect strangers to her mother's general untidiness, her want of intellectual Boston conversation, immoderate love of iced water and green corn, stinginess in the matter of candy, ignorance of the usages of the best Baltimore society, bodily ailments and the like. In fact, it may be truly said that no American child is ever blind to the deficiencies of its parents, no matter how much it may love them.

Yet, somehow, this educational system has not been so successful as it deserved. In many cases, no doubt, the material with which the children had to deal was crude and incapable of real development; but the fact remains that the American mother is a tedious person. The American father is better, for he is never seen in London. He passes his life entirely in Wall Street and communicates with his family once a month by means of a telegram in cipher. The mother, however, is always with us, and, lacking the quick imitative faculty of the younger generation, remains uninteresting and provincial to the last. In spite of her, however, the American girl is always welcome. She brightens our dull dinner parties for us and makes life go pleasantly by for a season. In the race for coronets she often carries off the prize; but, once she has gained the victory, she is generous and forgives her English rivals everything, even their beauty.

Warned by the example of her mother that American women do not grow old gracefully, she tries not to grow old at all and often succeeds. She has exquisite feet and hands, is always *bien chaussée et bien gantée*[2] and can talk brilliantly upon any subject, provided that she knows nothing about it.

Her sense of humour keeps her from the tragedy of a *grande passion*, and, as there is neither romance nor humility in her love, she makes an excellent wife. What her ultimate influence on English life will be it is difficult to estimate at present; but there can be no doubt that, of all the factors that have contributed to the social revolution of London, there are few more important, and none more delightful, than the American Invasion.

2. Well shod and well gloved.

SINCLAIR LEWIS

How I Wrote a Novel on Trains and beside the Kitchen Sink

I have a philosophical principle, a handy and portable key to achievement, for the twenty or thirty million young Americans who at the present second are wondering how they can attain it. It applies to shoemakers as much as to authors. It is: Six times one equals six. It sounds simple and rather foolish, and it is harder to carry out than an altitude flight.

Being a professional writer, not a good one but quite a hard-working one, I hear at least once a week: "What's the trick? How can I break into the magazine game? I want to write. I've been reading your stuff, and I think I could do something like it. What must I do?"

My first answer is: "Well, you can save a great deal of time by not reading my stuff. Read Thomas Hardy, Conrad, Anatole France. Or, if you want the younger men, look at Joseph Hergesheimer, James Branch Cabell, Henry Mencken; and all of these astonishing young Englishmen — Walpole, Maugham, Cannan, Lawrence, and the rest."

The achievement hunter ferrets an ancient envelope out of his pocket and solemnly notes down the names, as though they were magic formulas, and I have a private fit of despair in the most convenient corner, because young men who solemnly note down things rarely put their notes into life. And, to defend my own sex, let me say that frequently the young man in question is a young woman. One out of every three women of any leisure will, without much pressing, confide that she "wants to write" — not to write anything in particular, but just write.

After restoring the annotated envelope to a pocket where it will be lost for keeps, he, or she, confides that he — confound those pronouns — they confide that they are peculiar, quite different from all other humans, because, by the most extraordinary circumstances, they "haven't much time."

The young newspaperman boasts that after a night at the grind he is tired. And he says it with a haughty air of being the only person on the entire earth and suburban planets who works hard enough to get tired. And a young married woman tranquilly asserts that after a conference with cook, a bridge-tea, labouring at eating dinner, and watching the nurse put baby to bed, she is so exhausted that she cannot possibly carry out her acute ambition to write.

I want to add to recorded history the fact that there is no patent on being tired and no monopoly in it. Several people have been tired since the days of Assyria. It is not so novel a state that it is worth much publicity. When I hear of a marvellous new case of it on the part of a yearner, I sigh:

"But do you really want to write?"

"Oh, yessssss!"

"Why?"

"Oh, it must be such a fascinating life."

"Huh!" the boorish professional grunts, "I don't see anything very fascinating about sitting before a typewriter six or seven hours a day."

"Oh, yes, but the—the joy of self-expression, and the fame."

"Fame! Huh! I'll lay you nine to one that if Rudyard Kipling and Jack Dempsey arrived on the same train, Kipling wouldn't even be able to hire a taxi."

"I don't *care*," the yearner insists. "I think my present life is intolerably dull, and I do want to write."

"Very well, then. I'll tell you the trick. You have to do only one thing: Make black marks on white paper. That little detail of writing is one that is neglected by almost all the aspirants I meet."

He—and especially she—is horribly disappointed by my cynicism. He —and often she—finds nothing interesting in making marks on paper. What he, she, it, they, and sometimes W and Y, want to do is to sit dreaming purple visions, and have them automatically appear: (1) on a manuscript; (2) on a cheque from the editor. So he, and the rest of the pronouns, usually finds the same clever excuse:

"But I simply can't seem to find the time. Oh, I just lonnnnnnnnnng to write, but when I sit down to it, someone always comes and disturbs me, and I'm so tired, and—Well, I always tell Adolphus that some day I'll have six months free, and I'll devote them to writing, and then I just know I'll succeed. I always say to Dolph, I know I can write better stuff than I read in all these magazines."

"Look here. Could you get an hour free every day?"

After a certain amount of bullying, they usually admit the hour. The newspaper reporter who desires to follow Irv Cobb[1] confesses that he could make use of an hour while he is waiting for an assignment. The young housewife who wishes to produce a volume of fairy-stories for children— and 96.3 per cent of all young housewives do so wish—grants that if she hustled a little with her sewing and marketing and telephoning to other housewives, she could have an hour free.

"All right!" the discouraging philosopher concludes, "an hour a day for six days is six hours a week, twenty-five or so hours a month. Anybody who is not deaf, blind, and addicted to *dementia præcox*, can write between a hundred and a thousand words an hour. Making it a minimum of a hundred, you can do five thousand words in two months—and that is a fair-sized short story. At the maximum of a thousand, you could do a short story in a week.

"Very few writers produce more than one short story a month, in the long average, though they can use as much as they wish of twenty-four hours a day. That is because they become wearied of invention, of planning new stories; must spur themselves by the refreshment and recreation of real life. But that real life you are getting all day. You have, as far as time goes, just as much chance as they. If you concentrate an hour a day you can produce somewhere between half as much as, and four times as much as, a professional writer.

1. Irvin S. Cobb (1876–1944), a noted New York journalist and columnist who was best known for humorous stories reflecting his Kentucky background.

"Providing always — providing you can write. And providing you have enough will-power to use your ability. And providing you stop deceiving yourself about not having the time!"

Six times one is six, in hours as much as in the potatoes which William is always selling to John in the arithmetic. But you can vary the multiplication. Of those few people who cannot control an hour a day, there are probably none above the mental grade of *moron* who cannot get in a quarter of an hour daily. If the aspirant actually is too tired at night, he can get up a quarter of an hour earlier in the morning.

If a man wrote only twenty-five words a day, but kept that up for twelve years, he would have a full-length novel. Twelve years for one novel will seem slow to the get-literary-quick yearners. Yet most good writers toil through fifteen or twenty years of apprenticeship before they succeed, and a scholar thinks nothing of twenty years spent on a work of research which does well if it sells a thousand copies.

If you have it in you to produce one thundering good novel, one really big novel, just one, your place in American literature will be safe for the next hundred years. For very few even of the well-known novelists ever produce as much as one thoroughly good novel in all their lives, and still fewer produce more than one. You can rival or excel them with twenty-five words a day — if you have the ability — and *if you really want to*. If you haven't the ability, and if you don't violently want to, then you couldn't do it with twenty-four hours free every day.

But once you understand this principle, you must also grasp another thing: the need of concentration. Each daily hour must instantly hook on the hour of the day before. Concentration can be learned — and without any trick exercises. It is largely habit. The taxi-driver, calm and concentrated in traffic that would shatter an amateur, the policeman attending strictly to the crowd and ignoring the King driving by, the buttonmaker serene on the job all day long — none of them are heroic exceptions, but all of them are practising excellent concentration. It can be learned — if you want to. But for Heaven's sake, if you don't sufficiently want to, stop yearning for the almost entirely imaginary glories of the literary career.

Now, if all of this applied only to writing, it would scarce be worth recording. But it happens to apply equally to the ambition of almost every young man or woman, whether that ambition is the study of law, the designing of new types of aeroplanes — or of hats — the mastery of business detail, or gaining promotion and greater knowledge in your present work, your present office or shop.

A large percentage of people go on vaguely believing that they would like to be lawyers or executives, vaguely desiring to do something about it, vaguely talking about it, vaguely excusing themselves. And the years slip on, treacherous and swift and cruel; and by and by they are seventy, and the chance has gone — for want of understanding that six times one daily hour is six hours every week.

But let me tremulously endeavour to remove myself from the category of chest-pounding, imitate-me-and-you-will-be-successful inspiration-mongers by hastening to admit that I have had many years of laziness. I have beat the job in about all the known ways. Jack Dunnigan fired me from the San Francisco *Bulletin* because I was a rotten reporter;

and with amazing unanimity Charley Kloeber fired me from the Associated Press. But there did come a time when I desperately saw that if I was ever going to be free to write, I must—write!

I, too, 'had no time for it'. I was, by now, a rather busy editor for a publishing firm. I read manuscripts, saw authors and artists, answered telephone calls from the printer, wrote advertising, devised devilish ways of getting publicity, from nine-fifteen to five or six or seven, with forty miles a day of commuting besides. And, like the complainants of whom I complain, I was dead tired every evening—too tired to think of anything but the Krazy Kat pictures[2] and the inviting genius of the man who invented sleeping.

So I decided that I would not have time for being tired, instead of not having time for writing.

I wrote practically all of a novel on trains, and the rest of it I wrote at times when I didn't have time to write!

About one morning a week—not oftener, I confess—I had courage enough to get up an hour earlier than usual. Our Long Island bungalow took an hour to heat after the furnace had been fed; but the kitchen was warm, and before the cook arrived from her palatial mansion I got in most of an hour of writing—with the drain-board in the kitchen as my desk!

Between adjectives I made a cup of coffee on the gas range. By request, my wife did not get up to make it for me. I wanted to concentrate on the job. And I may say that no studio—I believe there are writers who have things called studios—and no Hepplewhite chairs and Spanish tapestries and Sheraton desks ever made a better environment for writing than a drain-board, with a cup of coffee steaming beside me in the sink.

There was an hour a week, at least; and that was fifty hours a year.

Commuting into New York took from thirty-five to fifty minutes. I finished the morning paper in seven or eight minutes, and after that I did not, as invariably I wanted to, gossip about golf, the water-rates, and Tammany[3] with my fellow commuters. I looked around, got ready to be queer, hauled out a plain manila filing folder, and began to write in pencil, with the folder on my knee as a desk. I got from fifty to five hundred words done almost every morning.

There are many paragraphs in *The Trail of the Hawk*—probably the only arousing ones in that not very interesting novel—which were composed in order to give a good bewildered time to some shoe merchant or broker sitting beside me in the train. At first their ponderously cautious curiosity bothered me, but as I gradually got the habit of concentration, it amused me.

Returning on the train at night, I was usually too tired to write again, but sometimes I did manage five minutes. And when I lunched alone I found that I could plan two or three days' work without having to 'find time'. I don't know that thinking about story plots took any longer than meditating on the impossibility of finding time to think about plots.

---

2. Newspaper comic strip that ran from 1916 to 1944.
3. A reference to the New York City Democratic Party machine. This political organization is derived historically from the Society of Tammany, founded in 1789, which took its name from a Delaware chief famed for his sagacity.

In the evening, after dinner and playing and loafing and perhaps reading a manuscript not finished in office hours, I could usually capture another hour or two. Oh, I didn't want to work. I was tired. I longed to go to bed. But I didn't let myself do it till midnight.

Nor did Saturday afternoon have to be devoted entirely to tramping or tennis or a swim. I compromised. I was home by one; wrote for two hours; then enjoyed ten times more the beautiful freedom of a hike across the Long Island hills.

A lot of you, my dear young friends, whose candid face I see here before me tonight—and let me say that I am always glad to get back to your beautiful little city, the loveliest spot on my entire Lyceum circuit— many of you will endeavour to avoid my prosaic principle of six times one is six by turning virtuous; by quoting some of my predecessors on this platform, and stating in pure and ringing accents that you can't write, or read law, or design frocks, or study for promotion in the office, at 6.30 a.m., on the drain-board, because that would be unfair to your present job.

I have yet to learn why excited, future-reaching, adventurous work at your real ambition should be more injurious to your job than sitting up half the night to play poker, or gossiping in a smoke-filled room till you are a pulp of aimlessness, or painstakingly cooking fudge, or yawning at a sentimental movie full of domestic virtues and kitties, or industriously reading the social column in a newspaper.

Oh, I've been guilty. I've dawdled through the movies, sat talking about things that did not interest me with people who bored me—because it was too much trouble to shake them off and go home. The last time I committed these two faults in one evening was something less than twenty-four hours before striking out these majestic chords on the type- writer.

But at least I have learned this: When I have not done the things I thought I wanted to do; if, in the future, I shall not do the things I now think I want to do, the one excuse I may *not* use is: "I can't find the time." I have, and you have, twenty-four hours a day. And that is, so far as I can find out, approximately the same amount of daily time that was granted to Michelangelo, Pasteur, Shakespeare, or Ty Cobb.

"I want to write." Well then, hang it—write!

If you decide that the one way to do the job is to do it, kindly get through it without the use of any of the following words: Pep, punch, jazz, hustle, snap, virile, and, most of all, red-blooded.

These words are the symbols of what may well be the worst fault in American philosophy—a belief that a shallow appearance of energy actu- ally is energy. In begging people to use the selvages and scraps of their time, I wish them to understand that I am not advocating the Pep creed: that religion of making a lot of noise about what you're going to do as soon as you can take time off from making a lot of noise.

There is no Pep, there is no phonographic bellowing of the cant phrases of the market-place, in a quiet, resolute desire for daily concentra- tion. In fact, the man who pounds his desk, and scatters papers all over the floor, and yells at the telephone operator, and bursts into flights of optimism, has no time to settle down to the job.

To the man with a sense of humour, this clamorous insistence on violently hustling nowhere in particular, and standing on one's hind legs to advocate that form of activity as contributing to the welfare of the nation, is simply impossible. To the man with a passionate desire for beauty, with a longing to build — whether it is to build novels or stone walls or shoes — there is only shrinking disgust at the yapping of the man whose entire creed is: "What you guys want to do is to jazz up the business and keep the iron men doing quick turnovers."

The real disciple of success is diligent about the Lord's affairs, yet he is curiously gentle. He uses his reason. And he does something more subtle than merely spending his spare quarter-hours in working for advancement. He thinks. Most people do not actively think about anything beyond the immediate details of food and the job. For it is not easy to detach one's self from pleased self-approbation and to see clearly one's relation to the round of life.

The builder, and he may be a builder in business as much as in any art, concentrates on his building, yet sees all of life expanding, as circle beyond circle of possible achievement is disclosed. He will neither whine "I can't find time," nor, at the other extreme, will he pound his own back and bellow "Oh, I'm one grand little worker." His idol is neither the young man sighing over a listless pipe, nor the human calliope. He works, persistently, swiftly, without jar.

GEORGE ORWELL

Politics and the English Language

Most people who bother with the matter at all would admit that the English language is in a bad way, but it is generally assumed that we cannot by conscious action do anything about it. Our civilization is decadent and our language — so the argument runs — must inevitably share in the general collapse. It follows that any struggle against the abuse of language is a sentimental archaism, like preferring candles to electric light or hansom cabs to aeroplanes. Underneath this lies the half-conscious belief that language is a natural growth and not an instrument which we shape for our own purposes.

Now, it is clear that the decline of a language must ultimately have political and economic causes: it is not due simply to the bad influence of this or that individual writer. But an effect can become a cause, reinforcing the original cause and producing the same effect in an intensified form, and so on indefinitely. A man may take to drink because he feels himself to be a failure, and then fail all the more completely because he drinks. It is rather the same thing that is happening to the English language. It becomes ugly and inaccurate because our thoughts are foolish, but the slovenliness of our language makes it easier for us to have foolish thoughts. The point is that the process is reversible. Modern English, especially written English, is full of bad habits which spread by imitation and which can be avoided if one is willing to take the necessary trouble. If one gets rid of these habits one can think more clearly, and to think clearly is a necessary first step towards political regeneration: so that the fight against bad English is not frivolous and is not the exclusive concern of professional writers. I will come back to this presently, and I hope that by that time the meaning of what I have said here will have become clearer. Meanwhile, here are five specimens of the English language as it is now habitually written.

These five passages have not been picked out because they are especially bad — I could have quoted far worse if I had chosen — but because they illustrate various of the mental vices from which we now suffer. They are a little below the average, but are fairly representative samples. I number them so that I can refer back to them when necessary:

[1] I am not, indeed, sure whether it is not true to say that the Milton who once seemed not unlike a seventeenth-century Shelley had not become, out of an experience ever more bitter in each year, more alien [sic]to the founder of that Jesuit sect which nothing could induce him to tolerate.
PROFESSOR HAROLD LASKI
Essay in 'Freedom of Expression'

[2] Above all, we cannot play ducks and drakes with a native battery of idioms which prescribes such egregious collocations of vocables

as the Basic *put up with* for *tolerate* or *put at a loss* for *bewilder*.
PROFESSOR LANCELOT HOGBEN
'*Interglossa*'

[3] On the one side we have the free personality: by definition it is not
neurotic, for it has neither conflict nor dream. Its desires, such as they
are, are transparent, for they are just what institutional approval
keeps in the forefront of consciousness; another institutional pattern
would alter their number and intensity; there is little in them that is
natural, irreducible, or culturally dangerous. But *on the other side*, the
social bond itself is nothing but the mutual reflection of these self-
secure integrities. Recall the definition of love. Is not this the very
picture of a small academic? Where is there a place in this hall of mirrors
for either personality or fraternity?
Essay on psychology in 'Politics' (New York)

[4] All the 'best people' from the gentlemen's clubs, and all the frantic
fascist captains, united in common hatred of Socialism and bestial
horror of the rising tide of the mass revolutionary movement, have
turned to acts of provocation, to foul incendiarism, to medieval legends
of poisoned wells, to legalize their own destruction of proletarian
organizations, and rouse the agitated petty-bourgeoisie to chauvinistic
fervour on behalf of the fight against the revolutionary way out of the
crises.
Communist pamphlet

[5] If a new spirit *is* to be infused into this old country, there is one thorny
and contentious reform which must be tackled, and that is the humani-
zation and galvanization of the B.B.C. Timidity here will bespeak
canker and atrophy of the soul. The heart of Britain may be sound and of
strong beat, for instance, but the British lion's roar at present is like
that of Bottom in Shakespeare's *Midsummer Night's Dream* — as gentle as any sucking dove. A virile new Britain cannot continue indefinitely to be traduced in the eyes, or rather ears, of the world by the
effete languors of Langham Place, brazenly masquerading as 'standard
English'. When the Voice of Britain is heard at nine o'clock, better far
and infinitely less ludicrous to hear aitches honestly dropped than the
present priggish, inflated, inhibited, school-ma'amish arch braying of
blameless bashful mewing maidens!
Letter in 'Tribune'

Each of these passages has faults of its own, but, quite apart from
avoidable ugliness, two qualities are common to all of them. The first is
staleness of imagery: the other is lack of precision. The writer either has a
meaning and cannot express it, or he inadvertently says something else, or
he is almost indifferent as to whether his words mean anything or not. This
mixture of vagueness and sheer incompetence is the most marked characteristic of modern English prose, and especially of any kind of political

writing. As soon as certain topics are raised, the concrete melts into the abstract and no one seems able to think of turns of speech that are not hackneyed: prose consists less and less of *words* chosen for the sake of their meaning, and more and more of *phrases* tacked together like the sections of a prefabricated hen-house. I list, below, with notes and examples, various of the tricks by means of which the work of prose construction is habitually dodged:

DYING METAPHORS. A newly invented metaphor assists thought by evoking a visual image, while on the other hand a metaphor which is technically 'dead' (e.g. *iron resolution*) has in effect reverted to being an ordinary word and can generally be used without loss of vividness. But in between these two classes there is a huge dump of worn-out metaphors which have lost all evocative power and are merely used because they save people the trouble of inventing phrases for themselves. Examples are: *Ring the changes on, take up the cudgels for, toe the line, ride roughshod over, stand shoulder to shoulder with, play into the hands of, no axe to grind, grist to the mill, fishing in troubled waters, rift within the lute, on the order of the day, Achilles' heel, swan song, hotbed.* Many of these are used without knowledge of their meaning (what is a 'rift', for instance?), and incompatible metaphors are frequently mixed, a sure sign that the writer is not interested in what he is saying. Some metaphors now current have been twisted out of their original meaning without those who use them even being aware of the fact. For example, *toe the line* is sometimes written *tow the line*. Another example is *the hammer and the anvil*, now always used with the implication that the anvil gets the worst of it. In real life it is always the anvil that breaks the hammer, never the other way about: a writer who stopped to think what he was saying would be aware of this, and would avoid perverting the original phrase.

OPERATORS or VERBAL FALSE LIMBS. These save the trouble of picking out appropriate verbs and nouns, and at the same time pad each sentence with extra syllables which give it an appearance of symmetry. Characteristic phrases are: *render inoperative, militate against, make contact with, be subjected to, give rise to, give grounds for, have the effect of, play a leading part (role) in, make itself felt, take effect, exhibit a tendency to, serve the purpose of,* etc., etc. The keynote is the elimination of simple verbs. Instead of being a single word, such as *break, stop, spoil, mend, kill,* a verb becomes a *phrase,* made up of a noun or adjective tacked on to some general-purpose verb such as *prove, serve, form, play, render.* In addition, the passive voice is wherever possible used in preference to the active, and noun constructions are used instead of gerunds (*by examination of* instead of *by examining*). The range of verbs is further cut down by means of the *-ize* and *de-* formations, and the banal statements are given an appearance of profundity by means of the *not un-* formation. Simple conjunctions and prepositions are replaced by such phrases as *with respect to, having regard to, the fact that, by dint of, in view of, in the interests of, on the hypothesis that,* and the ends of sentences are saved from anticlimax by such resounding commonplaces as *greatly to be desired, cannot be left out of account, a development to be expected in the near future, deserving* *of serious consideration*, *brought to a satisfactory conclusion*, and so on and so forth.

PRETENTIOUS DICTION. Words like *phenomenon, element, individual* (as noun), *objective, categorical, effective, virtual, basic, primary, promote, constitute, exhibit, exploit, utilize, eliminate, liquidate*, are used to dress up simple statements and give an air of scientific impartiality to biased judgments. Adjectives like *epoch-making, epic, historic, unforgettable, triumphant, age-old, inevitable, inexorable, veritable*, are used to dignify the sordid processes of international politics, while writing that aims at glorifying war usually takes on an archaic colour, its characteristic words being: *realm, throne, chariot, mailed fist, trident, sword, shield, buckler, banner, jackboot, clarion*. Foreign words and expression such as *cul de sac, ancien régime, deus ex machina, mutatis mutandis, status quo, gleichschaltung, weltanschauung*, are used to give an air of culture and elegance. Except for the useful abbreviations *i.e., e.g.,* and *etc.,* there is no real need for any of the hundreds of foreign phrases now current in English. Bad writers, and especially scientific, political and sociological writers, are nearly always haunted by the notion that Latin or Greek words are grander than Saxon ones, and unnecessary words like *expedite, ameliorate, predict, extraneous, deracinated, clandestine, subaqueous* and hundreds of others constantly gain ground from their Anglo-Saxon opposite numbers.[1] The jargon peculiar to Marxist writing (*hyena, hangman, cannibal, petty bourgeois, these gentry, lacquey, flunkey, mad dog, White Guard*, etc.) consists largely of words and phrases translated from Russian, German or French; but the normal way of coining a new word is to use a Latin or Greek root with the appropriate affix and, where necessary, the *-ize* formation. It is often easier to make up words of this kind (*deregionalize, impermissible, extramarital, non-fragmentatory* and so forth) than to think up the English words that will cover one's meaning. The result, in general, is an increase in slovenliness and vagueness.

MEANINGLESS WORDS. In certain kinds of writing, particularly in art criticism and literary criticism, it is normal to come across long passages which are almost completely lacking in meaning.[2] Words like *romantic, plastic, values, human, dead, sentimental, natural, vitality*, as used in art criticism, are strictly meaningless in the sense that they not only do not point to any discoverable object, but are hardly ever expected to do so by the reader. When one critic writes, 'The outstanding feature of Mr. X's

1. "An interesting illustration of this is the way in which the English flower names which were in use till very recently are being ousted by Greek ones, *snapdragon* becoming *antirrhinum*, *forget-me-not* becoming *myosotis*, etc. It is hard to see any practical reason for this change of fashion: it is probably due to an instinctive turning-away from the more homely word and a vague feeling that the Greek word is scientific" (Orwell's note).
2. "Example: 'Comfort's catholicity of percep-tion and image, strangely Whitmanesque in range, almost the exact opposite in aesthetic compulsion, continues to evoke that trembling atmospheric accumulative hinting at a cruel, an inexorably serene timelessness.... Wrey Gardiner scores by aiming at simple bullseyes with precision. Only they are not so simple, and through this contented sadness runs more than the surface bitter-sweet of resignation' (*Poetry Quarterly*)" (Orwell's note).

work is its living quality', while another writes, 'The immediately striking thing about Mr. X's work is its peculiar deadness', the reader accepts this as a simple difference of opinion. If words like *black* and *white* were involved, instead of the jargon words *dead* and *living*, he would see at once that the language was being used in an improper way. Many political words are similarly abused. The word *Fascism* has now no meaning except in so far as it signifies 'something not desirable'. The words *democracy, socialism, freedom, patriotic, realistic, justice*, have each of them several different meanings which cannot be reconciled with one another. In the case of a word like *democracy*, not only is there no agreed definition, but the attempt to make one is resisted from all sides. It is almost universally felt that when we call a country democratic we are praising it: consequently the defenders of every kind of régime claim that it is a democracy, and fear that they might have to stop using the word if it were tied down to any one meaning. Words of this kind are often used in a consciously dishonest way. That is, the person who uses them has his own private definition, but allows his hearer to think he means something quite different. Statements like *Marshal Pétain was a true patriot, The Soviet Press is the freest in the world, The Catholic Church is opposed to persecution*, are almost always made with intent to deceive. Other words used in variable meanings, in most cases more or less dishonestly, are: *class, totalitarian, science, progressive, reactionary, bourgeois, equality*.

Now that I have made this catalogue of swindles and perversions, let me give another example of the kind of writing that they lead to. This time it must of its nature be an imaginary one. I am going to translate a passage of good English into modern English of the worst sort. Here is a well-known verse from *Ecclesiastes*:

'I returned and saw under the sun, that the race is not to the swift, nor the battle to the strong, neither yet bread to the wise, nor yet riches to men of understanding, nor yet favour to men of skill; but time and chance happeneth to them all.'

Here it is in modern English:

'Objective consideration of contemporary phenomena compels the conclusion that success or failure in competitive activities exhibits no tendency to be commensurate with innate capacity, but that a considerable element of the unpredictable must invariably be taken into account.'

This is a parody, but not a very gross one. Exhibit (3), above, for instance, contains several patches of the same kind of English. It will be seen that I have not made a full translation. The beginning and ending of the sentence follow the original meaning fairly closely, but in the middle the concrete illustrations — race, battle, bread — dissolve into the vague phrase 'success or failure in competitive activities'. This had to be so, because no modern writer of the kind I am discussing — no one capable of using phrases like 'objective consideration of contemporary phenomena' — would ever tabulate his thoughts in that precise and detailed way. The whole tendency of modern prose is away from concreteness. Now analyse these two sentences a little more closely. The first contains forty-nine words but only sixty syllables, and all its words are those of everyday life. The second contains thirty-eight words of ninety syllables: eighteen of its words are from Latin roots, and one from Greek. The first sentence contains six vivid images, and only one phrase ('time and chance') that could be called vague. The second contains not a single fresh, arresting phrase, and in spite of its ninety syllables it gives only a shortened version of the meaning contained in the first. Yet without a doubt it is the second kind of sentence that is gaining ground in modern English. I do not want to exaggerate. This kind of writing is not yet universal, and outcrops of simplicity will occur here and there in the worst-written page. Still, if you or I were told to write a few lines on the uncertainty of human fortunes, we should probably come much nearer to my imaginary sentence than to the one from *Ecclesiastes*.

As I have tried to show, modern writing at its worst does not consist in picking out words for the sake of their meaning and inventing images in order to make the meaning clearer. It consists in gumming together long strips of words which have already been set in order by someone else, and making the results presentable by sheer humbug. The attraction of this way of writing is that it is easy. It is easier — even quicker, once you have the habit — to say *In my opinion it is a not unjustifiable assumption that* than to say *I think*. If you use ready-made phrases, you not only don't have to hunt about for words; you also don't have to bother with the rhythms of your sentences, since these phrases are generally so arranged as to be more or less euphonious. When you are composing in a hurry — when you are dictating to a stenographer, for instance, or making a public speech — it is natural to fall into a pretentious, Latinized style. Tags like *a consideration which we should do well to bear in mind* or *a conclusion to which all of us would readily assent* will save many a sentence from coming down with a bump. By using stale metaphors, similes and idioms, you save much mental effort, at the cost of leaving your meaning vague, not only for your reader but for yourself. This is the significance of mixed metaphors. The sole aim of a metaphor is to call up a visual image. When these images clash — as in *The Fascist octopus has sung its swan song, the jackboot is thrown into the melting pot* — it can be taken as certain that the writer is not seeing a mental image of the objects he is naming; in other words he is not really thinking. Look again at the examples I gave at the beginning of this essay. Professor Laski (1) uses five negatives in fifty-three words. One of these is superfluous, making nonsense of the whole passage, and in addition there is the slip *alien* for akin, making further nonsense, and several avoidable pieces of clumsiness which increase the general vagueness. Professor Hogben (2) plays ducks and drakes with a battery which is able to write prescriptions, and, while disapproving of the everyday phrase *put up with*, is unwilling to look *egregious* up in the dictionary and see what it means. (3), if one takes an uncharitable attitude towards it, is simply meaningless: probably one could work out its intended meaning by reading the whole of the article in which it occurs. In (4), the writer knows more or less what he wants to say, but an accumulation of stale phrases chokes him like tea leaves blocking a sink. In (5), words and meaning have almost parted company. People who write in this manner usually have a general emotional meaning — they dislike one thing and want to express solidarity with another — but they are not interested in the detail of what they are saying. A scrupulous writer, in every sentence that he writes, will ask himself at least four questions, thus: What am I trying to say? What words will express it? What image or idiom will make it clearer? Is this image fresh enough to have an effect? And he will probably ask himself two more: Could I put it more shortly? Have I said anything that is avoidably ugly? But you are not obliged to go to all this trouble. You can shirk it by simply throwing your mind open and letting the ready-made phrases come crowding in. They will construct your sentences for you—even think your thoughts for you, to a certain extent—and at need they will perform the important service of partially concealing your meaning even from yourself. It is at this point that the special connection between politics and the debasement of language becomes clear.

In our time it is broadly true that political writing is bad writing. Where it is not true, it will generally be found that the writer is some kind of rebel, expressing his private opinions and not a 'party line'. Orthodoxy, of whatever colour, seems to demand a lifeless, imitative style. The political dialects to be found in pamphlets, leading articles, manifestos, White Papers and the speeches of Under-Secretaries do, of course, vary from party to party, but they are all alike in that one almost never finds in them a fresh, vivid, home-made turn of speech. When one watches some tired hack on the platform mechanically repeating the familiar phrases—*bestial atrocities, iron heel, bloodstained tyranny, free peoples of the world, stand shoulder to shoulder*—one often has a curious feeling that one is not watching a live human being but some kind of dummy: a feeling which suddenly becomes stronger at moments when the light catches the speaker's spectacles and turns them into blank discs which seem to have no eyes behind them. And this is not altogether fanciful. A speaker who uses that kind of phraseology has gone some distance towards turning himself into a machine. The appropriate noises are coming out of his larynx, but his brain is not involved as it would be if he were choosing his words for himself. If the speech he is making is one that he is accustomed to make over and over again, he may be almost unconscious of what he is saying, as one is when one utters the responses in church. And this reduced state of consciousness, if not indispensable, is at any rate favourable to political conformity.

In our time, political speech and writing are largely the defence of the indefensible.[3] Things like the continuance of British rule in India, the Russian purges and deportations, the dropping of the atom bombs on Japan, can indeed be defended, but only by arguments which are too brutal for most people to face, and which do not square with the professed aims of political parties. Thus political language has to consist largely of euphemism, question-begging and sheer cloudy vagueness. Defenceless villages are bombarded from the air, the inhabitants driven out into the countryside, the cattle machine-gunned, the huts set on fire with incendiary bullets: this is called *pacification*. Millions of peasants are robbed of their farms and sent trudging along the roads with no more than they can carry: this is called *transfer of population* or *rectification of frontiers*. People are imprisoned for years without trial, or shot in the back of the neck or sent to die of scurvy in Arctic lumber camps: this is called *elimination of unreliable elements*. Such phraseology is needed if one wants to name things without calling up mental pictures of them. Consider for

3. This essay was written in 1946.

instance some comfortable English professor defending Russian totalitarianism. He cannot say outright, 'I believe in killing off your opponents when you can get good results by doing so.' Probably, therefore, he will say something like this:

'While freely conceding that the Soviet régime exhibits certain features which the humanitarian may be inclined to deplore, we must, I think, agree that a certain curtailment of the right to political opposition is an unavoidable concomitant of transitional periods, and that the rigours which the Russian people have been called upon to undergo have been amply justified in the sphere of concrete achievement.'

The inflated style is itself a kind of euphemism. A mass of Latin words falls upon the facts like soft snow, blurring the outlines and covering up all the details. The great enemy of clear language is insincerity. When there is a gap between one's real and one's declared aims, one turns as it were instinctively to long words and exhausted idioms, like a cuttlefish squirting out ink. In our age there is no such thing as 'keeping out of politics'. All issues are political issues, and politics itself is a mass of lies, evasions, folly, hatred and schizophrenia. When the general atmosphere is bad, language must suffer. I should expect to find—this is a guess which I have not sufficient knowledge to verify—that the German, Russian and Italian languages have all deteriorated in the last ten or fifteen years, as a result of dictatorship.

But if thought corrupts language, language can also corrupt thought. A bad usage can spread by tradition and imitation, even among people who should and do know better. The debased language that I have been discussing is in some ways very convenient. Phrases like *a not unjustifiable assumption*, *leaves much to be desired*, *would serve no good purpose*, *a consideration which we should do well to bear in mind*, are a continuous temptation, a packet of aspirins always at one's elbow. Look back through this essay, and for certain you will find that I have again and again committed the very faults I am protesting against. By this morning's post I have received a pamphlet dealing with conditions in Germany. The author tells me that he 'felt impelled' to write it. I open it at random, and here is almost the first sentence that I see: '[The Allies] have an opportunity not only of achieving a radical transformation of Germany's social and political structure in such a way as to avoid a nationalistic reaction in Germany itself, but at the same time of laying the foundations of a co-operative and unified Europe.' You see, he 'feels impelled' to write—feels, presumably, that he has something new to say—and yet his words, like cavalry horses answering the bugle, group themselves automatically into the familiar dreary pattern. This invasion of one's mind by ready-made phrases (*lay the foundations, achieve a radical transformation*) can only be prevented if one is constantly on guard against them, and every such phrase anaesthetizes a portion of one's brain.

I said earlier that the decadence of our language is probably curable. Those who deny this would argue, if they produced an argument at all, that language merely reflects existing social conditions, and that we cannot influence its development by any direct tinkering with words and constructions. So far as the general tone or spirit of a language goes, this may be true, but it is not true in detail. Silly words and expressions have often disappeared, not through any evolutionary process but owing to the conscious action of a minority. Two recent examples were *explore every avenue* and *leave no stone unturned*, which were killed by the jeers of a few journalists. There is a long list of flyblown metaphors which could similarly be got rid of if enough people would interest themselves in the job; and it should also be possible to laugh the *not un-* formation out of existence,[4] to reduce the amount of Latin and Greek in the average sentence, to drive out foreign phrases and strayed scientific words, and, in general, to make pretentiousness unfashionable. But all these are minor points. The defence of the English language implies more than this, and perhaps it is best to start by saying what it does *not* imply.

To begin with it has nothing to do with archaism, with the salvaging of obsolete words and turns of speech, or with the setting up of a 'standard English' which must never be departed from. On the contrary, it is especially concerned with the scrapping of every word or idiom which has outworn its usefulness. It has nothing to do with correct grammar and syntax, which are of no importance so long as one makes one's meaning clear, or with the avoidance of Americanisms, or with having what is called a 'good prose style'. On the other hand it is not concerned with fake simplicity and the attempt to make written English colloquial. Nor does it even imply in every case preferring the Saxon word to the Latin one, though it does imply using the fewest and shortest words that will cover one's meaning. What is above all needed is to let the meaning choose the word, and not the other way about. In prose, the worst thing one can do with words is to surrender to them. When you think of a concrete object, you think wordlessly, and then, if you want to describe the thing you have been visualizing you probably hunt about till you find the exact words that seem to fit. When you think of something abstract you are more inclined to use words from the start, and unless you make a conscious effort to prevent it, the existing dialect will come rushing in and do the job for you, at the expense of blurring or even changing your meaning. Probably it is better to put off using words as long as possible and get one's meaning as clear as one can through pictures or sensations. Afterwards one can choose — not simply *accept* — the phrases that will best cover the meaning, and then switch round and decide what impression one's words are likely to make on another person. This last effort of the mind cuts out all stale or mixed images, all prefabricated phrases, needless repetitions, and humbug and vagueness generally. But one can often be in doubt about the effect of a word or a phrase, and one needs rules that one can rely on when instinct fails. I think the following rules will cover most cases:

    (i) Never use a metaphor, simile or other figure of speech which you are used to seeing in print.

    (ii) Never use a long word where a short one will do.

    (iii) If it is possible to cut a word out, always cut it out.

    (iv) Never use the passive where you can use the active.

    (v) Never use a foreign phrase, a scientific word or a jargon word if you can think of an everyday English equivalent.

4. "One can cure oneself of the *not un-* formation by memorizing this sentence: *A not unblack dog was chasing a not unsmall rabbit across a not ungreen field*" (Orwell's note).

(vi) Break any of these rules sooner than say anything outright bar-
        barous.
These rules sound elementary, and so they are, but they demand a deep
change of attitude in anyone who has grown used to writing in the style
now fashionable. One could keep all of them and still write bad English, but
one could not write the kind of stuff that I quoted in those five specimens at
the beginning of this article.

I have not here been considering the literary use of language, but
merely language as an instrument for expressing and not for concealing or
preventing thought. Stuart Chase and others have come near to claiming
that all abstract words are meaningless, and have used this as a pretext for
advocating a kind of political quietism. Since you don't know what Fascism
is, how can you struggle against Fascism? One need not swallow such
absurdities as this, but one ought to recognize that the present political
chaos is connected with the decay of language, and that one can probably
bring about some improvement by starting at the verbal end. If you
simplify your English, you are freed from the worst follies of orthodoxy.
You cannot speak any of the necessary dialects, and when you make a
stupid remark its stupidity will be obvious, even to yourself. Political
language—and with variations this is true of all political parties, from
Conservatives to Anarchists—is designed to make lies sound truthful and
murder respectable, and to give an appearance of solidity to pure wind.
One cannot change this all in a moment, but one can at least change one's
own habits, and from time to time one can even, if one jeers loudly enough,
send some worn-out and useless phrase—some *jackboot, Achilles' heel,
hotbed, melting pot, acid test, veritable inferno*, or other lump of verbal
refuse—into the dustbin where it belongs.

— Orwell would like to see the individual make an attempt to improve one's language usage —

NORTHROP FRYE ✓

~~speaks about academic freedom~~
~~shows an elitist bias towards academics~~

Culture and the National Will *academics*

I am, of course, very deeply appreciative of the honour that Carleton University has done me. It is particularly an honour to receive this degree in the company of Mr. A. Y. Jackson, as well as a great pleasure, because Mr. Jackson is an old friend.[1] May I congratulate also those of you who are receiving your degrees, and who are leaving the real world of the university and going out to the confused illusions of the world outside. Here you are in contact with reality at every point: this is the engine room; this is where the great ideas and forces and symbols that shape human behaviour take their start. Soon you will be in the ivory towers of business, in the escapist retreats of the suburbs, in the charmless magic of teaching, or in the schizophrenic fantasies of government. Wherever you are, you will be in a labyrinth, and only your four years at Carleton will give you the clue to it.

I should like also to congratulate President Bissell and everyone else concerned on the graduating of Carleton College itself into Carleton University. A graduate school usually means, in practice, that the teaching staff has to do twice as much work for the same money: but teachers are curious people, and they seem to thrive on such arrangements.

Carleton University has some of the advantages that often go with being the youngest in a large family. It began its history when Canada was developing an entirely new attitude towards its universities.[2] The Canadian public didn't realize how important universities were until it was clear that we couldn't win a war without them. That gave us a sense of urgency about them: we began to realize that a nation has to take care of its universities or disappear from the modern world. Not long after Canadian universities started receiving federal grants. Now federal grants can never be the sole or even the main financial support of any university, but the fact that they exist sets up two essential principles in Canadian life. In the first place, universities are far too important to the country not to be recognized as essential non-profit industries like the postal service, for which the state is to some degree responsible.

In the second place, universities in a democracy must remain universities, and that means academic freedom, the unrestricted pursuit of undiscovered truth, and not the repeating of the truths that the different pressure groups in society think they already have. All pressure groups in society are anti-educational, no matter what they are pressing for. In Wilkie Collins' detective story *The Moonstone* there's an unpleasant nosy female who speaks of "the blessed prospect of interfering," and there are people like that in every country. But the more remote and diverse the

---

1. This essay was the Convocation Address at Carleton University, 17 May 1957. A.Y. Jackson (1882–1974), the well-known Canadian painter, was also honoured on this occasion.
2. Carleton was established during the Sec-ond World War (1942) as the Ottawa Association for the Advancement of Learning. It became Carleton College in 1952 and Carleton University in 1957.

34

— business & government distort the world
— distrusts society in general.
— do not believe in the wisdom of the people.

financial support of a university is, the less easy it is for them to get inspired by that prospect.

Now, with the Canada Council Act,[3] federal aid for universities is linked with federal aid for culture. The principles involved for culture are precisely the same. Federal aid cannot be the sole or even the main financial support of Canadian culture, but having it establishes the same double recognition of its necessity and its freedom: it has to be there, and it has to be left alone. It is logical to link the university and culture: in fact it could almost be said that the university today is to culture what the church is to religion: the social institution that makes it possible. It teaches the culture of the past, and it tries to build up an educated public for the culture of the present.

In the Soviet Union, as I understand it, culture is regarded as a function of the state, and hence all culture comes directly under political criticism. I dare say a great deal of lively discussion results, which may often be quite free in its own context, or even help the artist from a Marxist point of view. Still, the principle involved strikes us here in the democracies as pernicious. Yet it seems to me that a good deal of public thinking about culture here is still stuck in the laissez-faire economics of a century ago. For us the writer is still a small retailer, who has to be subsidized to compete with the mass media. This makes the writer an economic absurdity. A few novelists, most of them bad ones, may eke out a small living by writing, or even hit a best-seller jackpot; but a poet would have to be spectacularly bad before he could live on his poetry. The writer, unlike the painter, has nothing to sell that becomes the exclusive property of the buyer. Speaking of literature, which is the aspect of culture I know most about, I should say that the writer as such really has no economic position at all, and depends for his livng on various official and semi-official devices.

One obvious place for the writer to work in is the university, and most serious writers are now university employees, at least in the summer. Of course there is no reason why a university should employ writers who are not scholars or teachers, and not all good writers are. Still if it does employ a good writer, it also recognizes his social importance, and it covers his freedom with its own academic freedom.

A writer who does not feel that he is developing as well as reflecting public taste will lose his self-respect very quickly. In the mass media of radio and television, as everywhere else, the democratic way is a middle way between rigid control and the anarchy of laissez-faire. This applies also to the grants for writers through wealthy foundations which help them to devote a certain amount of free time to writing. Such assistance only goes so far, but here is still another way of recognizing the importance of the writer without trying to control what he says. Sometimes it may be a very moderate talent that is being encouraged, but you never know: if such

3. The Canada Council Act of 1957 enabled the government of Canada to create an independent body "to foster and promote the study and enjoyment of, and the production of, works in the arts, humanities and social sciences." The original mandate of the Council was amended in 1978 after another act had been passed that transferred the Council's reponsibility for the humanities and social sciences to a new organization, the Social Sciences and Humanities Research Council. Since the present mandate of the Canada Council is restricted to the arts, the link to which Frye refers, between federal aid to universities and federal aid to culture, has been dissolved.

a grant had been made to Keats in the summer of 1819 the whole sensibility of the modern world might have been very different. In all these fields democracy has to follow its own trial-and-error, inductive, illogical and well-meaning way. It will not solve large problems by this method, but it will do a great deal of piecemeal good. And as with the Canada Council Act we enter a new era in the recognition of culture by society, we may keep in mind the shrewd advice of William Blake:

He who would do good to another must do it in Minute Particulars: General Good is the plea of the scoundrel, hypocrite and flatterer.

Children in Canadian schools study Canadian geography, not because it is better than the geography of other nations, but because it is theirs; and similarly with Canadian history and politics. Canadian writing, too, has a value for Canadians independent of its international value. It tells us how Canadian imaginations have reacted to their environment, and therefore it tells us something about Canada that nothing else can tell us. Even if it were not very good in itself, still a Canadian who did not know something of his own literature would be as handicapped as if he had heard of Paris and Rome but never of Ottawa. The study of Canadian literature is not a painful patriotic duty like voting, but a simple necessity of getting one's bearings.

It is reasonable to assume that most Canadian literature would be roughly Canadian in subject-matter, not because it ought to be, but because a serious writer finds it easier to write if he knows what he is talking about. It is often assumed that there is something unique, or at least distinctive, about the Canadian environment or character, and that it is the duty of our writers to interpret those distinctive qualities. Well, this is, of course, the most hackneyed problem in Canadian culture: all our intellectuals are thoroughly tired of it, and very suspicious of attempts to revive it. But they would not feel tired or suspicious if it were or ever had been a genuine problem. The question is put the wrong way round. Writers don't interpret national characters; they create them. But what they create is a series of individual things, characters in novels, images in poems, landscapes in pictures. Types and distinctive qualities are second-hand conventions. If you see what you think is a typical Englishman, it's a hundred to one that you've got your notion of a typical Englishman from your second-hand reading. It is only in satire that types are properly used: a typical Englishman can exist only in such figures as Low's Colonel Blimp.[4] If you look at Mr. Jackson's paintings, you will see a most impressive pictorial survey of Canada: pictures of Georgian Bay and Lake Superior, pictures of the Quebec Laurentians, pictures of Great Bear Lake and the Mackenzie river. What you will not see is a typically Canadian landscape: no such place exists. In fiction too, there is nothing typically Canadian, and Canada would not be a very interesting place to live in if there were. Only the outsider to a country finds characters or patterns of behaviour that are seriously typical. *Maria Chapdelaine* has something of

4. Colonel Blimp was an editorial-cartoon figure created by David Low (1891–1963), the brilliant New Zealander who dominated British cartooning in the 1930–50 era. The Colonel was intended to caricature all that was isolationist and reactionary about the British political mentality, especially in the years immediately preceding the Second World War.

this typifying quality, but then *Maria Chapdelaine* is a tourist's novel.[5]
    I insist on this point because it's a special case of widespread misunderstanding about literature. It is often believed that a new environment is a creative influence: that because we have a lot of new things and experiences in Canada, we ought to have a new literature too. So we ought, except that novelty relates to content, not to form or technique. Form and technique don't exist outside literature, and a writer's technical power will depend, not on new experience or new feelings, but only on how well he can absorb what he reads. A hundred years ago Canada was a much newer experience than it is now, and critics were predicting that new Iliads and heroic sagas would emerge from the virgin forests. But what the poets produced was faint echoes of Tom Moore and a few bits of Byron and Wordsworth, because that was what they had absorbed from their reading. That is why the ultimate standards of Canadian literature have to be international ones. The forms in which Canadian writers must write are established in the literary world as a whole, chiefly in Great Britain and the United States for writers in English. The independent value of Canadian culture for Canadians that I just spoke of doesn't excuse the Canadian writer from being judged by world standards. So a good deal of serious Canadian writing is likely to seem like second-hand echoes of American or British writers, who are not only remote from the Canadian scene but often seem to be unreasonably difficult in themselves. Many people in that case would be apt to feel that if the Canada Council encourages the sort of culture that only a small minority can understand, or if it only helps Canadians to imitate writers who have nothing to do with Canada, it can only widen the gap between the Canadian writer and his public. I am not speaking of the Yahoos who sound off about feeding arty bums at the public trough and so forth; I am speaking of what a responsible citizen might reasonably feel.
    This raises the question of how far a serious Canadian literature can also be popular, in the sense of being a genuine possession of its people. There are several kinds of popular literature. One kind is the commercial or best-seller type of popular book, usually fiction: its popularity depends on its news value, and when that dies the book dies too. Or it depends on sexual stimulation, which is equally short-lived, as most of you have already discovered. Then there is the kind of book that appeals to the eternal bourgeois in the heart of man, the book that tells him how to get ahead in life and supplies him with inspiring slogans and proverbial philosophy. Books on the power of positive thinking and on winning friends and influencing people have been popular since the days of ancient Egypt: an eighteenth-century example was called "The Way to be Rich and Respectable," which is as good a title as any. Devotees of these books attach an exaggerated importance to such poems as Kipling's *If* or Longfellow's *Psalm of Life*, which represents the same kind of thing in poetry. There seems to be an inner law that prevents this proverbial philosophy from getting beyond a certain point of literary merit. I once heard a speaker recommending Shakespeare as a poet who said profound things about life,

5. This well-known account of habitant life was written by a visiting French writer, Louis Hémon (1889–1913), shortly before he was killed in a railway accident.

but this was the kind of poetry he liked, and I couldn't help noticing that all his quotations were from Polonius and Iago.

But there is another kind of popular literature which is more important. This comes into the reading and listening of the child, in the songs and the stories, the history and the wisdom, which are central in our cultural tradition. Whatever literature we learn early, from pre-school nursery rhymes to high-school Shakespeare and beyond, provides us with the keys to nearly all the imaginative experience that it is possible for us to have in life. The central part of this training consists of the Bible, the Classics, and the great heritage of our mother tongue. Such education includes genuinely popular literature: that is, literature which provides a simple and direct form of imaginative experience. In America this would include Rip van Winkle and Huckleberry Finn, the songs of Foster, the tall tales of the West and the comic strips that develop similar folklore cycles in the Tennessee hills and the Florida swamps. We have very little of it in Canada independent of its North American context. The popular in this sense is the contemporary primitive, what in previous ages was folk song and folk tale. Much of it is rubbish, and it includes the cheap fiction and comic books that the enormous (maw) and the ostrich digestion of a ten-year-old reader assimilate after school hours.

What is popular, in the sense of being permanently and genuinely well loved, is a by-product of education, and as one's education improves, the quality of what one likes improves too, until we reach the fully mature level at which the Bible and Shakespeare and the other staples of culture are popular. A good deal of the worry over the ten-year-old's comic books would be far better expended on making sure that the central educational structure is a sound one. I recently heard of a grade-eight teacher in an expensive regressive school in New York, welcoming a boy who had been away with some joke about the prodigal's return, and gradually realizing that no one in her class had heard the story of the prodigal son. Now a grade-eight student who does not know that story has not simply missed out on a piece of information that can be supplied at any time. He has been deprived of one of the keys to the whole imagination and thought of western culture, no less than if he had been deprived of the multiplication table. An educational theory which does not recognize this is not just a mistaken theory: it is criminally negligent.

If his elementary education is sound, no student will find contemporary literature remote from him. On the contrary, he will realize that T. S. Eliot and William Faulkner and Dylan Thomas have far more in common with popular literature, as I have defined it, than any positive thinker could ever have. But by this time he is beginning to feel something of the weight and power of the forces at work in society that are trying to prevent him from getting educated. Contemporary culture is very obviously about us, and it talks to us in a fully mature way. Society consists largely of adolescents and arrested adolescents, and departments of education who have to arrange high-school curricula are well aware of the fact. As a rule a student has to get to university before he can make much contact with the culture of his own time.

This suggests that much of what is now central in our cultural tradition was in its day equally disturbing in its impact, and still can be. The earliest of the prophets of Israel, we are told, was Amos, and the Book of Amos includes a few of the agonized squeals of his contemporaries: "the land is not able to bear all his words," they said. That has been the history of great culture ever since. When Wordsworth said:

> We must be free or die, who speak the tongue
> That Shakespeare spake; the faith and morals hold
> That Milton held.

> edit out obscene passages.

he meant what he said and he was telling the truth. But school texts of Shakespeare continue to be expurgated, for this fair land is still unable to bear all Shakespeare's words; the faith and morals of Milton are as violently resented today as they ever were. If we subsidize our culture properly, we are certain to encourage a good deal that will be described by a good many people as everything from longhair to filthy. If you think that society has outgrown such narrow-mindedness, I would call your attention to the fact that Canada, like all other countries, has laws of book censorship that no serious student of liteature can possibly have the slightest respect for. Or you might ask Mr. Jackson about some of the early reviews of Group of Seven exhibitions.[6]

This is where the class of 1957 at Carleton University comes in. As John Stuart Mill proved a century ago, the basis of all freedom is academic freedom of thought and discussion. You have had that here, because you are responsible for carrying it into society. I know the staff of Carleton fairly well, and I know that none of them would try to adjust you or integrate you with your society. They have done all they could to detach you from it, to wean you from the maternal bosom of Good Housekeeping and the Reader's Digest, the pneumatic bliss of the North American way of life. They have tried to teach you to compare your society's ideas with Plato's, its language with Shakespeare's, its calculations with Newton's, its love with the love of the saints. Being dissatisfied with society is the price we pay for being free men and women. And that should help you to understand the Canadian writer better, because he's so often forced to say most loudly what his audience least wants to hear. If people are morally smug, they will think their writers blasphemous; if they are sodden with integration and adjustment, they will think their writers neurotic; if they accept a way of life, they will think their writers subversive. Sometimes, of course, they will be right, but their rightness is not important, and poems which are immoral or hopelessly obscure today may be babbled happily from infant lips tomorrow. Whatever people do, most of their best writers will be doing the opposite. And if the worst of all came upon us, if we had to fight to the last ditch for our freedom, with our brothers killed and our cities in smoking ruins, our poets would still stand over against us, and break out in hymns to the glory of God and in praise of his beautiful world.

soart of air

---

6. Surviving members of the Algonquin school of landscape painters, A.Y. Jackson among them, gathered in Toronto after the First World War and began to mount joint exhibitions, calling themselves the Group of Seven. Although their work eventually became influential, the austere, simplified forms and bold colours of their paintings at first disturbed both the critics and the general public.

M. H. SCARGILL

Canadians Speak Canadian

It was only this year[1] that a distinguished philologist in Montreal was taken to task for giving a talk on "Canadian English". His critics claimed that he was talking about something that does not exist because Canadians, when not following British usage in speech, must be following American usage. That is, we English-speaking Canadians have developed no language of our own and must depend on Britain or the U.S.A. for all our ideas and for all the words to express them.

What a narrow view! Who discovered insulin, pray, and named it from the Latin? Who experimented with and named the splake?[2] And since when have Americans or British freely discussed Clear Grits, Digby chickens, Socreds, the Land of Little Sticks, separate schools, nitchies, longlinermen?

If the philologist's critics are so sure that they do speak nothing but a strange mixture of British with American English, why are they recognized as Canadians both in Britain and America as soon as they open their mouths? "I know you are a Canadian by the way you pronounce about, house, sir, and elm and because you use 'eh' instead of 'what'," says the American. "I know you aren't British because you pronounce cot and caught in the same way," says the Britisher. "And you do rhyme tomato with potato, a thing that we never do."

Since the Americans deny that we speak like them and since the British refuse to recognize us as speaking British English, we must speak something different from either one. Could this be Canadian English?

Moreover, not only are English-speaking Canadians easily recognized outside Canada by the way they talk, they are also recognized within Canada as coming from different areas. Once the native of Toronto pronounces the name of his city, he can be recognized anywhere. Which of us cannot pick out the Newfoundlander with his soft lilt and Celtic tones? And I well remember the Ottawa man holidaying (or is it vacationing?) in the West who looked at me askance when I pointed out a clump of trees as a bluff. The poor man was under the impression that a bluff is some sort of hill. He didn't know what a Manitoba wave was, either.

Of course, because of a lack of adequate research, it is hard to define Canadian English. That is why many people prefer to deny its existence. That and a strange belief that because many words which they use daily are not in the *Oxford English Dictionary* they must be figments of their imagination. We have no authoritative dictionary of Canadian English. We have no history of Canadian English. We do not have a single grammar based on the actual usage of Canadian English speakers and writers. Canadian teachers of English use books based on British or American

---

1. This essay was first published in December 1956. At that time, no authoritative dictionary of Canadian English existed. *A Dictionary of Canadianisms on Historical Principles* appeared in 1967.
2. A splake is a hybrid game fish of the trout family developed by Canadian biologists.

usage. Indeed, I doubt if there can be any people in the world as ignorant of its own language as we English-speaking Canadians are of ours.

I am surprised that in the course of arguments about bilingualism our *Canadien* compatriots have not pointed out that they can at least describe their language and produce dictionaries devoted to it, whereas the English-speaking Canadian seems anxious to deny that he himself speaks any particular language at all. Before we start talking about the "official" languages of Canada, we had better remember that the existence of one of them or, at least, its nature seems a matter of doubt.

It is obviously true that Canadian English shares certain features with British English and certain features with American English. Things could hardly be otherwise in view of the history of our country. The closer Canadians live to the American border, the greater is the influence of the Northern American speech area on them. In a city like Lethbridge, for instance, eighty per cent of the people have predominantly American habits of pronunciation. Indeed, in Alberta as a whole more than sixty per cent of the native-born population have a pronunciation which is predominantly American. Only one-half of one per cent have predominantly British habits of pronunciation. The rest can use either British or American pronunciations with equal facility and acceptability.

It seems unlikely that British English will have any influence at all on Canadian English in Alberta unless there is a great influx of British immigrants. That is, the people of Alberta will soon follow American habits of pronunciation entirely.

But this acknowledgment of the debt Canadian English owes to American English is not to say that we must derive Canadian English from American English wherever they are alike. There is often no reason for even seeing an American influence. For example, there is nothing against saying that, in many cases, similar features of Canadian and American English pronunciation which are no longer found in Standard British English are to be traced separately to the same source: earlier forms of British English. The unrounded vowel of "not," the short vowel in "grass," the pronunciation of tomato to rhyme with potato—where these are found in Canadian English—may well have been introduced directly from England and later strengthened by the fact that they occur in certain areas of American English.

A proper history of the English language in Canada would be useful in settling disputed points. But we have no such history as yet. One often hears that the English language in Canada is to be derived from American English by way of the Loyalists. But such a theory is hardly valid. It is very doubtful if any such thing as "American English" even existed for the Loyalists to bring. And even if it did exist, it seems unlikely that every immigrant into Canada has been influenced by it.

In any case, the fact that Canadian English does make use of both British and American pronunciations, spellings, and vocabulary throws no light on Canadian English as something completely independent. For Canadian English to be accepted at all as different from either British or American English we must show not that it shares features with both but that it differs from each of them.

Now where is this independence of both British and American English likely to be? Where has Canadian English developed quite independently of either of them? Obviously not in grammar, for I am using a grammatical structure that is understood by both British and Americans. Nor is this development in orthography. We do not have an orthography completely different from that of British or American English. Nor have we developed such a radically different system of pronunciation that we cannot be understood outside Canada—although this matter of pronunciation will, I think, bear investigation and show interesting results.

It is in vocabulary that Canadian English is often quite independent of either British or American English. And this is to be expected. Canadians do not live exactly as do the Americans and the British: we do not always talk about the same things because we do not always share the same things. The fact that we and the Americans prefer gas to British petrol proves only that we all use the same product under different names. But neither the British nor the Americans have mounties or fishing admirals or separate schools. And, therefore, they do not have the words for them unless they are borrowed from us. Canadian English shows independence in names for things distinctively Canadian: Bennett buggy, outage, Lakehead, aboideau, seigneury, Grit, corduroy road, tuladi, oomiak, mukluk, treaty Indian, rampike, Prairie Provinces, gumbo, tupek, ponasked, chuck races, parklands, Bluenose, Confederation, wood rights. Obviously some of these words are French in origin; some are Eskimo and American Indian. But they have little or no place in British or American English because what they describe has no place there.

The classes into which distinctively Canadian English words do fall have been listed for the *Journal of the Canadian Linguistic Association* by an eminent lexicographer, C. J. Lovell. Some of them are adoptions from native languages: comatik, shagannappi. Some are words from Canadian French: cariole, gaspereau. Some words are created in Canada: kerosene, splake, insulin. Some are geographical and descriptive names: Loyalist City, Rupert's Land, herring choker. Some are survivals from Scottish and English dialects: droke, knapp.

Many words now identified by leading dictionaries as being of American origin can easily be shown to have their source in Canada. Other words quite properly declared obsolete by British and American dictionaries are very much alive in Canadian English. For example, a leading American dictionary gives the first appearance of "Chinese laundry" as 1904. But it can be found in the *Moose Jaw Times* for 1890. The same dictionary lists "seed catalogue" for 1907. But the *Saskatchewan Herald* used it in 1880. The *Moose Jaw Times* used "binder twine" in 1890. But an excellent American dictionary knows of it only from 1946. The same dictionary lists "treaty Indian" and "treaty money" as obsolete; it is true of the United States, but not of Canada.

Many leading dictionaries do not list words which are used daily in Canadian English: Lakehead, kokanee, Siwash, Maritimer, separate school, check (in hockey). The *Concise Oxford Dictionary* does not give chinook, saskatoon, choke cherry, mukluk, wendigo, muskeg, malemute, jack pine and many others.

But then, of course, why should American or British dictionaries concern themselves with matters of Canadian English? The *Oxford Eng-*

lish Dictionary is not intended to be a record of the spelling, pronunciation, and vocabulary of Canadian English. Nor is the *Dictionary of Americanisms*. And we do not have a dictionary of Canadian English that is comparable to those two great works, that does for Canadian English what they do for British and for American English.

Surely it is time that we ended the widespread ignorance that exists about Canadian English. No scholar in Canada or anywhere else can say just what "Canadian English pronunciation" really is. It has not been thoroughly investigated. No university in Canada gives a course entitled "The History of the English Language in Canada". Other matters Canadian are now considered worthy of study: literature, politics, history, resources. Why not Canadian English? "Shibboleth" is defined as "a test word that reveals one's nationality". What is the shibboleth of English-speaking Canadians?

ROBERT WARSHOW

The Gangster as Tragic Hero

America, as a social and political organization, is committed to a cheerful view of life. It could not be otherwise. The sense of tragedy is a luxury of aristocratic societies, where the fate of the individual is not conceived of as having a direct and legitimate political importance, being determined by a fixed and supra-political—that is, non-controversial—moral order or fate. Modern equalitarian societies, however, whether democratic or authoritarian in their political forms, always base themselves on the claim that they are making life happier; the avowed function of the modern state, at least in its ultimate terms, is not only to regulate social relations, but also to determine the quality and the possibilities of human life in general. Happiness thus becomes the chief political issue—in a sense, the only political issue—and for that reason it can never be treated as an issue at all. If an American or a Russian is unhappy, it implies a certain reprobation of his society, and therefore, by a logic of which we can all recognize the necessity, it becomes an obligation of citizenship to be cheerful; if the authorities find it necessary, the citizen may even be compelled to make a public display of his cheerfulness on important occasions, just as he may be conscripted into the army in time of war.

Naturally, this civic responsibility rests most strongly upon the organs of mass culture. The individual citizen may still be permitted his private unhappiness so long as it does not take on political significance, the extent of this tolerance being determined by how large an area of private life the society can accommodate. But every production of mass culture is a public act and must conform with accepted notions of the public good. Nobody seriously questions the principle that it is the function of mass culture to maintain public morale, and certainly nobody in the mass audience objects to having his morale maintained.[1] At a time when the normal condition of the citizen is a state of anxiety, euphoria spreads over our culture like the broad smile of an idiot. In terms of attitudes towards life, there is very little difference between a "happy" movie like *Good News*, which ignores death and suffering, and a "sad" movie like *A Tree Grows in Brooklyn*, which uses death and suffering as incidents in the service of a higher optimism.

But, whatever its effectiveness as a source of consolation and a means of pressure for maintaining "positive" social attitudes, this optimism is fundamentally satisfying to no one, not even to those who would be most disoriented without its support. Even within the area of mass culture, there always exists a current of opposition, seeking to express by whatever means are available to it that sense of desperation and inevitable

---

1. "In her testimony before the House Committee on Un-American Activities, Mrs. Leila Rogers said that the movie *None But the Lonely Heart* was un-American because it was gloomy. Like so much else that was said during the unhappy investigation of Hollywood, this statement was at once stupid and illuminating. One knew immediately what Mrs. Rogers was talking about; she had simply been insensitive enough to carry her philistinism to its conclusion" (Warshow's note).

failure which optimism itself helps to create. Most often, this opposition is confined to rudimentary or semi-literate forms: in mob politics and journalism, for example, or in certain kinds of religious enthusiasm. When it does enter the field of art, it is likely to be disguised or attenuated; in an unspecific form of expression like jazz, in the basically harmless nihilism of the Marx Brothers, in the continually reasserted strain of hopelessness that often seems to be the real meaning of the soap opera. The gangster film is remarkable in that it fills the need for disguise (though not sufficiently to avoid arousing uneasiness) without requiring any serious distortion. From its beginnings, it has been a consistent and astonishingly complete presentation of the modern sense of tragedy.[2]

In its initial character, the gangster film is simply one example of the movies' constant tendency to create fixed dramatic patterns that can be repeated indefinitely with a reasonable expectation of profit. One gangster film follows another as one musical or one Western follows another. But this rigidity is not necessarily opposed to the requirements of art. There have been very successful types of art in the past which developed such specific and detailed conventions as almost to make individual examples of the type interchangeable. This is true, for example, of Elizabethan revenge tragedy and Restoration comedy.

For such a type to be successful means that its conventions have imposed themselves upon the general consciousness and become the accepted vehicles of a particular set of attitudes and a particular aesthetic effect. One goes to any individual example of the type with very definite expectations, and originality is to be welcomed only in the degree that it intensifies the expected experience without fundamentally altering it. Moreover, the relationship between the conventions which go to make up such a type and the real experience of its audience or the real facts of whatever situation it pretends to describe is of only secondary importance and does not determine its aesthetic force. It is only in an ultimate sense that the type appeals to its audience's experience of reality; much more immediately, it appeals to previous experience of the type itself: it creates its own field of reference.

Thus the importance of the gangster film, and the nature and intensity of its emotional and aesthetic impact, cannot be measured in terms of the place of the gangster himself or the importance of the problem of crime in American life. Those European movie-goers who think there is a gangster on every corner in New York are certainly deceived, but defenders of the "positive" side of American culture are equally deceived if they think it relevant to point out that most Americans have never seen a gangster. What matters is that the experience of the gangster *as an experience of art* is universal to Americans. There is almost nothing we understand better or react to more readily or with quicker intelligence. The Western film, though it seems never to diminish in popularity, is for most of us no more than the folklore of the past, familiar and understandable only because it

2. "Efforts have been made from time to time to bring the gangster film into line with the prevailing optimism and social constructiveness of our culture; *Kiss of Death* is a recent example. These efforts are usually unsuccessful; the reasons for their lack of success are interesting in themselves, but I shall not be able to discuss them here" (Warshow's note).

has been repeated so often. The gangster film comes much closer. In ways that we do not easily or willingly define, the gangster speaks for us, expressing that part of the American psyche which rejects the qualities and the demands of modern life, which rejects "Americanism" itself.

The gangster is the man of the city, with the city's language and knowledge, with its queer and dishonest skills and its terrible daring, carrying his life in his hands like a placard, like a club. For everyone else, there is at least the theoretical possibility of another world—in that happier American culture which the gangster denies, the city does not really exist; it is only a more crowded and more brightly lit country—but for the gangster there is only the city; he must inhabit it in order to personify it: not the real city, but that dangerous and sad city of the imagination which is so much more important, which is the modern world. And the gangster—though there are real gangsters—is also, and primarily, a creature of the imagination. The real city, one might say, produces only criminals; the imaginary city produces the gangster: he is what we want to be and what we are afraid we may become.

Thrown into the crowd without background or advantages, with only those ambiguous skills which the rest of us—the real people of the real city —can only pretend to have, the gangster is required to make his way, to make his life and impose it on others. Usually, when we come upon him, he has already made his choice or the choice has already been made for him, it doesn't matter which: we are not permitted to ask whether at some point he could have chosen to be something else than what he is.

The gangster's activity is actually a form of rational enterprise, involving fairly definite goals and various techniques for achieving them. But this rationality is usually no more than a vague background; we know, perhaps, that the gangster sells liquor or that he operates a numbers racket; often we are not given even that much information. So his activity becomes a kind of pure criminality: he hurts people. Certainly our response to the gangster film is most consistently and most universally a response to sadism; we gain the double satisfaction of participating vicariously in the gangster's sadism and then seeing it turned against the gangster himself.

But on another level the quality of irrational brutality and the quality of rational enterprise become one. Since we do not see the rational and routine aspects of the gangster's behavior, the practice of brutality—the quality of unmixed criminality—becomes the totality of his career. At the same time, we are always conscious that the whole meaning of this career is a drive for success: the typical gangster film presents a steady upward progress followed by a very precipitate fall. Thus brutality itself becomes at once the means to success and the content of success—a success that is defined in its most general terms, not as accomplishment or specific gain, but simply as the unlimited possibility of aggression. (In the same way, film presentations of businessmen tend to make it appear that they achieve their success by talking on the telephone and holding conferences and that success *is* talking on the telephone and holding conferences.)

From this point of view, the initial contact between the film and its audience is an agreed conception of human life: that man is a being with the possibilities of success or failure. This principle, too, belongs to the city; one must emerge from the crowd or else one is nothing. On that basis the necessity of the action is established, and it progresses by inalterable paths to the point where the gangster lies dead and the principle has been modified: there is really only one possibility—failure. The final meaning of the city is anonymity and death.

In the opening scene of *Scarface*, we are shown a successful man; we know he is successful because he has just given a party of opulent proportions and because he is called Big Louie. Through some monstrous lack of caution, he permits himself to be alone for a few moments. We understand from this immediately that he is about to be killed. No convention of the gangster film is more strongly established than this: it is dangerous to be alone. And yet the very conditions of success make it impossible not to be alone, for success is always the establishment of an *individual* preeminence that must be imposed on others, in whom it automatically arouses hatred; the successful man is an outlaw. The gangster's whole life is an effort to assert himself as an individual, to draw himself out of the crowd, and he always dies *because* he is an individual; the final bullet thrusts him back, makes him, after all, a failure. "Mother of God," says the dying Little Caesar, "is this the end of Rico?"—speaking of himself thus in the third person because what has been brought low is not the undifferentiated *man*, but the individual with a name, the gangster, the success; even to himself he is a creature of the imagination. (T. S. Eliot has pointed out that a number of Shakespeare's tragic heroes have this trick of looking at themselves dramatically; their true identity, the thing that is destroyed when they die, is something outside themselves—not a man, but a style of life, a kind of meaning.)

At bottom, the gangster is doomed because he is under the obligation to succeed, not because the means he employs are unlawful. In the deeper layers of the modern consciousness, *all* means are unlawful, every attempt to succeed is an act of aggression, leaving one alone and guilty and defenseless among enemies: one is *punished* for success. This is our intolerable dilemma: that failure is a kind of death and success is evil and dangerous, is —ultimately—impossible. The effect of the gangster film is to embody this dilemma in the person of the gangster and resolve it by his death. The dilemma is resolved because it is *his* death, not ours. We are safe; for the moment, we can acquiesce in our failure, we can choose to fail.

MORDECAI RICHLER

Why I Write

As I write, October 1970, I have just finished a novel of intimidating length, a fiction begun five years ago, on the other side of the moon, so I am, understandably enough, concerned by the state of the novel in general. Is it dead? Dead *again*. Like God or MGM. Father McLuhan says so (writing, 'The Age of Writing has passed') and Dylan Thomas's daughter recently pronounced stingingly from Rome, "Nobody reads novels any more."

I'm soon going to be forty. Too old to learn how to teach. Or play the guitar. Stuck, like the blacksmith, with the only craft I know. But brooding about the novel, and its present unmodishness, it's not the established practitioner I'm grieving for, it's the novice, that otherwise effervescent young man stricken with the wasting disease whose earliest symptom is the first novel. These are far from halcyon days for the fledgling novelist.

Look at it this way. Most publishers, confronted with a rectal polyp, hold on to hope, tempting the surgeon with a bigger advance. They know the score. What's truly terminal. Offered a first novel or worse news — infamy—a short story collection, they call for the ledgers which commemorate last season's calamities. The bright new talents nobody wanted to read. Now more to be remaindered than remembered, as *Time* once observed.

I know. Carting off my cumbersome manuscript to be xeroxed, it was my first novel that was uppermost in my mind, *The Acrobats*, published in 1954, when I was twenty-three years old. At the time, I was living in Montreal, and my British publisher, André Deutsch, urged me to visit his Canadian distributor before sailing for England. So I caught the overnight Greyhound bus to Toronto, arriving at 7 a.m. in a city where I knew nobody and walking the sweltering summer streets until 9.30, when offices would open.

The Canadian distributor, bracingly realistic, did not detain me overlong with *recherché*[1] chitchat about style, content or influences. "Have you written a thick book or a thin book?" he demanded.

A thin one, I allowed.

"Thick books sell better than thin ones here."

A slow learner, I published five more before I at last surfaced with a thick one, *St. Urbain's Horseman*, which was all of 180,000 words. And retrieving my seven xeroxed copies, I couldn't help but reflect that the £80 I forked out for them was only slightly less than the British advance against royalties I was paid for my first novel sixteen years ago. The American publisher, G. P. Putnam's Sons, was more generous; they sent me 750 dollars. But I was disheartened when I received their catalogue. Putnam's was, at the time, trying a new experiment in book selling. If you didn't enjoy one of their books, your bookseller would return you the money, no questions asked. Only two books listed in the autumn catalogue

---

1. Rare, choice.

conspicuously failed to carry this guarantee, mine, and another young writer's.

The Acrobats ultimately sold some 2,000 copies in England and less than a 1,000 in the U.S., but it was — as I pointed out to my aunt, on a visit to Montreal — translated into five foreign languages.

"There must," she said, smoothing out her skirt, "be a shortage of books."

My uncle, also a critic, was astonished when he computed my earnings against the time I had invested. I would have earned more mowing his lawn, and, furthermore, it would have been healthier for me.

The novel, the novel.

Write a study of the Pre-Columbian butterfly, compose an account of colonial administration in Tongo, and Nigel Dennis, that most perspicacious and witty of British reviewers, might perversely enshrine it in a 1,000 word essay in the *Sunday Telegraph*. Or Malcolm Muggeridge might take it as the text for a lengthy sermon, excoriating once more that generation of younger vipers who will continue to enjoy, enjoy, after he has passed on to his much-advertised rest. But novels, coming in batches of twenty weekly, seldom rate a notice of their own in England. Sixteen are instant losers. Or, looked at another way, payola from the literary editor. Badly-paid reviewer's perks. The reviewer is not even expected to read them, but it is understood he can flog them for half-price to a buyer from Fleet Street. Of the four that remain, comprising the typical novel column, one is made especially for skewering in the last deadly paragraph, and two are destined for the scales of critical balance. On the one hand, somewhat promising, on the other, ho-hum. Only one makes the lead. But it must lead in four of the five influential newspapers, say, the *Sunday Times*, *Observer*, *Times* and *Guardian*, if anybody's to take notice. Some even buying.

"Basically," a concerned New York editor told me, "the trouble is we are trying to market something nobody wants. Or needs."

The novel has had its day, we are assured, and in the Age of Aquarius, film, man, film's the stuff that will do more than fiction can to justify God's way to man. Given any rainy afternoon who wants to read Doris Lessing fully-clothed for forty bob when, for only ten, you can actually see Jane Fonda starkers, shaking it for you and art, and leaving you with sufficient change for a half-bottle of gin?

To be fair, everything has (and continues) to be tried. Novels like decks of playing cards. Shuffle, and read it anyway it comes up. Novels like jokes or mutual funds. You cut your potential time-investment loss by inviting everybody in the office to pound out a chapter. *Naked Came The Stranger. I Knew Daisy Smutten*. Or instead-of-sex. Why weary yourself, performing badly perhaps when, if only you lose yourself in *The Adventurers*, you can have better-hung Dax come for you? And, sooner or later, somebody's bound to turn to the cassette. No need to bruise your thumbs turning pages. You slip the thing into a machine and listen to Racquel Welch read it. "The latest Amis as read by. . . ."

On a recent visit to Canadian university campuses, I found myself a creature to be pitied, still writing novels when anybody could tell you that's no longer "where it's at." But I've tried the logical alternative, screen writing, and though I still write for the films from time to time, it's not really for me.

The trouble is, like most novelists, I am conditioned to working for years on material I discuss with nobody. To adjust from that to script writing is too much like what Truman Capote once described as group sports. Even so, five years in a room with a novel-in-progress can be more than gruelling. If getting up to it some mornings is a pleasure, it is, just as often, a punishment. A self-inflicted punishment. There have been false starts, wrong turns, and weeks with nothing to show except sharpened pencils and bookshelves rearranged. I have rewritten chapters ten times that in the end simply didn't belong and had to be cut. Ironically, even unforgivably, it usually seems to be those passages over which I have laboured most arduously, nurtured in the hot-house, as it were, that never really spring to life, and the pages that came too quickly, with utterly suspect ease, that read most felicitously.

Riding into my second year on *St. Urbain's Horseman*, disheartened by proliferating school bills, diminished savings, and only fitful progress, I finally got stuck so badly that there was nothing for it but to shove the manuscript aside. I started in on another novel, a year's heat, which yielded *Cocksure*. Anthony Burgess clapped hands in *Life*, *Time* approved, *Newsweek* cheered, and the British notices were almost uniformly fulsome. Encouraged and somewhat solvent again, I resolved to resume work on *Horseman*. After twelve years in London, I was to return to Montreal for a year with my wife and five children, to report for duty as writer-in-residence at Sir George Williams University, my *alma mater*. Or, put plainly, in return for taking a "creative writing" seminar one afternoon a week, I could get on with my novel, comparatively free of financial worry.

Ostensibly, conditions were ideal, winds couldn't be more favourable, and so I started in for the ninth time on page one of *St. Urbain's Horseman*. I didn't get much further before, my stomach crawling with fear, I began to feel I'd lost something somewhere.

I got stuck. Morning after morning, I'd switch to an article or a book review, already long overdue. Or compose self-pitying letters to friends. Or dawdle until eleven a.m., when it was too late to make a decent start on anything, and I was at last free to quit my room and stroll downtown. St. Catherine Street. Montreal's Main Stem, as the doyen of our gossip columnists has it. Pretending to browse for books by lesser novelists, I could surreptitiously check out the shops on stacks of the paperback edition of *Cocksure*.

Or take in a movie maybe.

Ego dividends. I could pick a movie that I had been asked to write myself, but declined. Whatever the movie, it was quite likely I would know the director or the script writer, maybe even one of the stars.

So there you have it. Cat's out of the bag. In London, I skitter on the periphery of festooned circles, know plenty of inside stories. Bomb-shells. Like which cabinet minister is an insatiable pederast. What best-selling novel was really stitched together by a cunning editor. Which wrinkled Hollywood glamour queen is predisposed toward gang shags with hirsute Neapolitan waiters from the Mirabelle. Yes, yes, I'll own up to it. I am, after eighteen years as a writer, not utterly unconnected or unknown, as witness the entry in the indispensable *Oxford Companion to Canadian Literature*.

> Richler, Mordecai (1931–) Born in Montreal, he was educated at Sir George Williams College and spent two years abroad. Returning to Canada in 1952, he joined the staff of the Canadian Broadcasting Corporation. He now lives in England, where he writes film scripts, novels, and short stories. The key to Richler's novels is...

After eighteen years and six novels there is nothing I cherish so much as the first and most vulnerable book, *The Acrobats*, not only because it marked the first time my name appeared in a Canadian newspaper, a prescient Toronto columnist writing from London, "You've not heard of Mordecai Richler yet, but, look out, she's a name to watch for"; but also because it was the one book I could write as a totally private act, with the deep, inner assurance that nobody would be such a damn fool as to publish it. That any editor would boot it back to me, a condescending rejection note enclosed, enabling me to quit Paris for Montreal, an honourable failure, and get down to the serious business of looking for a job. A real job.

I did in fact return to Montreal, broke, while my manuscript made the rounds. My father, who hadn't seen me for two years, took me out for a drive.

"I hear you wrote a novel in Europe," he said.

"Yes."

"What's it called?"

"*The Acrobats*."

"What in the hell do you know about the circus?"

I explained the title was a symbolic one.

"Is it about Jews or ordinary people?" my father asked.

To my astonishment, André Deutsch offered to publish the novel. Now, when somebody asked me what I did, I could reply, without seeming fraudulent to myself, that I was indeed a writer. If, returned to Hampstead once more, I still tended to doubt it in the early morning hours, now *The Acrobats*, in shop windows here and there, was the proof I needed. My novel on display side by side with real ones. There is no publication as agonizing or charged with elation as the first.

Gradually, you assume that what you write will be published. After the first book, composing a novel is no longer self-indulgent, a conceit. It becomes, among other things, a living. Though to this day reviews can still sting or delight, it's sales that buy you the time to get on with the next. Mind you, there are a number of critics whose esteem I prize, whose opprobrium can sear, but, for the most part, I, in common with other writers, have learned to read reviews like a market report. This one will help move the novel, that one not.

Writing a novel, as George Orwell has observed, is a horrible, exhausting struggle. "One would never undertake such a thing if one were not driven by some demon whom one can neither resist nor understand." Something else. Each novel is a failure, or there would be no compulsion to begin afresh. Critics don't help. Speaking as someone who fills that office on occasion, I must say that the critic's essential relationship is with the reader, not the writer. It is his duty to celebrate good books, eviscerate bad ones, lying ones.

When I first published, in 1954, it was commonly assumed that to commit a film script was to sell out (Daniel Fuchs, Christopher Isherwood, Irwin Shaw), and that the good and dedicated life was in academe. Now, the inverse seems to be the Canadian and, I daresay, American case. The creative young yearn to be in films, journeymen retire to the universities: *seems* to be the case, because, happily, there are exceptions.

All of us tend to romanticize the world we nearly chose. In my case, academe, where instead of having to bring home the meat, I would only be obliged to stamp it, rejecting this shoulder of beef as Hank James derivative, or that side of pork as sub-Jimmy Joyce. I saw myself no longer a perplexed free-lancer with an unpredictable income, balancing this magazine assignment, that film job, against the time it would buy me. No sir. Sipping Tio Pepe in the faculty club, snug in my leather winged-back armchair and the company of other disinterested scholars, I would not, given the assurance of a monthly cheque, chat about anything so coarse as money.

— Why don't you, um, write a novel yourself this summer, Professor Richler?

— Well, Dr. Lemming, like you, I have too much respect for the tradition to sully it with my own feeble scribblings.

— Quite.

— Just so.

Alas, academe, like girls, whisky, and literature, promised better than it paid. I now realize, after having ridden the academic gravy train for a season, that vaudeville hasn't disappeared or been killed by TV, but merely retired to small circuits, among them, the universities. Take the Canadian poets, for instance. Applying for Canada Council grants today, they no longer catalogue their publications (the obsolete accomplishments of linear man) but, instead, like TV actors on the make, they list their personal appearances, the campuses where they read aloud. Wowsy at Simon Fraser U., hotsy at Carleton. Working wrinkles out of the act in the stix, with a headliner coming up in the veritable Palace of the Canadian campus circuit, the University of Toronto.

If stand-up comics now employ batteries of gag writers because national TV exposure means they can only use their material once, then professors, playing to a new house every season, can peddle the same oneliners year after year, improving only on timing and delivery. For promos, they publish. Bringing out journals necessary to no known audience, but essential to their advancement.

Put plainly, these days everybody's in show business, all trades are riddled with impurities. And so, after a most enjoyable (and salaried) year in academe — a reverse sabbatical, if you like — I returned to the uncertain world of the free-lance writer, where nobody, as James Thurber once wrote, sits at anybody's feet unless he's been knocked there. I returned with my family to London, no deeper into *St. Urbain's Horseman* than when I had left.

Why do you write?

Doctors are seldom asked why they practise, shoemakers how come they cobble, or baseball players why they don't drive a coal truck instead, but again and again writers, like housebreakers, are asked why they do it.

Orwell, as might be expected, supplies the most honest answer in his essay, "Why I Write."

"1. Sheer egoism. Desire to seem clever, to be talked about, to be remembered after death, to get your own back on grownups who snubbed you in childhood, etc. etc." To this I would add egoism informed by imagination, style, and a desire to be known, yes, *but only on your own conditions*.

Nobody is more embitttered than the neglected writer and, obviously, allowed a certain recognition, I am a happier and more generous man than I would otherwise be. But nothing I have done to win this recognition appals me, has gone against my nature. I fervently believe that all a writer should send into the marketplace to be judged is his own work; the rest should remain private. I deplore the writer as a personality, however large and undoubted the talent, as is the case with Norman Mailer. I also do not believe in special licence for so-called artistic temperament. After all, my problems, as I grudgingly come within spitting distance of middle age, are the same as anybody else's. Easier maybe. I can bend my anxieties to subversive uses. Making stories of them. When I'm not writing, I'm a husband and a father of five. Worried about pollution. The population explosion. My sons' report cards.

"2. Aesthetic enthusiasm. Perception of beauty in the external world, or, on the other hand, in words and their right arrangement." The agonies involved in creating a novel, the unsatisfying draft, the scenes you never get right, are redeemed by those rare and memorable days when, seemingly without reason, everything falls right. Bonus days. Blessed days when, drawing on resources unsuspected, you pluck ideas and prose out of your skull that you never dreamt yourself capable of.

Such, such are the real joys.

Unfortunately, I don't feel that I've ever been able to sustain such flights for a novel's length. So the passages that flow are balanced with those which were forced in the hothouse. Of all the novels I've written, it is *The Apprenticeship of Duddy Kravitz* and *Cocksure* which come closest to my intentions and, therefore, give me the most pleasure. I should add that I'm still lumbered with the characters and ideas, the social concerns I first attempted in *The Acrobats*. Every serious writer has, I think, one theme, many variations to play on it.

Like any serious writer, I want to write one novel that will last, something that will make me remembered after death, and so I'm compelled to keep trying.

"3. Historical impulse. Desire to see things as they are. . . ."

No matter how long I continue to live abroad, I do feel forever rooted in Montreal's St. Urbain Street. That was my time, my place, and I have elected myself to get it right.

"4. Political purpose — using the word 'political' in the widest possible sense. Desire to push the world in a certain direction, to alter other people's idea of the kind of society that they should strive after."

Not an overlarge consideration in my work, though I would say that any serious writer is a moralist and only incidentally an entertainer.

After a year on the academic payroll, I returned to London in August 1969, abysmally depressed, because after four years *St. Urbain's Horseman* was no nearer to completion and, once more, my savings were running down. I retired to my room each morning, ostensibly to work, but actually to prepare highly impressive schedules. Starting next Monday, without fail, I would write three pages a day. Meanwhile, I would train for this ordeal by taking a nap every afternoon, followed by trips to the movies I simply had to see, thereby steeling myself against future fatigue and distractions. Next Monday, however, nothing came. Instead, taking the sports pages of the *International Herald-Tribune* as my text, I calculated, based on present standings and won-lost ratios, where each team in both major baseball leagues would end the season. Monday, falling on the eighth of the month, was a bad date, anyway. Neither here nor there. I would seriously begin work, I decided, on the 15th of the month, writing *six* pages daily. After all, if Simenon could write a novel in a week, surely. . . . When I failed to write even a paragraph on the 15th, I was not upset. Finally, I grasped the real nature of my problem. Wrong typewriter. Wrong colour ribbon. Wrong texture paper. I traded in my machine for one with a new type face, bought six blue ribbons, and three boxes of heavy bond paper, but still nothing came. Absolutely nothing.

Then, suddenly, in September, I began to put in long hours in my room, writing with ease, one day's work more gratifying than the next, and within a year the novel was done, all 550 typewritten pages.

The first person to read the manuscript, my wife, was, like all writers' wives, in an invidious position. I depend on my wife's taste and honesty. It is she, unenviably, who must tell me if I've gone wrong. If she disapproved, however diplomatically, there would be angry words, some things I would have to say about her own deficiencies, say her choice of clothes, her cooking, and the mess she was making of raising our children. I would also point out that it was gratuitously cruel of her to laugh aloud in bed, reading *Portnoy's Complaint*, when I was having such a struggle with my own novel. All the same, I would not submit the manuscript. If she found it wanting, I would put it aside for six months to be considered afresh. Another year, another draft. And yet—and yet—even if she proclaimed the manuscript a masterpiece, radiating delight, I would immediately discount her praise, thinking she's only my wife, loyal and loving, and therefore dangerously prejudiced. Maybe a liar. Certainly beyond the critical pale.

After my wife had pronounced, foolishly saying *St. Urbain's Horseman* was the best novel I'd written by far (making me resentful, because this obviously meant she hadn't enjoyed my earlier work as much as she should have done) I submitted the manuscript to my editors. Another hurdle, another intricate relationship. I deal with editors who are commonly taken to be among the most prescient in publishing—Robert Gottlieb at Knopf and, in England, Tony Godwin at Weidenfeld & Nicolson —but once I had sent them my manuscript, and they had obviously not dropped everything to read it overnight, wakening me with fulsome cables, long distance calls, champagne and caviar, I began to arm myself with fancied resentments and the case that could be made against their much-advertised (but as I had reason to suspect) over-rated acumen. As each morning's mail failed to yield a letter, and the telephone didn't ring, I lay seething on the living room sofa, ticking off, in my mind's eye, all the lesser novelists on their lists, those they flattered with larger ads, bigger first prints, more generous advances, more expensive lunches, than they had ever allowed me. In fact I had all but decided it was time to move on to other, more appreciative publishers when, only a week after I had submitted the manuscript, both editors wrote me enthusiastic letters. Enthusiastic letters, that is, until you have scrutinized them for the ninth time, reading between the lines, and grasp that the compliments are forced, the praise false, and that the sour truth hidden beneath the clichés is that they don't really like the novel. Or even if they did, their taste is demonstrably fallible, and corrupted by the fact that they are personal friends, especially fond of my wife.

Put plainly, nothing helps.

LAURA BOHANNAN

Shakespeare in the Bush

Just before I left Oxford for the Tiv in West Africa, conversation turned to the season at Stratford. "You Americans," said a friend, "often have difficulty with Shakespeare. He was, after all, a very English poet, and one can easily misinterpret the universal by misunderstanding the particular."

I protested that human nature is pretty much the same the whole world over; at least the general plot and motivation of the greater tragedies would always be clear — everywhere — although some details of custom might have to be explained and difficulties of translation might produce other slight changes. To end an argument we could not conclude, my friend gave me a copy of *Hamlet* to study in the African bush: it would, he hoped, lift my mind above its primitive surroundings, and possibly I might, by prolonged meditation, achieve the grace of correct interpretation.

It was my second field trip to that African tribe, and I thought myself ready to live in one of its remote sections — an area difficult to cross even on foot. I eventually settled on the hillock of a very knowledgeable old man, the head of a homestead of some hundred and forty people, all of whom were either his close relatives or their wives and children. Like the other elders of the vicinity, the old man spent most of his time performing ceremonies seldom seen these days in the more accessible parts of the tribe. I was delighted. Soon there would be three months of enforced isolation and leisure, between the harvest that takes place just before the rising of the swamps and the clearing of new farms when the water goes down. Then, I thought, they would have even more time to perform ceremonies and explain them to me.

I was quite mistaken. Most of the ceremonies demanded the presence of elders from several homesteads. As the swamps rose, the old men found it too difficult to walk from one homestead to the next, and the ceremonies gradually ceased. As the swamps rose even higher, all activities but one came to an end. The women brewed beer from maize and millet. Men, women, and children sat on their hillocks and drank it.

People began to drink at dawn. By midmorning the whole homestead was singing, dancing, and drumming. When it rained, people had to sit inside their huts: there they drank and sang or they drank and told stories. In any case, by noon or before, I either had to join the party or retire to my own hut and my books. "One does not discuss serious matters when there is beer. Come, drink with us." Since I lacked their capacity for the thick native beer, I spent more and more time with *Hamlet*. Before the end of the second month, grace descended on me. I was quite sure that *Hamlet* had only one possible interpretation, and that one universally obvious.

Early every morning, in the hope of having some serious talk before the beer party, I used to call on the old man at his reception hut — a circle of posts supporting a thatched roof above a low mud wall to keep out wind and rain. One day I crawled through the low doorway and found most of the men of the homestead sitting huddled in their ragged cloths on stools, low plank beds, and reclining chairs, warming themselves against the chill of the rain around a smoky fire. In the center were three pots of beer. The party had started.

The old man greeted me cordially. "Sit down and drink." I accepted a large calabash full of beer, poured some into a small drinking gourd, and tossed it down. Then I poured some more into the same gourd for the man second in seniority to my host before I handed my calabash over to a young man for further distribution. Important people shouldn't ladle beer themselves.

"It is better like this," the old man said, looking at me approvingly and plucking at the thatch that had caught in my hair. "You should sit and drink with us more often. Your servants tell me that when you are not with us, you sit inside your hut looking at a paper."

The old man was acquainted with four kinds of "papers": tax receipts, bride price receipts, court free receipts, and letters. The messenger who brought him letters from the chief used them mainly as a badge of office, for he always knew what was in them and told the old man. Personal letters for the few who had relatives in the government or mission stations were kept until someone went to a large market where there was a letter writer and reader. Since my arrival, letters were brought to me to be read. A few men also brought me bride price receipts, privately, with requests to change the figures to a higher sum. I found moral arguments were of no avail, since in-laws are fair game, and the technical hazards of forgery difficult to explain to an illiterate people. I did not wish them to think me silly enough to look at any such papers for days on end, and I hastily explained that my "paper" was one of the "things of long ago" of my country.

"Ah," said the old man. "Tell us."

I protested that I was not a storyteller. Storytelling is a skilled art among them; their standards are high, and the audiences critical—and vocal in their criticism. I protested in vain. This morning they wanted to hear a story while they drank. They threatened to tell me no more stories until I told them one of mine. Finally, the old man promised that no one would criticize my style "for we know you are struggling with our language." "But," put in one of the elders, "you must explain what we do not understand, as we do when we tell you our stories." Realizing that here was my chance to prove *Hamlet* universally intelligible, I agreed.

The old man handed me some more beer to help me on with my storytelling. Men filled their long wooden pipes and knocked coals from the fire to place in the pipe bowls; then, puffing contentedly, they sat back to listen. I began in the proper style, "Not yesterday, not yesterday, but long ago, a thing occurred. One night three men were keeping watch outside the homestead of the great chief, when suddenly they saw the former chief approach them."

"Why was he no longer their chief?"

"He was dead," I explained. "That is why they were troubled and afraid when they saw him."

"Impossible," began one of the elders, handing his pipe on to his neighbor, who interrupted, "Of course it wasn't the dead chief. It was an omen sent by a witch. Go on."

Slightly shaken, I continued. "One of these three was a man who knew things"—the closest translation for scholar, but unfortunately it also meant witch. The second elder looked triumphantly at the first. "So he spoke to the dead chief saying, 'Tell us what we must do so you may rest in your grave,' but the dead chief did not answer. He vanished, and they could see him no more. Then the man who knew things—his name was Horatio—said this event was the affair of the dead chief's son, Hamlet."

There was a general shaking of heads around the circle. "Had the dead chief no living brothers? Or was this son the chief?"

"No," I replied. "That is, he had one living brother who became the chief when the elder brother died."

The old men muttered: such omens were matters for chiefs and elders, not for youngsters; no good could come of going behind a chief's back; clearly Horatio was not a man who knew things.

"Yes, he was," I insisted, shooing a chicken away from my beer. "In our country the son is next to the father. The dead chief's younger brother had become the great chief. He had also married his elder brother's widow only about a month after the funeral."

"He did well," the old man beamed and announced to the others, "I told you that if we knew more about Europeans, we would find they really were very like us. In our country also," he added to me, "the younger brother marries the elder brother's widow and becomes the father of his children. Now, if your uncle, who married your widowed mother, is your father's full brother, then he will be a real father to you. Did Hamlet's father and uncle have one mother?"

His question barely penetrated my mind; I was too upset and thrown too far off balance by having one of the most important elements of *Hamlet* knocked straight out of the picture. Rather uncertainly I said that I thought they had the same mother, but I wasn't sure—the story didn't say. The old man told me severely that these genealogical details made all the difference and that when I got home I must ask the elders about it. He shouted out the door to one of his younger wives to bring his goatskin bag.

Determined to save what I could of the mother motif, I took a deep breath and began again. "The son Hamlet was very sad because his mother had married again so quickly. There was no need for her to do so, and it is our custom for a widow not to go to her next husband until she has mourned for two years."

"Two years is too long," objected the wife, who had appeared with the old man's battered goatskin bag. "Who will hoe your farms for you while you have no husband?"

"Hamlet," I retorted without thinking, "was old enough to hoe his mother's farms himself. There was no need for her to remarry." No one looked convinced. I gave up. "His mother and the great chief told Hamlet not to be sad, for the great chief himself would be a father to Hamlet. Furthermore, Hamlet would be the next chief: therefore he must stay to learn the things of a chief. Hamlet agreed to remain, and all the rest went off to drink beer."

While I paused, perplexed at how to render Hamlet's disgusted soliloquy to an audience convinced that Claudius and Gertrude had behaved in the best possible manner, one of the younger men asked me who had married the other wives of the dead chief.

"He had no other wives," I told him.

"But a chief must have many wives! How else can he brew beer and prepare food for all his guests?"

I said firmly that in our country even chiefs had only one wife, that they had servants to do their work, and that they paid them from tax money.

It was better, they returned, for a chief to have many wives and sons who would help him hoe his farms and feed his people; then everyone loved the chief who gave much and took nothing—taxes were a bad thing.

I agreed with the last comment, but for the rest fell back on their favorite way of fobbing off my questions: "That is the way it is done, so that is how we do it."

I decided to skip the soliloquy. Even if Claudius was here thought quite right to marry his brother's widow, there remained the poison motif, and I knew they would disapprove of fratricide. More hopefully I resumed, "That night Hamlet kept watch with the three who had seen his dead father. The dead chief again appeared, and although the others were afraid, Hamlet followed his dead father off to one side. When they were alone, Hamlet's dead father spoke."

"Omens can't talk!" The old man was emphatic.

"Hamlet's dead father wasn't an omen. Seeing him might have been an omen, but he was not." My audience looked as confused as I sounded. "It *was* Hamlet's dead father. It was a thing we call a 'ghost.' " I had to use the English word, for unlike many of the neighboring tribes, these people didn't believe in the survival after death of any individuating part of the personality.

"What is a 'ghost'? An omen?"

"No, a 'ghost' is someone who is dead but who walks around and can talk, and people can hear him and see him but not touch him."

They objected. "One can touch zombis."

"No, no! It was not a dead body the witches had animated to sacrifice and eat. No one else made Hamlet's dead father walk. He did it himself."

"Dead men can't walk," protested my audience as one man.

I was quite willing to compromise. "A 'ghost' is the dead man's shadow."

But again they objected. "Dead men cast no shadows."

"They do in my country," I snapped.

The old man quelled the babble of disbelief that arose immediately and told me with that insincere, but courteous, agreement one extends to the fancies of the young, ignorant, and superstitious, "No doubt in your country the dead can also walk without being zombis." From the depths of his bag he produced a withered fragment of kola nut, bit off one end to show it wasn't poisoned, and handed me the rest as a peace offering.

"Anyhow," I resumed, "Hamlet's dead father said that his own brother, the one who became chief, had poisoned him. He wanted Hamlet to avenge him. Hamlet believed this in his heart, for he did not like his father's brother." I took another swallow of beer. "In the country of the great chief, living in the same homestead, for it was a very large one, was an important elder who was often with the chief to advise and help him. His name was Polonius. Hamlet was courting his daughter, but her father and her brother ...[I cast hastily about for some tribal analogy] warned her not to let Hamlet visit her when she was alone on her farm, for he would be a great chief and so could not marry her."

"Why not?" asked the wife, who had settled down on the edge of the old man's chair. He frowned at her for asking stupid questions and growled, "They lived in the same homestead."

"That was not the reason," I informed them. "Polonius was a stranger who lived in the homestead because he helped the chief, not because he was a relative."

"Then why couldn't Hamlet marry her?"

"He could have," I explained, "but Polonius didn't think he would. After all, Hamlet was a man of great importance who ought to marry a chief's daughter, for in his country a man could have only one wife. Polonius was afraid that if Hamlet made love to his daughter, then no one else would give a high price for her."

"That might be true," remarked one of the shrewder elders, "but a chief's son would give his mistress's father enough presents and patronage to more than make up the difference. Polonius sounds like a fool to me."

"Many people think he was," I agreed. "Meanwhile Polonius sent his son Laertes off to Paris to learn the things of that country, for it was the homestead of a very great chief indeed. Because he was afraid that Laertes might waste a lot of money on beer and women and gambling, or get into trouble by fighting, he sent one of his servants to Paris secretly, to spy out what Laertes was doing. One day Hamlet came upon Polonius's daughter Ophelia. He behaved so oddly he frightened her. Indeed" — I was fumbling for words to express the dubious quality of Hamlet's madness — "the chief and many others had also noticed that when Hamlet talked one could understand the words but not what they meant. Many people thought that he had become mad." My audience suddenly became much more attentive. "The great chief wanted to know what was wrong with Hamlet, so he sent for two of Hamlet's age mates [school friends would have taken long explanation] to talk to Hamlet and find out what troubled his heart. Hamlet, seeing that they had been bribed by the chief to betray him, told them nothing. Polonius, however, insisted that Hamlet was mad because he had been forbidden to see Ophelia, whom he loved."

"Why," inquired a bewildered voice, "should anyone bewitch Hamlet on that account?"

"Bewitch him?"

"Yes, only witchcraft can make anyone mad, unless, of course, one sees the beings that lurk in the forest."

I stopped being a storyteller, took out my notebook and demanded to be told more about these two causes of madness. Even while they spoke and I jotted notes, I tried to calculate the effect of this new factor on the plot. Hamlet had not been exposed to the beings that lurk in the forest.

Only his relatives in the male line could bewitch him. Barring relatives not mentioned by Shakespeare, it had to be Claudius who was attempting to harm him. And, of course, it was.

For the moment I staved off questions by saying that the great chief also refused to believe that Hamlet was mad for the love of Ophelia and nothing else. "He was sure that something much more important was troubling Hamlet's heart."

"Now Hamlet's age mates," I continued, "had brought with them a famous storyteller. Hamlet decided to have this man tell the chief and all his homestead a story about a man who had poisoned his brother because he desired his brother's wife and wished to be chief himself. Hamlet was sure the great chief could not hear the story without making a sign if he was indeed guilty, and then he would discover whether his dead father had told him the truth."

The old man interrupted, with deep cunning, "Why should a father lie to his son?" he asked.

I hedged: "Hamlet wasn't sure that it really was his dead father." It was impossible to say anything, in that language, about devil-inspired visions.

"You mean," he said, "it actually was an omen, and he knew witches sometimes send false ones. Hamlet was a fool not to go to one skilled in reading omens and divining the truth in the first place. A man-who-sees-the-truth could have told him how his father died, if he really had been poisoned, and if there was witchcraft in it; then Hamlet could have called the elders to settle the matter."

The shrewd elder ventured to disagree. "Because his father's brother was a great chief, one-who-sees-the-truth might therefore have been afraid to tell it. I think it was for that reason that a friend of Hamlet's father—a witch and an elder—sent an omen so his friend's son would know. Was the omen true?"

"Yes," I said, abandoning ghosts and the devil; a witch-sent omen it would have to be. "It was true, for when the storyteller was telling his tale before all the homestead, the great chief rose in fear. Afraid that Hamlet knew his secret he planned to have him killed."

The stage set of the next bit presented some difficulties of translation. I began cautiously. "The great chief told Hamlet's mother to find out from her son what he knew. But because a woman's children are always first in her heart, he had the important elder Polonius hide behind a cloth that hung against the wall of Hamlet's mother's sleeping hut. Hamlet started to scold his mother for what she had done."

There was a shocked murmur from everyone. A man should never scold his mother.

"She called out in fear, and Polonius moved behind the cloth. Shouting, 'A rat!' Hamlet took his machete and slashed through the cloth." I paused for dramatic effect. "He had killed Polonius!"

The old men looked at each other in supreme disgust. "That Polonius truly was a fool and a man who knew nothing! What child would not know enough to shout, 'It's me!' " With a pang, I remembered that these people are ardent hunters, always armed with bow, arrow, and machete; at the first rustle in the grass an arrow is aimed and ready, and the hunter shouts

"Game!" If no human voice answers immediately, the arrow speeds on its way. Like a good hunter Hamlet had shouted, "A rat!"

I rushed in to save Polonius's reputation. "Polonius did speak. Hamlet heard him. But he thought it was the chief and wished to kill him to avenge his father. He had meant to kill him earlier that evening. . . ." I broke down, unable to describe to these pagans, who had no belief in individual afterlife, the difference between dying at one's prayers and dying "unhousell'd, disappointed, unaneled."[1]

This time I had shocked my audience seriously. "For a man to raise his hand against his father's brother and the one who has become his father — that is a terrible thing. The elders ought to let such a man be bewitched."

I nibbled at my kola nut in some perplexity, then pointed out that after all the man had killed Hamlet's father.

"No," pronounced the old man, speaking less to me than to the young men sitting behind the elders. "If your father's brother has killed your father, you must appeal to your father's age mates; *they* may avenge him. No man may use violence against his senior relatives." Another thought struck him. "But if his father's brother had indeed been wicked enough to bewitch Hamlet and make him mad that would be a good story indeed, for it would be his fault that Hamlet, being mad, no longer had any sense and thus was ready to kill his father's brother."

There was a murmur of applause. *Hamlet* was again a good story to them, but it no longer seemed quite the same story to me. As I thought over the coming complications of plot and motive, I lost courage and decided to skim over dangerous ground quickly.

"The great chief," I went on, "was not sorry that Hamlet had killed Polonius. It gave him a reason to send Hamlet away, with his two treacherous age mates, with letters to a chief of a far country, saying that Hamlet should be killed. But Hamlet changed the writing on their papers, so that the chief killed his age mates instead." I encountered a reproachful glare from one of the men whom I had told undetectable forgery was not merely immoral but beyond human skill. I looked the other way.

"Before Hamlet could return, Laertes came back for his father's funeral. The great chief told him Hamlet had killed Polonius. Laertes swore to kill Hamlet because of this, and because his sister Ophelia, hearing her father had been killed by the man she loved, went mad and drowned in the river."

"Have you already forgotten what we told you?" The old man was reproachful. "One cannot take vengeance on a madman; Hamlet killed Polonius in his madness. As for the girl, she not only went mad, she was drowned. Only witches can make people drown. Water itself can't hurt anything. It is merely something one drinks and bathes in."

I began to get cross. "If you don't like the story, I'll stop."

The old man made soothing noises and himself poured me some more beer. "You tell the story well, and we are listening. But it is clear that the elders of your country have never told you what the story really means. No, don't interrupt! We believe you when you say your marriage customs

---

1. See *Hamlet* I.iv.77.

are different, or your clothes and weapons. But people are the same everywhere; therefore, there are always witches and it is we, the elders, who know how witches work. We told you it was the great chief who wished to kill Hamlet, and now your own words have proved us right. Who were Ophelia's male relatives?"

"There were only her father and her brother." Hamlet was clearly out of my hands.

"There must have been many more; this also you must ask of your elders when you get back to your country. From what you tell us, since Polonius was dead, it must have been Laertes who killed Ophelia, although I do not see the reason for it."

We had emptied one pot of beer, and the old men argued the point with slightly tipsy interest. Finally one of them demanded of me, "What did the servant of Polonius say on his return?"

With difficulty I recollected Reynaldo and his mission. "I don't think he did return before Polonius was killed."

"Listen," said the elder, "and I will tell you how it was and how your story will go, then you may tell me if I am right. Polonius knew his son would get into trouble, and so he did. He had many fines to pay for fighting, and debts from gambling. But he had only two ways of getting money quickly. One was to marry off his sister at once, but it is difficult to find a man who will marry a woman desired by the son of a chief. For if the chief's heir commits adultery with your wife, what can you do? Only a fool calls a case against a man who will someday be his judge. Therefore Laertes had to take the second way: he killed his sister by witchcraft, drowning her so he could secretly sell her body to the witches."

I raised an objection. "They found her body and buried it. Indeed Laertes jumped into the grave to see his sister once more—so, you see, the body was truly there. Hamlet, who had just come back, jumped in after him."

"What did I tell you?" The elder appealed to the others. "Laertes was up to no good with his sister's body. Hamlet prevented him, because the chief's heir, like a chief, does not wish any other man to grow rich and powerful. Laertes would be angry, because he would have killed his sister without benefit to himself. In our country he would try to kill Hamlet for that reason. Is this not what happened?"

"More or less," I admitted. "When the great chief found Hamlet was still alive, he encouraged Laertes to try to kill Hamlet and arranged a fight with machetes between them. In the fight both the young men were wounded to death. Hamlet's mother drank the poisoned beer that the chief meant for Hamlet in case he won the fight. When he saw his mother die of poison, Hamlet, dying, managed to kill his father's brother with his machete."

"You see, I was right!" exclaimed the elder.

"That was a very good story," added the old man, "and you told it with very few mistakes. There was just one more error, at the very end. The poison Hamlet's mother drank was obviously meant for the survivor of the fight, whichever it was. If Laertes had won, the great chief would have poisoned him, for no one would know that he arranged Hamlet's death.

Then, too, he need not fear Laertes' witchcraft; it takes a strong heart to kill one's only sister by witchcraft.

"Sometime," concluded the old man, gathering his ragged toga about him, "you must tell us some more stories of your country. We, who are elders, will instruct you in their true meaning, so that when you return to your own land your elders will see that you have not been sitting in the bush, but among those who know things and who have taught you wisdom."

ALLEEN PACE NILSEN

Sexism in English: A Feminist View

Does culture shape language? Or does language shape culture? This is as difficult a question as the old puzzler of which came first, the chicken or the egg, because there's no clear separation between language and culture.

A well-accepted linguistic principle is that as culture changes so will the language. The reverse of this—as a language changes so will the culture—is not so readily accepted. This is why some linguists smile (or even scoff) at feminist attempts to replace *Mrs.* and *Miss* with *Ms.* and to find replacements for those all-inclusive words which specify masculinity, e.g., *chairman, mankind, brotherhood, freshman,* etc.

Perhaps they are amused for the same reason that it is the doctor at a cocktail party who laughs the loudest at the joke about the man who couldn't afford an operation so he offered the doctor a little something to touch up the X-ray. A person working constantly with language is likely to be more aware of how really deep-seated sexism is in our communication system.

Last winter I took a standard desk dictionary and gave it a place of honor on my night table. Every night that I didn't have anything more interesting to do, I read myself to sleep making a card for each entry that seemed to tell something about male and female. By spring I had a rather dog-eared dictionary, but I also had a collection of note cards filling two shoe boxes. The cards tell some rather interesting things about American English.

First, in our culture it is a woman's body which is considered important while it is a man's mind or his activities which are valued. A woman is sexy. A man is successful.

I made a card for all the words which came into modern English from somebody's name. I have a two-and-one-half-inch stack of cards which are men's names now used as everyday words. The women's stack is less than a half inch high and most of them came from Greek mythology. Words coming from the names of famous American men include *lynch, sousaphone, sideburns, Pullman, rickettsia, Shick test, Winchester rifle, Franklin stove, Bartlett pear, teddy bear,* and *boysenberry.* The only really common words coming from the names of American women are *bloomers* (after Amelia Jenks Bloomer) and *Mae West jacket.* Both of these words are related in some way to a woman's physical anatomy, while the male words (except for *sideburns* after General Burnsides) have nothing to do with the namesake's body.

This reminded me of an earlier observation that my husband and I made about geographical names. A few years ago we became interested in what we called "Topless Topography" when we learned that the Grand Tetons used to be simply called *The Tetons* by French explorers and *The Teats* by American frontiersmen. We wrote letters to several map makers and found the following listings: *Nippletop* and *Little Nipple Top* near Mt. Marcy in the Adirondacks, *Nipple Mountain* in Archuleta County, Colorado, *Nipple Peak* in Coke County, Texas, *Nipple Butte* in Pennington,

South Dakota, *Squaw Peak* in Placer County, California (and many other places), *Maiden's Peak* and *Squaw Tit* (they're the same mountain) in the Cascade Range in Oregon, *Jane Russell Peaks* near Stark, New Hampshire, and *Mary's Nipple* near Salt Lake City, Utah.

We might compare these names to Jackson Hole, Wyoming, or Pikes Peak, Colorado. I'm sure we would get all kinds of protests from the Jackson and Pike descendants if we tried to say that these topographical features were named because they in some way resembled the bodies of Jackson and Pike, respectively.

This preoccupation with women's breasts is neither new nor strictly American. I was amused to read the derivation of the word *Amazon*. According to Greek folk etymology, the *a* means "without" as in *atypical* or *amoral* while *mazon* comes from *mazós* meaning "breast". According to the legend, these women cut off one breast so that they could better shoot their bows. Perhaps the feeling was that the women had to trade in part of their femininity in exchange for their active or masculine role.

There are certain pairs of words which illustrate the way in which sexual connotations are given to feminine words while the masculine words retain a serious, businesslike aura. For example, being a *callboy* is perfectly respectable. It simply refers to a person who calls actors when it is time for them to go on stage, but being a *call girl* is being a prostitute.

Also we might compare *sir* and *madam*. *Sir* is a term of respect while *madam* has acquired the meaning of a brothel manager. The same thing has happened to the formerly cognate terms, *master* and *mistress*. Because of its acquired sexual connotations, *mistress* is now carefully avoided in certain contexts. For example, the Boy Scouts have *scoutmasters* but certainly not *scoutmistresses*. And in a dog show the female owner of a dog is never referred to as the *dog's mistress*, but rather as the *dog's master*.

Master appears in such terms as *master plan, concert master, schoolmaster, mixmaster, master charge, master craftsman*, etc. But *mistress* appears in very few compounds. This is the way it is with dozens of words which have male and female counterparts. I found two hundred such terms, e.g., *usher-usherette, heir-heiress, hero-heroine*, etc. In nearly all cases it is the masculine word which is the base with a feminine suffix being added for the alternate word. The masculine word also travels into compounds while the feminine word is a dead end; e.g., from *king-queen* comes *kingdom* but not *queendom*, from *sportsman-sportslady* comes *sportsmanship* but not *sportsladyship*, etc. There is one — and only one — semantic area in which the masculine word is not the base or more powerful word. This is in the area dealing with sex and marriage. Here it is the feminine word which is dominant. *Prostitute* is the base word with *male prostitute* being the derived term. *Bride* appears in *bridal shower, bridal gown, bridal attendant, bridesmaid*, and even in *bridegroom*, while *groom* in the sense of *bridegroom* does not appear in any compounds, not even to name the groom's attendants or his prenuptial party.

At the end of a marriage, this same emphasis is on the female. If it ends in divorce, the woman gets the title of *divorcée* while the man is usually described with a statement, such as, "He's divorced." When the marriage ends in death, the woman is a *widow* and the *-er* suffix which seems to connote masculine (probably because it is an agentive or actor type suffix) is added to make *widower*. *Widower* doesn't appear in any compounds (except for *grass widower*, which is another companion term), but *widow* appears in several compounds and in addition has some acquired meanings, such as the extra hand dealt to the table in certain card games and an undesirable leftover line of type in printing.

If I were an anthropological linguist making observations about a strange and primitive tribe, I would duly note on my tape recorder that I had found linguistic evidence to show that in the area of sex and marriage the female appears to be more important than the male, but in all other areas of the culture, it seems that the reverse is true.

But since I am not an anthropological linguist, I will simply go on to my second observation, which is that women are expected to play a passive role while men play an active one.

One indication of women's passive role is the fact that they are often identified as something to eat. What's more passive than a plate of food? Last spring I saw an announcement advertising the Indiana University English Department picnic. It read "Good Food! Delicious Women!" The publicity committee was probably jumped on by local feminists, but it's nothing new to look on women as "delectable morsels." Even women compliment each other with "You look good enough to eat," or "You have a peaches and cream complexion." Modern slang constantly comes up with new terms, but some of the old standbys for women are: *cute tomato, dish, peach, sharp cookie, cheese cake, honey, sugar,* and *sweetie-pie*. A man may occasionally be addressed as *honey* or described as a *hunk of meat*, but certainly men are not laid out on a buffet and labeled as women are.

Women's passivity is also shown in the comparisons made to plants. For example, to *deflower* a woman is to take away her virginity. A girl can be described as a *clinging vine*, a *shrinking violet*, or a *wall flower*. On the other hand, men are too active to be thought of as plants. The only time we make the comparison is when insulting a man we say he is like a woman by calling him a *pansy*.

We also see the active-passive contrast in the animal terms used with males and females. Men are referred to as *studs, bucks,* and *wolves,* and they go *tomcatting around*. These are all aggressive roles, but women have such pet names as *kitten, bunny, beaver, bird, chick, lamb,* and *fox*. The idea of being a pet seems much more closely related to females than to males. For instance, little girls grow up wearing *pigtails* and *ponytails* and they dress in *halters* and *dog collars*.

The active-passive contrast is also seen in the proper names given to boy babies and girl babies. Girls are much more likely to be given names like *Ivy, Rose, Ruby, Jewel, Pearl, Flora, Joy,* etc., while boys are given names describing active roles such as *Martin* (warlike), *Leo* (lion), *William* (protector), *Ernest* (resolute fighter), and so on.

Another way that women play a passive role is that they are defined in relationship to someone else. This is what feminists are protesting when they ask to be identified as *Ms.* rather than as *Mrs.* or *Miss*. It is a constant source of irritation to women's organizations that when they turn in items to newspapers under their own names, that is, Susan Glascoe, Jeanette Jones, and so forth, the editors consistently rewrite the item so that the names read Mrs. John Glascoe, Mrs. Robert E. Jones.

In the dictionary I found what appears to be an attitude on the part of editors that it is almost indecent to let a respectable woman's name march unaccompanied across the pages of a dictionary. A woman's name must somehow be escorted by a male's name regardless of whether or not the male contributed to the woman's reason for being in the dictionary, or in his own right, was as famous as the woman. For example, Charlotte Brontë is identified as Mrs. Arthur B. Nicholls, Amelia Earhart is identified as Mrs. George Palmer Putnam, Helen Hayes is identified as Mrs. Charles MacArthur, Zona Gale is identified as Mrs. William Llewelyn Breese, and Jenny Lind is identified as Mme. Otto Goldschmidt.

Although most of the women are identified as Mrs. ——— or as the wife of ———, other women are listed with brothers, fathers, or lovers. Cornelia Otis Skinner is identified as the daughter of Otis, Harriet Beecher Stowe is identified as the sister of Henry Ward Beecher, Edith Sitwell is identified as the sister of Osbert and Sacheverell, Nell Gwyn is identified as the mistress of Charles II, and Madame Pompadour is identified as the mistress of Louis XV.

The women who did get into the dictionary without the benefit of a masculine escort are a group sort of on the fringes of respectability. They are the rebels and the crusaders: temperance leaders Frances Elizabeth Caroline Willard and Carry Nation, women's rights leaders Carrie Chapman Catt and Elizabeth Cady Stanton, birth control educator Margaret Sanger, religious leader Mary Baker Eddy, and slaves Harriet Tubman and Phillis Wheatley.

I would estimate that far more than fifty percent of the women listed in the dictionary were identified as someone's wife. But of all the men—and there are probably ten times as many men as women—only one was identified as "the husband of . . . ." This was the unusual case of Frederic Joliot who took the last name of Joliot-Curie and was identified as "husband of Irene." Apparently Irene, the daughter of Pierre and Marie Curie, did not want to give up her maiden name when she married and so the couple took the hyphenated last name.

There are several pairs of words which also illustrate the more powerful role of the male and the relational role of the female. For example a *count* is a high political officer with a *countess* being simply the wife of a count. The same is true for a *duke* and a *duchess* and a *king* and a *queen*. The fact that a king is usually more powerful than a queen might be the reason that Queen Elizabeth's husband is given the title of *prince* rather than *king*. Since *king* is a stronger word than *queen*, it is reserved for a true heir to the throne because if it were given to someone coming into the royal family by marriage, then the subjects might forget where the true power lies. With the weaker word of *queen*, this would not be a problem; so a woman marrying a ruling monarch is given the title without question.

My third observation is that there are many positive connotations connected with the concept of masculine, while there are either trivial or negative connotations connected with the corresponding feminine concept. Conditioning toward the superiority of the masculine role starts very early in life. Child psychologists point out that the only area in which a girl has more freedom than a boy is in experimenting with an appropriate sex role. She is much freer to be a *tomboy* than is her brother to be a *sissy*. The proper names given to children reflect this same attitude. It's perfectly all right for a girl to have a boy's name, but not the other way around. As girls are given more and more of the boys' names, parents shy away from using boy names that might be mistaken for girl names, so the number of available masculine names is constantly shrinking. Fifty years ago *Hazel*, *Beverly*, *Marion*, *Frances*, and *Shirley* were all perfectly acceptable boys' names. Today few parents give these names to baby boys and adult men who are stuck with them self-consciously go by their initials or by abbreviated forms such as *Haze* or *Shirl*. But parents of little girls keep crowding the masculine set and currently popular girls' names include *Jo*, *Kelly*, *Teri*, *Cris*, *Pat*, *Shawn*, *Toni*, and *Sam*.

When the mother of one of these little girls tells her to *be a lady*, she means for her to sit with her knees together. But when the father of a little boy tells him to *be a man*, he means for him to be noble, strong, and virtuous. The whole concept of manliness has such positive connotations that it is a compliment to call a male a *he-man*, a *manly man*, or a *virile man* (*virile* comes from the Indo-European *vir*, meaning "man"). In each of these three terms, we are implying that someone is doubly good because he is doubly a man.

Compare *chef* with *cook*, *tailor* and *seamstress*, and *poet* with *poetess*. In each case, the masculine form carries with it an added degree of excellence. In comparing the masculine *governor* with the feminine *governess* and the masculine *major* with the feminine *majorette*, the added feature is power.

The difference between positive male and negative female connotations can be seen in several pairs of words which differ denotatively only in the matter of sex. For instance compare *bachelor* with the terms *spinster* and *old maid*. *Bachelor* has such positive connotations that modern girls have tried to borrow the feeling in the term *bachelor-girl*. *Bachelor* appears in glamorous terms such as *bachelor pad*, *bachelor party*, and *bachelor button*. But *old maid* has such strong negative feelings that it has been adopted into other areas, taking with it the feeling of undesirability. It has the metaphorical meaning of shriveled and unwanted kernels of pop corn, and it's the name of the last unwanted card in a popular game for children.

Patron and *matron* (Middle English for *father* and *mother*) are another set where women have tried to borrow the positive masculine connotations, this time through the word *patroness*, which literally means "female father." Such a peculiar term came about because of the high prestige attached to the word *patron* in such phrases as "*a patron of the arts*" or "*a patron saint*." *Matron* is more apt to be used in talking about a woman who is in charge of a jail or a public restroom.

Even *lord* and *lady* have different levels of connotation. *Our Lord* is used as a title for deity, while the corresponding *Our Lady* is a relational title for Mary, the moral mother of Jesus. *Landlord* has more dignity than *landlady* probably because the landlord is more likely to be thought of as the owner while the landlady is the person who collects the rent and enforces the rules. *Lady* is used in many insignificant places where the corresponding *lord* would never be used, for example, *ladies room, ladies sizes, ladies aid society, ladybug,* etc.

This overuse of *lady* might be compared to the overuse of *queen* which is rapidly losing its prestige as compared to *king.* Hundreds of beauty queens are crowned each year and nearly every community in the United States has its *Dairy Queen* or its *Freezer Queen*, etc. Male homosexuals have adopted the term to identify the "feminine" partner. And advertisers who are constantly on the lookout for euphemisms to make unpleasant sounding products salable have recently dealt what might be a death blow to the prestige of the word *queen.* They have begun to use it as an indication of size. For example, *queen-size* panty hose are panty hose for fat women. The meaning comes through a comparison with *king-size,* meaning big. However, there's a subtle difference in that our culture considers it desirable for males to be big because size is an indication of power, but we prefer that females be small and petite. So using *king-size* as a term to indicate bigness partially enhances the prestige of *king,* but using *queen-size* to indicate bigness brings unpleasant associations to the word *queen.*

Another set that might be compared are *brave* and *squaw.* The word *brave* carries with it the connotations of youth, vigor, and courage, while *squaw* implies almost opposite characteristics. With the set *wizard* and *witch,* the main difference is that *wizard* implies skill and wisdom combined with magic, while *witch* implies evil intentions combined with magic. Part of the unattractiveness of both *squaw* and *witch* is that they suggest old age, which in women is particularly undesirable. When I lived in Afghanistan (1967–1969), I was horrified to hear a proverb stating that when you see an old man you should sit down and take a lesson, but when you see an old woman you should throw a stone. I was equally startled when I went to compare the connotations of our two phrases *grandfatherly advice* and *old wives' tales.* Certainly it isn't expressed with the same force as in the Afghan proverb, but the implication is similar.

In some of the animal terms used for women the extreme undesirability of female old age is also seen. For instance consider the unattractiveness of *old nag* as compared to *filly,* of *old crow* or *old bat* as compared to *bird,* and of being *catty* as compared to being *kittenish.* The chicken metaphor tells the whole story of a girl's life. In her youth she is a *chick,* then she marries and begins feeling *cooped up,* so she goes to *hen parties* where she *cackles* with her friends. Then she has her *brood* and begins to *henpeck* her husband. Finally she turns into *an old biddy.*

BIL GILBERT

Fast as an Elephant, Strong as an Ant

One day recently I was reading a story about the San Diego Chargers when I came across the following sentence describing Mr. Ernie Ladd, a tackle who is said to be 6 feet 9 inches tall and to weigh 300 pounds. Ladd, the report stated, has "a body that a grizzly bear could be proud of." Now, this is an example of the falsely anthropomorphic and the factually inaccurate natural-history metaphor, a literary device widely used by sportswriters and one that I have long thought should be reported to authorities and stamped out.

The description of Ernie Ladd is objectionable on two counts. First, there is no evidence that bears take pride in their personal appearance, physical prowess or muscular development. Among animals, only men seem susceptible to narcissism. And even if grizzlies did have the emotions of a beach boy and sat about the woods admiring their physiques, no bear would be proud of having a body like that of Mr. Ladd.

According to my copy of *Mammals of the World* (Ernest P. Walker, The Johns Hopkins Press, 1964, page 1173), "Grizzlies 2.5 meters [about 8 feet] in length and 360 kg. [800 pounds] in weight have been recorded...." In brief, Mr. Ladd is simply too puny to impress a grizzly even if grizzlies were impressionable in these matters.

I have never been one to criticize without offering constructive alternatives. Additional reading of *Mammals of the World* has uncovered some statistics that may prove useful in the future. Should the need arise, one might accurately (though still anthropomorphically) write that Mr. Ernie Ladd has a body that a female gray seal (150 kg., 2 meters) or a pygmy hippopotamus (160 kg., 1.9 meters, counting tail) might be proud of.

It is not my purpose to embarrass or harass the man who wrote the story. Rather, it is to point out that he is the inheritor, the victim, of a bad journalistic tradition. Sportswriters have been comparing such and such an athlete to this or that animal since the dawn of sports. Many of these long-standing figures, metaphors, similes and tropes are even more wildly inaccurate and ridiculous than the comparison of Mr. Ladd to a grizzly bear.

An example that comes quickly to mind is the expression "wild as a hawk," used to describe either erratic performance (a baseball pitcher who cannot throw the ball across the plate) or untamable behavior (a fractious horse). In both senses the phrase is misleading. As far as control goes, the birds of prey are the antithesis of wildness (in the baseball use of the word). A duck hawk, for example, flying a mile high in the sky, can suddenly turn, dive earthward at 175 mph and strike a tiny sandpiper flying just a few feet above the ground. Sandy Koufax should be so accurate. As to being untamable, I, as a falconer, have often captured a feral adult hawk and in a month had the bird flying free, returning to my hand in response to a whistled command.

My own suggestion is that "wild as a heron" would better suggest the kind of behavior that wild as a hawk is supposed to describe. In many situations herons appear uncoordinated, almost spastic. Seeing a long-legged, gangly heron trying to land or take off from the ground is an experience. Furthermore, herons are far wilder (in the ferocious sense) than hawks. The most painful injury I ever received from an animal was given me by an American bittern (a heron type), who gouged a large hole in my wrist as I was attempting to free him from a fish trap.

"Loose as a goose" is an avian simile, supposedly suggesting extreme suppleness. Actually, geese have rigid pinions and are more or less bound like weight lifters by a heavy layer of pectoral muscle. Straight as a goose, stiff as a goose, pompous as a goose would be all right. But loose as a goose? Never. A better expression of the notion would be: "Though Slats Slattern has been a stellar NBA performer for 12 seasons, he remains young in spirit and loose as a mink." The slim-bodied minks, as well as weasels, ferrets and otters, are designed along the lines of a wet noodle. They look, and in fact are, far looser than a goose can possibly be.

Turning to mammals, an agility simile is "quick as a cat," often used in connection with such athletes as shortstops and goalies. It is true that cats are quicker than some things — turtles, mice, goldfish in bowls, for example — but they are much less quick than many other creatures. Any wheezing old dog worth its salt can catch a cat. I once had a crow so quick that it could fly down and deliver three pecks between the eyes of a cat (which the crow despised) before the feline could raise a paw in self-defense. Not long ago I was watching a tame baboon which had the run of a yard in which was caged an ocelot. The baboon, even though working through bars, would reach into the cage and, while the ocelot was trying to get her reflexes in order, grab the cat by both her handsome tail and pointed ears. Baboon-quick is accurate and has a nice exotic ring to it.

Cats may not be the quickest animals, but at least one of the family, the cheetah, is the swiftest mammal as far as straight-ahead sprinting goes. It would seem that "run like a cheetah" would be a natural simile for sportswriters, but what do we have? "Ziggy Zagowski, slashing left half for the Keokuk Kidneys, ran like a rabbit through the defending Sioux City Spleens." Now, for a few jumps a rabbit can move at a rate of 30 or 35 miles an hour, but 20 mph is its pace for a distance as great as 100 yards. This rate is about the same as — or a bit slower than — that of a journeyman human sprinter over the same course. The chances are that if old Zig could not out-leg a bunny he would not have even made his high school team. If, however, he could run like a cheetah, it would be a different matter, since those cats can do the 440 at 71 mph.

Since an elephant can skip along as fast as 25 mph (a bit faster than Bob Hayes or the average cottontail), it would be highly complimentary to say of an athlete that he runs like an elephant. However, the expression "elephantine" is actually used in sports as a term of derision, to twit a ponderous, slow-moving, clumsy performer. Actually, elephants are not only swift beasts but graceful ones. Despite their size, they are almost as quick as a baboon or as loose as a mink. They can slip quietly through the jungle, stand on a barrel or a ballerina at the behest of a ringmaster. "Horsine" would be a better term to designate a stumblebum. Horses are forever falling over small pebbles, ropes and their own feet. When a horse and rider start down even a gradual incline or up a path slightly narrower than the Pennsylvania Turnpike, the rider must dismount, and it is he who must lead, guide and, in general, prop up the horse.

Great strength has its place in sports, and it is traditional to describe the athlete who possesses it as being "strong as an ox." As in the case of quick cats and fast rabbits, the simile is not completely false, only inadequate. In proportion to their bulk, oxen are relatively strong but not overpoweringly so. A team of oxen weighing 3,400 pounds can move a dead weight, say a block of granite, equal to about three times its own weight. This is a fair feat when compared to a 150-pound weight lifter who can dead-lift 300 pounds. However, it is a feeble effort when one considers the ant, which can pick up a load 50 times heavier than itself. To speak of a fullback as being strong as an ant would be high praise indeed, since it would signify that the player could, without undue strain, carry the entire opposing team not only across the goal line, but right up into Row E.

Held in high regard by coaches, reporters and fans is the athlete who works incessantly at mastering the fundamentals of his game. Often such persevering types are admired as "beavers." This, of course, is a contraction of the folksy expressions "to work like a beaver" or "to be as busy as a beaver," both of which are based upon a misunderstanding of the beaver's nature and misobservation of the animal's customary behavior. Unlike some animals that must travel many miles a day just to rustle up a square meal, beavers seldom forage more than a hundred yards from their home. Beavers construct their well-publicized dams and lodges only when it is absolutely impossible to find a suitable natural waterscape. The lowly mole, on the other hand, may dig several hundred yards of tunnel in a day in an incessant effort to keep body and soul together. "I like that boy, all spring long he's been moling away," would be an apt way for a coach to describe and praise industriousness.

Canines have a strong attraction for scribes looking for a vivid, if fallacious, phrase. There is, for example, the veteran who is a "sly, foxy" competitor. (If foxes are so sly, how come they never run down the hounds? Who ever heard of a hunt catching a skunk?) Then there is the prizefighter about to addle the brains of his opponent or the fast-ball pitcher poised to stick one in a batter's ear. These violent men, we are often told, have a "wolfish grin" on their faces.

One of the few naturalists who have been close enough long enough to *au naturel* wolves to observe their facial expressions is Farley Mowat, who spent a summer camped virtually on the den step of a family of Arctic wolves. Mowat in his delightful book, *Never Cry Wolf*, claims that *his* wolves were kindly, affectionate, tolerant animals who looked and acted more like diplomats than thugs. This stands to reason. Many creatures besides man are predatory, but hardly any species except man tries to do real violence to its own kind in play while contemplating the prospect with a grin. If such a premayhem facial expression as a "wolfish grin" actually exists, it is probably unique to man. If this peculiar look of violence must be compared to that of some other animal, I recommend the short-tailed shrew.

The short-tailed shrew is one of the commonest animals of North America and one of the most perpetually predatory. Ounce for ounce (which is what a large shrew weighs), there is no busier killer in the world. Awake, the shrew is almost always preparing to kill, is killing or has just killed, and its victims include rodents, reptiles, birds and mammals several times its own size. The shrew, like almost all other mammals, does not kill out of capriciousness or playfulness, but rather because it has an extraordinarily high metabolic rate. It must daily consume the equivalent of its own body weight in order to keep the inner fires burning. (Eat like a shrew, rather than eat like a horse, would better describe the habits of a first baseman who is such a formidable trencherman that he can no longer bend down to scoop up low throws.) When a shrew closes in to kill something, say a white-footed mouse, it wears a really dreadful expression. A shrew is chinless, and its long mouth slashes across the underpart of its muzzle in a cruel, sharklike line. As the tiny killer closes in, its eyes glitter with excitement and two long brown fangs (which, incidentally, drip with a venomous saliva) are exposed. If Sonny Liston looked only half as wicked as a short-tailed shrew he might still be heavyweight champion of the world.

I fully realize that many of the criticisms and suggestions offered here do violence to some of the most cherished traditions of sports journalism, but there is no holding back literary and scientific progress. Consider, for example, the manner in which the style I advocate, high-fidelity zoological metaphor, injects color as well as accuracy into the following interview with Sig Schock of the Pardy Pumas:

"Sig Schock, a big horsine man, grizzled as a Norway rat, leaned back against the plywood bench, taking up a position so that the hot sun beat down on his ant-like shoulders. The eyes, old but still sharp as a barn owl's, flicked over the practice field, where the young Pumas cavorted as quick as so many baboons. 'I'll tell you,' Sig confided in his disconcertingly high, spring-peeperlike voice. 'These kids has got it. The most of them can run like elephants, a couple like cheetahs. And size. We finally got some. We got six boys with builds like a female gray seal's. Course, they're still young, some of them are wild as herons—that's O.K., they got the old desire. Every one of them is a snapping turtle or a raccoon. And I'll tell you something,' the sly, skunky veteran added, lowering his squeaky voice. 'We'll chew 'em up and lay 'em out this season.' A shrewish grin spread across the battered old face."

Leaving you with that, I remain pretty as a peacock, sassy as a jay-bird, happy as a clam.

Introduction to Poetry

The word "poetry," in the most widely used sense of the term, refers simply to composition in verse form. Verse, like prose, usually follows all the normal patterns of grammar, syntax, and punctuation. As a mode of composition, it differs from prose in providing the reader with additional conventions such as delimited line lengths, rhythmic patterns, and sometimes rhyme, all of which are devices for regularizing, or putting into measured form, the flow of language. Since some purists insist that only good or excellent verse deserves to be called poetry, there is some confusion about the term. The first sense of the word is a descriptive one: "poetry" used roughly as an equivalent for verse. As an evaluative term, "poetry" signifies approval of the expressive quality of a given use of language. In this use of the term, we not only speak approvingly of some works in verse as "poetry" and not so approvingly of other works as mere "verse," but we also speak of some prose that is "poetic" and some that is not. "Poetry", then, is both a descriptive and an evaluative term. For our purposes in this introduction, the term will be used in its more customary descriptive sense.

Poetry is the oldest literary form. Wherever we look in the history of literature we find that poetry, in its various forms, existed long before any form of literature in prose. Similarly, in our own lives we find that children take great pleasure in words used rhythmically long before they are able to enjoy being told a story. The rhythm of poetry, like that of music, seems to appeal to something quite basic in our physical and emotional beings, something that affects us prior to but anticipates our understanding of the actual language. It is this rhythm that makes demands on the order of the words, phrases, and clauses of a poem; and it is this rhythm again that leads, through its pattern, to a line that is distinctly poetic and enables us to distinguish it from prose.

Much of the earliest poetry in English was composed in order to be sung. For example, all of the ballads included here would originally have been sung rather than spoken. Although most of the later poetry in this section was not written for musical accompaniment, almost all of it can be readily seen to embody a musical element in the use of rhythm and in the choice of words not only for their meaning but also for the sound they produce. This sound of poetry is perhaps its most important characteristic; a poem has to be heard as well as seen. Indeed, Ezra Pound has said that "poetry begins to atrophy when it gets too far from music."

All rhythm, which makes the poem a poem, is heard in the poetic voice. The speaker of a poem, that is, its voice, is the poetic equivalent of the narrator in a short story. The poet usually creates, in more or less detail, an individual speaker who has a separate creative existence. In the dramatic monologue, a kind of poem in which the speaker converses with a silent listener (see, for example, Browning's "My Last Duchess" or T.S. Eliot's "The Love Song of J. Alfred Prufrock"), we find a clearly identifiable character. Others are not so obviously fictional characters, and some seem almost indistinguishable from the poets themselves. Some speakers

75

use a formal, others an informal, tone. Some use voices that are prophetic, political, philosophical, or otherwise public; others are altogether private. In all cases, however, the speaker views, experiences, and interprets life to varying degrees; and our understanding of a particular poem is contingent upon our understanding of the speaker's role.

In many cases, students who take the trouble to understand a poem's speaker are initially motivated to do so by particular interest in the subject of the poem, although such subjects are infinitely diverse. We would be faced with a nearly impossible task if we were to try to define the subject matter of poetry in our own or any other age. Particular subjects have a long poetic tradition, whereas others have held sway with different fashions at different times. It is a mistake to imagine that some subject, scene, or experience is naturally poetic. Poetic emotions are stimulated by a variety of experiences and scenes. Religion has inspired the creative minds of poets like Donne, Herbert, Hopkins, Larkin, Eliot, and Yeats. Wilfred Owen, Siegfried Sassoon, and Randall Jarrell have all written poems about war. The city and other social themes have become poetic material for, among others, John Betjeman, Ezra Pound, Dorothy Livesay, and P.K. Page. Landscapes and seascapes appear in the poems of, for example, Wordsworth, Coleridge, Shelley, Keats, Arnold, Auden, Purdy, Lochhead, Roberts, Carman, and Thomas. Tennyson, Gray, Cowper, Plath, Hughes, and Atwood all have written poems about animals. Spenser, Shakespeare, Marlowe, Donne, Marvell, and Auden have all written poems on love. Death is the focus of "Death, Be Not Proud," "Do Not Go Gentle into That Good Night," "Home Burial," "How Annandale Went Out," and "Keine Lazarovitch." Some of the poems in this selection are about poetry itself — Housman's "Terence, This Is Stupid Stuff," Marianne Moore's "Poetry," and Auden's "In Memory of W.B. Yeats." Whatever the subject — and the ones mentioned here are the most traditional — it is the poet's craft and sensibility that determine the quality of any poem.

The nature of a poem is also determined by its place in its particular poetic tradition. Some, like ballads or narrative poems ("David," by Earle Birney, and "Out, Out —," by Robert Frost) tell a complete story. Others may hint at a story (see Marvell's "To His Coy Mistress"), but their main focus is elsewhere. Some of the earlier poems, like Henry King's "Exequy," were written for specific occasions — in King's case to formally commemorate the death of his wife. Modern poets characteristically focus on events or perceptions that are especially significant in the context of the poet's particular sensibility but not necessarily a matter of public record. Margaret Atwood's "This Is a Photograph of Me" plays off the public nature of a photograph against the private sensibility that responds to it. In fact, the lyric poem, which is an intensely personal poetic expression, is now the most frequently used poetic form. The ode, the sonnet, the dramatic monologue, and the elegy, for example, are all different kinds of lyrical expressions. Students wishing more specific details regarding poetic tradition should consult one of the many fine handbooks to literature that are currently available.

Poetry often makes considerable demands on the reader because it tends to concentrate and compress expression rather than to offer lengthy explanations. Consequently, the reader is required to provide some of the connections and explanations that have been distilled out of the poem. For this reason, poetry is frequently both more involving and more memorable than prose. As readers of the poem, we thus become more active participants in the creative process. Students being introduced to poetry at the introductory level should understand something about the kind of language by which the poet best achieves concentration and compression. Figurative language is language that is used in a nonliteral way — a way that departs from the meaning of the word or phrase or construction in order to achieve a particular effect. When Owen says that the soldiers in "Dulce et Decorum Est" were "Bent double, like old beggars under sacks," he is using a simile, a fairly simple figurative device. When Shakespeare says in Sonnet 116 that love is "an ever fixèd mark/That looks on tempests and is never shaken," he is using a metaphor, a device with even greater potential for complexity of expression. As these examples indicate, figurative language demands that we see pictures or images of the thing being described. Imagery comprehends all aspects of poetic diction including, among other things, figurative language, connotative meanings, symbolism, and auditory impact. Critical terminology requires greater explication than can be offered here. We expect that classroom discussion will complement and amplify our remarks.

Finally, a few words on the subject of versification: traditionally, English versification has been based on so-called metrical principles. Metre is a device for producing and controlling intensity in the expression of feeling. It has been developed in English out of the natural tendency of our language to express emotion by heavily accentuating certain syllables in relation to others. A single line is a sort of verse sentence, and a popular poetic device is to play off grammatical pauses and sentences against the line length. The relationship in a verse line between the stressed syllables and the relatively unstressed ones is another important factor in the way poetry expresses emotion. The highly stressed quality of the English language tends to impart what we call a "rising rhythm" to our speech. We have an inclination when phrasing things to begin with an unstressed syllable and proceed immediately to a stressed syllable — for example, thĕ sún, thĕ móon, tŏdáy, tŏníght, or Marvell's "Hăd wé bŭt wórld eñoúgh aňd tíme." The result is that one rising rhythm phrase tends to follow another, and the pattern of unstressed and then stressed syllables seems to approximate the natural rhythm of our speech. This metrical pattern is called iambic, and the iambic foot is the most commonly employed metrical unit in the language.

Good poetry varies a great deal from strict metrical rhythm, and iambic and other stress patterns are guides rather than prescriptions for versification. In fact, whatever metre or combination of metres is used as the basis for the rhythm of a poem, some sort of controlled variation from the metrical norm is desirable. A stanza in which there is no variation ignores the expressive capacities of speech and shows, in its monotony, the dangers of excessive rhythmic regularity. Other measuring devices besides metre have been used (and been found to work) in much modern poetry as a basis for versification. What we call "free verse" is "free" only in the sense that it has liberated itself from the traditional preference for keeping strict count of stresses and syllables. It is not without its own unit of measurement. Whether the unit be the line, the cadenced phrase, the recurrence of images, or whatever, the onus of verse quality is placed mainly on the sensitivity of the poet's ear. The poetry in this anthology encompasses a variety of traditional and free versification methods.

However moving the "sound" of a poem, words have a referential meaning and say something about the world in which we live. If our discussion has taken us away from this very important aspect of poetry in order to concentrate on rather more formal aspects of the genre, the emphasis should be seen as a practical and not a philosophical one. It is our hope that these remarks will go some way to bringing students closer to poetry not only so that they may understand how a poem achieves its effect, but so that they may prepare to be affected.

ANONYMOUS

Sir Patrick Spence

The king sits in Dumferling toune,
　　Drinking the blude-reid wine;
"O whar will I get guid sailor,
　　To sail this ship of mine?"

5　Up and spak an eldern knight,
　　Sat at the king's richt knee:
"Sir Patrick Spence is the best sailor,
　　That sails upon the sea.

The king has written a braid[1] letter,
10　　And signed it wi' his hand,
And sent it to Sir Patrick Spence,
　　Was walking on the sand.

The first line that Sir Patrick red,
　　A loud laugh laughed he;
15　The next line that Sir Patrick red,
　　The tear blinded his ee.

"O wha is this has don this deed,
　　This ill deed don to me,
To send me out this time o' the year,
20　　To sail upon the sea!

"Mak haste, mak haste, my merry men all,
　　Our guid ship sails the morne."
"O say no sae, my master dear,
　　For I fear a deadly storme.

25　"Late, late yestreen I saw the new moone,
　　Wi' the auld moone in her arme,
And I fear, I fear, my dear master,
　　That we will come to harme."

O our Scots nobles were richt laith
30　　To weet their cork-heel'd schoone;
Bot lang owre a' the play were play'd,
　　Their hats they swam aboone.

O lang, lang may their ladies sit,
　　Wi' their fans into their hand,

---

1. Literally broad, possibly official.

35   Or ere they see Sir Patrick Spence
            Come sailing to the land.

        O lang, lang may the ladies stand,
            Wi' their gold kems² in their hair,
        Waiting for their ain dear lords,
40   For they'll see thame na mair.

        Haf owre,³ haf owre, to Aberdour,
            It's fiftie fadom deep,
        And their lies guid Sir Patrick Spence,
            Wi' the Scots lords at his feet.

Lord Randal

        "O where ha you been, Lord Randal, my son?
        And where ha you been, my handsome young man?"
        "I ha' been at the greenwood; mother, mak my bed soon,
        For I'm wearied wi' huntin', and fain wad lie down."

5   "And wha met ye there, Lord Randal, my son?
        And wha met you there, my handsome young man?"
        "O I met wi' my true-love; mother, mak my bed soon,
        For I'm wearied wi' huntin', and fain wad lie down."

        "And what did she give you, Lord Randal, my son?
10   And what did she give you, my handsome young man?"
        "Eels fried in a pan; mother, mak my bed soon,
        For I'm wearied wi' huntin', and fain wad lie down."

        "And wha gat your leavin's, Lord Randal, my son?
        And wha gat your leavin's, my handsome young man?"
15   "My hawks and my hounds; mother, mak my bed soon,
        For I'm wearied wi' huntin', and fain wad lie down."

        "And what becam of them, Lord Randal, my son?
        And what becam of them, my handsome young man?"
        "They stretched their legs out and died; mother, mak my bed soon,
20   For I'm wearied wi' huntin', and fain wad lie down."

        "Oh I fear you are poisoned, Lord Randal, my son!
        I fear you are poisoned, my handsome young man!"
        "O yes, I am poisoned; mother, mak my bed soon,
        For I'm sick at the heart, and I fain wad lie down."

2. Combs.
3. Half-way.

25 "What d' ye leave to your mother, Lord Randal, my son?
What d' ye leave to your mother, my handsome young man?"
"Four and twenty milk kye;[1] mother, mak my bed soon,
For I'm sick at the heart, and I fain wad lie down."

"What d' ye leave to your sister, Lord Randal, my son?
30 What d' ye leave to your sister, my handsome young man?"
"My gold and my silver; mother, mak my bed soon,
For I'm sick at the heart, and I fain wad lie down."

"What d' ye leave to your brother, Lord Randal, my son?
What d' ye leave to your brother, my handsome young man?"
35 "My houses and my lands; mother, mak my bed soon,
For I'm sick at the heart, and I fain wad lie down."

"What d' ye leave to your true-love, Lord Randal, my son?
What d' ye leave to your true-love, my handsome young man?"
"I leave her hell and fire; mother, mak my bed soon,
40 For I'm sick at the heart, and I fain wad lie down."

The Twa Corbies

A

There were three ravens sat on a tree,
   Downe a downe, hay down, hay downe
There were three ravens sat on a tree,
   With a downe
5 There were three ravens sat on a tree,
They were as blacke as they might be,
   With a downe derrie, derrie, derrie, downe, downe.

The one of them said to his mate,
"Where shall we our breakfast take?"

10 "Down in yonder greene field,
There lies a knight slain under his shield.

"His hounds they lie downe at his feete,
So well they can their master keepe.

"His haukes they flie so eagerly,
15 There's no fowle dare him come nie."

Downe there comes a fallow doe,
As great with yong as she might goe.

---

1. Dairy cows.

She lift up his bloudy hed,
And kist his wounds that were so red.

20   She got him up upon her backe,
And carried him to earthen lake.[1]

She buried him before the prime,
She was dead herselfe ere even-song time.

God send every gentleman
25   Such haukes, such hounds, and such a leman.[2]

B

As I was walking all alane,
I heard twa corbies making a mane;[1]
The tane[2] unto the t'other say,
"Where sall we gang and dine today?"

"In behint yon auld fail dyke,[3]
I wot there lies a new-slain knight;
And naebody kens that he lies there,
But his hawk, his hound, and lady fair.

"His hound is to the hunting gane,
His hawk to fetch the wild-fowl hame,
His lady's ta'en another mate,
So we may mak our dinner sweet.

"Ye'll sit on his white hause-bane,[4]
And I'll pick out his bonny blue een;
Wi' ae lock o' his gowden hair
We'll theek[5] our nest when it grows bare.

"Mony a one for him makes mane,
But nane sall ken where he is gane;
O'er his white banes when they are bare,
The wind sall blaw for evermair."

1. Pit.   2. One.
2. Sweetheart.   3. Old turf wall.
                           4. Neck.
1. Moan   5. Thatch.

Little Musgrave and the Lady Barnard

As it fell one holy-day
    As many be in the year,
When young men and maids together did go,
    Their mattins and masses to hear,

5   Little Musgrave came to the church-door;
    The priest was at private mass,
But he had more mind of the fair women
    Then he had of our Lady's grace.

The one of them was clad in green,
10   Another was clad in pall,
And then came in Lord Barnard's wife,
    The fairest amongst them all.

She cast an eye on Little Musgrave,
    As bright as the summer sun;
15   And then bethought this Little Musgrave,
    This lady's heart have I won.

Quoth she, "I have loved thee, Little Musgrave,
    Full long and many a day;"
"So have I loved you, fair lady,
20   Yet never a word durst I say."

"I have a bower at Buckelsfordbery,
    Full daintily it is dight;[1]
If thou wilt wend thither, thou Little Musgrave
    Thou's lie in mine arms all night."

25   Quoth he, "I thank ye, fair lady,
    This kindness thou showest to me;
But whether it be to my weal or woe,
    This night I will lie with thee."

With that he heard, a little tiny page,
30   By his lady's coach as he ran:
"All though I am my lady's foot-page,
    Yet I am Lord Barnard's man.

"My lord Barnard shall know of this,
    Whether I sink or swim;"
35   And ever where the bridges were broake
    He laid him down to swim.

---

1. Furnished.

"A sleep or wake, thou Lord Barnard,
   As thou art a man of life,
For Little Musgrave is at Bucklesfordbery,
40   A bed with thy own wedded wife."

"If this be true, thou little tiny page,
   This thing thou tellest to me,
Then all the land in Bucklesfordbery,
   I freely will give to thee.

45 "But if it be a lie, thou little tiny page,
   This thing thou tellst to me,
On the highest tree in Bucklesfordbery
   Then hanged shalt thou be."

He called up his merry men all:
50   "Come saddle me my steed;
This night must I go to Bucklesfordbery,
   For I never had greater need."

And some of them whistl'd, and some of them sung,
   And some these words did say,
55 And ever when my lord Barnard's horn blew,
   "Away, Musgrave, away!"

"Methinks I hear the thresel-cock,[2]
   Methinks I hear the jay;
Methinks I hear my lord Barnard,
60   And I would I were away."

"Lie still, lie still, thou Little Musgrave,
   And huggell me from the cold;
'Tis nothing but a shepherd's boy,
   A driving his sheep to the fold.

65 "Is not thy hawk upon a perch?
   Thy steed eats oats and hay;
And thou a fair lady in thine arms,
   And wouldst thou be away?"

With that my lord Barnard came to the door,
70   And lit a stone upon;
He plucked out three silver keys,
   And he opened the doors each one.

He lifted up the coverlet,
   He lifted up the sheet:

---

2. Thrush.

75 "How now, how now, thou Little Musgrave,
  Dost thou find my lady sweet?"

 "I find her sweet," quoth Little Musgrave,
  "The more 'tis to my pain;
 I would gladly give three hundred pounds
80 That I were on yonder plain."

 "Arise, arise, thou Little Musgrave,
  And put thy clothës on;
 It shall nere be said in my country
  I have killed a naked man.

85 "I have two swords in one scabbard,
  Full dear they cost my purse;
 And thou shalt have the best of them,
  And I will have the worse."

 The first stroke that Little Musgrave stroke,
90 He hurt Lord Barnard sore;
 The next stroke that Lord Barnard stroke,
  Little Musgrave nere struck more.

 With that bespake this fair lady,
  In bed whereas she lay:
95 "Although thou'rt dead, thou Little Musgrave,
  Yet I for thee will pray.

 "And wish well to thy soul will I,
  So long as I have life;
 So will I not for thee, Barnard,
100 Although I am thy wedded wife."

 He cut her paps from off her breast;
  Great pity it was to see
 That some drops of this lady's heart's blood
  Ran trickling down her knee.

105 "Woe worth you,[3] woe worth, my merry men all
  You were not borne for my good;
 Why did you not offer to stay my hand,
  When you see me wax so wood?[4]

 "For I have slain the bravest sir knight
110 That ever rode on a steed;
 So have I done the fairest lady
  That ever did woman's deed.

3. May woe betide you.
4. Become so insane.

"A grave, a grave," Lord Barnard cried,
"To put these lovers in;
115 But lay my lady on the upper hand,
For she came of the better kin."

He's Young but He's Daily A-Growing

The leaves they are green and the trees they are tall,
All those happy summer days are all past and gone:
Here I am left on the coldest winter day,
He's young but he's daily a-growing.

"O father, dear father, you've done me much wrong
For you have married me to a boy that's too young,
For I am twice twelve and he's only thirteen,
He's young but he's daily a-growing."

"O daughter, dear daughter, I've done you no wrong
For I have married you to a rich farmer's son,
And if you do but love him he'll be your lord and king
He's young but he's daily a-growing."

At the age of thirteen a married man was he,
At the age of fourteen his oldest son was born,
At the age of sixteen on his grave the grass grows green,
He's young but he's daily a-growing.

SIR THOMAS WYATT

They Flee from Me

They flee from me, that sometime did me seek,
With naked foot, stalking in my chamber:
I have seen them gentle, tame, and meek,
That now are wild, and do not remember
5   That sometime they put themselves in danger
To take bread at my hand; and now they range,
Busily seeking with a continual change.

Thanked be fortune, it hath been otherwise
Twenty times better; but once, in special,
10   In thin array, after a pleasant guise,
When her loose gown from her shoulders did fall,
And she me caught in her arms long and small,
Therewithal sweetly did me kiss,
And softly said, "Dear heart, how like you this?"

15   It was no dream; I lay broad waking.
But all is turned, thorough my gentleness,
Into a strange fashion of forsaking;
And I have leave to go of her goodness,
And she also to use new-fangledness.
20   But since that I so kindely am served,
I would fain know what she hath deserved.

CHIDIOCK TICHBORNE

Tichborne's Elegy
Written with His Own Hand in the Tower before His Execution

My prime of youth is but a frost of cares,
My feast of joy is but a dish of pain,
My crop of corn is but a field of tares,
And all my good is but vain hope of gain;
The day is past, and yet I saw no sun,
And now I live, and now my life is done.

My tale was heard and yet it was not told,
My fruit is fallen and yet my leaves are green,
My youth is spent and yet I am not old,
I saw the world and yet I was not seen;
My thread is cut and yet it is not spun,
And now I live, and now my life is done.

I sought my death and found it in my womb,
I looked for life and saw it was a shade,
I trod the earth and knew it was my tomb,
And now I die, and now I was but made;
My glass is full, and now my glass is run,
And now I live, and now my life is done.

EDMUND SPENSER

One Day I Wrote Her Name upon the Strand

One day I wrote her name upon the strand,
But came the waves and washéd it away.
Again I wrote it with a second hand,
But came the tide, and made my pains his prey.
Vain man, said she, that dost in vain assay
A mortal thing so to immortalize,

For I myself shall, like to this, decay,
And eke[1] my name be wipéd out likewise.
Not so, quoth I; let baser things devise[2]
To die in dust, but you shall live by fame:
My verse your virtues rare shall eternize,
And in the heavens write your glorious name.
Where, whenas death shall all the world subdue,
Our love shall live, and later life renew.

MICHAEL DRAYTON

Since There's No Help

Since there's no help, come let us kiss and part;
Nay, I have done, you get no more of me;
And I am glad, yea, glad with all my heart,
That thus so cleanly I myself can free.
Shake hands for ever, cancel all our vows,
And when we meet at any time again,
Be it not seen in either of our brows
That we one jot of former love retain.
Now at the last gasp of love's latest breath,
When, his pulse failing, passion speechless lies,
When faith is kneeling by his bed of death,
And innocence is closing up his eyes,
Now if thou wouldst, when all have given him over,
From death to life thou might'st him yet recover.

WILLIAM SHAKESPEARE

Sonnet 29

When in disgrace with fortune and men's eyes
I all alone beweep my outcast state,
And trouble deaf heaven with my bootless cries,
And look upon myself, and curse my fate,
Wishing me like to one more rich in hope,
Featured like him, like him with friends possessed,
Desiring this man's art, and that man's scope,
With what I most enjoy contented least;
Yet in these thoughts myself almost despising,
Haply I think on thee, and then my state,

1. Also.
2. Expect, plan.

Like to the lark at break of day arising
From sullen earth, sings hymns at heaven's gate;
For thy sweet love remembered such wealth brings
That then I scorn to change my state with kings.

Sonnet 60

Like as the waves make toward the pebbled shore,
So do our minutes hasten to their end,
Each changing place with that which goes before,
In sequent toil all forward do contend.
Nativity, once in the main of light,
Crawls to maturity, wherewith being crowned,
Crookèd eclipses 'gainst his glory fight,
And Time that gave doth now his gift confound.
Time doth transfix the flourish set on youth
And delves the parallels in beauty's brow,
Feeds on the rarities of nature's truth,
And nothing stands but for his scythe to mow.
And yet to times in hope my verse shall stand,
Praising thy worth, despite his cruel hand.

Sonnet 73

That time of year thou mayst in me behold
When yellow leaves, or none, or few, do hang
Upon those boughs which shake against the cold,
Bare ruined choirs, where late the sweet birds sang.
In me thou see'st the twilight of such day
As after sunset fadeth in the west,
Which by and by black night doth take away,
Death's second self that seals up all in rest.
In me thou see'st the glowing of such fire,
That on the ashes of his youth doth lie,
As the death-bed whereon it must expire
Consumed with that which it was nourished by.
This thou perceiv'st, which makes thy love more strong
To love that well, which thou must leave ere long.

Sonnet 116

Let me not to the marriage of true minds
Admit impediments. Love is not love
Which alters when it alteration finds,
Or bends with the remover to remove.
Oh, no! It is an ever-fixèd mark
That looks on tempests and is never shaken;
It is the star to every wand'ring bark,

Whose worth's unknown, although his height be taken.
Love's not Time's fool, though rosy lips and cheeks
Within his bending sickle's compass come.
Love alters not with his brief hours and weeks,
But bears it out even to the edge of doom.
If this be error, and upon me proved,
I never writ, nor no man ever loved.

pastoral, carpe diem.

CHRISTOPHER MARLOWE

The Passionate Shepherd to His Love

Come live with me and be my love,
And we will all the pleasures prove
That valleys, groves, hills, and fields,
Woods, or steepy mountain yields.

5   And we will sit upon the rocks,
Seeing the shepherds feed their flocks,
By shallow rivers to whose falls
Melodious birds sing madrigals.

And I will make thee beds of roses
10   And a thousand fragrant posies,
A cap of flowers, and a kirtle[1]
Embroidered all with leaves of myrtle;

A gown made of the finest wool
Which from our pretty lambs we pull;
15   Fair lined slippers for the cold,
With buckles of the purest gold;

A belt of straw and ivy buds,
With coral clasps and amber studs:
And if these pleasures may thee move,
20   Come live with me, and be my love.

The shepherd swains shall dance and sing
For thy delight each May morning:
If these delights thy mind may move,
Then live with me and be my love.

---

1. Woman's gown, skirt, or outer petticoat.

SIR WALTER RALEIGH

The Nymph's Reply to the Shepherd

If all the world and love were young,
And truth in every shepherd's tongue,
These pretty pleasures might me move
To live with thee and be thy love.

5   Time drives the flocks from field to fold,
When rivers rage, and rocks grow cold,
And Philomel[1] becometh dumb;
The rest complain of cares to come.

The flowers do fade, and wanton fields
10   To wayward winter reckoning yields:
A honey tongue, a heart of gall,
Is fancy's spring, but sorrow's fall.

Thy gowns, thy shoes, thy beds of roses,
Thy cap, thy kirtle, and thy posies
15   Soon break, soon wither, soon forgotten;
In folly ripe, in reason rotten.

Thy belt of straw and ivy buds,
Thy coral clasps and amber studs,
All these in me no means can move
20   To come to thee and be thy love.

But could youth last, and love still breed,
Had joys no date, nor age no need,
Then these delights my mind might move
To live with thee and be thy love.

JOHN DONNE

The Flea

Mark but this flea, and mark in this,
How little that which thou deniest me is;
It sucked me first, and now sucks thee,
And in this flea our two bloods mingled be;
5   Thou know'st that this cannot be said

---

1. Poetic name for the nightingale.

A sin, nor shame, nor loss of maidenhead;
  Yet this enjoys before it woo,
  And, pampered, swells with one blood made of two;
  And this, alas, is more than we would do.

10   Oh stay, three lives in one flea spare,
Where we almost, yea, more than married are.
This flea is you and I, and this
Our marriage bed and marriage temple is;
Though parents grudge, and you, we're met,
15   And cloistered in these living walls of jet.
  Though use make you apt to kill me,
  Let not to that, self-murder added be,
  And sacrilege, three sins in killing three.

Cruel and sudden, hast thou since
20   Purpled thy nail in blood of innocence?
Wherein could this flea guilty be,
Except in that drop which it sucked from thee?
Yet thou triumph'st and say'st that thou
Find'st not thyself, nor me, the weaker now.
25   'Tis true, then learn how false fears be:
  Just so much honor, when thou yield'st to me,
  Will waste, as this flea's death took life from thee.

A Valediction Forbidding Mourning

As virtuous men pass mildly away,
  And whisper to their souls to go,
Whilst some of their sad friends do say,
  The breath goes now, and some say, no;

5   So let us melt and make no noise,
  No tear-floods nor sigh-tempests move;
  'Twere profanation of our joys
  To tell the laity our love.

Moving of th'earth brings harms and fears:
10   Men reckon what it did and meant;
But trepidation of the spheres,
  Though greater far, is innocent.

Dull sublunary lovers' love,
  Whose soul is sense, cannot admit
15   Absence, because it doth remove
  Those things which elemented it.

But we, by a love so much refined
  That ourselves know not what it is,

Inter-assurèd of the mind,
20   Care less eyes, lips, hands to miss.

Our two souls, therefore, which are one,
     Though I must go, endure not yet
A breach, but an expansìon,
     Like gold to airy thinness beat.

25 If they be two, they are two so
     As stiff twin compasses are two;
Thy soul, the fixed foot, makes no show
     To move, but doth if th'other do.

And though it in the center sit,
30   Yet when the other far doth roam,
It leans, and hearkens after it,
     And grows erect as that comes home.

Such wilt thou be to me, who must,
     Like th'other foot, obliquely run;
35 Thy firmness makes my circle just,
     And makes me end where I begun.

The Bait

Come live with me and be my love,
And we will some new pleasures prove
Of golden sands and crystal brooks,
With silken lines and silver hooks.

5 There will the river whispering run,
Warm'd by thine eyes more than the sun,
And there th' enamor'd fish will stay,
Begging themselves they may betray.

When thou wilt swim in that live bath,
10 Each fish which every channel hath
Will amorously to thee swim,
Gladder to catch thee than thou him.

If thou to be so seen be'st loath,
By sun or moon, thou dark'nest both,
15 And if myself have leave to see,
I need not their light, having thee.

Let others freeze with angling reeds,
And cut their legs with shells and weeds,
Or treacherously poor fish beset
20 With strangling snare or windowy net;

Let coarse bold hands from slimy nest
The bedded fish in banks outwrest,
Or curious traitors, sleave-silk flies,
Bewitch poor fishes' wand'ring eyes,

25   For thee, thou need'st no such deceit,
For thou thyself art thine own bait;
That fish that is not catch'd thereby,
Alas, is wiser far than I.

Death, Be Not Proud

Death, be not proud, though some have called thee
Mighty and dreadful, for thou art not so.
For those whom thou think'st thou dost overthrow
Die not, poor death; nor yet canst thou kill me.
From rest and sleep, which but thy pictures be,
Much pleasure; then from thee much more must flow;
And soonest our best men with thee do go,
Rest of their bones, and soul's delivery.
Thou 'rt slave to fate, chance, kings, and desperate men,
And dost with poison, war, and sickness dwell;
And poppy or charms can make us sleep as well
And better than thy stroke. Why swell'st thou then?
One short sleep past, we wake eternally,
And death shall be no more: Death, thou shalt die.

ROBERT HERRICK

To the Virgins, to Make Much of Time

Gather ye rosebuds while ye may:
    Old Time is still a-flying;
And this same flower that smiles today,
    Tomorrow will be dying.

The glorious lamp of heaven, the sun,
    The higher he's a-getting,
The sooner will his race be run,
    And nearer he's to setting.

That age is best which is the first,
    When youth and blood are warmer;
But being spent, the worse, and worst
    Times, still succeed the former.

Then be not coy, but use your time;
   And while ye may, go marry:
For, having lost but once your prime,
   You may for ever tarry.

HENRY KING

The Exequy[1]

Accept, thou shrine of my dead saint,
Instead of dirges, this complaint;
And for sweet flowers to crown thy hearse,
Receive a strew of weeping verse
5   From thy grieved friend, whom thou might'st see
Quite melted into tears for thee.

Dear loss! since thy untimely fate
My task hath been to meditate
On thee, on thee; thou art the book,
10   The library whereon I look,
Though almost blind. For thee, loved clay,
I languish out, not live, the day,
Using no other exercise
But what I practise with mine eyes;
15   By which wet glasses I find out
How lazily time creeps about
To one that mourns; this, only this,
My exercise and business is.
So I compute the weary hours
20   With sighs dissolvèd into showers.

Nor wonder if my time go thus
Backward and most preposterous;
Thou has't benighted me; thy set
This eve of blackness did beget,
25   Who wast my day, though overcast
Before thou hadst thy noon-tide passed;
And I remember must in tears,
Thou scarce hadst seen so many years
As day tells hours. By thy clear sun
30   My love and fortune first did run;
But thou wilt never more appear

1. Funeral rite. Written in memory of King's
first wife, Anne.

Folded within my hemisphere,
Since both thy light and motion
Like a fled star is fall'n and gone;
35   And 'twixt me and my soul's dear wish
An earth now interposèd is,
Which such a strange eclipse doth make
As ne'er was read in almanac.

I could allow thee for a time
40   To darken me and my sad clime;
Were it a month, a year, or ten,
I would thy exile live till then,
And all that space my mirth adjourn,
So thou wouldst promise to return,
45   And putting off thy ashy shroud,
At length disperse this sorrow's cloud.

But woe is me! the longest date
Too narrow is to calculate
These empty hopes; never shall I
50   Be so much blest as to descry
A glimpse of thee, till that day come
Which shall the earth to cinders doom,
And a fierce fever must calcine[2]
The body of this world like thine,
55   My little world. That fit of fire
Once off, our bodies shall aspire
To our souls' bliss; then we shall rise
And view ourselves with clearer eyes
In that calm region where no night
60   Can hide us from each other's sight.

Meantime, thou hast her, earth; much good
May my harm do thee. Since it stood
With heaven's will I might not call
Her longer mine, I give thee all
65   My short-lived right and interest
In her whom living I loved best;
With a most free and bounteous grief,
I give thee what I could not keep.
Be kind to her, and prithee look
70   Thou write into thy doomsday book
Each parcel of this rarity
Which in thy casket shrined doth lie.

See that thou make thy reck'ning straight,
And yield her back again by weight;

2. Consume, purify by heat or fire.

75   For thou must audit on thy trust
     Each grain and atom of this dust,
     As thou wilt answer Him that lent,
     Not gave thee, my dear monument.

     So close the ground, and 'bout her shade
80   Black curtains draw, my bride is laid.
     Sleep on, my love, in thy cold bed,
     Never to be disquieted!
     My last good-night! Thou wilt not wake
     Till I thy fate shall overtake;
85   Till age, or grief, or sickness must
     Marry my body to that dust
     It so much loves, and fill the room
     My heart keeps empty in thy tomb.
     Stay for me there, I will not fail
90   To meet thee in that hollow vale.
     And think not much of my delay;
     I am already on the way,
     And follow thee with all the speed
     Desire can make, or sorrows breed.
95   Each minute is a short degree,
     And every hour a step towards thee.
     At night when I betake to rest,
     Next morn I rise nearer my west
     Of life, almost by eight hours' sail,
100 Than when sleep breathed his drowsy gale.

     Thus from the sun my bottom[3] steers,
     And my day's compass downward bears;
     Nor labor I to stem the tide
     Through which to thee I swiftly glide.

105 'Tis true, with shame and grief I yield,
     Thou like the van[4] first tookst the field,
     And gotten hath the victory
     In thus adventuring to die
     Before me, whose more years might crave
110 A just precedence in the grave.
     But hark! my pulse like a soft drum
     Beats my approach, tells thee I come;
     And slow howe'er my marches be,
     I shall at last sit down by thee.

115 The thought of this bids me go on,
     And wait my dissolution

---

3. Foundation, figuratively, boat.
4. Vanguard, front line.

With hope and comfort. Dear, forgive
The crime, I am content to live
Divided, with but half a heart,
120   Till we shall meet and never part.

GEORGE HERBERT

The Collar

I struck the board and cried, No more!
    I will abroad.
What? shall I ever sigh and pine?
My lines and life are free, free as the road,
5   Loose as the wind, and large as store.[1]
      Shall I be still in suit?[2]
Have I no harvest but a thorn
To let me blood, and not restore
What I have lost with cordial[3] fruit?
10   Sure there was wine
Before my sighs did dry it; there was corn
    Before my tears did drown it.
    Is the year only lost to me?
    Have I no bays[4] to crown it?
15   No flowers, no garlands gay? all blasted?
      All wasted?
    Not so, my heart: but there is fruit,
     And thou hast hands.
    Recover all thy sigh-blown age
20 On double pleasures: leave thy cold dispute
Of what is fit and not; forsake thy cage,
     Thy rope of sands,
Which petty thoughts have made, and made to thee
    Good cable, to enforce and draw,
25   And be thy law,
While thou didst wink and wouldst not see.
     Away! Take heed!
     I will abroad.
Call in thy death's-head[5] there; tie up thy fears.
30   He that forbears
    To suit and serve his need,
     Deserves his load.

---

1. Abundance.
2. Obligation.
3. Comforting, cheering.
4. A garland of laurel, symbolic of honour.
5. A skull, symbolic of mortality.

But as I raved and grew more fierce and wild
    At every word,
35   Methought I heard one calling, *Child!*
    And I replied, *My Lord*.

Virtue

Sweet day, so cool, so calm, so bright,
The bridal of the earth and sky:
The dew shall weep thy fall tonight,
    For thou must die.

Sweet rose, whose hue, angry and brave,
Bids the rash gazer wipe his eye:
Thy root is ever in its grave,
    And thou must die.

Sweet spring, full of sweet days and roses,
A box where sweets compacted lie:
My music shows ye have your closes,
    And all must die.

Only a sweet and virtuous soul,
Like seasoned timber, never gives;
But though the whole world turn to coal,
    Then chiefly lives.

JOHN MILTON

On His Blindness

When I consider how my light is spent,
Ere half my days, in this dark world and wide,
And that one talent[1] which is death to hide
Lodged with me useless, though my soul more bent
To serve therewith my Maker, and present
My true account, lest he returning chide,
"Doth God exact day labour, light denied?"
I fondly[2] ask; but Patience, to prevent
That murmur, soon replies: "God doth not need
Either man's work or his own gifts; who best
Bear his mild yoke, they serve him best. His state
Is kingly: thousands at his bidding speed
And post[3] o'er land and ocean without rest.
They also serve who only stand and wait."

---

1. Matthew xxv.14–30. See "The Parable of
the Talents" in the short-fiction section.

2. Foolishly.
3. Travel quickly.

ANDREW MARVELL

To His Coy Mistress

Had we but world enough, and time,
This coyness, lady, were no crime.
We would sit down, and think which way
To walk, and pass our long love's day.
5   Thou by the Indian Ganges' side
Shouldst rubies[1] find; I by the tide
Of Humber would complain. I would
Love you ten years before the Flood,
And you should, if you please, refuse
10   Till the conversion of the Jews.
My vegetable love should grow
Vaster than empires, and more slow;
An hundred years should go to praise
Thine eyes and on thy forehead gaze,
15   Two hundred to adore each breast,
But thirty thousand to the rest:
An age at least to every part,
And the last age should show your heart.
For, lady, you deserve this state,
20   Nor would I love at lower rate.
    But at my back I always hear
Time's wingèd chariot hurrying near;
And yonder all before us lie
Deserts of vast eternity.
25   Thy beauty shall no more be found,
Nor in thy marble vault shall sound
My echoing song; then worms shall try
That long preserved virginity,
And your quaint honour turn to dust,
30   And into ashes all my lust.
The grave's a fine and private place,
But none, I think, do there embrace.
    Now, therefore, while the youthful hue
Sits on thy skin like morning dew,
35   And while thy willing soul transpires
At every pore with instant fires,
Now let us sport us while we may,
Rather at once our time devour
Than languish in his slow-chapped[2] power.
40   Let us roll all our strength and all

1. Because of its colour the ruby reputedly removed evil thoughts, banished sadness, gave protection against the plague, and controlled amorous desires.
2. Slow-jawed (i.e., slowly devouring).

Our sweetness up into one ball,
And tear our pleasures with rough strife
Thorough the iron gates of life.
Thus, though we cannot make our sun
45 Stand still, yet we will make him run.

HENRY VAUGHAN

The Retreat

Happy those early days when I
Shined in my angel-infancy:
Before I understood this place
Appointed for my second race,
5   Or taught my soul to fancy aught
But a white, celestial thought;
When yet I had not walked above
A mile or two from my first love,
And looking back, at that short space,
10 Could see a glimpse of His bright face;
When on some gilded cloud or flower
My gazing soul would dwell an hour,
And in those weaker glories spy
Some shadows of eternity;
15 Before I taught my tongue to wound
My conscience with a sinful sound,
Or had the black art to dispense
A several[1] sin to every sense,
But felt through all this fleshly dress
20 Bright shoots of everlastingness.
    O how I long to travel back
And tread again that ancient track!
That I might once more reach that plain
Where first I left my glorious train,
25 From whence th'enlightened spirit sees
That shady city of palm trees.[2]
But, ah, my soul with too much stay
Is drunk, and staggers in the way.
Some men a forward motion love,
30 But I by backward steps would move;
And when this dust falls to the urn,
In that state I came, return.

1. Distinct, separate.
2. Jericho: a reference to the vision that

Moses had of the promised land (Deut.
xxxiv.1-4).

MATTHEW PRIOR

Jinny the Just[1]

Releas'd from the noise of the butcher and baker,
Who, my old friends be thanked, did seldom forsake her,
And from the soft duns[2] of my landlord the Quaker,

From chiding the footmen and watching the lasses,
5   From Nel that burn't milk too, and Tom that brake glasses
(Sad mischiefs through which a good housekeeper passes!),

From some real care but more fancied vexation,
From a life partly-colour'd half reason half passion,
Here lies after all the best wench in the Nation.

10   From the Rhine to the Po, from the Thames to the Rhone
Joanna or Janneton, Jinny or Joan
Twas all one to her by what name she was known.

For the idiom of words very little she heeded,
Provided the matter she drove at succeeded,
15   She took and gave languages just as she needed:

So for kitchen and market, for bargain and sale
She paid English or Dutch or French down on the nail,
But in telling a story she sometimes did fail;

Then begging excuse as she happen'd to stammer,
20   With respect to her betters but none to her grammar,
Her blush helpt her out and her jargon became her.

Her habit and mien she endeavour'd to frame
To the different gout[3] of the place where she came,
Her outside still chang'd, but her inside the same:

25   At the Hague in her slippers and hair as the mode is,
At Paris all falbalow'd[4] fine as a Goddess,
And at censuring London in smock sleeves and bodice,

She order'd affairs that few people could tell
In what part about her that mixture did dwell
30   Of Vrough[5] or Mistress or Mademoiselle.

---

1. Jinny was Prior's mistress and house-keeper who accompanied him on his many European travels.
2. Demands for payment.
3. Taste or manners.
4. A falbalow or furbelow was a flounce or pleated border on a petticoat or gown.
5. Matron.

For her sirname and race let the Heralds e'en answer,[6]
For her own proper worth was enough to advance her,
And he who lik'd her little valu'd her Grandsire.

But from what House soever her lineage may come
35   I wish my own Jinny but out of her tomb,
Though all her relations were there in her room.

Of such terrible beauty she never could boast
As with absolute sway o'er all hearts rules the roast
When Jacob[7] bawls out to the Chair for a toast;

40   But of good household features her person was made,
Nor by faction cried up nor of censure afraid,
And her beauty was rather for use than Parade;

Her blood so well mixt and flesh so well pasted[8]
That though her youth faded her comliness lasted,
45   The blue was worn off but the plum was well tasted.

Less smooth than her skin and less white than her breast
Was this polisht stone beneath which she lies prest:
Stop, reader and sigh while thou think'st on the rest.

With a just trim of virtue her soul was endued,
50   Not affectedly pious nor secretly lewd
She cut even between the coquette and the prude,

And her will with her duty so equally stood
That seldom oppos'd she was commonly good
And did pretty well, doing just what she would.

55   Declining all power she found means to persuade,
Was then most regarded, when most she obey'd,
The Mistress in truth when she seem'd but the Maid.

Such care of her own proper actions she took
That on other folks lives she had no time to look,
60   So censure and pride were struck out of her book.

Her thought still confin'd to its own little sphere
She minded not who did excell or did err
But just as the matter related to her.

6. From the reign of Henry VIII up to the accession of William and Mary, heralds travelled the English countryside registering the genealogies of its inhabitants, their main interest being in the coats of arms of the aristocracy and gentry. The genealogies that the heralds compiled were notoriously inac- curate since they depended heavily on hearsay and word-of-mouth claims of ancestry.
7. Probably refers to Jacob Tonson (1656– 1736) who was secretary of the Kit-Cat club to which Prior belonged.
8. Well made-up.

Then too when her private tribunal was rear'd
65   Her mercy so mixt with her judgement appear'd
That her foes were condemned and her friends always clear'd.

Her religion so well with her learning did suit
That in practice sincere, and in controverse mute
She show'd she knew better to live than dispute.

70   Some parts of the Bible by heart she recited
And much in historical chapters delighted
But in points about faith she was something short-sighted;

So notions and modes she referr'd to the Schools[9]
And in matters of Conscience adher'd to two rules,
75   To advise with no bigots and jest with no fools;

And scrupling but little, enough she believ'd,
By Charity ample small sins she retriev'd,
And when she had new clothes she always receiv'd.

Thus still whilst her morning unseen fled away
80   In ordering the linen and making the tea
That she scarce could have time for the Psalms of the Day;

And while after dinner the night came so soon
That half she propos'd very seldom was done,
With twenty God bless Me's how this day is gone;

85   While she read and accounted and pay'd and abated,[10]
Eat and drank, play'd and work'd, laugh'd and cried, lov'd and hated
As answer'd the End of her being created:

In the midst of her Age came a cruel disease
Which neither her broths nor receipts could appease,
90   So down dropt her Clay, may her Soul be at Peace.

Retire from this Sepulchre all the profane,
Ye that love for debauch or that marry for gain,
Retire least ye trouble the Manes[11] of Jane.

But thou that know'st love above Interest or lust,
95   Strew the Myrtle and rose on this once belov'd dust,
And shed one pious tear upon Jinny the Just.

Tread soft on her grave, and do right to her honour,
Let neither rude hand nor ill tongue light upon her,
Do all the small favours that now can be done her.

9. To professional theologians.
10. Deducted.   11. The soul of the dead.

100 And when what thou lik'd shall return to her clay,
For so I'm persuaded she must do one day,
What ever fantastic John Asgill[12] may say,

When as I have done now thou shalt set up a Stone
For something however distinguish'd or known,
105 May some pious friend the misfortune bemoan
And make thy Concern by reflexion his own.

JONATHAN SWIFT

Clever Tom Clinch Going to Be Hanged

As clever Tom Clinch, while the rabble was bawling,
Rode stately through Holborn,[1] to die in his calling;
He stopped at the George for a bottle of sack,
And promised to pay for it when he'd come back.
5 His waistcoat and stockings, and breeches were white,
His cap had a new cherry ribbon to tie 't.
The maids to the doors and the balconies ran,
And said, lack-a-day! he's a proper young man.
But, as from the windows the ladies he spied,
10 Like a beau in the box, he bowed low on each side;
And when his last speech the loud hawkers did cry,[2]
He swore from his cart, it was all a damned lie.
The hangman for pardon fell down on his knee;
Tom gave him a kick in the guts for his fee.
15 Then said, I must speak to the people a little,
But I'll see you all damned before I will *whittle*.[3]
My honest friend Wild,[4] may he long hold his place,
He lengthened my life with a whole year of grace.
Take courage, dear comrades, and be not afraid,
20 Nor slip this occasion to follow your trade.
My conscience is clear, and my spirits are calm,
And thus I go off without Pray'r-Book or Psalm.
Then follow the practice of clever Tom Clinch,
Who hung like a hero, and never would flinch.

12. John Asgill (1659–1738) wrote a tract in 1700 that set out to prove that Christians need not die. This "blasphemous pamphlet" was ordered burnt and Asgill was expelled from both the Irish and English parliaments.

1. The London street which ran to the gallows at Tyburn.
2. Broadsides relating the execution of a criminal and the criminal's supposed last words, the latter often in ballad form, were sold at public hangings. The producers of these broadsides were printers, who published the sheets and then employed hawkers in London and elsewhere.
3. Confess at the gallows.
4. Jonathan Wild (1683–1725) maintained a thriving gang of thieves in London but escaped punishment for a long time by helping the authorities catch other criminals. He was hanged at Tyburn.

ALEXANDER POPE

From An Essay on Criticism

A *little learning* is a dang'rous thing;
Drink deep, or taste not the Pierian spring: [1]
There shallow draughts intoxicate the brain,
And drinking largely sobers us again.
Fir'd at first sight with what the Muse imparts,
In fearless youth we tempt[2] the heights of Arts,
While from the bounded level of our mind,
Short views we take, nor see the lengths behind;
But, more advanc'd, behold with strange surprise,
New distant scenes of endless science rise!
So pleas'd at first the tow'ring Alps we try,
Mount o'er the vales, and seem to tread the sky,
Th' eternal snows appear already past,
And the first clouds and mountains seem the last:
But, those attain'd, we tremble to survey
The growing labours of the lengthen'd way,
Th' increasing prospect tires our wand'ring eyes,
Hills peep o'er hills, and Alps on Alps arise!

From The Rape of the Lock

And now, unveil'd, the Toilet stands display'd,
Each silver Vase in mystic order laid.
First, rob'd in white, the Nymph intent adores,
With head uncover'd, the Cosmetic pow'rs.
5   A heav'nly Image in the glass appears,
To that she bends, to that her eyes she rears;
Th' inferior Priestess, at her altar's side,
Trembling begins the sacred rites of Pride.
Unnumber'd treasures ope at once, and here
10   The various off'rings of the world appear;
From each she nicely culls with curious toil,
And decks the Goddess with the glitt'ring spoil.
This casket India's glowing gems unlocks,
And all Arabia breathes from yonder box.
15   The Tortoise here and Elephant unite,
Transform'd to combs, the speckled, and the white.
Here files of pins[1] extend their shining rows,
Puffs, Powders, Patches,[2] Bibles, Billet-doux.[3]

---

1. Spring sacred to the Pierides (Muses),
derived from Pieria near Mt. Olympus, where
it was first worshipped by the Thracians.
2. Attempt.

1. Brooches.
2. Artificial beauty spots.
3. Love-letters.

Now awful Beauty puts on all its arms;
20 The fair each moment rises in her charms,
Repairs her smiles, awakens ev'ry grace,
And calls forth all the wonders of her face;
Sees by degrees a purer blush arise,
And keener lightnings quicken in her eyes.
25 The busy Sylphs surround their darling care,
These set the head, and those divide the hair,
Some fold the sleeve, whilst others plait the gown;
And Betty's prais'd for labours not her own.

THOMAS GRAY

Ode on the Death of a Favourite Cat, Drowned in a Tub of Gold Fishes

'Twas on a lofty vase's side,
Where China's gayest art had dy'd
   The azure flowers, that blow;
Demurest of the tabby kind,
5 The pensive Selima reclin'd,
   Gazed on the lake below.

Her conscious tail her joy declar'd;
The fair round face, the snowy beard,
   The velvet of her paws,
10 Her coat, that with the tortoise vies,
Her ears of jet, and emerald eyes,
   She saw; and purr'd applause.

Still had she gaz'd; but 'midst the tide
Two angel forms were seen to glide,
15   The Genii of the stream:
Their scaly armour's Tyrian hue[1]
Thro' richest purple to the view
   Betray'd a golden gleam.

The hapless Nymph with wonder saw:
20 A whisker first and then a claw,
   With many an ardent wish,
She stretch'd in vain to reach the prize.
What female heart can gold despise?
   What Cat's averse to fish?

1. A purple dye of great importance in antiq-
uity, obtained from the secretion of the
Mediterranean sea snail.

25   Presumptuous Maid! with looks intent
       Again she stretch'd, again she bent,
          Nor knew the gulf between.
       (Malignant Fate sat by, and smil'd)
       The slipp'ry verge her feet beguil'd,
30   She tumbled headlong in.

       Eight times emerging from the flood
       She mew'd to ev'ry watry God,
          Some speedy aid to send.
       No Dolphin[2] came, no Nereid[3] stirr'd:
35   Nor cruel *Tom*, nor *Susan* heard.
          A Fav'rite has no friend!

       From hence, ye Beauties, undeceiv'd,
       Know, one false step is ne'er retriev'd,
          And be with caution bold.
40   Not all that tempts your wand'ring eyes
       And heedless hearts, is lawful prize;
          Nor all, that glisters, gold.

WILLIAM COWPER

The Retired Cat

       A poet's cat, sedate and grave,
       As poet well could wish to have,
       Was much addicted to inquire
       For nooks, to which she might retire,
5   And where, secure as mouse in chink,
       She might repose, or sit and think.
       I know not where she caught the trick—
       Nature perhaps herself had cast her
       In such a mould PHILOSOPHIQUE,
10   Or else she learn'd it of her master.
       Sometimes ascending, debonair,
       An apple-tree or lofty pear,
       Lodg'd with convenience in the fork,
       She watch'd the gard'ner at his work;
15   Sometimes her ease and solace sought
       In any old empty wat'ring pot,
       There wanting nothing, save a fan,
       To seem some nymph in her sedan,

---

2. A reference to the story of Arion who was
rescued from the sea by a dolphin.
3. Water nymph.

Apparell'd in exactest sort,
20 And ready to be borne to court.
　　But love of change it seems has place
Not only in our wiser race;
Cats also feel as well as we
That passion's force, and so did she.
25 Her climbing, she began to find,
Expos'd her too much to the wind,
And the old utensil of tin
Was cold and comfortless within:
She therefore wish'd instead of those,
30 Some place of more serene repose,
Where neither cold might come, nor air
Too rudely wanton with her hair,
And sought it in the likeliest mode
Within her master's snug abode.
35 　　A draw'r, — it chanc'd, at bottom lin'd
With linen of the softest kind,
With such as merchants introduce
From India, for the ladies' use, —
A draw'r impending o'er the rest,
40 Half open in the topmost chest,
Of depth enough, and none to spare,
Invited her to slumber there.
Puss with delight beyond expression,
Survey'd the scene, and took possession.
45 Recumbent at her ease ere long,
And lull'd by her own hum-drum song,
She left the cares of life behind,
And slept as she would sleep her last,
When in came, housewifely inclin'd,
50 The chambermaid, and shut it fast,
By no malignity impell'd,
But all unconscious whom it held.
　　Awaken'd by the shock (cried puss)
Was ever cat attended thus!
55 The open draw'r was left, I see,
Merely to prove a nest for me,
For soon as I was well compos'd,
Then came the maid, and it was clos'd:
How smooth these 'kerchiefs, and how sweet,
60 O what a delicate retreat!
I will resign myself to rest
Till Sol, declining in the west,
Shall call to supper; when, no doubt,
Susan will come and let me out.
65 　　The evening came, the sun descended,
And puss remain'd still unattended.
The night roll'd tardily away,
(With her indeed 'twas never day)

The sprightly morn her course renew'd,
70   The evening gray again ensued,
And puss came into mind no more
Than if entomb'd the day before.
With hunger pinch'd, and pinch'd for room,
She now presag'd approaching doom,
75   Nor slept a single wink, nor purr'd,
Conscious of jeopardy incurr'd.
   That night, by chance, the poet watching,
Heard an inexplicable scratching,
His noble heart went pit-a-pat,
80   And to himself he said — What's that?
He drew the curtain at his side,
And forth he peep'd, but nothing spied.
Yet, by his ear directed, guess'd
Something imprison'd in the chest,
85   And doubtful what, with prudent care,
Resolv'd it should continue there.
At length a voice, which well he knew,
A long and melancholy mew,
Saluting his poetic ears,
90   Consol'd him, and dispell'd his fears;
He left his bed, he trod the floor,
He 'gan in haste the draw'rs explore,
The lowest first, and without stop,
The rest in order to the top.
95   For 'tis a truth well known to most,
That whatsoever thing is lost,
We seek it, ere it come to light.
In ev'ry cranny but the right.
Forth skipp'd the cat; not now replete
100 As erst with airy self-conceit,
Nor in her own fond apprehension,
A theme for all the world's attention,
But modest, sober, cur'd of all
Her notions hyperbolical,
105 And wishing for a place of rest
Anything rather than a chest:
Then stept the poet into bed,
With this reflexion in his head:

Moral

Beware of too sublime a sense
110 Of your own worth and consequence!
The man who dreams himself so great,
And his importance of such weight,
That all around, in all that's done,
Must move and act for him alone,
115 Will learn, in school of tribulation,
The folly of his expectation.

Epitaph on a Hare

Here lies, whom hound did ne'er pursue;
    Nor swifter greyhound follow,
Whose foot ne'er tainted morning dew,
    Nor ear heard huntsman's hallo',

5   Old Tiney, surliest of his kind,
    Who, nurs'd with tender care,
And to domestic bounds confin'd,
    Was still a wild Jack-hare.

Though duly from my hand he took
10   His pittance ev'ry night,
He did it with a jealous look,
    And, when he could, would bite.

His diet was of wheaten bread,
    And milk, and oats, and straw,
15   Thistles, or lettuces instead,
    With sand to scour his maw.

On twigs of hawthorn he regal'd,
    On pippins' russet peel;
And, when his juicy salads fail'd,
20   Slic'd carrot pleas'd him well.

A Turkey carpet was his lawn,
    Whereon he lov'd to bound,
To skip and gambol like a fawn,
    And swing his rump around.

25   His frisking was at evening hours,
    For then he lost his fear;
But most before approaching show'rs,
    Or when a storm drew near.

Eight years and five round-rolling moons
30   He thus saw steal away,
Dozing out all his idle noons,
    And ev'ry night at play.

I kept him for his humour' sake,
    For he would oft beguile
35   My heart of thoughts that made it ache,
    And force me to a smile.

But now, beneath this walnut-shade
    He finds his long, last home,
And waits in snug concealment laid,
40   Till gentler Puss shall come.

He, still more aged, feels the shocks
  From which no care can save,
And, partner once of Tiney's box,
  Must soon partake his grave.

WILLIAM BLAKE

London

I wander thro' each charter'd[1] street,
Near where the charter'd Thames does flow,
And mark in every face I meet
Marks of weakness, marks of woe.

In every cry of every Man,
In every Infant's cry of fear,
In every voice, in every ban,[2]
The mind-forg'd manacles I hear.

How the Chimney-sweeper's cry
Every blackning Church appalls;
And the hapless Soldier's sigh
Runs in blood down Palace walls.

But most thro' midnight streets I hear
How the youthful Harlot's curse
Blasts the new-born Infant's tear,
And blights with plagues the Marriage hearse.

The Sick Rose

O rose, thou art sick.
The invisible worm
That flies in the night
In the howling storm

Has found out thy bed
Of crimson joy,
And his dark secret love
Does thy life destroy.

1. The Charter of the City of London once represented its source of freedom, by which citizens held certain liberties and privileges.

2. A ban is a political or legal prohibition but can also be a public condemnation or a curse. Cf. also "banns" in the sense of a marriage proclamation.

The Lamb

Little Lamb, who made thee?
Dost thou know who made thee?
Gave thee life & bid thee feed,
By the stream & o'er the mead;
Gave thee clothing of delight,
Softest clothing wooly bright;
Gave thee such a tender voice,
Making all the vales rejoice!
Little Lamb who made thee?
Dost thou know who made thee?

Little Lamb I'll tell thee,
Little Lamb I'll tell thee!
He is callèd by thy name,
For he calls himself a Lamb:
He is meek & he is mild,
He became a little child:
I a child & thou a lamb,
We are callèd by his name.
Little Lamb God bless thee.
Little Lamb God bless thee.

The Tyger

Tyger! Tyger! burning bright
In the forests of the night,
What immortal hand or eye
Could frame thy fearful symmetry?

5   In what distant deeps or skies
Burnt the fire of thine eyes?
On what wings dare he aspire?
What the hand, dare seize the fire?

And what shoulder, & what art,
10   Could twist the sinews of thy heart?
And when thy heart began to beat,
What dread hand? & what dread feet?

What the hammer? what the chain?
In what furnace was thy brain?
15   What the anvil? what dread grasp
Dare its deadly terrors clasp?

When the stars threw down their spears,
And water'd heaven with their tears,
Did he smile his work to see?
20   Did he who made the Lamb make thee?

Tyger! Tyger! burning bright
In the forests of the night,
What immortal hand or eye
Dare frame thy fearful symmetry?

ROBERT BURNS

A Red, Red Rose

O, my luve's like a red, red rose
That's newly sprung in June.
O, my luve is like the melodie
That's sweetly played in tune.

As fair art thou, my bonnie lass,
So deep in luve am I;
And I will luve thee still, my dear,
Till a' the seas gang dry.

Till a' the seas gang dry, my dear,
And the rocks melt wi' the sun;
And I will luve thee still, my dear,
While the sands o' life shall run.

And fare thee weel, my only luve,
And fare thee weel a while!
And I will come again, my luve,
Though it were ten thousand mile.

WILLIAM WORDSWORTH

Ode
Intimations of Immortality from Recollections of Early Childhood

The Child is father of the Man;
And I could wish my days to be
Bound each to each by natural piety.[1]

1
There was a time when meadow, grove, and stream,
The earth, and every common sight,
    To me did seem
    Appareled in celestial light,

---

1. Final lines of Wordsworth's "My Heart
Leaps Up."

5 The glory and the freshness of a dream.
   It is not now as it hath been of yore —
       Turn whereso'er I may,
         By night or day,
   The things which I have seen I now can see no more.

       2
10   The Rainbow comes and goes,
           And lovely is the Rose,
           The Moon doth with delight
   Look round her when the heavens are bare,
         Waters on a starry night
15   Are beautiful and fair;
       The sunshine is a glorious birth;
       But yet I know, where'er I go,
   That there hath passed away a glory from the earth.

       3
   Now, while the birds thus sing a joyous song,
20   And while the young lambs bound
         As to the tabor's[2] sound,
   To me alone there came a thought of grief:
   A timely utterance gave that thought relief,
         And I again am strong:
25 The cataracts blow their trumpets from the steep;
   No more shall grief of mine the season wrong;
   I hear the Echoes through the mountains throng,
   The Winds come to me from the fields of sleep,
         And all the earth is gay;
30   Land and sea
         Give themselves up to jollity,
           And with the heart of May
           Doth every Beast keep holiday —
             Thou Child of Joy,
35 Shout round me, let me hear thy shouts, thou happy Shepherd-boy!

       4
   Ye blessèd Creatures, I have heard the call
     Ye to each other make; I see
   The heavens laugh with you in your jubilee;
       My heart is at your festival,
40   My head hath its coronal,
   The fullness of your bliss, I feel — I feel it all.
         Oh, evil day! if I were sullen
           While Earth herself is adorning,
             This sweet May morning,

---

2. A tabor is a small drum.

45   And the Children are culling
            On every side,
        In a thousand valleys far and wide,
        Fresh flowers; while the sun shines warm,
        And the Babe leaps up on his Mother's arm—
50   I hear, I hear, with joy I hear!
        —But there's a Tree, of many, one,
        A single Field which I have looked upon,
        Both of them speak of something that is gone:
            The Pansy at my feet
55   Doth the same tale repeat:
        Whither is fled the visionary gleam?
        Where is it now, the glory and the dream?

        5
        Our birth is but a sleep and a forgetting:
        The Soul that rises with us, our life's Star,
60   Hath had elsewhere its setting,
            And cometh from afar:
            Not in entire forgetfulness,
            And not in utter nakedness,
        But trailing clouds of glory do we come
65   From God, who is our home:
        Heaven lies about us in our infancy!
        Shades of the prison-house begin to close
            Upon the growing Boy
            But he
70   Beholds the light, and whence it flows,
            He sees it in his joy;
        The Youth, who daily farther from the east
            Must travel, still is Nature's Priest,
            And by the vision splendid
75   Is on his way attended;
        At length the Man perceives it die away,
        And fade into the light of common day.

        6
        Earth fills her lap with pleasures of her own;
        Yearnings she hath in her own natural kind,
80   And, even with something of a Mother's mind,
            And no unworthy aim,
            The homely Nurse doth all she can
        To make her foster child, her Inmate Man,
            Forget the glories he hath known,
85   And that imperial palace whence he came.

        7
        Behold the Child among his new-born blisses,
        A six years' Darling of a pigmy size!
        See, where 'mid work of his own hand he lies,
        Fretted by sallies of his mother's kisses,

90   With light upon him from his father's eyes!
See, at his feet, some little plan or chart,
Some fragment from his dream of human life,
Shaped by himself with newly-learnéd art;
      A wedding or a festival,
95   A mourning or a funeral;
        And this hath now his heart,
      And unto this he frames his song;
        Then will he fit his tongue
To dialogues of business, love, or strife;
100   But it will not be long
      Ere this be thrown aside,
      And with new joy and pride
The little Actor cons another part;
Filling from time to time his "humorous stage"[3]
105   With all the Persons, down to palsied Age,
That Life brings with her in her equipage;
      As if his whole vocation
      Were endless imitation.

8

Thou, whose exterior semblance doth belie
110   Thy Soul's immensity;
Thou best Philosopher, who yet dost keep
Thy heritage, thou Eye among the blind,
That, deaf and silent, read'st the eternal deep,
Haunted forever by the eternal mind—
115   Mighty Prophet! Seer blest!
      On whom those truths do rest,
Which we are toiling all our lives to find,
In darkness lost, the darkness of the grave;
Thou, over whom thy Immortality
120   Broods like the Day, a Master o'er a Slave,
A Presence which is not to be put by;
Thou little Child, yet glorious in the might
Of heaven-born freedom on thy being's height,
Why with such earnest pains dost thou provoke
125   The years to bring the inevitable yoke,
Thus blindly with thy blessedness at strife?
Full soon thy Soul shall have her earthly freight,
And custom lie upon thee with a weight,
Heavy as frost, and deep almost as life!

9

130   O joy! that in our embers
      Is something that doth live,
      That nature yet remembers
      What was so fugitive!

---

3. Exhibiting the "humours," or characteristic
physical and mental qualities, of people.

The thought of our past years in me doth breed
135   Perpetual benediction: not indeed
For that which is most worthy to be blest;
Delight and liberty, the simple creed
Of Childhood, whether busy or at rest,
With new-fledged hope still fluttering in his breast—
140   Not for these I raise
         The song of thanks and praise;
         But for those obstinate questionings
         Of sense and outward things,
         Fallings from us, vanishings;
145   Blank misgivings of a Creature
Moving about in worlds not realized,
High instincts before which our mortal Nature
Did tremble like a guilty Thing surprised;
         But for those first affections,
150   Those shadowy recollections,
         Which, be they what they may,
Are yet the fountain light of all our day,
Are yet a master light of all our seeing;
         Uphold us, cherish, and have power to make
155   Our noisy years seem moments in the being
Of the eternal Silence: truths that wake,
         To perish never;
Which neither listlessness, nor mad endeavor,
         Nor Man nor Boy,
160   Nor all that is at enmity with joy,
Can utterly abolish or destroy!
         Hence in a season of calm weather
         Though inland far we be,
Our Souls have sight of that immortal sea
165   Which brought us hither,
         Can in a moment travel thither,
And see the Children sport upon the shore,
And hear the mighty waters rolling evermore.

10
Then sing, ye Birds, sing, sing a joyous song!
170   And let the young Lambs bound
         As to the tabor's sound!
We in thought will join your throng,
         Ye that pipe and ye that play,
         Ye that through your hearts today
175   Feel the gladness of the May!
What though the radiance which was once so bright
Be now forever taken from my sight,
         Though nothing can bring back the hour
Of splendor in the grass, of glory in the flower;
180   We will grieve not, rather find
         Strength in what remains behind;

In the primal sympathy
Which having been must ever be;
In the soothing thoughts that spring
185   Out of human suffering;
In the faith that looks through death,
In years that bring the philosophic mind.

11
And O, ye Fountains, Meadows, Hills, and Groves,
Forebode not any severing of our loves!
190   Yet in my heart of hearts I feel your might;
I only have relinquished one delight
To live beneath your more habitual sway.
I love the Brooks which down their channels fret,
Even more than when I tripped lightly as they;
195   The innocent brightness of a new-born Day
        Is lovely yet;
The clouds that gather round the setting sun
Do take a sober coloring from an eye
That hath kept watch o'er man's mortality;
200   Another race hath been, and other palms are won.
Thanks to the human heart by which we live,
Thanks to its tenderness, its joys, and fears,
To me the meanest flower that blows can give
Thoughts that do often lie too deep for tears.

Lines Composed a Few Miles above Tintern Abbey,[1] on Revisiting the Banks of the Wye during a Tour, July 13, 1798

Five years have past; five summers, with the length
Of five long winters! and again I hear
These waters, rolling from their mountain-springs
With a soft inland murmur. — Once again
5   Do I behold these steep and lofty cliffs,
That on a wild secluded scene impress
Thoughts of more deep seclusion; and connect
The landscape with the quiet of the sky.
The day is come when I again repose
10   Here, under this dark sycamore, and view
These plots of cottage-ground, these orchard-tufts,
Which at this season, with their unripe fruits,
Are clad in one green hue, and lose themselves
'Mid groves and copses. Once again I see
15   These hedge-rows, hardly hedge-rows, little lines
Of sportive wood run wild: these pastoral farms,

---

1. Ruins of a medieval abbey in the valley of
the river Wye.

Green to the very door; and wreaths of smoke
Sent up, in silence, from among the trees!
With some uncertain notice, as might seem
20   Of vagrant dwellers in the houseless woods,
Or of some Hermit's cave, where by his fire
The Hermit sits alone.
                              These beauteous forms,
Through a long absence, have not been to me
As is a landscape to a blind man's eye:
25   But oft, in lonely rooms, and 'mid the din
Of towns and cities, I have owed to them
In hours of weariness, sensations sweet,
Felt in the blood, and felt along the heart;
And passing even into my purer mind,
30   With tranquil restoration: — feelings too
Of unremembered pleasure: such, perhaps,
As have no slight or trivial influence
On that best portion of a good man's life,
His little, nameless, unremembered acts
35   Of kindness and of love. Nor less, I trust,
To them I may have owed another gift,
Of aspect more sublime; that blessed mood,
In which the burthen of the mystery,
In which the heavy and the weary weight
40   Of all this unintelligible world,
Is lightened: — that serene and blessed mood,
In which the affections gently lead us on, —
Until, the breath of this corporeal frame
And even the motion of our human blood
45   Almost suspended, we are laid asleep
In body, and become a living soul:
While with an eye made quiet by the power
Of harmony, and the deep power of joy,
We see into the life of things.
                                        If this
50   Be but a vain belief, yet, oh! how oft —
In darkness and amid the many shapes
Of joyless daylight; when the fretful stir
Unprofitable, and the fever of the world,
Have hung upon the beatings of my heart —
55   How oft, in spirit, have I turned to thee,
O sylvan Wye! thou wanderer thro' the woods,
How often has my spirit turned to thee!
   And now, with gleams of half-extinguished thought,
With many recognitions dim and faint,
60   And somewhat of a sad perplexity,
The picture of the mind revives again:
While here I stand, not only with the sense
Of present pleasure, but with pleasing thoughts
That in this moment there is life and food

65 For future years. And so I dare to hope,
    Though changed, no doubt, from what I was when first
    I came among these hills; when like a roe
    I bounded o'er the mountains, by the sides
    Of the deep rivers, and the lonely streams,
70 Wherever nature led: more like a man
    Flying from something that he dreads, than one
    Who sought the thing he loved. For nature then
    (The coarser pleasures of my boyish days,
    And their glad animal movements all gone by)
75 To me was all in all. — I cannot paint
    What then I was. The sounding cataract
    Haunted me like a passion: the tall rock,
    The mountain, and the deep and gloomy wood,
    Their colours and their forms, were then to me
80 An appetite; a feeling and a love,
    That had no need of a remoter charm,
    By thought supplied, nor any interest
    Unborrowed from the eye. — That time is past,
    And all its aching joys are now no more,
85 And all its dizzy raptures. Not for this
    Faint I, nor mourn nor murmur; other gifts
    Have followed; for such loss, I would believe,
    Abundant recompense. For I have learned
    To look on nature, not as in the hour
90 Of thoughtless youth; but hearing oftentimes
    The still, sad music of humanity,
    Nor harsh nor grating, though of ample power
    To chasten and subdue. And I have felt
    A presence that disturbs me with the joy
95 Of elevated thoughts; a sense sublime
    Of something far more deeply interfused,
    Whose dwelling is the light of setting suns,
    And the round ocean and the living air,
    And the blue sky, and in the mind of man;
100 A motion and a spirit, that impels
    All thinking things, all objects of all thought,
    And rolls through all things. Therefore am I still
    A lover of the meadows and the woods,
    And mountains; and of all that we behold
105 From this green earth; of all the mighty world
    Of eye, and ear, — both what they half create,
    And what perceive; well pleased to recognise
    In nature and the language of the sense,
    The anchor of my purest thoughts, the nurse,
110 The guide, the guardian of my heart, and soul
    Of all my moral being.
                          Nor perchance,
    If I were not thus taught, should I the more
    Suffer my genial spirits to decay:

For thou art with me here upon the banks
115 Of this fair river; thou my dearest Friend,[2]
My dear, dear Friend; and in thy voice I catch
The language of my former heart, and read
My former pleasures in the shooting lights
Of thy wild eyes. Oh! yet a little while
120 May I behold in thee what I was once,
My dear, dear Sister! and this prayer I make,
Knowing that Nature never did betray
The heart that loved her; 'tis her privilege,
Through all the years of this our life, to lead
125 From joy to joy: for she can so inform
The mind that is within us, so impress
With quietness and beauty, and so feed
With lofty thoughts, that neither evil tongues,
Rash judgments, nor the sneers of selfish men,
130 Nor greetings where no kindness is, nor all
The dreary intercourse of daily life,
Shall e'er prevail against us, or disturb
Our cheerful faith, that all which we behold
Is full of blessings. Therefore let the moon
135 Shine on thee in thy solitary walk;
And let the misty mountain-winds be free
To blow against thee: and, in after years,
When these wild ecstasies shall be matured
Into a sober pleasure; when thy mind
140 Shall be a mansion for all lovely forms,
Thy memory be as a dwelling-place
For all sweet sounds and harmonies; oh! then,
If solitude, or fear, or pain, or grief,
Should be thy portion, with what healing thoughts
145 Of tender joy wilt thou remember me,
And these my exhortations! Nor, perchance—
If I should be where I no more can hear
Thy voice, nor catch from thy wild eyes these gleams
Of past existence—wilt thou then forget
150 That on the banks of this delightful stream
We stood together; and that I, so long
A worshipper of Nature, hither came
Unwearied in that service: rather say
With warmer love—oh! with far deeper zeal
155 Of holier love. Nor wilt thou then forget,
That after many wanderings, many years
Of absence, these steep woods and lofty cliffs,
And this green pastoral landscape, were to me
More dear, both for themselves and for thy sake!

---

2. His sister, Dorothy, with whom he was on a
walking tour when he composed the poem.

SAMUEL TAYLOR COLERIDGE

Frost at Midnight

The Frost performs its secret ministry,
Unhelped by any wind. The owlet's cry
Came loud—and hark, again! loud as before.
The inmates of my cottage, all at rest,
5   Have left me to that solitude, which suits
Abstruser musings: save that at my side
My cradled infant slumbers peacefully.
'Tis calm indeed! so calm, that it disturbs
And vexes meditation with its strange
10   And extreme silentness. Sea, hill, and wood,
This populous village! Sea, and hill, and wood,
With all the numberless goings-on of life,
Inaudible as dreams! the thin blue flame
Lies on my low-burnt fire, and quivers not;
15   Only that film,[1] which fluttered on the grate,
Still flutters there, the sole unquiet thing.
Methinks its motion in this hush of nature
Gives it dim sympathies with me who live,
Making it a companionable form,
20   Whose puny flaps and freaks the idling Spirit
By its own moods interprets, everywhere
Echo or mirror seeking of itself,
And makes a toy of Thought.
                      But O! how oft,
How oft, at school, with most believing mind,
25   Presageful, have I gazed upon the bars,
To watch that fluttering *stranger!* and as oft
With unclosed lids, already had I dreamt
Of my sweet birthplace, and the old church tower,
Whose bells, the poor man's only music, rang
30   From morn to evening, all the hot Fair-day,
So sweetly, that they stirred and haunted me
With a wild pleasure, falling on mine ear
Most like articulate sounds of things to come!
So gazed I, till the soothing things, I dreamt,
35   Lulled me to sleep, and sleep prolonged my dreams!
And so I brooded all the following morn,
Awed by the stern preceptor's face, mine eye
Fixed with mock study on my swimming book:
Save if the door half opened, and I snatched
40   A hasty glance, and still my heart leaped up,

---

1. Coleridge noted that "In all parts of the kingdom these films are called *strangers* and supposed to portend the arrival of some absent friend."

For still I hoped to see the *stranger's* face,
Townsman, or aunt, or sister more beloved,
My playmate when we both were clothed alike!

Dear Babe, that sleepest cradled by my side,
45   Whose gentle breathings, heard in this deep calm,
Fill up the interspersèd vacancies
And momentary pauses of the thought!
My babe so beautiful! it thrills my heart
With tender gladness, thus to look at thee,
50   And think that thou shalt learn far other lore,
And in far other scenes! For I was reared
In the great city, pent 'mid cloisters dim,
And saw nought lovely but the sky and stars.
But *thou*, my babe! shalt wander like a breeze
55   By lakes and sandy shores, beneath the crags
Of ancient mountain, and beneath the clouds,
Which image in their bulk both lakes and shores
And mountain crags: so shalt thou see and hear
The lovely shapes and sounds intelligible
60   Of that eternal language, which thy God
Utters, who from eternity doth teach
Himself in all, and all things in himself.
Great universal Teacher! he shall mold
Thy spirit, and by giving make it ask.

65   Therefore all seasons shall be sweet to thee,
Whether the summer clothe the general earth
With greenness, or the redbreast sit and sing
Betwixt the tufts of snow on the bare branch
Of mossy apple tree, while the nigh thatch
70   Smokes in the sun-thaw; whether the eave-drops fall
Heard only in the trances of the blast,
Or if the secret ministry of frost
Shall hang them up in silent icicles,
Quietly shining to the quiet Moon.

Kubla Khan
Or a Vision in a Dream. A Fragment[1]

In Xanadu did Kubla Khan
A stately pleasure dome decree:
Where Alph, the sacred river, ran
Through caverns measureless to man
5   Down to a sunless sea.
So twice five miles of fertile ground
With walls and towers were girdled round:
And there were gardens bright with sinuous rills,
Where blossomed many an incense-bearing tree;
10   And here were forests ancient as the hills,
Enfolding sunny spots of greenery.

But oh! that deep romantic chasm which slanted
Down the green hill athwart a cedarn cover!
A savage place! as holy and enchanted
15   As e'er beneath a waning moon was haunted
By woman wailing for her demon lover!
And from this chasm, with ceaseless turmoil seething,
As if this earth in fast thick pants were breathing,
A mighty fountain momently was forced:
20   Amid whose swift half-intermitted burst
Huge fragments vaulted like rebounding hail,
Or chaffy grain beneath the thresher's flail:
And 'mid these dancing rocks at once and ever
It flung up momently the sacred river.
25   Five miles meandering with a mazy motion
Through wood and dale the sacred river ran,
Then reached the caverns measureless to man,
And sank in tumult to a lifeless ocean:

---

1. Kubla Khan was a Mongol emperor in thirteenth-century China. In an introductory note to the poem, Coleridge gave the following explanation of its composition: "In the summer of the year 1797, the author, then in ill health, had retired to a lonely farmhouse between Porlock and Linton, on the Exmoor confines of Somerset and Devonshire. In consequence of a slight indisposition, an anodyne had been prescribed, from the effects of which he fell asleep in his chair at the moment that he was reading the following sentence, or words of the same substance, in *Purchas's Pilgrimage*: "Here the Khan Kubla commanded a palace to be built, and a stately garden thereunto. And thus ten miles of fertile ground were inclosed with a wall." The author continued for about three hours in a profound sleep, at least of the external sense, during which time he has the most vivid confidence that he could not have composed less than from two to three hundred lines; if that indeed can be called composition in which all the images rose up before him as *things*, with a parallel production of the correspondent expressions, without any sensation or consciousness of effort. On awaking he appeared to himself to have a distinct recollection of the whole, and taking his pen, ink, and paper, instantly and eagerly wrote down the lines that are here preserved. At this moment he was unfortunately called out by a person on business from Porlock, and detained by him above an hour, and on his return to his room, found, to his no small surprise and mortification, that though he still retained some vague and dim recollection of the general purport of the vision, yet, with the exception of some eight or ten scattered lines and images, all the rest had passed away like the images on the surface of a stream into which a stone has been cast, but, alas! without the after restoration of the latter!"

And 'mid this tumult Kubla heard from far
30   Ancestral voices prophesying war!

The shadow of the dome of pleasure
Floated midway on the waves;
Where was heard the mingled measure
From the fountain and the caves.
35   It was a miracle of rare device,
A sunny pleasure dome with caves of ice!

A damsel with a dulcimer
In a vision once I saw:
It was an Abyssinian maid,
40   And on her dulcimer she played,
Singing of Mount Abora.
Could I revive within me
Her symphony and song,
To such a deep delight 'twould win me,
45   That with music loud and long,
I would build that dome in air,
That sunny dome! those caves of ice!
And all who heard should see them there,
And all should cry, Beware! Beware!
50   His flashing eyes, his floating hair!
Weave a circle round him thrice,
And close your eyes with holy dread,
For he on honey-dew hath fed,
And drunk the milk of Paradise.

GEORGE GORDON, LORD BYRON

On This Day I Complete My Thirty-Sixth Year
Missolonghi,[1] January 22, 1824

'Tis time this heart should be unmoved,
    Since others it hath ceased to move:
Yet, though I cannot be beloved,
    Still let me love!

5   My days are in the yellow leaf;
    The flowers and fruits of love are gone;
The worm, the canker, and the grief
    Are mine alone!

The fire that on my bosom preys
10   Is lone as some volcanic isle;

1. In Greece, where Byron had gone to support the Greek insurgents against the forces of the Ottoman Empire in the Greek War of Independence. Byron died there on 19 April 1824.

No torch is kindled at its blaze—
    A funeral pile.

The hope, the fear, the jealous care,
    The exalted portion of the pain
15 And power of love, I cannot share,
    But wear the chain.

But 'tis not *thus* —and 'tis not *here* —
    Such thoughts should shake my soul, nor *now*,
Where glory decks the hero's bier,
20   Or binds his brow.

The sword, the banner, and the field,
    Glory and Greece, around me see!
The Spartan, borne upon his shield,
    Was not more free.

25 Awake! (not Greece—she *is* awake!)
    Awake, my spirit! Think through *whom*
Thy life-blood tracks its parent lake,
    And then strike home!

Tread those reviving passions down,
30   Unworthy manhood!—unto thee
Indifferent should the smile or frown
    Of beauty be.

If thou regrett'st thy youth, *why live?*
    The land of honourable death
35 Is here:—up to the field, and give
    Away thy breath!

Seek out—less often sought than found—
    A soldier's grave, for thee the best;
Then look around, and choose thy ground,
40   And take thy rest.

Stanzas
When a Man Hath No Freedom to Fight for at Home

When a man hath no freedom to fight for at home,
    Let him combat for that of his neighbours;
Let him think of the glories of Greece and of Rome,
    And get knocked on his head for his labours.

To do good to mankind is the chivalrous plan,
    And is always as nobly requited;
Then battle for freedom wherever you can,
    And, if not shot or hanged, you'll get knighted.

PERCY BYSSHE SHELLEY

Ode to the West Wind

1

O wild West Wind, thou breath of Autumn's being,
Thou, from whose unseen presence the leaves dead
Are driven, like ghosts from an enchanter fleeing,

Yellow, and black, and pale, and hectic red,
5   Pestilence-stricken multitudes: O thou,
Who chariotest to their dark wintry bed

The wingéd seeds, where they lie cold and low,
Each like a corpse within its grave, until
Thine azure sister of the Spring shall blow

10   Her clarion o'er the dreaming earth, and fill
(Driving sweet buds like flocks to feed in air)
With living hues and odours plain and hill:

Wild Spirit, which are moving everywhere;
Destroyer and preserver; hear, oh, hear!

2

15   Thou on whose stream, mid the steep sky's commotion,
Loose clouds like earth's decaying leaves are shed,
Shook from the tangled boughs of Heaven and Ocean,

Angels of rain and lightning: there are spread
On the blue surface of thine aëry surge,
20   Like the bright hair uplifted from the head

Of some fierce Maenad,[1] even from the dim verge
Of the horizon to the zenith's height,
The locks of the approaching storm. Thou dirge

25   Of the dying year, to which this closing night
Will be the dome of a vast sepulcher,
Vaulted with all thy congregated might

Of vapours, from whose solid atmosphere
Black rain, and fire, and hail will burst: oh, hear!

---

1. Maenads, in Greek mythology, were female devotees of Dionysus, god of wine and fertility. When they danced they frequently worked themselves into an ecstatic frenzy.

3

Thou who didst waken from his summer dreams
30   The blue Mediterranean, where he lay,
Lulled by the coil of his crystálline streams,

Beside a pumice isle in Baiae's bay,[2]
And saw in sleep old palaces and towers
Quivering within the wave's intenser day,

35   All overgrown with azure moss and flowers
So sweet, the sense faints picturing them! Thou
For whose path the Atlantic's level powers

Cleave themselves into chasms, while far below
The sea-blooms and the oozy woods which wear
40   The sapless foliage of the ocean, know

Thy voice, and suddenly grow gray with fear,
And tremble and despoil themselves: oh, hear!

4

If I were a dead leaf thou mightest bear,
If I were a swift cloud to fly with thee;
45   A wave to pant beneath thy power, and share

The impulse of thy strength, only less free
Than thou, O uncontrollable! If even
I were as in my boyhood, and could be

The comrade of thy wanderings over Heaven,
50   As then, when to outstrip thy skyey speed
Scarce seemed a vision; I would ne'er have striven

As thus with thee in prayer in my sore need.
Oh, lift me as a wave, a leaf, a cloud!
I fall upon the thorns of life! I bleed!

55   A heavy weight of hours has chained and bowed
One too like thee: tameless, and swift, and proud.

5

Make me thy lyre, even as the forest is:
What if my leaves are falling like its own!
The tumult of thy mighty harmonies

2. Near Naples, Italy.

60   Will take from both a deep, autumnal tone,
     Sweet though in sadness. Be thou, Spirit fierce,
     My spirit! Be thou me, impetuous one!

     Drive my dead thoughts over the universe
     Like withered leaves to quicken a new birth!
65   And, by the incantation of this verse,

     Scatter, as from an unextinguished hearth
     Ashes and sparks, my words among mankind!
     Be through my lips to unawakened earth

     The trumpet of a prophecy! O Wind,
70   If Winter comes, can Spring be far behind?

JOHN CLARE

I Am

I am: yet what I am none cares or knows
    My friends forsake me like a memory lost,
I am the self-consumer of my woes —
    They rise and vanish in oblivious host,
Like shadows in love's frenzied, stifled throes —
And yet I am, and live — like vapours tossed

Into the nothingness of scorn and noise,
    Into the living sea of waking dreams,
Where there is neither sense of life or joys,
    But the vast shipwreck of my life's esteems;
Even the dearest, that I love the best,
Are strange — nay, rather stranger than the rest.

I long for scenes, where man hath never trod,
    A place where woman never smiled or wept —
There to abide with my Creator, God,
    And sleep as I in childhood sweetly slept,
Untroubling, and untroubled where I lie,
The grass below — above the vaulted sky.

JOHN KEATS

Ode to a Nightingale

1

My heart aches, and a drowsy numbness pains
　My sense, as though of hemlock[1] I had drunk,
Or emptied some dull opiate to the drains
　One minute past, and Lethe-wards[2] had sunk:
5　'Tis not through envy of thy happy lot,
　　But being too happy in thine happiness —
　　　That thou, light-wingéd Dryad[3] of the trees,
　　　　In some melodious plot
　　Of beechen green, and shadows numberless,
10　　Singest of summer in full-throated ease.

2

O, for a draught of vintage! that hath been
　Cooled a long age in the deep-delvéd earth,
Tasting of Flora[4] and the country green,
　Dance, and Provençal song,[5] and sunburnt mirth!
15　O for a beaker full of the warm South,
　　Full of the true, the blushful Hippocrene,[6]
　　　With beaded bubbles winking at the brim,
　　　　And purple-stainéd mouth;
　　That I might drink, and leave the world unseen,
20　　And with thee fade away into the forest dim:

3

Fade far away, dissolve, and quite forget
　What thou among the leaves hast never known,
The weariness, the fever, and the fret
　Here, where men sit and hear each other groan;
25　Where palsy shakes a few, sad, last gray hairs,
　　Where youth grows pale, and specter-thin, and dies,
　　　Where but to think is to be full of sorrow
　　　　And leaden-eyed despairs,
　　Where Beauty cannot keep her lustrous eyes,
30　　Or new Love pine at them beyond tomorrow.

1. Poisonous plant used as a powerful sedative.
2. Towards the river of forgetfulness, Lethe, in Hades.
3. Wood nymph.
4. Roman goddess of springtime and flowers.
5. The medieval troubadours of Provence, in southern France, were very famous.
6. Fountain on Mount Helicon in Greece sacred to the Muses (goddesses of poetry and the arts); its waters provide poetic inspiration.

4

Away! away! for I will fly to thee,
   Not charioted by Bacchus and his pards,[7]
But on the viewless wings of Poesy,
   Though the dull brain perplexes and retards:
35 Already with thee! tender is the night,
     And haply the Queen-Moon is on her throne,
       Clustered around by all her starry Fays;
         But here there is no light,
     Save what from heaven is with the breezes blown
40   Through verdurous glooms and winding mossy ways.

5

I cannot see what flowers are at my feet,
   Nor what soft incense hangs upon the boughs,
But, in embalmèd darkness, guess each sweet
   Wherewith the seasonable month endows
45 The grass, the thicket, and the fruit tree wild;
     White hawthorn, and the pastoral eglantine;
       Fast fading violets covered up in leaves;
         And mid-May's eldest child,
     The coming musk-rose, full of dewy wine,
50   The murmurous haunt of flies on summer eves.

6

Darkling I listen; and for many a time
   I have been half in love with easeful Death,
Called him soft names in many a musèd rhyme,
   To take into the air my quiet breath;
55 Now more than ever seems it rich to die,
     To cease upon the midnight with no pain,
       While thou art pouring forth thy soul abroad
         In such an ecstasy!
     Still wouldst thou sing, and I have ears in vain—
60   To thy high requiem become a sod.

7

Thou wast not born for death, immortal Bird!
   No hungry generations tread thee down;
The voice I hear this passing night was heard
   In ancient days by emperor and clown:
65 Perhaps the selfsame song that found a path
     Through the sad heart of Ruth,[8] when, sick for home,
       She stood in tears amid the alien corn;
         The same that ofttimes hath
     Charmed magic casements, opening on the foam
70   Of perilous seas, in faery lands forlorn.

7. Bacchus, Roman god of wine and fertility, was sometimes portrayed in a chariot drawn by leopards.
8. See Ruth ii.

8

Forlorn! the very word is like a bell
 To toll me back from thee to my sole self!
Adieu! the fancy cannot cheat so well
 As she is famed to do, deceiving elf.
75 Adieu! adieu! thy plaintive anthem fades
 Past the near meadows, over the still stream,
  Up the hill side; and now 'tis buried deep
   In the next valley-glades:
 Was it a vision, or waking dream?
80 Fled is that music:—Do I wake or sleep?

To Autumn

1

Season of mists and mellow fruitfulness,
 Close bosom-friend of the maturing sun;
Conspiring with him how to load and bless
 With fruit the vines that round the thatch-eves run;
5 To bend with apples the mossed cottage-trees,
 And fill all fruit with ripeness to the core;
  To swell the gourd, and plump the hazel shells
With a sweet kernel; to set budding more,
 And still more, later flowers for the bees,
10 Until they think warm days will never cease,
  For Summer has o'er-brimmed their clammy cells.

2

Who hath not seen thee oft amid thy store?
 Sometimes whoever seeks abroad may find
Thee sitting careless on a granary floor,
15 Thy hair soft-lifted by the winnowing wind;
Or on a half-reaped furrow sound asleep,
 Drowsed with the fume of poppies, while thy hook
  Spares the next swath and all its twinéd flowers:
And sometimes like a gleaner thou dost keep
20 Steady thy laden head across a brook;
 Or by a cider-press, with patient look,
  Thou watchest the last oozings hours by hours.

3

Where are the songs of Spring? Ay, where are they?
 Think not of them, thou hast thy music too—
25 While barréd clouds bloom the soft-dying day,
 And touch the stubble-plains with rosy hue;
Then in a wailful choir the small gnats mourn
 Among the river sallows, borne aloft
  Or sinking as the light wind lives or dies;

30   And full-grown lambs loud bleat from hilly bourn;
     Hedge-crickets sing; and now with treble soft
     The red-breast whistles from a garden-croft;
     And gathering swallows twitter in the skies.

ALFRED, LORD TENNYSON

The Kraken[1]

Below the thunders of the upper deep;
Far, far beneath in the abysmal sea,
His ancient, dreamless, uninvaded sleep
The Kraken sleepeth: faintest sunlights flee
About his shadowy sides: above him swell
Huge sponges of millennial growth and height;
And far away into the sickly light,
From many a wondrous grot and secret cell
Unnumbered and enormous polypi
Winnow with giant arms the slumbering green.
There hath he lain for ages and will lie
Battening upon hugh seaworms in his sleep,
Until the latter fire shall heat the deep;
Then once by man and angels to be seen,
In roaring he shall rise and on the surface die.

The Eagle

He clasps the crag with crooked hands;
Close to the sun in lonely lands,
Ringed with the azure world, he stands.

The wrinkled sea beneath him crawls;
He watches from his mountain walls,
And like a thunderbolt he falls.

Dark House, by Which Once More I Stand[1]

Dark house, by which once more I stand
    Here in the long unlovely street,
    Doors where my heart was used to beat
So quickly, waiting for a hand,

---

1. A mythical sea-monster of enormous size,
said to have been seen at times off the coast of
Norway.

1. From Tennyson's *In Memoriam*, 7.

A hand that can be clasped no more —
  Behold me, for I cannot sleep,
  And like a guilty thing I creep
At earliest morning to the door.

He is not here; but far away
  The noise of life begins again,
  And ghastly through the drizzling rain
On the bald street breaks the blank day.

ROBERT BROWNING

My Last Duchess

Ferrara[1]

That's my last duchess painted on the wall,
Looking as if she were alive. I call
That piece a wonder, now: Frà Pandolf's hands
Worked busily a day, and there she stands.
5 Will't please you sit and look at her? I said
"Frà Pandolf" by design, for never read
Strangers like you that pictured countenance,
The depth and passion of its earnest glance,
But to myself they turned (since none puts by
10 The curtain I have drawn for you, but I)
And seemed as they would ask me, if they durst,
How such a glance came there; so, not the first
Are you to turn and ask thus. Sir, 'twas not
Her husband's presence only, called that spot
15 Of joy into the Duchess' cheek: perhaps
Frà Pandolf chanced to say "Her mantle laps
"Over my lady's wrist too much," or "Paint
"Must never hope to reproduce the faint
"Half-flush that dies along her throat": such stuff
20 Was courtesy, she thought, and cause enough
For calling up that spot of joy. She had
A heart — how shall I say? — too soon made glad,
Too easily impressed; she liked whate'er
She looked on, and her looks went everywhere.
25 Sir, 'twas all one! My favor at her breast,
The dropping of the daylight in the West,
The bough of cherries some officious fool
Broke in the orchard for her, the white mule

1. In 1564 Alfonso II, duke of Ferrara in Italy, was negotiating through an agent for the hand of the niece of the Count of Tyrol. His previous wife had died three years earlier at age seventeen, apparently as the result of poisoning.

30 She rode with round the terrace — all and each
Would draw from her alike the approving speech,
Or blush, at least. She thanked men — good! but thanked
Somehow — I know not how — as if she ranked
My gift of a nine-hundred-years-old name
With anybody's gift. Who'd stoop to blame
35 This sort of trifling? Even had you skill
In speech — which I have not — to make your will
Quite clear to such an one, and say, "Just this
"Or that in you disgusts me; here you miss,
"Or there exceed the mark" — and if she let
40 Herself be lessoned so, nor plainly set
Her wits to yours, forsooth, and made excuse,
— E'en then would be some stooping; and I choose
Never to stoop. Oh sir, she smiled, no doubt,
Whene'er I passed her; but who passed without
45 Much the same smile? This grew; I gave commands;
Then all smiles stopped together. There she stands
As if alive. Will't please you rise? We'll meet
The company below, then. I repeat,
The Count your master's known munificence
50 Is ample warrant that no just pretense
Of mine for dowry will be disallowed;
Though his fair daughter's self, as I avowed
At starting, is my object. Nay, we'll go
Together down, sir. Notice Neptune, though,
55 Taming a sea-horse, thought a rarity,
Which Claus of Innsbruck[2] cast in bronze for me!

WALT WHITMAN

To a Locomotive in Winter

Thee for my recitative,
Thee in the driving storm even as now, the snow, the winter-day
declining,
Thee in thy panoply, thy measured dual throbbing and thy beat
convulsive,
Thy black cylindric body, golden brass and silvery steel,
5 Thy ponderous side-bars, parallel and connecting rods, gyrating,
shuttling at thy sides,
Thy metrical, now swelling pant and roar, now tapering in the distance,
Thy great protruding head-light fixed in front,
Thy long, pale, floating vapor-pennants, tinged with delicate purple,
The dense and murky clouds out-belching from thy smoke-stack,

2. Claus of Innsbruck, like Frà Pandolf
(l. 3), is a fictitious artist.

10 Thy knitted frame, thy springs and valves, the tremulous twinkle of thy
                                                                        wheels,
    Thy train of cars behind, obedient, merrily following,
    Through gale or calm, now swift, now slack, yet steadily careering;
    Type of the modern—emblem of motion and power—pulse of the
                                                              continent,
    For once come serve the Muse and merge in verse, even as here I see
                                                                      thee,
15 With storm and buffeting gusts of wind and falling snow,
    By day thy warning ringing bell to sound its notes,
    By night thy silent signal lamps to swing.

    Fierce-throated beauty!
    Roll through my chant with all thy lawless music, thy swinging lamps at
                                                                       night,
20 Thy madly-whistled laughter, echoing, rumbling like an earthquake,
                                                               rousing all,
    Law of thyself complete, thine own track firmly holding,
    (No sweetness debonair of tearful harp or glib piano thine,)
    Thy trills of shrieks by rocks and hills return'd,
    Launch'd o'er the prairies wide, across the lakes
25 To the free skies unpent and glad and strong.

MATTHEW ARNOLD

Dover Beach[1]

    The sea is calm to-night.
    The tide is full, the moon lies fair
    Upon the straits;—on the French coast, the light
    Gleams, and is gone; the cliffs of England stand,
5   Glimmering and vast, out in the tranquil bay.
    Come to the window, sweet is the night air!
    Only, from the lone line of spray
    Where the sea meets the moon-blanched land,
    Listen! you hear the grating roar
10 Of pebbles which the waves draw back, and fling,
    At their return, up the high strand,
    Begin, and cease, and then again begin,
    With tremulous cadence slow, and bring
    The eternal note of sadness in.

1. The Strait of Dover is a narrow channel that connects the North Sea with the English Channel and separates England and France at their closest points. The lights on the French coast (see ll. 3–4) would be almost twenty-one miles away.

15   Sophocles² long ago
      Heard it on the Ægæan, and it brought
      Into his mind the turbid ebb and flow
      Of human misery; we
      Find also in the sound a thought,
20   Hearing it by this distant northern sea.

      The Sea of Faith
      Was once, too, at the full, and round earth's shore
      Lay like the folds of a bright girdle furled.
      But now I only hear
25   Its melancholy, long, withdrawing roar,
      Retreating, to the breath
      Of the night-wind down the vast edges drear
      And naked shingles of the world.

      Ah, love, let us be true
30   To one another! for the world, which seems
      To lie before us like a land of dreams,
      So various, so beautiful, so new,
      Hath really neither joy, nor love, nor light,
      Nor certitude, nor peace, nor help for pain;
35   And we are here as on a darkling plain
      Swept with confused alarms of struggle and flight,
      Where ignorant armies clash by night.

EMILY DICKINSON

There's a Certain Slant of Light

There's a certain Slant of light,
Winter Afternoons —
That oppresses, like the Heft¹
Of Cathedral Tunes —

Heavenly Hurt, it gives us —
We can find no scar,
But internal difference,
Where the Meanings, are —

None may teach it — Any —
'Tis the Seal Despair —
An imperial affliction
Sent us of the Air —

---

2. Greek dramatist of the fifth century B.C.   1. Weight.

When it comes, the Landscape listens—
Shadows—hold their breath—
When it goes, 'tis like the Distance
On the look of Death—

I Heard a Fly Buzz

I heard a Fly buzz—when I died—
The Stillness in the Room
Was like the Stillness in the Air—
Between the Heaves of Storm—

The Eyes around—had wrung them dry—
And Breaths were gathering firm
For that last Onset—when the King
Be witnessed—in the Room—

I willed my Keepsakes—Signed away
What portion of me be
Assignable—and then it was
There interposed a Fly—

With Blue—uncertain stumbling Buzz—
Between the light—and me—
And then the Windows failed—and then
I could not see to see—

LEWIS CARROLL

Jabberwocky

'Twas brillig, and the slithy toves
    Did gyre and gimble in the wabe;
All mimsy were the borogoves,
      And the mome raths outgrabe.

5   "Beware the Jabberwock, my son!
    The jaws that bite, the claws that catch!
Beware the Jubjub bird, and shun
      The frumious Bandersnatch!"

He took his vorpal sword in hand:
10   Long time the manxome foe he sought—
So rested he by the Tumtum tree,
      And stood awhile in thought.

And as in uffish thought he stood,
    The Jabberwock, with eyes of flame,
15 Came whiffling through the tulgey wood,
    And burbled as it came!

One, two! One, two! And through and through
    The vorpal blade went snicker-snack!
He left it dead, and with its head
20   He went galumphing back.

"And hast thou slain the Jabberwock?
    Come to my arms, my beamish boy!
O frabjous day! Callooh! Callay!"
    He chortled in his joy.

25 'Twas brillig, and the slithy toves
    Did gyre and gimble in the wabe;
All mimsy were the borogoves,
    And the mome raths outgrabe.

THOMAS HARDY

The Ruined Maid

"O 'Melia, my dear, this does everything crown!
Who could have supposed I should meet you in Town?
And whence such fair garments, such prosperi-ty?" —
"O didn't you know I'd been ruined?" said she.

5   — "You left us in tatters, without shoes or socks,
Tired of digging potatoes, and spudding up docks;[1]
And now you've gay bracelets and bright feathers three!" —
"Yes: that's how we dress when we're ruined," said she.

    — "At home in the barton[2] you said 'thee' and 'thou,'
10 And 'thik oon,' and 'theäs oon,'[3] and 't'other'; but now
Your talking quite fits 'ee for high compa-ny!" —
"Some polish is gained with one's ruin," said she.

    — "Your hands were like paws then, your face blue and bleak
But now I'm bewitched by your delicate cheek,
15 And your little gloves fit as on any la-dy!" —
"We never do work when we're ruined," said she.

---

1. Digging up dock weeds.
2. Farmyard.   3. That one and this one.

—"You used to call home-life a hag-ridden dream,
And you'd sigh, and you'd sock; but at present you seem
To know not of megrims[4] or melancho-ly!"—
20   "True. One's pretty lively when ruined," said she.

—"I wish I had feathers, a fine sweeping gown,
And a delicate face, and could strut about Town!"—
"My dear—a raw country girl, such as you be,
Cannot quite expect that. You ain't ruined," said she.

At Castle Boterel

As I drive to the junction of lane and highway,
    And the drizzle bedrenches the waggonette,
I look behind at the fading byway,
    And see on its slope, now glistening wet,
5   Distinctly yet

Myself and a girlish form benighted
    In dry March weather. We climb the road
Beside a chaise. We had just alighted
    To ease the sturdy pony's load
10   When he sighed and slowed.

What we did as we climbed, and what we talked of
    Matters not much, nor to what it led, —
Something that life will not be balked of
    Without rude reason till hope is dead,
15   And feeling fled.

It filled but a minute. But was there ever
    A time of such quality, since or before,
In that hill's story? To one mind never,
    Though it has been climbed, foot-swift, foot-sore,
20   By thousands more.

Primaeval rocks form the road's steep border,
    And much have they faced there, first and last,
Of the transitory in Earth's long order;
    But what they record in colour and cast
25   Is—that we two passed.

And to me, though Time's unflinching rigour,
    In mindless rote, has ruled from sight
The substance now, one phantom figure
    Remains on the slope, as when that night
30   Saw us alight.

4. A form of headache; also low spirits.

I look and see it there, shrinking, shrinking,
  I look back at it amid the rain
For the very last time; for my sand is sinking,
  And I shall traverse old love's domain
35   Never again.

Afterwards

When the Present has latched its postern behind my tremulous stay,
  And the May month flaps its glad green leaves like wings,
Delicate-filmed as new-spun silk, will the neighbours say,
  'He was a man who used to notice such things'?

If it be in the dusk when, like an eyelid's soundless blink,
  The dewfall-hawk comes crossing the shades to alight
Upon the wind-warped upland thorn, a gazer may think,
  'To him this must have been a familiar sight.'

If I pass during some nocturnal blackness, mothy and warm,
  When the hedgehog travels furtively over the lawn,
One may say, 'He strove that such innocent creatures should come to no
                                                                    harm,
But he could do little for them; and now he is gone.'

If, when hearing that I have been stilled at last, they stand at the door,
  Watching the full-starred heavens that winter sees,
Will this thought rise on those who will meet my face no more,
  'He was one who had an eye for such mysteries'?

And will any say when my bell of quittance is heard in the gloom,
  And a crossing breeze cuts a pause in its outrollings,
Till they rise again, as they were a new bell's boom,
  'He hears it now, but used to notice such things'?

GERARD MANLEY HOPKINS

God's Grandeur

The world is charged with the grandeur of God.
  It will flame out, like shining from shook foil;[1]
  It gathers to a greatness, like the ooze of oil
Crushed. Why do men then now not reck his rod?
Generations have trod, have trod, have trod;

---

1. "I mean foil in its sense of leaf or tinsel. . . .
Shaken goldfoil gives off broad glares like
sheet lightning and also, and this is true of
nothing else, owing to its zigzag dents and
creasings and network of small many cornered
facets, a sort of fork lightning too" (Hopkins,
Letters).

And all is seared with trade; bleared, smeared with toil;
And wears man's smudge and shares man's smell: the soil
Is bare now, nor can foot feel, being shod.

And for all this, nature is never spent;
    There lives the dearest freshness deep down things;
And though the last lights off the black West went
    Oh, morning at the brown brink eastward, springs —
Because the Holy Ghost over the bent
    World broods with warm breast and with ah! bright wings.

The Windhover[1]
To Christ Our Lord

I caught this morning morning's minion, king-
    dom of daylight's dauphin, dapple-dawn-drawn Falcon, in his riding
    Of the rolling level underneath him steady air, and striding
High there, how he rung upon the rein of a wimpling wing
In his ecstasy! then off, off forth on swing,
    As a skate's heel sweeps smooth on a bow-bend: the hurl and gliding
    Rebuffed the big wind. My heart in hiding
Stirred for a bird, —the achieve of, the mastery of the thing!

Brute beauty and valor and act, oh, air, pride, plume, here
    Buckle! AND the fire that breaks from thee then, a billion
Times told lovelier, more dangerous, O my chevalier!

    No wonder of it: shéer plód makes plough down sillion[2]
Shine, and blue-bleak embers, ah my dear,
    Fall, gall themselves, and gash gold-vermilion.

Spring and Fall
To a Young Child

Márgarét, are you griéving
Over Goldengrove unleaving?[1]
Leáves, like the things of man, you
With your fresh thoughts care for can you?
Áh! ás the heart grows older
It will come to such sights colder
By and by, nor spare a sigh
Though worlds of wanwood leafmeal lie;

---

1. Name for a small hawk, the kestrel, from
its habit of hovering or hanging in the air with
its head to the wind.
2. A ridge or narrow strip lying between two
furrows formed in dividing an open field.

1. "Goldengrove" and "unleaving," along with
"wanwood" and "leafmeal" (see l. 8), are
coined words.

And yet you will weep and know why.
Now no matter, child, the name:
Sórrow's springs áre the same.
Nor mouth had, no nor mind, expressed
What heart heard of, ghost guessed:
It ís the blight man was born for,
It is Margaret you mourn for.

Pied Beauty

Glory be to God for dappled things —
    For skies of couple-colour as a brinded cow;
      For rose-moles all in stipple upon trout that swim;
Fresh-firecoal chestnut-falls; finches' wings;
    Landscape plotted and pieced — fold, fallow, and plow;
      And all trades, their gear and tackle and trim.
All things counter, original, spare, strange;
    Whatever is fickle, freckled (who knows how?)
      With swift, slow; sweet, sour; adazzle, dim;
He fathers-forth whose beauty is past change:
              Praise him.

A. E. HOUSMAN

Terence,[1] This Is Stupid Stuff

    "Terence, this is stupid stuff:
You eat your victuals fast enough;
There can't be much amiss, 'tis clear,
To see the rate you drink your beer.
5   But oh, good Lord, the verse you make,
It gives a chap the belly-ache.
The cow, the old cow, she is dead;
It sleeps well, the horned head:
We poor lads, 'tis our turn now
10   To hear such tunes as killed the cow.
Pretty friendship 'tis to rhyme
Your friends to death before their time
Moping melancholy mad:
Come, pipe a tune to dance to, lad."

1. The volume in which this poem originally appeared is called *A Shropshire Lad*, originally to be called *The Poems of Terence Hearsay*. Housman, a classical scholar and Professor of Latin at Cambridge, may have named his fictive poet after Terence the Roman writer of comedies.

15   Why, if 'tis dancing you would be,
There's brisker pipes than poetry.
Say, for what were hop-yards meant,
Or why was Burton built on Trent?[2]
Oh many a peer of England brews
20   Livelier liquor than the Muse,
And malt does more than Milton can
To justify God's ways to man.[3]
Ale, man, ale's the stuff to drink
For fellows whom it hurts to think:
25   Look into the pewter pot
To see the world as the world's not.
And faith, 'tis pleasant till 'tis past:
The mischief is that 'twill not last.
Oh I have been to Ludlow fair
30   And left my necktie God knows where,
And carried half-way home, or near,
Pints and quarts of Ludlow beer:
Then the world seemed none so bad,
And I myself a sterling lad;
35   And down in lovely muck I've lain,
Happy till I woke again.
Then I saw the morning sky:
Heigho, the tale was all a lie;
The world, it was the old world yet,
40   I was I, my things were wet,
And nothing now remained to do
But begin the game anew.

    Therefore, since the world has still
Much good, but much less good than ill,
45   And while the sun and moon endure
Luck's a chance, but trouble's sure,
I'd face it as a wise man would,
And train for ill and not for good.
'Tis true, the stuff I bring for sale
50   Is not so brisk a brew as ale:
Out of a stem that scored the hand
I wrung it in a weary land.
But take it: if the smack is sour,
The better for the embittered hour;
55   It should do good to heart and head
When your soul is in my soul's stead;
And I will friend you, if I may,
In the dark and cloudy day.

2. Burton-on-Trent is a town whose most famous industry is the brewing of ale.
3. Seventeenth-century English poet John Milton tried to "justify the ways of God to man" in his *Paradise Lost*.

There was a king reigned in the East:
60   There, when kings will sit to feast,
They get their fill before they think
With poisoned meat and poisoned drink.
He gathered all that springs to birth
From the many-venomed earth;
65   First a little, thence to more,
He sampled all her killing store;
And easy, smiling, seasoned sound,
Sate the king when healths went round.
They put arsenic in his meat
70   And stared aghast to watch him eat;
They poured strychnine in his cup
And shook to see him drink it up:
They shook, they stared as white's their shirt:
Them it was their poison hurt.
75   —I tell the tale that I heard told.
Mithridates,[4] he died old.

RUDYARD KIPLING

Danny Deever

'What are the bugles blowin' for?' said Files-on-Parade.
'To turn you out, to turn you out,' the Colour-Sergeant said.
'What makes you look so white, so white?' said Files-on-Parade.
'I'm dreadin' what I've got to watch,' the Colour-Sergeant said.
5   For they're hangin' Danny Deever, you can hear the Dead March play,
The Regiment's in 'ollow square—they're hangin' him to-day;
They've taken of his buttons off an' cut his stripes away,
An' they're hangin' Danny Deever in the mornin'.

'What makes the rear-rank breathe so 'ard?' said Files-on-Parade.
10   'It's bitter cold, it's bitter cold,' the Colour-Sergeant said.
'What makes that front-rank man fall down?' said Files-on-Parade.
'A touch o' sun, a touch o' sun,' the Colour-Sergeant said.
They are hangin' Danny Deever, they are marchin' of 'im round,
They 'ave 'alted Danny Deever by 'is coffin on the ground;
15   An' 'e'll swing in 'arf a minute for a sneakin' shootin' hound—
O they're hangin' Danny Deever in the mornin'!

''Is cot was right-'and cot to mine,' said Files-on-Parade.
''E's sleepin' out an' far to-night,' the Colour-Sergeant said.
'I've drunk 'is beer a score o' times,' said Files-on-Parade.
20   ''E's drinkin' bitter beer alone,' the Colour-Sergeant said.

4. King of Pontus in Asia Minor in the first century B.C.; he developed an immunity to particular poisons by taking them in small doses.

They are hangin' Danny Deever, you must mark 'im to 'is place,
For 'e shot a comrade sleepin'—you must look 'im in the face;
Nine 'undred of 'is county an' the Regiment's disgrace,
While they're hangin' Danny Deever in the mornin'.

25   'What's that so black agin the sun?' said Files-on-Parade.
'It's Danny fightin' 'ard for life,' the Colour-Sergeant said.
'What's that that whimpers over'ead?' said Files-on-Parade.
'It's Danny's soul that's passin' now,' the Colour-Sergeant said.
For they're done with Danny Deever, you can 'ear the quickstep play,
The Regiment's in column, an' they're marchin' us away;
Ho! the young recruits are shakin', an' they'll want their beer to-day,
After hangin' Danny Deever in the mornin'!

CHARLES G. D. ROBERTS

The Tantramar[1] Revisited

Summers and summers have come, and gone with the flight of the
                                                      swallow;
Sunshine and thunder have been, storm, and winter, and frost;
Many and many a sorrow has all but died from remembrance,
Many a dream of joy fall'n in the shadow of pain.
5   Hands of chance and change have marred, or moulded, or broken,
Busy with spirit or flesh, all I most have adored;
Even the bosom of Earth is strewn with heavier shadows,—
Only in these green hills, aslant to the sea, no change!
Here where the road that has climbed from the inland valleys and
                                                      woodlands,
10   Dips from the hill-tops down, straight to the base of the hills,—
Here, from my vantage-ground,[2] I can see the scattering houses,
Stained with time, set warm in orchards, and meadows, and wheat,
Dotting the broad bright slopes outspread to southward and eastward,
Wind-swept all day long, blown by the south-east wind.
15   Skirting the sunbright uplands stretches a riband of meadow,
Shorn of the laboring grass, bulwarked well from the sea,
Fenced on its seaward border with long clay dikes from the turbid
Surge and flow of the tides vexing the Westmoreland shores.
Yonder, toward the left, lie broad the Westmoreland marshes,—
20   Miles on miles they extend, level, and grassy, and dim,
Clear from the long red sweep of flats to the sky in the distance,
Save for the outlying heights, green-rampired Cumberland Point;

1. The Tantramar Marshes are located at the head of Cumberland Basin, a body of water bounded by Westmoreland County, New Brunswick, on the north, and Cumberland County, Nova Scotia, on the south.

2. Westcock, New Brunswick, near Sackville. Minudie, Nova Scotia (see l. 25), is directly across the Cumberland Basin from this location.

Miles on miles outrolled, and the river-channels divide them, —
Miles on miles of green barred by the hurtling gusts.

25   Miles on miles beyond the tawny bay is Minudie.
There are the low blue hills; villages gleam at their feet.
Nearer a white sail shines across the water, and nearer
Still are the slim, gray masts of fishing boats dry on the flats.
Ah, how well I remember those wide red flats, above tide-mark
30   Pale with scurf of the salt, seamed and baked in the sun!
Well I remember the piles of blocks and ropes, and the net-reels
Wound with the beaded nets, dripping and dark from the sea!
Now at this season the nets are unwound; they hang from the rafters
Over the fresh-stowed hay in upland barns, and the wind
35   Blows all day through the chinks, with the streaks of sunlight, and sways
them
Softly at will; or they lie heaped in the gloom of a loft.

Now at this season the reels are empty and idle; I see them
Over the lines of the dikes, over the gossiping grass.
Now at this season they swing in the long strong wind, thro' the lonesome
40   Golden afternoon, shunned by the foraging gulls.
Near about sunset the crane will journey homeward above them;
Round them, under the moon, all the calm night long,
Winnowing soft gray wings of marsh-owls wander and wander,
Now to the broad, lit marsh, now to the dusk of the dike.
45   Soon, thro' their dew-wet frames, in the live keen freshness of morning,
Out of the teeth of the dawn blows back the awakening wind.
Then, as the blue day mounts, and the low-shot shafts of the sunlight
Glance from the tide to the shore, gossamers jewelled with dew
Sparkle and wave, where late sea-spoiling fathoms of drift-net
50   Myriad-meshed, uploomed sombrely over the land.

Well I remember it all. The salt raw scent of the margin;[3]
While, with men at the windlass, groaned each reel, and the net,
Surging in ponderous lengths, uprose and coiled in its station;
Then each man to his home, — well I remember it all!

55   Yet, as I sit and watch, this present peace of the landscape, —
Stranded boats, these reels empty and idle, the hush,
One gray hawk slow-wheeling above yon cluster of haystacks, —
More than the old-time stir this stillness welcomes me home.
Ah the old-time stir, how once it stung me with rapture, —
60   Old-time sweetness, the winds freighted with honey and salt!
Yet will I stay my steps and not go down to the marsh-land, —
Muse and recall far off, rather remember than see, —
Lest on too close sight I miss the darling illusion,
Spy at their task even here the hands of chance and change.

3. The beach immediately adjacent to the
water.

ARCHIBALD LAMPMAN

Solitude

How still it is here in the woods. The trees
Stand motionless, as if they did not dare
To stir, lest it should break the spell. The air
Hangs quiet as spaces in a marble frieze.
Even this little brook, that runs at ease,
Whispering and gurgling in its knotted bed,
Seems but to deepen, with its curling thread
Of sound, the shadowy sun-pierced silences.
Sometimes a hawk screams or a woodpecker
Startles the stillness from its fixéd mood
With his loud careless tap. Sometimes I hear
The dreamy white-throat from some far off tree
Pipe slowly on the listening solitude,
His five pure notes succeeding pensively.

BLISS CARMAN

Low Tide on Grand Pré[1]

The sun goes down, and over all
    These barren reaches by the tide
Such unelusive glories fall,
    I almost dream they yet will bide
5   Until the coming of the tide.

And yet I know that not for us,
    By any ecstasy of dream,
He lingers to keep luminous
    A little while the grievous stream,
10 Which frets, uncomforted of dream—

A grievous stream, that to and fro
    Athrough the fields of Acadie
Goes wandering, as if to know
    Why one beloved face should be
15 So long from home and Acadie.

1. Marshlands near Wolfville, Nova Scotia,
reclaimed by the Acadians in the seventeenth
century.

Was it a year or lives ago
   We took the grasses in our hands,
And caught the summer flying low
   Over the waving meadow lands,
20   And held it there between our hands?

The while the river at our feet —
   A drowsy inland meadow stream —
At set of sun the after-heat
   Made running gold, and in the gleam
25   We freed our birch upon the stream.

There down along the elms at dusk
   We lifted dripping blade to drift,
Through twilight scented fine like musk,
   Where night and gloom awhile uplift,
30   Nor sunder soul and soul adrift.

And that we took into our hands
   Spirit of life or subtler thing —
Breathed on us there, and loosed the bands
   Of death, and taught us, whispering,
35   The secret of some wonder-thing.

Then all your face grew light, and seemed
   To hold the shadow of the sun;
The evening faltered, and I deemed
   That time was ripe, and years had done
40   Their wheeling underneath the sun.

So all desire and all regret,
   And fear and memory, were naught;
One to remember or forget
   The keen delight our hands had caught;
45   Morrow and yesterday were naught.

The night has fallen, and the tide...
   Now and again comes drifting home,
Across these aching barrens wide,
   A sigh like driven wind or foam:
50   In grief the flood is bursting home.

DUNCAN CAMPBELL SCOTT

The Forsaken

1
Once in the winter
Out on a lake
In the heart of the north-land,
Far from the Fort
5   And far from the hunters,
A Chippewa[1] woman
With her sick baby,
Crouched in the last hours
Of a great storm.
10   Frozen and hungry,
She fished through the ice
With a line of the twisted
Bark of the cedar,
And a rabbit-bone hook
15   Polished and barbed;
Fished with the bare hook
All through the wild day,
Fished and caught nothing;
While the young chieftain
20   Tugged at her breasts,
Or slept in the lacings
Of the warm *tikanagan*.[2]
All the lake-surface
Streamed with the hissing
25   Of millions of iceflakes
Hurled by the wind;
Behind her the round
Of a lonely island
Roared like a fire
30   With the voice of the storm
In the deeps of the cedars.
Valiant, unshaken,
She took of her own flesh,
Baited the fish-hook,
35   Drew in a grey-trout,
Drew in his fellows,
Heaped them beside her,
Dead in the snow.
Valiant, unshaken,
40   She faced the long distance,

1. Or Ojibwa, an Indian tribe inhabiting the region around Lake Superior and westward.

2. Cradleboard or infant's cot that rests on a frame and is portable.

Wolf-haunted and lonely,
Sure of her goal
And the life of her dear one:
Tramped for two days,
45 On the third in the morning,
Saw the strong bulk
Of the Fort by the river,
Saw the wood-smoke
Hang soft in the spruces,
50 Heard the keen yelp
Of the ravenous huskies
Fighting for whitefish:
Then she had rest.

2

Years and years after,
55 When she was old and withered,
When her son was an old man
And his children filled with vigour,
They came in their northern tour on the verge of winter,
To an island in a lonely lake.
60 There one night they camped, and on the morrow
Gathered their kettles and birch-bark
Their rabbit-skin robes and their mink-traps,
Launched their canoes and slunk away through the islands,
Left her alone forever,
65 Without a word of farewell,
Because she was old and useless,
Like a paddle broken and warped,
Or a pole that was splintered.
Then, without a sigh,
70 Valiant, unshaken,
She smoothed her dark locks under her kerchief,
Composed her shawl in state,
Then folded her hands ridged with sinews and corded with veins,
Folded them across her breasts spent with the nourishing of children,
75 Gazed at the sky past the tops of the cedars,
Saw two spangled nights arise out of the twilight,
Saw two days go by filled with the tranquil sunshine,
Saw, without pain, or dread, or even a moment of longing:
Then on the third great night there came thronging and thronging
80 Millions of snowflakes out of a windless cloud;
They covered her close with a beautiful crystal shroud,
Covered her deep and silent.
But in the frost of the dawn,
Up from the life below,
85 Rose a column of breath
Through a tiny cleft in the snow,
Fragile, delicately drawn,
Wavering with its own weakness,

90
In the wilderness a sign of the spirit,
Persisting still in the sight of the sun
Till day was done.
Then all light was gathered up by the hand of God and hid in His breast,
Then there was born a silence deeper than silence,
Then she had rest.

WILLIAM BUTLER YEATS

The Magi[1]

Now as at all times I can see in the mind's eye,
In their stiff, painted clothes, the pale unsatisfied ones
Appear and disappear in the blue depth of the sky
With all their ancient faces like rain-beaten stones,
And all their helms of silver hovering side by side,
And all their eyes still fixed, hoping to find once more,
Being by Calvary's turbulence unsatisfied.
The uncontrollable mystery on the bestial floor.

Leda[1] and the Swan

A sudden blow: the great wings beating still
Above the staggering girl, her thighs caressed
By the dark webs, her nape caught in his bill,
He holds her helpless breast upon his breast.

How can those terrified vague fingers push
The feathered glory from her loosening thighs?
And how can body, laid in that white rush,
But feel the strange heart beating where it lies?

A shudder in the loins engenders there
The broken wall, the burning roof and tower
And Agamemnon dead.
                              Being so caught up,
So mastered by the brute blood of the air,
Did she put on his knowledge with his power
Before the indifferent beak could let her drop?

---

1. Three Kings or Wise Men of the East who followed the Star of Bethlehem and brought gifts to the infant Jesus.

1. Wife of the King of Sparta who, in Greek legend, was raped by Zeus (disguised as a swan), thus begetting Helen of Troy. Leda was also mother of Clytemnestra, who murdered her husband, Agamemnon (see l. 11), when he returned from leading the Greek armies in the Trojan war.

Sailing to Byzantium[1]

I

That is no country for old men. The young
In one another's arms, birds in the trees
—Those dying generations—at their song,
The salmon-falls, the mackerel-crowded seas
5   Fish, flesh, or fowl, commend all summer long
Whatever is begotten, born, and dies.
Caught in that sensual music all neglect
Monuments of unaging intellect.

II

An aged man is but a paltry thing,
10   A tattered coat upon a stick, unless
Soul clap its hands and sing, and louder sing
For every tatter in its mortal dress,
Nor is there singing school but studying
Monuments of its own magnificence;
15   And therefore I have sailed the seas and come
To the holy city of Byzantium.

III

O sages standing in God's holy fire
As in the gold mosaic of a wall,
Come from the holy fire, perne in a gyre,[2]
20   And be the singing-masters of my soul.
Consume my heart away; sick with desire
And fastened to a dying animal
It knows not what it is; and gather me
Into the artifice of eternity.

IV

25   Once out of nature I shall never take
My bodily form from any natural thing,
But such a form as Grecian goldsmiths make
Of hammered gold and gold enameling
To keep a drowsy Emperor awake;[3]
30   Or set upon a golden bough to sing
To lords and ladies of Byzantium
Of what is past, or passing, or to come.

1. Ancient city on the site of present-day
Istanbul. As Constantinople it was the capital
of a Byzantine Empire that had its most
glorious period (in art and architecture at
least) in the sixth century A.D.

2. Spin in a gyrating pattern.
3. "I have read somewhere that in the Emper-
or's palace at Byzantium was a tree made of
gold and silver, and artificial birds that sang"
(Yeats's note).

The Choice

The intellect of man is forced to choose
Perfection of the life, or of the work,
And if it take the second must refuse
A heavenly mansion, raging in the dark.
When all that story's finished, what's the news?
In luck or out the toil has left its mark:
That old perplexity an empty purse,
Or the day's vanity, the night's remorse.

Lapis Lazuli[1]

For Harry Clifton

I have heard that hysterical women say
They are sick of the palette and fiddle-bow,
Of poets that are always gay,
For everybody knows or else should know
5   That if nothing drastic is done
Aeroplane and Zeppelin will come out,
Pitch like King Billy[2] bomb-balls in
Until the town lie beaten flat.

All perform their tragic play,
10 There struts Hamlet, there is Lear,
That's Ophelia, that Cordelia;
Yet they, should the last scene be there,
The great stage curtain about to drop,
If worthy their prominent part in the play,
15 Do not break up their lines to weep.
They know that Hamlet and Lear are gay;
Gaiety transfiguring all that dread.
All men have aimed at, found and lost;
Black out; Heaven blazing into the head:
20 Tragedy wrought to its uttermost.
Though Hamlet rambles and Lear rages,
And all the drop-scenes drop at once
Upon a hundred thousand stages,
It cannot grow by an inch or an ounce.

1. Literally, from the Latin, "stone of azure."
An opaque blue-green semiprecious gem. In a
letter (6 July 1935), Yeats wrote, "Someone
has sent me a present of a great piece [of lapis
lazuli] carved by some Chinese sculptor into
the semblance of a mountain with temple,
trees, paths and an ascetic and pupil about to
climb the mountain. Ascetic, pupil, hard
stone, eternal theme of the sensual east. The
heroic cry in the midst of despair. But no, I am
wrong, the east has its solutions always and
therefore knows nothing of tragedy. It is we,
not the east, that must raise the heroic cry."
2. At the Battle of the Boyne on 1 July 1690,
William III, king of England since 1689, had
defeated the forces of the deposed king,
James II.

25   On their own feet they came, or on shipboard,
      Camel-back, horse-back, ass-back, mule-back,
      Old civilizations put to the sword.
      Then they and their wisdom went to rack:
      No handiwork of Callimachus,[3]
30   Who handled marble as if it were bronze,
      Made draperies that seemed to rise
      When sea-wind swept the corner, stands;
      His long lamp-chimney shaped like the stem
      Of a slender palm, stood but a day;
35   All things fall and are built again,
      And those that build them again are gay.

      Two Chinamen, behind them a third,
      Are carved in lapis lazuli,
      Over them flies a long-legged bird,
40   A symbol of longevity;
      The third, doubtless a serving-man,
      Carries a musical instrument.

      Every discoloration of the stone,
      Every accidental crack or dent,
45   Seems a water-course or an avalanche,
      Or lofty slope where it still snows
      Though doubtless plum or cherry-branch
      Sweetens the little half-way house
      Those Chinamen climb towards, and I
50   Delight to imagine them seated there;
      There, on the mountain and the sky,
      On all the tragic scene they stare.
      One asks for mournful melodies;
      Accomplished fingers begin to play.
55   Their eyes mid many wrinkles, their eyes,
      Their ancient, glittering eyes, are gay.

EDWIN ARLINGTON ROBINSON

How Annandale Went Out

"They called it Annandale—and I was there
To flourish, to find words, and to attend:
Liar, physician, hypocrite, and friend,
I watched him; and the sight was not so fair
As one or two that I have seen elsewhere:

3. A Greek sculptor of the fifth century B.C.
who reputedly designed the Corinthian column.

An apparatus not for me to mend—
A wreck, with hell between him and the end,
Remained of Annandale; and I was there.

"I knew the ruin as I knew the man;
So put the two together, if you can,
Remembering the worst you know of me.
Now view yourself as I was, on the spot—
With a slight kind of engine. Do you see?
Like this ... You wouldn't hang me? I thought not."

Karma[1]

Christmas was in the air and all was well
With him, but for a few confusing flaws
In divers of God's images. Because
A friend of his would neither buy nor sell,
Was he to answer for the axe that fell?
He pondered; and the reason for it was,
Partly, a slowly freezing Santa Claus
Upon the corner, with his beard and bell.
Acknowledging an improvident surprise,
He magnified a fancy that he wished
The friend whom he had wrecked were here again.
Not sure of that, he found a compromise;
And from the fulness of his heart he fished
A dime for Jesus who had died for men.

ROBERT FROST

The Oven Bird

There is a singer everyone has heard,
Loud, a mid-summer and a mid-wood bird,
Who makes the solid tree trunks sound again.
He says that leaves are old and that for flowers
Mid-summer is to spring as one to ten.
He says the early petal-fall is past,
When pear and cherry bloom went down in showers
On sunny days a moment overcast;
And comes that other fall we name the fall.
He says the highway dust is over all.

---

1. Basic concept common to Hinduism, Buddhism, and Jainism. The doctrine of karma states that one's present existence is the result of actions in past incarnations, and action in this life can determine one's destiny in future incarnations.

The bird would cease and be as other birds
But that he knows in singing not to sing.
The question that he frames in all but words
Is what to make of a diminished thing.

Home Burial

He saw her from the bottom of the stairs
Before she saw him. She was starting down,
Looking back over her shoulder at some fear.
She took a doubtful step and then undid it
5   To raise herself and look again. He spoke
Advancing toward her: "What is it you see
From up there always?—for I want to know."
She turned and sank upon her skirts at that,
And her face changed from terrified to dull.
10   He said to gain time: "What is it you see?"
Mounting until she cowered under him.
"I will find out now—you must tell me, dear."
She, in her place, refused him any help,
With the least stiffening of her neck and silence.
15   She let him look, sure that he wouldn't see,
Blind creature; and awhile he didn't see.
But at last he murmured, "Oh," and again, "Oh."

"What is it—what?" she said.

                              "Just that I see."

"You don't," she challenged. "Tell me what it is."

20   "The wonder is I didn't see at once.
I never noticed it from here before.
I must be wonted to it—that's the reason.
The little graveyard where my people are!
So small the window frames the whole of it.
25   Not so much larger than a bedroom, is it?
There are three stones of slate and one of marble,
Broad-shouldered little slabs there in the sunlight
On the sidehill. We haven't to mind *those*.
But I understand: it is not the stones,
But the child's mound————"

                              "Don't, don't, don't,

30   don't" she cried.

She withdrew, shrinking from beneath his arm
That rested on the banister, and slid downstairs;

And turned on him with such a daunting look,
He said twice over before he knew himself:
35 "Can't a man speak of his own child he's lost?"

"Not you!—Oh, where's my hat? Oh, I don't need it!
I must get out of here. I must get air. —
I don't know rightly whether any man can."

"Amy! Don't go to someone else this time.
40 Listen to me. I won't come down the stairs."
He sat and fixed his chin between his fists.
"There's something I should like to ask you, dear."

"You don't know how to ask it."

                    "Help me, then."

Her fingers moved the latch for all reply.

45 "My words are nearly always an offense.
I don't know how to speak of anything
So as to please you. But I might be taught,
I should suppose. I can't say I see how.
A man must partly give up being a man
50 With womenfolk. We could have some arrangement
By which I'd bind myself to keep hands off
Anything special you're a-mind to name.
Though I don't like such things 'twixt those that love.
Two that don't love can't live together without them.
55 But two that do can't live together with them."
She moved the latch a little. "Don't—don't go.
Don't carry it to someone else this time.
Tell me about it if it's something human.
Let me into your grief. I'm not so much
60 Unlike other folks as your standing there
Apart would make me out. Give me my chance.
I do think, though, you overdo it a little.
What was it brought you up to think it the thing
To take your mother-loss of a first child
65 So inconsolably—in the face of love.
You'd think his memory might be satisfied—"

"There you go sneering now!"
                    "I'm not, I'm not!
You make me angry. I'll come down to you.
God, what a woman! And it's come to this,
70 A man can't speak of his own child that's dead."

"You can't because you don't know how to speak.
If you had any feelings, you that dug

With your own hand—how could you?—his little grave;
I saw you from that very window there,
75   Making the gravel leap and leap in air,
Leap up, like that, like that, and land so lightly
And roll back down the mound beside the hole.
I thought, Who is that man? I didn't know you.
And I crept down the stairs and up the stairs
80   To look again, and still your spade kept lifting.
Then you came in. I heard your rumbling voice.
Out in the kitchen, and I don't know why,
But I went near to see with my own eyes.
You could sit there with the stains on your shoes
85   Of the fresh earth from your own baby's grave
And talk about your everyday concerns.
You had stood the spade up against the wall
Outside there in the entry, for I saw it."

"I shall laugh the worst laugh I ever laughed.
90   I'm cursed. God, if I don't believe I'm cursed."

"I can repeat the very words you were saying:
'Three foggy mornings and one rainy day
Will rot the best birch fence a man can build.'
Think of it, talk like that at such a time!
95   What had how long it takes a birch to rot
To do with what was in the darkened parlor?
You *couldn't* care! The nearest friends can go
With anyone to death, comes so far short
They might as well not try to go at all.
100   No, from the time when one is sick to death,
One is alone, and he dies more alone.
Friends make pretense of following to the grave,
But before one is in it, their minds are turned
And making the best of their way back to life
105   And living people, and things they understand.
But the world's evil. I won't have grief so
If I can change it. Oh, I won't, I won't!"

"There, you have said it all and you feel better.
You won't go now. You're crying. Close the door.
110   The heart's gone out of it: why keep it up?
Amy! There's someone coming down the road!"

"*You*—oh, you think the talk is all. I must go—
Somewhere out of this house. How can I make you———"

"If—you—do!" She was opening the door wider.
115   "Where do you mean to go? First tell me that.
I'll follow and bring you back by force. I *will!* —"

"Out, Out—"[1]

The buzz saw snarled and rattled in the yard
And made dust and dropped stove-length sticks of wood,
Sweet-scented stuff when the breeze drew across it.
And from there those that lifted eyes could count
5   Five mountain ranges one behind the other
Under the sunset far into Vermont.
And the saw snarled and rattled, snarled and rattled,
As it ran light, or had to bear a load.
And nothing happened: day was all but done.
10 Call it a day, I wish they might have said
To please the boy by giving him the half hour
That a boy counts so much when saved from work.
His sister stood beside them in her apron
To tell them "Supper." At the word, the saw,
15 As if to prove saws knew what supper meant,
Leaped out at the boy's hand, or seemed to leap—
He must have given the hand. However it was,
Neither refused the meeting. But the hand!
The boy's first outcry was a rueful laugh,
20 As he swung toward them holding up the hand
Half in appeal, but half as if to keep
The life from spilling. Then the boy saw all—
Since he was old enough to know, big boy
Doing a man's work, though a child at heart—
25 He saw all spoiled. "Don't let him cut my hand off—
The doctor, when he comes. Don't let him, sister!"
So. But the hand was gone already.
The doctor put him in the dark of ether.
He lay and puffed his lips out with his breath.
30 And then—the watcher at his pulse took fright.
No one believed. They listened at his heart.
Little—less—nothing!—and that ended it.
No more to build on there. And they, since they
Were not the one dead, turned to their affairs.

The Road Not Taken

Two roads diverged in a yellow wood,
And sorry I could not travel both
And be one traveler, long I stood
And looked down one as far as I could
To where it bent in the undergrowth;

---

1. See Shakespeare's *Macbeth* V.v.19–28.

Then took the other, as just as fair,
And having perhaps the better claim,
Because it was grassy and wanted wear;
Though as for that, the passing there
Had worn them really about the same,

And both that morning equally lay
In leaves no step had trodden black.
Oh, I kept the first for another day!
Yet knowing how way leads on to way,
I doubted if I should ever come back.

I shall be telling this with a sigh
Somewhere ages and ages hence:
Two roads diverged in a wood, and I—
I took the one less traveled by,
And that has made all the difference.

EDWARD THOMAS

Old Man[1]

Old Man, or Lad's-love, —in the name there's nothing
To one that knows not Lad's-love, or Old Man,
The hoar-green feathery herb, almost a tree,
Growing with rosemary and lavender.
5   Even to one that knows it well, the names
Half decorate, half perplex, the thing it is:
At least, what that is clings not to the names
In spite of time. And yet I like the names.

The herb itself I like not, but for certain
10   I love it, as some day the child will love it
Who plucks a feather from the door-side bush
Whenever she goes in or out of the house.
Often she waits there, snipping the tips and shrivelling
The shreds at last on to the path, perhaps
15   Thinking, perhaps of nothing, till she sniffs
Her fingers and runs off. The bush is still
But half as tall as she, though it is as old;
So well she clips it. Not a word she says;
And I can only wonder how much hereafter

1. Old Man and Lad's Love are both common names for southernwood (*Artemisia abrotanum*), one of the wormwood family and a popular garden shrub.

20 She will remember, with that bitter scent,
Of garden rows, and ancient damson trees
Topping a hedge, a bent path to a door,
A low thick bush beside the door, and me
Forbidding her to pick.
25   As for myself,
Where first I met the bitter scent is lost.
I, too, often shrivel the grey shreds,
Sniff them and think and sniff again and try
Once more to think what it is I am remembering,
30 Always in vain. I cannot like the scent,
Yet I would rather give up others more sweet,
With no meaning, than this bitter one.

I have mislaid the key. I sniff the spray
And think of nothing; I see and I hear nothing;
35 Yet seem, too, to be listening, lying in wait
For what I should, yet never can, remember:
No garden appears, no path, no hoar-green bush
Of Lad's-love, or Old Man, no child beside,
Neither father nor mother, nor any playmate;
40 Only an avenue, dark, nameless, without end.

WALLACE STEVENS

Thirteen Ways of Looking at a Blackbird

1
Among twenty snowy mountains,
The only moving thing
Was the eye of the blackbird.

2
I was of three minds,
5 Like a tree
In which there are three blackbirds.

3
The blackbird whirled in the autumn winds.
It was a small part of the pantomime.

4
A man and a woman
10 Are one.
A man and a woman and a blackbird
Are one.

5

I do not know which to prefer,
The beauty of inflections
15   Or the beauty of innuendoes,
The blackbird whistling
Or just after.

6

Icicles filled the long window
With barbaric glass.
20   The shadow of the blackbird
Crossed it, to and fro.
The mood
Traced in the shadow
An indecipherable cause.

7

25   O thin men of Haddam,[1]
Why do you imagine golden birds?
Do you not see how the blackbird
Walks around the feet
Of the women about you?

8

30   I know noble accents
And lucid, inescapable rhythms;
But I know, too,
That the blackbird is involved
In what I know.

9

35   When the blackbird flew out of sight,
It marked the edge
Of one of many circles.

10

At the sight of blackbirds
Flying in a green light,
40   Even the bawds of euphony
Would cry out sharply.

11

He rode over Connecticut
In a glass coach.
Once, a fear pierced him,
45   In that he mistook
The shadow of his equipage
For blackbirds.

1. Haddam is a town in Connecticut.

12
The river is moving.
The blackbird must be flying.

13
50 It was evening all afternoon.
It was snowing
And it was going to snow.
The blackbird sat
In the cedar-limbs.

E. J. PRATT

The Shark

He seemed to know the harbour,
So leisurely he swam;
His fin,
Like a piece of sheet-iron,
5 Three-cornered,
And with knife-edge,
Stirred not a bubble
As it moved
With its base-line on the water.

10 His body was tubular
And tapered
And smoke-blue,
And as he passed the wharf
He turned,
15 And snapped at a flat-fish
That was dead and floating.
And I saw the flash of a white throat,
And a double row of white teeth,
And eyes of metallic grey,
20 Hard and narrow and slit.

Then out of the harbour,
With that three-cornered fin
Shearing without a bubble the water
Lithely,
25 Leisurely,
He swam—
That strange fish,
Tubular, tapered, smoke-blue,
Part vulture, part wolf,
30 Part neither—for his blood was cold.

Silences

There is no silence upon the earth or under the earth like the silence
                                                                under the sea;
No cries announcing birth,
No sounds declaring death.
There is silence when the milt[1] is laid on the spawn in the weeds and
                                                fungus of the rock-clefts;
5   And silence in the growth and struggle for life.
The bonitoes pounce upon the mackerel,
And are themselves caught by the barracudas,
The sharks kill the barracudas
And the great molluscs rend the sharks,
10 And all noiselessly—
Though swift be the action and final the conflict,
The drama is silent.

There is no fury upon the earth like the fury under the sea.
For growl and cough and snarl are the tokens of spendthrifts who know
                                        not the ultimate economy of rage.
15 Moreover, the pace of the blood is too fast.
But under the waves the blood is sluggard and has the same temperature
                                                        as that of the sea.

There is something pre-reptilian about a silent kill.

Two men may end their hostilities just with their battle-cries.
"The devil take you," says one.
20 "I'll see you in hell first," says the other.
And these introductory salutes followed by a hail of gutturals and
            sibilants are often the beginning of friendship, for who would not
                prefer to be lustily damned than to be half-heartedly blessed?
No one need fear oaths that are properly enunciated, for they belong to the
            inheritance of just men made perfect, and, for all we know, of such
                                        may be the Kingdom of Heaven.
But let silent hate be put away for it feeds upon the heart of the hater.
Today I watched two pairs of eyes. One pair was black and the other
            grey. And while the owners thereof, for the space of five seconds,
                walked past each other, the grey snapped at the black and the
                                        black riddled the grey.
25 One looked to say—"The cat,"
And the other—"The cur."
But no words were spoken;

1. Roe of male fish.

Not so much as a hiss or a murmur came through the perfect enamel of
the teeth; not so much as a gesture of enmity.
If the right upper lip curled over the canine, it went unnoticed.
30   The lashes veiled the eyes not for an instant in the passing.
And as between the two in respect to candour of intention or eternity of
wish, there was no choice, for the stare was mutual and absolute.
A word would have dulled the exquisite edge of the feeling,
An oath would have flawed the crystallization of the hate.
For only such culture could grow in a climate of silence, —
35   Away back before the emergence of fur or feather, back to the unvocal
sea and down deep where the darkness spills its wash on the
threshold of light, where the lids never close upon the eyes, where
the inhabitants slay in silence and are as silently slain.

WILLIAM CARLOS WILLIAMS

The Dance

In Breughel's great picture, The Kermess,
the dancers go round, they go round and
around, the squeal and the blare and the
tweedle of bagpipes, a bugle and fiddles
tipping their bellies (round as the thick-
sided glasses whose wash they impound)
their hips and their bellies off balance
to turn them. Kicking and rolling about
the Fair Grounds, swinging their butts, those
shanks must be sound to bear up under such
rollicking measures, prance as they dance
in Breughel's great picture, The Kermess.

EZRA POUND

In a Station of the Metro

The apparition of these faces in the crowd;
Petals on a wet, black bough.

H.D. (HILDA DOOLITTLE)

Heat

O wind, rend open the heat,
cut apart the heat,
rend it to tatters.

Fruit cannot drop
through this thick air —
fruit cannot fall into heat
that presses up and blunts
the points of pears
and rounds the grapes.

Cut the heat —
plough through it,
turning it on either side
of your path.

SIEGFRIED SASSOON

Everyone Sang

Everyone suddenly burst out singing;
And I was filled with such delight
As prisoned birds must find in freedom,
Winging wildly across the white
Orchards and dark-green fields; on — on — and out of sight.

Everyone's voice was suddenly lifted;
And beauty came like the setting sun:
My heart was shaken with tears; and horror
Drifted away . . . O, but Everyone
Was a bird; and the song was wordless; the singing will never be done.

MARIANNE MOORE

Poetry

I, too, dislike it: there are things that are important beyond all this fiddle.
   Reading it, however, with a perfect contempt for it, one discovers in
   it after all, a place for the genuine.

      Hands that can grasp, eyes
5   that can dilate, hair that can rise
          if it must, these things are important not because a

high-sounding interpretation can be put upon them but because they are
    useful. When they become so derivative as to become unintelligible,
    the same thing may be said for all of us, that we
10   do not admire what
        we cannot understand: the bat
          holding on upside down or in quest of something to

eat, elephants pushing, a wild horse taking a roll, a tireless wolf under
    a tree, the immovable critic twitching his skin like a horse that feels a
                         flea, the base-
15   ball fan, the statistician —
        nor is it valid
          to discriminate against "business documents and

school-books";[1] all these phenomena are important. One must make a
                                     distinction
    however: when dragged into prominence by half poets, the result is not
                                      poetry,
20   nor till the poets among us can be
        "literalists of
        the imagination"[2] — above
          insolence and triviality and can present

for inspection, "imaginary gardens with real toads in them," shall we
                                     have
25   it. In the meantime, if you demand on the one hand,
      the raw material of poetry in
        all its rawness and
        that which is on the other hand
          genuine, you are interested in poetry.

---

1. *Diary of Tolstoy* (Dutton), p. 84. 'Where the boundary between prose and poetry lies, I shall never be able to understand. The question is raised in manuals of style, yet the answer to it lies beyond me. Poetry is verse: prose is not verse. Or else poetry is everything with the exception of business documents and school books' (Moore's note).
2. 'Literalists of the imagination.' Yeats: *Ideas of Good and Evil*, London, 1903, p. 182.

'The limitation of his [Blake's] view was from the very intensity of his vision; he was a too literal realist of imagination, as others are of nature; and because he believed that the figures seen by the mind's eye, when exalted by inspiration, were "eternal existences", symbols of divine essences, he hated every grace of style that might obscure their lineaments' (Moore's note).

JOHN CROWE RANSOM

Piazza Piece

—I am a gentleman in a dustcoat trying
To make you hear. Your ears are soft and small
And listen to an old man not at all,
They want the young men's whispering and sighing.
But see the roses on your trellis dying
And hear the spectral singing of the moon;
For I must have my lovely lady soon,
I am a gentleman in a dustcoat trying.

—I am a lady young in beauty waiting
Until my truelove comes, and then we kiss.
But what grey man among the vines is this
Whose words are dry and faint as in a dream?
Back from my trellis, Sir, before I scream!
I am a lady young in beauty waiting.

T. S. ELIOT

The Love Song of J. Alfred Prufrock

S'io credesse che mia risposta fosse
A persona che mai tornasse al mondo,
Questa fiamma staria senza piu scosse.
Ma perciocche giammai di questo fondo
Non torno vivo alcun, s'i'odo il vero,
Senza tema d'infamia ti rispondo.[1]

Let us go then, you and I,
When the evening is spread out against the sky
Like a patient etherized upon a table;
Let us go, through certain half-deserted streets,
5   The muttering retreats
Of restless nights in one-night cheap hotels
And sawdust restaurants with oyster-shells:
Streets that follow like a tedious argument
Of insidious intent
10   To lead you to an overwhelming question . . .

1. The epigraph is taken from Dante's *Inferno* (xxvii.61–6), where the poet encounters a fraudulent papal counsellor, Guido Da Montefeltro. In responding to the request to reveal his identity, the man, having sinned with his tongue in life, is now obliged to speak through the tongue of flame that encircles him: "If I thought that my reply were to one who would ever go back to the world, this flame would rest from further movement. But since no one, if what I hear is true, has ever returned alive from this abyss, I answer you without fear of infamy."

Oh, do not ask, "What is it?"
Let us go and make our visit.

In the room the women come and go
Talking of Michelangelo.

15   The yellow fog that rubs its back upon the window-panes,
The yellow smoke that rubs its muzzle on the window-panes
Licked its tongue into the corners of the evening,
Lingered upon the pools that stand in drains,
Let fall upon its back the soot that falls from chimneys,
20   Slipped by the terrace, made a sudden leap,
And seeing that it was a soft October night,
Curled once about the house, and fell asleep.

And indeed there will be time
For the yellow smoke that slides along the street,   '
25   Rubbing its back upon the window-panes;
There will be time, there will be time
To prepare a face to meet the faces that you meet;
There will be time to murder and create,
And time for all the works and days of hands
30   That lift and drop a question on your plate;
Time for you and time for me,
And time yet for a hundred indecisions,
And for a hundred visions and revisions,
Before the taking of a toast and tea.

35   In the room the women come and go
Talking of Michelangelo.

And indeed there will be time
To wonder, "Do I dare?" and, "Do I dare?"
Time to turn back and descend the stair,
40   With a bald spot in the middle of my hair—
(They will say: "How his hair is growing thin!")
My morning coat, my collar mounting firmly to the chin,
My necktie rich and modest, but asserted by a simple pin—
(They will say: "But how his arms and legs are thin!")
45   Do I dare
Disturb the universe?

In a minute there is time
For decisions and revisions which a minute will reverse.

For I have known them all already, known them all—
50   Have known the evenings, mornings, afternoons,
I have measured out my life with coffee spoons;
I know the voices dying with a dying fall
Beneath the music from a farther room.
       So how should I presume?

55   And I have known the eyes already, known them all —
      The eyes that fix you in a formulated phrase,
      And when I am formulated, sprawling on a pin,
      When I am pinned and wriggling on the wall,
      Then how should I begin
60   To spit out all the butt-ends of my days and ways?
          And how should I presume?

      And I have known the arms already, known them all —
      Arms that are braceleted and white and bare
      (But in the lamplight, downed with light brown hair!)
65   Is it perfume from a dress
      That makes me so digress?
      Arms that lie along a table, or wrap about a shawl.
          And should I then presume?
          And how should I begin?

70   Shall I say, I have gone at dusk through narrow streets
      And watched the smoke that rises from the pipes
      Of lonely men in shirt-sleeves, leaning out of windows? . . .

      I should have been a pair of ragged claws
      Scuttling across the floors of silent seas.

75   And the afternoon, the evening, sleeps so peacefully!
      Smoothed by long fingers,
      Asleep . . . tired . . . or it malingers,
      Stretched on the floor, here beside you and me.
      Should I, after tea and cakes and ices,
80   Have the strength to force the moment to its crisis?
      But though I have wept and fasted, wept and prayed,
      Though I have seen my head (grown slightly bald) brought in upon a
                                                                  platter,[2]
      I am no prophet — and here's no great matter;
      I have seen the moment of my greatness flicker,
85   And I have seen the eternal Footman hold my coat, and snicker,
      And in short, I was afraid.

      And would it have been worth it, after all,
      After the cups, the marmalade, the tea,
      Among the porcelain, among some talk of you and me,
90   Would it have been worth while,
      To have bitten off the matter with a smile,
      To have squeezed the universe into a ball[3]
      To roll it toward some overwhelming question,

---

2. Salome, rejected in love by John the Baptist, persuaded Herod to have John's severed head brought to her (Matthew xiv.3–11).

3. See Marvell, "To His Coy Mistress" (ll. 40-1).

To say: "I am Lazarus,⁴ come from the dead,
95 Come back to tell you all, I shall tell you all"—
If one, settling a pillow by her head,
      Should say: "That is not what I meant at all.
      That is not it, at all."

      And would it have been worth it, after all,
100 Would it have been worth while,
After the sunsets and the dooryards and the sprinkled streets,
After the novels, after the teacups, after the skirts that trail along the
                                                floor—
And this, and so much more?—
It is impossible to say just what I mean!
105 But as if a magic lantern threw the nerves in patterns on a screen:
Would it have been worth while
If one, settling a pillow or throwing off a shawl,
And turning toward the window, should say:
      "That is not it at all,
110 That is not what I meant, at all."

No! I am not Prince Hamlet, nor was meant to be;
Am an attendant lord, one that will do
To swell a progress, start a scene or two,
Advise the prince; no doubt, an easy tool,
115 Deferential, glad to be of use,
Politic, cautious, and meticulous;
Full of high sentence, but a bit obtuse;
At times, indeed, almost ridiculous—
Almost, at times, the Fool.

120 I grow old ... I grow old ...
I shall wear the bottoms of my trousers rolled.

      Shall I part my hair behind? Do I dare to eat a peach?
I shall wear white flannel trousers, and walk upon the beach.
I have heard the mermaids singing, each to each.

125 I do not think that they will sing to me.

      I have seen them riding seaward on the waves
Combing the white hair of the waves blown back
When the wind blows the water white and black.

      We have lingered in the chambers of the sea
130 By sea-girls wreathed with seaweed red and brown
Till human voices wake us, and we drown.

4. This reference may not be only to the Lazarus whom Christ raised from the dead (John xi.1–44) but also to the beggar Lazarus (Luke xvi.19–31), who was not permitted to return from the dead to warn the wealthy about hell.

Journey of the Magi[1]

"A cold coming we had of it,
Just the worst time of the year
For a journey, and such a long journey:
The ways deep and the weather sharp,
5　The very dead of winter."[2]
And the camels galled, sore-footed, refractory,
Lying down in the melting snow.
There were times we regretted
The summer palaces on slopes, the terraces,
10　And the silken girls bringing sherbet.
Then the camel men cursing and grumbling
And running away, and wanting their liquor and women,
And the night-fires going out, and the lack of shelters,
And the cities hostile and the towns unfriendly
15　And the villages dirty and charging high prices:
A hard time we had of it.
At the end we preferred to travel all night,
Sleeping in snatches,
With the voices singing in our ears, saying
20　That this was all folly.

　　Then at dawn we came down to a temperate valley,
Wet, below the snow line, smelling of vegetation;
With a running stream and a water-mill beating the darkness,
And three trees on the low sky,
25　And an old white horse galloped away in the meadow.
Then we came to a tavern with vine-leaves over the lintel,
Six hands at an open door dicing for pieces of silver,
And feet kicking the empty wine-skins.
But there was no information, and so we continued
30　And arrived at evening, not a moment too soon
Finding the place; it was (you may say) satisfactory.

　　All this was a long time ago, I remember,
And I would do it again, but set down
This set down
35　This: were we led all that way for
Birth or Death? There was a Birth, certainly,
We had evidence and no doubt. I had seen birth and death,
But had thought they were different; this Birth was
Hard and bitter agony for us, like Death, our death.

---

1. Three Kings or Wise Men of the East who
followed the star of Bethlehem and brought
gifts to the infant Jesus.
2. Adapted from a passage in a Nativity sermon by the seventeenth-century divine Lancelot Andrewes: "A cold coming they had of it
at this time of the year, just the worst time of
the year to take a journey, and specially a long
journey in. The ways deep, the weather sharp,
the days short, the sun farthest off, *in sol-
stitio brumali*, 'the very dead of winter.'"

40   We returned to our places, these Kingdoms,
     But no longer at ease here, in the old dispensation,
     With an alien people clutching their gods.
     I should be glad of another death.

KENNETH LESLIE

Halibut Cove Harvest

     The kettle sang the boy to a half-sleep;
     and the stir, stir of the kettle's lid
     drummed a new age
     into the boy's day-dream.
5   His mind strove with the mind of steam
     and conquered it
     and pressed it down and shaped it
     to the panting giant
     whose breath lies heavy on the world.

10   This is a song of harvest;
     the weather thickens with a harsh wind
     on this salt-seared coast;
     offshore a trawler, smoke-smearing the horizon,
     reaps the sea.

15   Here on the beach
     in the cove of the handliner[1]
     rain flattens the ungathered dulse
     and no cheek reddens to the rain.
     From the knock-kneed landing
20   a faltering path is lost among the rocks
     to a door that is closed with a nail.
     Seams widen and the paint falls off in curling flakes
     from the brave, the bold so little time ago,
     the dory high and dry,
25   anchored in hungry grass.

     This is the song of harvest:
     the belching trawler raping the sea,
     the cobweb ghosts against the window
     watching the wilderness uproot the doorsill with a weed.

---

1. Small fishing vessel.

WILFRED OWEN

Dulce et Decorum Est

Bent double, like old beggars under sacks,
Knock-kneed, coughing like hags, we cursed through sludge,
Till on the haunting flares we turned our backs
And towards our distant rest began to trudge.
5   Men marched asleep. Many had lost their boots
But limped on, blood-shod. All went lame; all blind;
Drunk with fatigue; deaf even to the hoots
Of tired, outstripped Five-Nines[1] that dropped behind.

Gas! Gas! Quick, boys! — An ecstasy of fumbling,
10   Fitting the clumsy helmets just in time;
But someone still was yelling out and stumbling
And floundering like a man in fire or lime[2] . . .
Dim, through the misty panes and thick green light,
As under a green sea, I saw him drowning.

15   In all my dreams, before my helpless sight,
He plunges at me, guttering, choking, drowning.

If in some smothering dreams you too could pace
Behind the wagon that we flung him in,
And watch the white eyes writhing in his face,
20   His hanging face, like a devil's sick of sin;
If you could hear, at every jolt, the blood
Come gargling from the froth-corrupted lungs,
Obscene as cancer, bitter as the cud
Of vile, incurable sores on innocent tongues, —
25   My friend, you would not tell with such high zest
To children ardent for some desperate glory,
The old lie: *Dulce et decorum est
Pro patria mori.*[3]

Miners[1]

There was a whispering in my hearth,
    A sigh of the coal,
Grown wistful of a former earth
    It might recall.

---

1. A 59 mm shell, fired from a mortar.
2. Quicklime, which becomes hot when exposed to air.
3. "It is sweet and proper to die for one's country" (Horace, *Odes* iii.2.13).

1. Inspired by an explosion at Podmore Hall Colliery, Halmer End, England, on 12 January 1918, when 155 men and boys were killed. Owen told his mother that he had written a poem about the colliery disaster but had got it mixed up with the war at the end.

5   I listened for a tale of leaves
       And smothered ferns,
     Frond-forests, and the low sly lives
       Before the fawns.

     My fire might show steam-phantoms simmer
10   From Time's old cauldron,
     Before the birds made nests in summer,
       Or men had children.

     But the coals were murmuring of their mine,
       And moans down there
15   Of boys that slept wry sleep, and men
       Writhing for air.

     I saw white bones in the cinder-shard,
       Bones without number.
     For many hearts with coal are charred,
20   And few remember.

     I thought of all that worked dark pits
       Of war, and died
     Digging the rock where Death reputes
       Peace lies indeed:

25   Comforted years will sit soft-chaired,
       In rooms of amber,
     The years will stretch their hands, well-cheered
       By our life's ember;

     The centuries will burn rich loads
30   With which we groaned,
     Whose warmth shall lull their dreaming lids,
       While songs are crooned;
     But they will not dream of us poor lads
       Lost in the ground.

Strange Meeting

     It seemed that out of the battle I escaped
     Down some profound dull tunnel, long since scooped
     Through granites which Titanic wars had groined.
     Yet also there encumbered sleepers groaned,
5   Too fast in thought or death to be bestirred,
     Then, as I probed them, one sprang up, and stared
     With piteous recognition in fixed eyes,
     Lifting distressful hands as if to bless.
     And by his smile, I knew that sullen hall.

10   With a thousand fears that vision's face was grained;
      Yet no blood reached there from the upper ground,
      And no guns thumped, or down the flues made moan.
      "Strange friend," I said, "here is no cause to mourn."
      "None," said the other, "save the undone years,
15   The hopelessness. Whatever hope is yours,
      Was my life also; I went hunting wild
      After the wildest beauty in the world,
      Which lies not calm in eyes, or braided hair,
      But mocks the steady running of the hour,
20   And if it grieves, grieves richlier than here.
      For by my glee might many men have laughed,
      And of my weeping something has been left,
      Which must die now. I mean the truth untold,
      The pity of war, the pity war distilled.
25   Now men will go content with what we spoiled,
      Or, discontent, boil bloody, and be spilled.
      They will be swift with swiftness of the tigress,
      None will break ranks, though nations trek from progress.
      Courage was mine, and I had mystery,
30   Wisdom was mine, and I had mastery;
      To miss the march of this retreating world
      Into vain citadels that are not walled.
      Then, when much blood had clogged their chariot-wheels
      I would go up and wash them from sweet wells,
35   Even with truths that lie too deep for taint.
      I would have poured my spirit without stint
      But not through wounds; not on the cess of war.
      Foreheads of men have bled where no wounds were.
      I am the enemy you killed, my friend.
40   I knew you in this death: for so you frowned
      Yesterday through me as you jabbed and killed.
      I parried; but my hands were loath and cold.
      Let us sleep now.... "

Anthem for Doomed Youth

"What passing-bells for these who died as cattle?
    Only the monstrous anger of the guns.
    Only the stuttering rifles' rapid rattle
Can patter out their hasty orisons.
No mockeries for them; no prayers or bells,
Nor any voice of mourning save the choirs, —
The shrill demented choirs of wailing shells;
And bugles calling for them from sad shires.

"What candles may be held to speed them all?
  Not in the hands of boys, but in their eyes
Shall shine the holy glimmers of good-byes.
  The pallor of girls' brows shall be their pall;
Their flowers the tenderness of patient minds,
And each slow dusk a drawing-down of blinds."

COLE PORTER

Miss Otis Regrets

Miss Otis regrets she's unable to lunch today,
Madam, Miss Otis regrets she's unable to lunch today.
She is sorry to be delayed,
But last evening down in lovers' lane she strayed,
Madam, Miss Otis regrets she's unable to lunch today.

When she woke up and found that her dream of love was gone,
Madam, she ran to the man who had led her so far astray,
And from under her velvet gown
She drew a gun and shot her lover down,
Madam, Miss Otis regrets she's unable to lunch today.

When the mob came and got her and dragged her from the jail,
Madam, they strung her upon the old willow across the way,
And the moment before she died
She lifted up her lovely head and cried,
Madam, "Miss Otis regrets she's unable to lunch today."

e. e. cummings

my father moved through dooms of love

my father moved through dooms of love
through sames of am through haves of give,
singing each morning out of each night
my father moved through depths of height

this motionless forgetful where
turned at his glance to shining here;
that if (so timid air is firm)
under his eyes would stir and squirm

newly as from unburied which
10   floats the fist who, his april touch
drove sleeping selves to swarm their fates
woke dreamers to their ghostly roots

and should some why completely weep
my father's fingers brought her sleep:
15   vainly no smallest voice might cry
for he could feel the mountains grow.

Lifting the valleys of the sea
my father moved through griefs of joy;
praising a forehead called the moon
20   singing desire into begin

joy was his song and joy so pure
a heart of star by him could steer
and pure so now and now so yes
the wrists of twilight would rejoice

25   keen as midsummer's keen beyond
conceiving mind of sun will stand,
so strictly (over utmost him
so hugely) stood my father's dream

his flesh was flesh his blood was blood:
30   no hungry man but wished him food;
No cripple wouldn't creep one mile
uphill to only see him smile.

Scorning the pomp of must and shall
my father moved through dooms of feel;
35   his anger was as right as rain
his pity was as green as grain

septembering arms of year extend
less humbly wealth to foe and friend
than he to foolish and to wise
40   offered immeasurable is

proudly and (by octobering flame
beckoned) as earth will downward climb,
so naked for immortal work
his shoulders marched against the dark

45   his sorrow was as true as bread:
no liar looked him in the head;
if every friend became his foe
he'd laugh and build a world with snow.

My father moved through theys of we,
50 singing each new leaf out of each tree
(and every child was sure that spring
danced when she heard my father sing)

then let men kill which cannot share,
let blood and flesh be mud and mire,
55 scheming imagine, passion willed,
freedom a drug that's bought and sold

giving to steal and cruel kind,
a heart to fear, to doubt a mind,
to differ a disease of same,
60 conform the pinnacle of am

though dull were all we taste as bright,
bitter all utterly things sweet,
maggoty minus and dumb death
all we inherit, all bequeath

65 and nothing quite so least as truth
—i say though hate were why men breathe—
because my father lived his soul
love is the whole and more than all

anyone lived in a pretty how town

anyone lived in a pretty how town
(with up so floating many bells down)
spring summer autumn winter
he sang his didn't he danced his did.

5 Women and men (both little and small)
cared for anyone not at all
they sowed their isn't they reaped their same
sun moon stars rain

children guessed (but only a few
10 and down they forgot as up they grew
autumn winter spring summer)
that noone loved him more by more

when by now and tree by leaf
she laughed his joy she cried his grief
15 bird by snow and stir by still
anyone's any was all to her

someones married their everyones
laughed their cryings and did their dance

(sleep wake hope and then) they
20　said their nevers they slept their dream

stars rain sun moon
(and only the snow can begin to explain
how children are apt to forget to remember
with up so floating many bells down)

25　one day anyone died i guess
(and noone stooped to kiss her face)
busy folk buried them side by side
little by little and was by was

all by all and deep by deep
30　and more by more they dream their sleep
noone and anyone earth by april
wish by spirit and if by yes.

Women and men (both dong and ding)
summer autumn winter spring
35　reaped their sowing and went their came
sun moon stars rain

next to of course god america i

"next to of course god america i
love you land of the pilgrims and so forth oh
say can you see by the dawn's early my
country 'tis of centuries come and go
and are no more what of it we should worry
in every language even deafanddumb
thy sons acclaim your glorious name by gorry
by jingo by gee by gosh by gum
why talk of beauty what could be more beautiful than these heroic happy dead
who rushed like lions to the roaring slaughter
they did not stop to think they died instead
then shall the voices of liberty be mute?"

He spoke. And drank rapidly a glass of water

ROBERT GRAVES

Warning to Children

Children, if you dare to think
Of the greatness, rareness, muchness,
Fewness of this precious only
Endless world in which you say
5   You live, you think of things like this:
Blocks of slate enclosing dappled
Red and green, enclosing tawny
Yellow nets, enclosing white
And black acres of dominoes,
10 Where a neat brown paper parcel
Tempts you to untie the string.
In the parcel a small island,
On the island a large tree,
On the tree a husky fruit.
15 Strip the husk and pare the rind off:
In the kernel you will see
Blocks of slate enclosed by dappled
Red and green, enclosed by tawny
Yellow nets, enclosed by white
20 And black acres of dominoes,
Where the same brown paper parcel—
Children, leave the string untied!
For who dares undo the parcel
Finds himself at once inside it,
25 On the island, in the fruit,
Blocks of slate about his head,
Finds himself enclosed by dappled
Green and red, enclosed by yellow
Tawny nets, enclosed by black
30 And white acres of dominoes,
With the same brown paper parcel
Still untied upon his knee.
And, if he then should dare to think
Of the fewness, muchness, rareness,
35 Greatness of this endless only
Precious world in which he says
He lives—he then unties the string.

The Cool Web

Children are dumb to say how hot the day is,
How hot the scent is of the summer rose,
How dreadful the black wastes of evening sky,
How dreadful the tall soldiers drumming by.

But we have speech, to chill the angry day,
And speech, to dull the rose's cruel scent.
We spell away the overhanging night,
We spell away the soldiers and the fright.

There's a cool web of language winds us in,
Retreat from too much joy or too much fear:
We grow sea-green at last and coldly die
In brininess and volubility.

But if we let our tongues lose self-possession,
Throwing off language and its watery clasp
Before our death, instead of when death comes,
Facing the wide glare of the children's day,
Facing the rose, the dark sky and the drums,
We shall go mad no doubt and die that way.

The Naked and the Nude

For me, the naked and the nude
(By lexicographers construed
As synonyms that should express
The same deficiency of dress
5   Or shelter) stand as wide apart
As love from lies, or truth from art.

Lovers without reproach will gaze
On bodies naked and ablaze;
The hippocratic eye will see
10   In nakedness, anatomy;
And naked shines the Goddess when
She mounts her lion among men.

The nude are bold, the nude are sly
To hold each treasonable eye.
15   While draping by a showman's trick
Their dishabille in rhetoric,
They grin a mock-religious grin
Of scorn at those of naked skin.

The naked, therefore, who compete
20   Against the nude may know defeat;

Yet when they both together tread
The briary pastures of the dead,
By Gorgons[1] with long whips pursued,
How naked go the sometime nude!

F. R. SCOTT

The Canadian Authors Meet

Expansive puppets percolate self-unction *—the act of annointing.*
Beneath a portrait of the Prince of Wales.
Miss Crotchet's muse has somehow failed to function,
Yet she's a poetess.   Beaming, she sails

5 From group to chattering group, with such a dear
Victorian saintliness, as is her fashion,
Greeting the other unknowns with a cheer—
Virgins of sixty who still write of passion.

The air is heavy with Canadian topics,
10 And Carman, Lampman, Roberts, Campbell, Scott,
Are measured for their faith and philanthropics, *—> humaneness.*
Their zeal for God and King, their earnest thought.

The cakes are sweet, but sweeter is the feeling
That one is missing with the *literati*;
15 It warms the old, and melts the most congealing.
Really, it is a most delightful party.

Shall we go round the mulberry bush, or shall
We gather at the river, or shall we
Appoint a Poet Laureate this fall,
20 Or shall we have another cup of tea?

O Canada, O Canada, Oh can
A day go by without new authors springing
To paint the native maple, and to plan
More ways to set the selfsame welkin ringing?

1. Gorgons (literally "the grim ones") figure frequently in Greek mythology. In Graves's own study of Greek mythology, *The Greek Myths* (1955), he suggests that a gorgon's head with its characteristic scowl, glaring eyes, and protruding tongue was traditionally used to warn off the idly curious from prying into divine mysteries.

W.L.M.K.[1]

How shall we speak of Canada,
Mackenzie King dead?
The Mother's boy in the lonely room
With his dog, his medium and his ruins?

5 He blunted us.

We had no shape
Because he never took sides,
And no sides
Because he never allowed them to take shape.

10 He skilfully avoided what was wrong
Without saying what was right,
And never let his on the one hand
Know what his on the other hand was doing.

The height of his ambition
15 Was to pile a Parliamentary Committee on a Royal Commission,
To have 'conscription if necessary
But not necessarily conscription',
To let Parliament decide —
Later.

20 Postpone, postpone, abstain.

Only one thread was certain:
After World War I
Business as usual,
After World War II
25 Orderly decontrol.
Always he led us back to where we were before.

He seemed to be in the centre
Because we had no centre,
No vision
30 To pierce the smoke-screen of his politics.

Truly he will be remembered
Wherever men honour ingenuity,
Ambiguity, inactivity, and political longevity.

Let us raise up a temple
35 To the cult of mediocrity,
Do nothing by halves
Which can be done by quarters.

1. William Lyon MacKenzie King (1874–1950), long-time Liberal Party leader (1919–48) and Canadian prime minister (1921–6, 1926–30, and 1935–48).

Calamity

A laundry truck
Rolled down the hill
And crashed into my maple tree.
It was a truly North American calamity.
5   Three cans of beer fell out
(Which in itself was revealing)
And a jumble of skirts and shirts
Spilled onto the ploughed grass.
Dogs barked, and the children
10   Sprouted like dandelions on my lawn.
Normally we do not speak to one another on this avenue,
But the excitement made us suddenly neighbours.
People exchanged remarks
Who had never been introduced
15   And for a while we were quite human.
Then the policeman came —
Sedately, for this was Westmount —
And carefully took down all names and numbers.
The towing truck soon followed,
20   Order was restored.
The starch came raining down.

A. J. M. SMITH

The Lonely Land

Cedar and jagged fir
uplift sharp barbs
against the gray
and cloud-piled sky;
5   and in the bay
blown spume and windrift
and thin, bitter spray
snap
at the whirling sky;
10   and the pine trees
lean one way.

A wild duck calls
to her mate,
and the ragged
15   and passionate tones
stagger and fall,
and recover,
and stagger and fall,
on these stones —

20   are lost
        in the lapping of water
        on smooth, flat stones.

        This is a beauty
        of dissonance,
25   this resonance
        of stony strand,
        this smoky cry
        curled over a black pine
        like a broken
30   and wind-battered branch
        when the wind
        bends the tops of the pines
        and curdles the sky
        from the north.

35   This is the beauty
        of strength
        broken by strength
        and still strong.

STEVIE SMITH

Not Waving but Drowning

Nobody heard him, the dead man,
But still he lay moaning:
I was much further out than you thought
And not waving but drowning.

Poor chap, he always loved larking
And now he's dead
It must have been too cold for him his heart gave way,
They said.

Oh, no no no, it was too cold always
(Still the dead one lay moaning)
I was much too far out all my life
And not waving but drowning.

The Best Beast of the Fat-Stock Show at Earls Court
(In monosyllables)

The Best Beast of the Show
Is fat,
He goes by the lift—
They all do that.

5   This lift, large as a room,
(Yet the beasts bunch),
Goes up with a groan,
They have not oiled the winch.

Not yet to the lift
10   Goes the Best Beast,
He has to walk on the floor to make a show
First.

Great are his horns,
Long his fur,
15   The Beast came from the North
To walk here.

Is he not fat?
Is he not fit?
Now in a crown he walks
20   To the lift.

When he lay in his pen,
In the close heat,
His head lolled, his eyes
Were not shut for sleep.

25 Slam the lift door,
Push it up with a groan,
Will they kill the Beast now?
Where has he gone?

When he lay in the straw
30 His heart beat so fast
His sides heaved, I touched his side
As I walked past.

I touched his side,
I touched the root of his horns;
35 The breath of the Beast
Came in low moans.

C. DAY LEWIS

Song

Come, live with me and be my love,[1]
And we will all the pleasures prove
Of peace and plenty, bed and board,
That chance employment may afford.

I'll handle dainties on the docks
And thou shalt read of summer frocks:
At evening by the sour canals
We'll hope to hear some madrigals.

Care on thy maiden brow shall put   *ambiguity or*
A wreath of wrinkles, and thy foot   *plurisignation.*
Be shod with pain: not silken dress
But toil shall tire thy loveliness.
            attire ?^ wear out.
Hunger shall make thy modest zone *belt.*
And cheat fond death of all but bone—
If these delights thy mind may move,
Then live with me and be my love.

---

1. See Christopher Marlowe, "The Passionate
Shepherd to His Love."

PATRICK KAVANAGH

The Great Hunger[1]

I

Clay is the word and clay is the flesh
Where the potato-gatherers like mechanised scare-crows move
Along the side-fall of the hill—Maguire and his men.
If we watch them an hour is there anything we can prove
5   Of life as it is broken-backed over the Book
Of Death? Here crows gabble over worms and frogs
And the gulls like old newspapers are blown clear of the hedges, luckily.
Is there some light of imagination in these wet clods?
Or why do we stand here shivering?
10   Which of these men
Loved the light and the queen
Too long virgin? Yesterday was summer. Who was it promised marriage
                       to himself
Before apples were hung from the ceilings for Halloween?
We will wait and watch the tragedy to the last curtain
15   Till the last soul passively like a bag of wet clay
Rolls down the side of the hill, diverted by the angles
Where the plough missed or a spade stands, straitening the way.

A dog lying on a torn jacket under a heeled-up cart,
A horse nosing along the posied headland, trailing
20   A rusty plough. Three heads hanging between wide-apart
Legs. October playing a symphony on a slack wire paling
Maguire watches the drills flattened out
And the flints that lit a candle for him on a June altar
Flameless. The drills slipped by and the days slipped by
25   And he trembled his head away and ran free from the world's halter,
And thought himself wiser than any man in the townland[2]
When he laughed over pints of porter
Of how he came free from every net spread
In the gaps of experience. He shook a knowing head
30   And pretended to his soul
That children are tedious in hurrying fields of April
Where men are spanging[3] across wide furrows.
Lost in the passion that never needs a wife—
The pricks that pricked were the pointed pins of harrows.
35   Children scream so loud that the crows could bring
The seed of an acre away with crow-rude jeers.

---

1. This is the introductory section of Kavanagh's long poem, *The Great Hunger* (1942), which takes its title from the Irish potato famine of the 1840s.

2. An Irish term for an area of land comparable to a township.
3. Leaping.

Patrick Maguire, he called his dog and he flung a stone in the air
And hallooed the birds away that were the birds of the years.

Turn over the weedy clods and tease out the tangled skeins.
40   What is he looking for there?
He thinks it is a potato, but we know better
Than his mud-gloved fingers probe in this insensitive hair.

"Move forward the basket and balance it steady
In this hollow. Pull down the shafts of that cart, Joe,
45   And straddle the horse" Maguire calls.
"The wind's over Brannagan's now that means rain.
Graip⁴ up some withered stalks and see that no potato falls
Over the tail-board going down the ruckety pass—
And *that's* a job we'll have to do in December,
50   Gravel it and build a kerb on the bog-side. Is that Cassidy's ass
Out in my clover? Curse o' God—
Where is that dog?
Never where he's wanted." Maguire grunts and spits
Through a clay-wattled moustache and stares about him from the height.
55   His dream changes again like the cloud-swung wind
And he is not so sure now if his mother was right
When she praised the man who made a field his bride.

Watch him, watch him, that man on a hill whose spirit
Is a wet sack flapping about the knees of time.
60   He lives that his little fields may stay fertile when his own body
Is spread in the bottom of a ditch under two coulters crossed in Christ's
                                                                        Name.

He was suspicious in his youth as a rat near strange bread.
When girls laughed; when they screamed he knew that meant
The cry of fillies in season. He could not walk
65   The easy road to his destiny. He dreamt
The innocence of young brambles to hooked treachery.
O the grip, O the grip of irregular fields! No man escapes.
It could not be that back of the hills love was free
And ditches straight.
70   No monster hand lifted up children and put down apes
As here.
                    "O God if I had been wiser!"
That was his sigh like the brown breeze in the thistles.
He looks towards his house and haggard.⁵ "O God if I had been wiser!"
75   But now a crumpled leaf from the whitethorn bushes
Darts like a frightened robin, and the fence
Shows the green of after-grass through a little window,

4. Fork.
5. Farmyard.

And he knows that his own heart is calling his mother a liar.
God's truth is life—even the grotesque shapes of its foulest fire.

80   The horse lifts its head and crashes
Through the whins and stones
To lip late passion in the crawling clover.
In the gap there's a bush weighted with boulders like morality
The fools of life bleed if they climb over.

85   The wind leans from Brady's, and the coltsfoot leaves are holed with rust,
Rain fills the cart-tracks and the sole-plate grooves;
A yellow sun reflects in Donaghmoyne[6]
The poignant light in puddles shaped by hooves.

Come with me, Imagination, into this iron house
90   And we will watch from the doorway the years run back,
And we will know what a peasant's left hand wrote on the page.
Be easy October. No cackle hen, horse neigh, tree-sough, duck quack.

what is this alluding to?

EARLE BIRNEY

David

I

David and I that summer cut trails on the Survey,
All week in the valley for wages, in air that was steeped
In the wail of mosquitoes, but over the sunalive week-ends
We climbed, to get from the ruck of the camp, the surly

5   Poker, the wrangling, the snoring under the fetid
Tents, and because we had joy in our lengthening coltish
Muscles, and mountains for David were made to see over,
Stairs from the valleys and steps to the sun's retreats.

II

Our first was Mount Gleam. We hiked in the long afternoon
10   To a curling lake and lost the lure of the faceted
Cone in the swell of its sprawling shoulders. Past
The inlet we grilled our bacon, the strips festooned

On a poplar prong, in the hurrying slant of the sunset.
Then the two of us rolled in the blanket while round us the cold
15   Pines thrust at the stars. The dawn was a floating
Of mists till we reached to the slopes above timber, and won

6. A stream in County Monaghan.

To snow like fire in the sunlight. The peak was upthrust
Like a fist in a frozen ocean of rock that swirled
Into valleys the moon could be rolled in. Remotely unfurling
20　Eastward the alien prairie glittered. Down through the dusty

Skree on the west we descended, and David showed me
How to use the give of shale for giant incredible
Strides. I remember, before the larches' edge,
That I jumped a long green surf of juniper flowing

25　Away from the wind, and landed in gentian and saxifrage
Spilled on the moss. Then the darkening firs
And the sudden whirring of water that knifed down a fern-hidden
Cliff and splashed unseen into mist in the shadows.

III
One Sunday on Rampart's arête[1] a rainsquall caught us,
30　And passed, and we clung by our blueing fingers and bootnails
An endless hour in the sun, not daring to move
Till the ice had steamed from the slate. And David taught me

How time on a knife-edge can pass with the guessing of fragments
Remembered from poets, the naming of strata beside one,
35　And matching of stories from schooldays. . . . We crawled astride
The peak to feast on the marching ranges flagged

By the fading shreds of the shattered stormcloud. Lingering
There it was David who spied to the south, remote,
And unmapped, a sunlit spire on Sawback, an overhang
40　Crooked like a talon. David named it the Finger.

That day we chanced on the skull and the splayed white ribs
Of a mountain goat underneath a cliff-face, caught
On a rock. Around were the silken feathers of hawks.
And that was the first I knew that a goat could slip.

IV
45　And then Inglismaldie. Now I remember only
The long ascent of the lonely valley, the live
Pine spirally scarred by lightning, the slicing pipe
Of invisible pika,[2] and great prints, by the lowest

Snow, of a grizzly. There it was too that David
50　Taught me to read the scroll of coral in limestone
And the beetle-seal in the shale of ghostly trilobites,[3]
Letters delivered to man from the Cambrian waves.

---

1. A sharp ascending ridge or edge of a mountain.
2. A small rodent.
3. Their fossil remains are found abundantly in Palaeozoic rocks.

V

On Sundance we tried from the col and the going was hard.
The air howled from our feet to the smudged rocks
55 And the papery lake below. At an outthrust we baulked
Till David clung with his left to a dint in the scarp,

Lobbed the iceaxe over the rocky lip,
Slipped from his holds and hung by the quivering pick,
Twisted his long legs up into space and kicked
60 To the crest. Then grinning, he reached with his freckled wrist

And drew me up after. We set a new time for that climb.
That day returning we found a robin gyrating
In grass, wing-broken. I caught it to tame but David
Took and killed it, and said, "Could you teach it to fly?"

VI

65 In August, the second attempt, we ascended The Fortress,
By the forks of the Spray we caught five trout and fried them
Over a balsam fire. The woods were alive
With the vaulting of mule-deer and drenched with clouds all the morning,

Till we burst at noon to the flashing and floating round
70 Of the peaks. Coming down we picked in our hats the bright
And sunhot raspberries, eating them under a mighty
Spruce, while a marten moving like quicksilver scouted us.

VII

But always we talked of the Finger on Sawback, unknown
And hooked, till the first afternoon in September we slogged
75 Through the musky woods, past a swamp that quivered with frog-song,
And camped by a bottle-green lake. But under the cold

Breath of the glacier sleep would not come, the moon-light
Etching the Finger. We rose and trod past the feathery
Larch, while the stars went out, and the quiet heather
80 Flushed, and the skyline pulsed with the surging bloom

Of incredible dawn in the Rockies. David spotted
Bighorns across the moraine and sent them leaping
With yodels the ramparts redoubled and rolled to the peaks,
And the peaks to the sun. The ice in the morning thaw

85 Was a gurgling world of crystal and cold blue chasms,
And seracs[4] that shone like frozen saltgreen waves.
At the base of the Finger we tried once and failed. Then David
Edged to the west and discovered the chimney; the last

4. An irregularly shaped pinnacle of ice on a
glacier, formed by the intersection of crevasses.

Hundred feet we fought the rock and shouldered and kneed
90   Our way for an hour and made it. Unroping we formed
A cairn on the rotting tip. Then I turned to look north
At the glistening wedge of giant Assiniboine, heedless

Of handhold. And one foot gave. I swayed and shouted.
David turned sharp and reached out his arm and steadied me,
95   Turning again with a grin and his lips ready
To jest. But the strain crumbled his foothold. Without

A gasp he was gone. I froze to the sound of grating
Edge-nails and fingers, the slither of stones, the lone
Second of silence, the nightmare thud. Then only
100   The wind and the muted beat of unknowing cascades.

VIII
Somehow I worked down the fifty impossible feet
To the ledge, calling and getting no answer but echoes
Released in the cirque,⁵ and trying not to reflect
What an answer would mean. He lay still, with his lean

105   Young face upturned and strangely unmarred, but his legs
Splayed beneath him, beside the final drop,
Six hundred feet sheer to the ice. My throat stopped
When I reached him, for he was alive. He opened his gray

Straight eyes and brokenly murmured "over . . . over."
110   And I, feeling beneath him a cruel fang
Of the ledge thrust in his back, but not understanding,
Mumbled stupidly, "Best not to move," and spoke

Of his pain. But he said, "I can't move. . . .If only I felt
Some pain." Then my shame stung the tears to my eyes
115   As I crouched, and I cursed myself, but he cried,
Louder, "No, Bobbie! Don't ever blame yourself.

I didn't test my foothold." He shut the lids
Of his eyes to the stare of the sky, while I moistened his lips
From our water flask and tearing my shirt into strips
120   I swabbed the shredded hands. But the blood slid

From his side and stained the stone and the thirsting lichens,
And yet I dared not lift him up from the gore
Of the rock. Then he whispered, "Bob, I want to go over!"
This time I knew what he meant and I grasped for a lie

125   And said, "I'll be back here by midnight with ropes
And men from the camp and we'll cradle you out." But I knew

5. A natural amphitheatre, a rounded hollow
or plain encircled by heights.

That the day and the night must pass and the cold dews
Of another morning before such men unknowing

The ways of mountains could win to the chimney's top.
130 And then, how long? And he knew. . . and the hell of hours
After that, if he lived till we came, roping him out.
But I curled beside him and whispered, "The bleeding will stop.

You can last." He said only, "Perhaps. . . . For what? A wheelchair,
Bob?" His eyes brightening with fever upbraided me.
135 I could not look at him more and said, "Then I'll stay
With you." But he did not speak, for the clouding fever.

I lay dazed and stared at the long valley,
The glistening hair of a creek on the rug stretched
By the firs, while the sun leaned round and flooded the ledge,
140 The moss, and David still as a broken doll.

I hunched to my knees to leave, but he called and his voice
Now was sharpened with fear. "For Christ's sake push me over!
If I could move. . . . Or die. . . ." The sweat ran from his forehead,
But only his eyes moved. A hawk was buoying

145 Blackly its wings over the wrinkled ice.
The purr of a waterfall rose and sank with the wind.
Above us climbed the last joint of the Finger
Beckoning bleakly the wide indifferent sky.

Even then in the sun it grew cold lying there. . . . And I knew
150 He had tested his holds. It was I who had not. . . . I looked
At the blood on the ledge, and the far valley. I looked
At last in his eyes. He breathed, "I'd do it for you, Bob."

IX
I will not remember how nor why I could twist
Up the wind-devilled peak, and down through the chimney's empty
155 Horror, and over the traverse alone. I remember
Only the pounding fear I would stumble on It

When I came to the grave-cold maw of the bergschrund[6] . . . reeling
Over the sun-cankered snowbridge, shying the caves
In the névé[7] . . . the fear, and the need to make sure It was there
160 On the ice, the running and falling and running, leaping

Of gaping greenthroated crevasses, alone and pursued
By the Finger's lengthening shadow. At last through the fanged
And blinding seracs I slid to the milky wrangling
Falls at the glacier's snout, through the rocks piled huge

6. Crevice.
7. A field or bed of frozen snow.

165   On the humped moraine, and into the spectral larches,
      Alone. By the glooming lake I sank and chilled
      My mouth but I could not rest and stumbled still
      To the valley, losing my way in the ragged marsh.

      I was glad of the mire that covered the stains, on my ripped
170   Boots, of his blood, but panic was on me, the reek
      Of the bog, the purple glimmer of toadstools obscene
      In the twilight. I staggered clear to a firewaste, tripped

      And fell with a shriek on my shoulder. It somehow eased
      My heart to know I was hurt, but I did not faint
175   And I could not stop while over me hung the range
      Of the Sawback. In blackness I searched for the trail by the creek

      And found it. . . . My feet squelched a slug and horror
      Rose again in my nostrils. I hurled myself
      Down the path. In the woods behind some animal yelped.
180   Then I saw the glimmer of tents and babbled my story.

      I said that he fell straight to the ice where they found him,
      And none but the sun and incurious clouds have lingered
      Around the marks of that day on the ledge of the Finger,
      That day, the last of my youth, on the last of our mountains.

      Toronto 1940

Way to the West

      11 pm & sunset still going on
      but that cd be the latitude
      whats wrongs the colour
      everywhere horseshit ochre & roiling
5   like paper that twists/browns
      before firing up on hot ashes
      theres somebodys hell ahead
      meantime our lips prick
      & the trees are dead

10   but it's another 20 miles before the sign
                  You Are Entering
                  S U D B U R Y
            Home of the world's largest
      & christ there on the skull of a hill
15   3 manhattan-high stacks   a phallic calvary
      ejaculating some essence of rotted semen
      straight up like mass sabotage at cape kennedy

the damned are all over   the young
shrieking (looking much like anyone)
20   drag-race with radios up
from one smouldering stoplight to another—
under neon the older faces
assembled from half europe
screwcheeked/pitted all the same way
25   have something dignified about their devilship
that stares us down   till they come human
& houck brown on the cement

    WELCOME TO . . .   73% OF THE FREE
    WORLD'S NICKEL IS CREATED HERE
30   & the free world invented a special cough
not even 100 taverns can dampen
nor all the jukes drown in the doorways
of pandemonium   milton thou shouldst
be living[1] etc

35   DEAD END   wheres west?   sunset folded
our headlights finger dumped cans
wriggle through streets like crevasses
blasted in bedrock pink & folded
like glazed guts on a butchers marble

40   out of the starless dark falls the roar
of golgotha   how long before one stops
noticing?   & the sting in the eyes?

by a raped old car an indian sits
praying?   puking
45   *You Are Leaving*
      S U D B U R Y
    Center of Free Enterprise
& 20 more miles of battlefield

at last a moon looms up
50   we are into the dumb firs again
    TURN OUT   300 YDS
      HISTORIC SITE
      FRENCH RIVER
what?   canoe route the Hurons found
55   & showed the whites—
the way to the west   silks   buffalo
vietnam   the moon
shines over the middle of nowhere—
dumb as the trees

1. The opening of a sonnet by Wordsworth.

60   we stop for a leak   silence
     too late for other cars
     the trees listen back
     nothing   the owls dead too?

     suddenly some kind of low growl
65   coming up!   we head back for the car—
     only a night jet

     but after it passes we realize
     we'd been hearing the river all along

The Bear on the Delhi Road

     Unreal   tall as a myth
     by the road the Himalayan bear
     is beating the brilliant air
     with his crooked arms
5   About him two men   bare
     spindly as locusts   leap

     One pulls on a ring
     in the great soft nose   His mate
     flicks   flicks with a stick
10   up at the rolling eyes

     They have not led him here
     down from the fabulous hills
     to this bald alien plain
     and the clamorous world   to kill
15   but simply to teach him to dance

     They are peaceful both   these spare
     men of Kashmir   and the bear
     alive is their living   too
     If   far on the Delhi way
20   around him galvanic they dance
     it is merely to wear   wear
     from his shaggy body the tranced
     wish forever to stay
     only an ambling bear
25   four-footed in berries

     It is no more joyous for them
     in this hot dust to prance
     out of reach of the praying claws
     sharpened to paw for ants

30   in the shadows of deodars
     It is not easy to free
     myth from reality
     or rear this fellow up
     to lurch   lurch with them
35   in the tranced dancing of men

Meeting of Strangers

"Nice jacket you got dere, man"

     He swerved his bicycle toward my curb
     to call   then flashed round the corner
     a blur in the dusk   of somebody big
5   redshirted   young   dark   unsmiling

     As I stood hoping for a taxi to show
     I thought him droll at least
     A passing pleasantry?   It was frayed
     a sixdollar coat   tropical weight
10   in this heat only something with pockets
     to carry things in

     Now all four streets were empty
     Dockland   everything shut

     It was a sound no bigger than a breath
15   that made me wheel

     He was ten feet away   redshirt
     The cycle leant by a post farther off
     where an alley came in   What?!

     My turning froze him
20   in the middle of some elaborate stealth
     He looked almost comic   splayed
     but there was a glitter
     under the downheld hand
     and something smoked from his eyes

25   By God if I was going to be stabbed
     for my wallet (adrenalin suffused me)
     it would have to be done in plain sight
     I made a flying leap
     to the middle of the crossing
30   White man   tourist   surrogate   yes
     but not guilty enough
     to be skewered in the guts for it

without raising all Trinidad first
with shouts   fists   feet   whatever
35   — I squared round to meet him

and there was a beautiful taxi
lumbering in from a sidestreet
empty!

As I rolled away   safe as Elijah[1]
40   lucky as Ganymede[2]
there on the curb I'd leaped from
stood that damned cyclist solemnly
shouting

"What did he say?"   I asked the driver
45   He shrugged at the windshield
"Man dat a crazy boogoo
He soun like he say
'dat a nice jump you got too' "

Port-of-Spain 1962

JOHN BETJEMAN

In Westminster Abbey

Let me take this other glove off
      As the *vox humana*[1] swells,
And the beauteous fields of Eden
      Bask beneath the Abbey bells.
5   Here, where England's statesmen lie,
Listen to a lady's cry.

Gracious Lord, oh bomb the Germans.
      Spare their women for Thy Sake,
And if that is not too easy
10   We will pardon Thy Mistake.
But, gracious Lord, whate'er shall be,
Don't let anyone bomb me.

Keep our Empire undismembered
      Guide our Forces by Thy Hand,
15   Gallant blacks from far Jamaica,

1. Old Testament prophet.
2. Cupbearer to the gods.

1. The organ stop that produces a sound
imitative of the human voice.

Honduras and Togoland;
Protect them Lord in all their fights,
And, even more, protect the whites.

Think of what our Nation stands for,
20   Books from Boots'[2] and country lanes,
Free speech, free passes, class distinction,
   Democracy and proper drains.
Lord, put beneath Thy special care
One-eighty-nine Cadogan Square.[3]

25   Although dear Lord I am a sinner,
   I have done no major crime;
Now I'll come to Evening Service
   Whensoever I have the time.
So, Lord, reserve for me a crown,
30   And do not let my shares go down.

I will labour for Thy Kingdom,
   Help our lads to win the war,
Send white feathers to the cowards
   Join the Women's Army Corps,
35   Then wash the Steps around Thy Throne
In the Eternal Safety Zone.

Now I feel a little better,
   What a treat to hear Thy Word,
Where the bones of leading statesmen,
40   Have so often been interr'd.
And now, dear Lord, I cannot wait
Because I have a luncheon date.

The City

Business men with awkward hips
And dirty jokes upon their lips,
And large behinds and jingling chains,
And riddled teeth and riddling brains,
And plump white fingers made to curl
Round some anaemic city girl,
And so lend colour to the lives
And old suspicions of their wives.

2. A chain drug-store. At one time branches
in English country towns had lending libraries
patronized mainly by the genteel.

3. A fashionable square near Knightsbridge,
London, not far from Hyde Park.

Young men who wear on office stools
The ties of minor public schools,[1]
Each learning how to be a sinner
And tell "a good one" after dinner,
And so discover it is rather
Fun to go one more than father.
But father, son and clerk join up
To talk about the Football Cup.[2]

The Licorice Fields at Pontefract[1]

In the licorice fields at Pontefract
   My love and I did meet
And many a burdened licorice bush
   Was blooming round our feet;
5   Red hair she had and golden skin,
Her sulky lips were shaped for sin,
Her sturdy legs were flannel-slack'd,
The strongest legs in Pontefract.

The light and dangling licorice flowers
10   Gave off the sweetest smells;
From various black Victorian towers
   The Sunday evening bells
Came pealing over dales and hills
And tanneries and silent mills
15   And lowly streets where country stops
And little shuttered corner shops.

She cast her blazing eyes on me
   And plucked a licorice leaf;
I was her captive slave and she
20   My red-haired robber chief.
Oh love! for love I could not speak,
It left me winded, wilting, weak
And held in brown arms strong and bare
And wound with flaming ropes of hair.

1. British private schools.
2. Football Association (soccer) knock-out competition.

1. An industrial town in Yorkshire, England, known, among other things, for the manufacture of licorice. Home of the "Pomfret" or Pontefract Cake.

W. H. AUDEN

A Summer Night 1933[1]
(To Geoffrey Hoyland)

Out on the lawn I lie in bed,
Vega[2] conspicuous overhead
   In the windless nights of June,
As congregated leaves complete
5   Their day's activity; my feet
   Point to the rising moon.

Lucky, this point in time and space
Is chosen as my working-place,
   Where the sexy airs of summer,
10 The bathing hours and the bare arms,
The leisured drives through a land of farms
   Are good to the newcomer.

Equal with colleagues in a ring
I sit on each calm evening
15   Enchanted as the flowers
The opening light draws out of hiding
With all its gradual dove-like pleading,
   Its logic and its powers

That later we, though parted then,
20 May still recall these evenings when
   Fear gave his watch no look;
The lion griefs loped from the shade
And on our knees their muzzles laid,
   And Death put down his book

25 Now north and south and east and west
Those I love lie down to rest;
   The moon looks on them all,
The healers and the brilliant talkers
The eccentrics and the silent walkers,
30   The dumpy and the tall.

1. In February 1933 Hitler came to power in Germany. In June of that year Sir Oswald Mosley's British Union of Fascists rallied at Olympia, London, causing unprecedented scenes of violence.
2. The fourth brightest star in the night sky.

She climbs the European sky,
Churches and power-station lie
   Alike among earth's fixtures:
Into the galleries she peers
35   And blankly as a butcher stares
   Upon the marvellous pictures

To gravity attentive, she
Can notice nothing here, though we
   Whom hunger does not move,
40   From gardens where we feel secure
Look up and with a sigh endure
   The tyrannies of love:

And, gentle, do not care to know,
Where Poland[3] draws her eastern bow,
45   What violence is done,
Nor ask what doubtful act allows
Our freedom in this English house,
   Our picnics in the sun.

Soon, soon, through dykes of our content
50   The crumpling flood will force a rent
   And, taller than a tree,
Hold sudden death before our eyes
Whose river dreams long hid the size
   And vigours of the sea.

55   But when the waters make retreat
And through the black mud first the wheat
   In shy green stalks appears,
When stranded monsters gasping lie,
And sounds of riveting terrify
60   Their whorled unsubtle ears,

May these delights we dread to lose,
This privacy, need no excuse
   But to that strength belong,
As through a child's rash happy cries
65   The drowned parental voices rise
   In unlamenting song.

After discharges of alarm
All unpredicted let them calm
   The pulse of nervous nations,
70   Forgive the murderer in his glass,
Tough in their patience to surpass
   The tigress her swift motions.

3. Possibly suggested by riots in Galicia, June,
1933.

Madrigal

O lurcher-loving[1] collier, black as night,
Follow your love across the smokeless hill;
Your lamp is out and all the cages still;
Course for her heart and do not miss,
For Sunday noon is past and, Kate, fly not so fast,
For Monday comes when none may kiss:
Be marble to his soot, and to his black be white.

Seascape

Look, stranger, on this island now
The leaping light for your delight discovers,
Stand stable here
And silent be,
5   That through the channels of the ear
May wander like a river
The swaying sound of the sea.

Here at a small field's ending pause
When the chalk wall falls to the foam and its tall ledges
10   Oppose the pluck
And knock of the tide,
And the shingle scrambles after the suck-
ing surf,
And a gull lodges
15   A moment on its sheer side.

Far off like floating seeds the ships
Diverge on urgent voluntary errands,
And this full view
Indeed may enter
20   And move in memory as now these clouds do,
That pass the harbour mirror
And all the summer through the water saunter.

One Evening

As I walked out one evening,
    Walking down Bristol Street,
The crowds upon the pavement
    Were fields of harvest wheat.

---

1. The lurcher is a kind of greyhound used for
poaching and racing.

5 And down by the brimming river
       I heard a lover sing
   Under an arch of the railway:
       'Love has no ending.

   'I'll love you, dear, I'll love you
10   Till China and Africa meet,
   And the river jumps over the mountain
       And the salmon sing in the street.

   'I'll love you till the ocean
       Is folded and hung up to dry,
15 And the seven stars go squawking
       Like geese about the sky.

   'The years shall run like rabbits,
       For in my arms I hold
   The Flower of the Ages,
20   And the first love of the world.'

   But all the clocks in the city
       Began to whirr and chime:
   'O let not Time deceive you,
       You cannot conquer Time.

25 'In the burrows of the Nightmare
       Where Justice naked is,
   Time watches from the shadow
       And coughs when you would kiss.

   'In headaches and in worry
30   Vaguely life leaks away,
   And Time will have his fancy
       To-morrow or to-day.

   'Into many a green valley
       Drifts the appalling snow;
35 Time breaks the threaded dances
       And the diver's brilliant bow.

   'O plunge your hands in water,
       Plunge them in up to the wrist;
   Stare, stare in the basin
40   And wonder what you've missed.

   'The glacier knocks in the cupboard,
       The desert sighs in the bed,
   And the crack in the tea-cup opens
       A lane to the land of the dead.

45 'Where the beggars raffle the banknotes
 And the Giant is enchanting to Jack,
And the Lily-white Boy[1] is a Roarer,
 And Jill goes down on her back.

'O look, look in the mirror,
50 O look in your distress;
Life remains a blessing
 Although you cannot bless.

'O stand, stand at the window
 As the tears scald and start;
55 You shall love your crooked neighbour
 With your crooked heart.'

It was late, late in the evening
 The lovers they were gone;
The clocks had ceased their chiming,
60 And the deep river ran on.

The Quarry

O what is that sound which so thrills the ear
 Down in the valley drumming, drumming?
Only the scarlet soldiers, dear,
 The soldiers coming.

5 O what is that light I see flashing so clear
 Over the distance brightly, brightly?
Only the sun on their weapons, dear,
 As they step lightly.

O what are they doing with all that gear,
10 What are they doing this morning, this morning?
Only their usual manœuvres, dear,
 Or perhaps a warning.

O why have they left the road down there,
 Why are they suddenly wheeling, wheeling?
15 Perhaps a change in their orders, dear.
 Why are you kneeling?

O haven't they stopped for the doctor's care,
 Haven't they reined their horses, their horses?
Why, they are none of them wounded, dear,
20 None of these forces.

1. Like the "seven stars" (l. 15), this is
derived from the folk song "Green Grow the

Rushes," which Auden included in his edition
of *The Oxford Book of Light Verse*.

O is it the parson they want, with white hair,
  Is it the parson, is it, is it?
No, they are passing his gateway, dear,
  Without a visit.

25   O it must be the farmer who lives so near.
  It must be the farmer so cunning, so cunning?
They have passed the farmyard already, dear,
  And now they are running.

O where are you going? Stay with me here!
30   Were the vows you swore deceiving, deceiving?
No, I promised to love you, dear,
  But I must be leaving.

O it's broken the lock and splintered the door,
  O it's the gate where they're turning, turning;
35   Their boots are heavy on the floor
  And their eyes are burning.

In Memory of W. B. Yeats[1]

(d. Jan. 1939)

I

He disappeared in the dead of winter:
The brooks were frozen, the airports almost deserted,
And snow disfigured the public statues;
The mercury sank in the mouth of the dying day.
5   What instruments we have agree
The day of his death was a dark cold day.

Far from his illness
The wolves ran on through the evergreen forests,
The peasant river was untempted by the fashionable quays;
10   By mourning tongues
The death of the poet was kept from his poems.

But for him it was his last afternoon as himself,
An afternoon of nurses and rumours;
The provinces of his body revolted,
15   The squares of his mind were empty,
Silence invaded the suburbs,
The current of his feeling failed; he became his admirers.

Now he is scattered among a hundred cities
And wholly given over to unfamiliar affections;

---

1. Auden and his friend Christopher
Isherwood arrived to live in New York on
26 January 1939. Yeats died two days
later.

20 To find his happiness in another kind of wood
    And be punished under a foreign code of conscience.
    The words of a dead man
    Are modified in the guts of the living.

    But in the importance and noise of to-morrow
25 When the brokers are roaring like beasts on the floor of the Bourse,[2]
    And the poor have the sufferings to which they are fairly accustomed,
    And each in the cell of himself is almost convinced of his freedom,
    A few thousand will think of this day
    As one thinks of a day when one did something slightly unusual.
30 What instruments we have agree
    The day of his death was a dark cold day.

II

    You were silly like us; your gift survived it all;
    The parish of rich women,[3] physical decay,
    Yourself: mad Ireland hurt you into poetry.
35 Now Ireland has her madness and her weather still,
    For poetry makes nothing happen: it survives
    In the valley of its saying where executives
    Would never want to tamper; it flows south
    From ranches of isolation and the busy griefs,
40 Raw towns that we believe and die in; it survives,
    A way of happening, a mouth.

III

    Earth, receive an honoured guest:
    William Yeats is laid to rest.
    Let the Irish vessel lie
45 Emptied of its poetry.

    In the nightmare of the dark
    All the dogs of Europe bark,
    And the living nations wait,
    Each sequestered in its hate;[4]

50 Intellectual disgrace
    Stares from every human face,
    And the seas of pity lie
    Locked and frozen in each eye.

    Follow, poet, follow right
55 To the bottom of the night,
    With your unconstraining voice
    Still persuade us to rejoice;

2. Stock exchange in Paris.
3. A reference to women such as Lady Greg-
ory, with whom Yeats had collaborated to
found the Irish Dramatic Movement.
4. Europe was on the verge of catastrophe
(see notes to "A Summer Night 1933" above).

With the farming of a verse
Make a vineyard of the curse,
60 Sing of human unsuccess
In a rapture of distress;

In the deserts of the heart
Let the healing fountain start,
In the prison of his days
65 Teach the free man how to praise.

LOUIS MACNEICE

Snow

The room was suddenly rich and the great bay-window was
Spawning snow and pink roses against it
Soundlessly collateral and incompatible:
World is suddener than we fancy it.

World is crazier and more of it than we think,
Incorrigibly plural. I peel and portion
A tangerine and spit the pips and feel
The drunkenness of things being various.

And the fire flames with a bubbling sound for world
Is more spiteful and gay than one supposes —
On the tongue on the eyes on the ears in the palms of one's hands —
There is more than glass between the snow and the huge roses.

Bagpipe Music

It's no go the merrygoround, it's no go the rickshaw,
All we want is a limousine and a ticket for the peepshow.
Their knickers[1] are made of crêpe-de-chine, their shoes are made of
                                                python,
Their halls are lined with tiger rugs and their walls with heads of bison.

5 John MacDonald found a corpse, put it under the sofa,
Waited till it came to life and hit it with a poker,
Sold its eyes for souvenirs, sold its blood for whiskey,
Kept its bones for dumb-bells to use when he was fifty.

It's no go the Yogi-Man,[2] it's no go Blavatsky,[3]
10 All we want is a bank balance and a bit of skirt in a taxi.

1. Panties.
2. Indian devotee practising Yoga.
3. Madame Blavatsky (1831–91), spiritualist
and co-founder of the Theosophical Society,
which aimed to express the ultimate spiritual
relationship between humanity and the
universe. A controversial figure, often
condemned as a charlatan.

Annie MacDougall went to milk, caught her foot in the heather,
Woke to hear a dance record playing of Old Vienna.
It's no go your maidenheads, it's no go your culture,
All we want is a Dunlop tyre and the devil mend the puncture.

15 The Laird o' Phelps spent Hogmanay[4] declaring he was sober,
Counted his feet to prove the fact and found he had one foot over.
Mrs Carmichael had her fifth, looked at the job with repulsion,
Said to the midwife, 'Take it away; I'm through with over-production.'

It's no go the gossip column, it's no go the Ceilidh,[5]
20 All we want is a mother's help and a sugar-stick for the baby.

Willie Murray cut his thumb, couldn't count the damage,
Took the hide of an Ayrshire cow and used it for a bandage.
His brother caught three hundred cran[6] when the seas were lavish,
Threw the bleeders back in the sea and went upon the parish.

25 It's no go the Herring Board, it's no go the Bible,
All we want is a packet of fags[7] when our hands are idle.

It's no go the picture palace,[8] it's no go the stadium,
It's no go the country cot with a pot of pink geraniums.
It's no go the Government grants, it's no go the elections,
30 Sit on your arse for fifty years and hang your hat on a pension.

It's no go my honey love, it's no go my poppet;
Work your hands from day to day, the winds will blow the profit.
The glass[9] is falling hour by hour, the glass will fall for ever,
But if you break the bloody glass you won't hold up the weather.

THEODORE ROETHKE

In a Dark Time

In a dark time, the eye begins to see,
I meet my shadow in the deepening shade;
I hear my echo in the echoing wood —
A lord of nature weeping to a tree.
5 I live between the heron and the wren,
Beasts of the hill and serpents of the den.

---

4. Last day of the year, specially celebrated in
Scotland.
5. Party with traditional music, story-telling,
or dancing in Scotland.

6. A measure of fresh herring.
7. Cigarettes.
8. Movie theatre.
9. Barometer.

What's madness but nobility of soul
At odds with circumstance? The day's on fire!
I know the purity of pure despair,
10   My shadow pinned against a sweating wall.
That place among the rocks—is it a cave,
Or winding path? The edge is what I have.

A steady storm of correspondences!
A night flowing with birds, a ragged moon,
15   And in broad day the midnight come again!
A man goes far to find out what he is—
Death of the self in a long, tearless night,
All natural shapes blazing unnatural light.

Dark, dark my light, and darker my desire.
20   My soul, like some heat-maddened summer fly,
Keeps buzzing at the sill. Which I is *I*?
A fallen man, I climb out of my fear.
The mind enters itself, and God the mind,
And one is One, free in the tearing wind.

[handwritten annotation: paradox]
[handwritten annotation: reference to Jove.]

STEPHEN SPENDER

The Landscape near an Aerodrome

[handwritten annotation: metaphor.]

More beautiful and soft than any moth
With burring furred antennae feeling its huge path
Through dusk, the air-liner with shut-off engines
Glides over suburbs and the sleeves set trailing tall
5   To point the wind. Gently, broadly, she falls
Scarcely disturbing charted currents of air.

Lulled by descent, the travellers across sea
And across feminine land indulging its easy limbs
In miles of softness, now let their eyes trained by watching
10   Penetrate through dusk the outskirts of this town
Here where industry shows a fraying edge.
Here they may see what is being done.

Beyond the winking masthead light
And the landing-ground, they observe the outposts
15   Of work: chimneys like lank black fingers
Or figures frightening and mad: and squat buildings
With their strange air behind trees, like women's faces
Shattered by grief. Here where few houses
Moan with faint light behind their blinds
20   They remark the unhomely sense of complaint, like a dog
Shut out and shivering at the foreign moon.

In the last sweep of love, they pass over fields
Behind the aerodrome, where boys play all day
Hacking dead grass: whose cries, like wild birds,
25 Settle upon the nearest roofs
But soon are hid under the loud city.

Then, as they land, they hear the tolling bell
Reaching across the landscape of hysteria
To where, larger than all the charcoaled batteries
30 And imaged towers against that dying sky,
Religion stands, the church blocking the sun.

DOROTHY LIVESAY

Day and Night

1
Dawn, red and angry, whistles loud and sends
A geysered shaft of steam searching the air.
Scream after scream announces that the churn
Of life must move, the giant arm command.
5 Men in a stream, a human moving belt
Move into sockets, every one a bolt.
The fun begins, a humming whirring drum—
Men do a dance in time to the machines.

One step forward
10 Two steps back
Shove the lever,
Push it back

While Arnot whirls
A roundabout
15 And Geoghan shuffles
Bolts about

One step forward
Hear it crack
Smashing rhythm—
20 Two steps back.

Your heart-beat pounds
Against your throat
The roaring voices
Drown your shout

25   Across the way
      A writhing whack
      Sets you spinning
      Two steps back—

      One step forward
30   Two steps back.

      2
      Day and night rising and falling
      Night and day shift gears and slip rattling
      Down the runway, shot into storerooms
      Where only eyes and a notebook remember
35   The record of evil, the sum of commitments.
      We move as through sleep's revolving memories
      Piling up hatred, stealing the remnants
      Doors forever folding before us—
      And where is the recompense, on what agenda
40   Will you set love down? Who knows of peace?

      Day and night
      Night and day
      Light rips into ribbons
      What we say

45   I called to love
      Deep in dream:
      Be with me in the daylight
      As in gloom.

      Be with me in the pounding
50   In the knives against my back
      Set your voice resounding
      Above the steel's whip crack.

      High and sweet
      Sweet and high
55   Hold, hold up the sunlight
      In the sky!

      Day and night
      Night and day
      Tear up all the silence
60   Find the words I could not say...

      3
      We were stoking coal in the furnaces; red hot
      They gleamed, burning our skins away, his and mine.
      We were working, together, night and day, and knew
      Each other's stroke; and without words exchanged

65   An understanding about kids at home,
      The landlord's jaw, wage-cuts and overtime.

      We were like buddies, see? Until they said
      That nigger is too smart the way he smiles
      And sauces back the foreman; he might say
70   Too much one day, to others changing shifts.
      Therefore they cut him down, who flowered at night
      And raised me up, day hanging over night —
      So furnaces could still consume our withered skin.

      Shadrack, Mechak and Abednego[1]
75   Turn in the furnace, whirling slow.

          Lord, I'm burnin' in the fire
          Lord, I'm steppin' on the coal
          Lord, I'm blacker than my brother
          Blow your breath down here.

80   Boss, I'm smothered in the darkness
          Boss, I'm shrivellin' in the flames
          Boss, I'm blacker than my brother
          Blow your breath down here.

      Shadrack, Mechak and Abednego
85   Burn in the furnace, whirling slow.

      4
      Up in the roller room, men swing steel
      Swing it, zoom; and cut it, crash.
      Up in the dark the welder's torch
      Makes sparks fly like lightning's reel.

90   Now I remember storm on a field:
      The trees bow tense before the blow
      Even the jittering sparrow's talk
      Ripples into the still tree shield.

      We are in storm that has no cease
95   No lull before, no after time
      When green with rain the grasses grow
      And air is sweet with fresh increase.

      We bear the burden home to bed
      The furnace glows within our hearts:
100   Our bodies hammered through the night
      Are welded into bitter bread.

1. Daniel iii. See short-fiction section.

Bitter, yes:
But listen, friend,
We are mightier
105   In the end

We have ears
Alert to seize
A weakness in
The foreman's ease.

110   We have eyes
To look across
The bosses' profit
At our loss.

Are you waiting?
115   Wait with us
Every evening
There's a hush

Use it not
For love's slow count:
120   Add up hate
And let it mount—

One step forward
Two steps back
Will soon be over:
125   Hear it crack!

The wheels may whirr
A roundabout
And neighbour's shuffle
Drown your shout

130   The wheel must limp
Till it hangs still
And crumpled men
Pour down the hill:

Day and night
135   Night and day—
Till life is turned
The other way!

A. M. KLEIN

Autobiographical

Out of the ghetto streets where a Jewboy
Dreamed pavement into pleasant Bible-land,
Out of the Yiddish slums where childhood met
The friendly beard the loutish Sabbath-goy,[1]
5   Or followed, proud, the Torah-escorting[2] band,
Out of the jargoning city I regret,
Rise memories, like sparrows rising from
The gutter-scattered oats,
Like sadness sweet of synagogal hum,
10   Like Hebrew violins
Sobbing delight upon their Eastern notes.

Again they ring their little bells, those doors
Deemed by the tender-year'd, magnificent:
Old Ashkenazi's[3] cellar, sharp with spice;
15   The widows' double-parlored candy-stores
And nuggets sweet bought for one sweaty cent;
The warm fresh-smelling bakery, its pies,
Its cakes, its navel'd bellies of black bread;
The lintels candy-poled
20   Of barber-shop, bright-bottled, green, blue, red;
And fruit-stall piled, exotic,
And the big synagogue door, with letters of gold.

Again my kindergarten home is full—
Saturday night—with kin and compatriot:
25   My brothers playing Russian card-games; my
Mirroring sisters looking beautiful,
Humming the evening's imminent fox-trot;
My uncle Mayer, of blessed memory,
Still murmuring maariv,[4] counting holy words;
30   And the two strangers, come
Fiery from Volhynia's[5] murderous hordes—
The cards and humming stop.
And I too swear revenge for that pogrom.

---

1. A person employed by Orthodox Jewish families to do certain tasks forbidden on the Sabbath, such as switching the lights on and off.
2. The Torah or Pentateuch consists of the first five books of the Old Testament taken collectively.
3. The Polish-German Jews, the Ashkenazim, traditionally Yiddish-speaking, are distinguished from the Sephardim or Spanish-Portuguese Jews.
4. Evening prayer (Hebrew).
5. Pogroms were organized massacres, especially of Jews in Eastern Europe. Volhynia, now a province in the northwest Ukraine, was a Hasidic centre and the scene of Nazi and other pogroms.

Occasions dear: the four-legged aleph[6] named
35   And angel pennies dropping on my book;
The rabbi patting a coming scholar-head;
My mother, blessing candles, Sabbath-flamed,
Queenly in her Warsovian perruque;
My father pickabacking me to bed
40   To tell tall tales about the Baal Shem Tov[7] —
Letting me curl his beard.
Oh memory of unsurpassing love,
Love leading a brave child
Through childhood's ogred corridors, unfear'd!

45   The week in the country at my brother's —(May
He own fat cattle in the fields of heaven!)
Its picking of strawberries from grassy ditch,
Its odor of dogrose and of yellowing hay —
Dusty, adventurous, sunny days, all seven! —
50   Still follow me, still warm me, still are rich
With the cow-tinkling peace of pastureland.
The meadow'd memory
Is sodded with its clover, and is spanned
By that same pillow'd sky
55   A boy on his back one day watched enviously.

And paved again the street: the shouting boys,
Oblivious of mothers on the stoops,
Playing the robust robbers and police,
The corncob battle — all high-spirited noise
60   Competitive among the lot-drawn groups.
Another day, of shaken apple trees
In the rich suburbs, and a furious dog,
And guilty boys in flight;
Hazelnut games, and games in the synagogue —
65   The burrs, the Haman rattle,[8]
The Torah dance on Simchas Torah[9] night.

6. The first letter of the Hebrew alphabet.
7. Israel Ben Eliezer (c. 1700–60), founder of modern Hasidism, a pietist movement in Judaism that arose in southeastern Poland (Volhynia, Podolia). The appellation "Baal Shem Tov" refers to men who possessed the secret meaning of God's name, although in this particular case the appellation refers specifically to the teacher/leader Israel Ben Eliezer.
8. On the festival of Purim, which commemorates the deliverance of the Jews from the hands of the Persian Haman, young children are given noisy rattles that they must shake each time the name of Haman is mentioned during the reading of the Book of Esther.
9. The Simchas Torah (Hebrew: The Rejoicing of the Torah) is a festival commemorating the handing of the Law to Moses and marking the completion and new start of the annual reading in the synagogue of the Sabbath portions of the Torah. It is customary on Simchas Torah night to carry parchment scrolls of the Law seven or more times around the synagogue with dances that may continue for some hours.

Immortal days of the picture calendar
Dear to me always with the virgin joy
Of the first flowering of senses five,
70 Discovering birds, or textures or a star,
Or tastes sweet, sour, acid, those that cloy;
And perfumes. Never was I more alive.
All days thereafter are a dying off,
A wandering away
75 From home and the familiar. The years doff
Their innocence.
No other day is ever like that day.

I am no old man fatuously intent
On memoirs, but in memory I seek
80 The strength and vividness of nonage days,
Not tranquil recollection of event.
It is a fabled city that I seek;
It stands in Space's vapors and Time's haze;
Thence comes my sadness in remembered joy
85 Constrictive of the throat;
Thence do I hear, as heard by a Jewboy,
The Hebrew violins,
Delighting in the sobbed Oriental note.

The Rocking Chair

It seconds the crickets of the province. Heard
in the clean lamplit farmhouses of Quebec, —
wooden, — it is no less a national bird;
and rivals, in its cage, the mere stuttering clock.
5 To its time, the evenings are rolled away;
and in its peace the pensive mother knits
contentment to be worn by her family,
grown-up, but still cradled by the chair in which she sits.

It is also the old man's pet, pair to his pipe,
10 the two aids of his arithmetic and plans,
plans rocking and puffing into market-shape;
and it is the toddler's game and dangerous dance.
Moved to the verandah, on summer Sundays, it is,
among the hanging plants, the girls, the boy-friends,
15 sabbatical and clumsy, like the white haloes
dangling above the blue serge suits of the young men.

It has a personality of its own;
is a character (like that old drunk Lacoste,
exhaling amber, and toppling on his pins);

20   it is alive; individual; and no less
an identity than those about it. And
it is tradition. Centuries have been flicked
from its arcs, alternately flicked and pinned.
It rolls with the gait of St Malo. It is act

25   and symbol, symbol of this static folk
which moves in segments, and returns to base, —
a sunken pendulum: *invoke, revoke;*
loosed yon, leashed hither, motion on no space.
O, like some Anjou ballad, all refrain,
30   which turns about its longing, and seems to move
to make a pleasure out of repeated pain,
its music moves, as if always back to a first love.

ELIZABETH BISHOP

First Death in Nova Scotia

In the cold, cold parlor
my mother laid out Arthur
beneath the chromographs:
Edward, Prince of Wales,
5   with Princess Alexandra,
and King George with Queen Mary.
Below them on the table
stood a stuffed loon
shot and stuffed by Uncle
10   Arthur, Arthur's father.

Since Uncle Arthur fired
a bullet into him,
he hadn't said a word.
He kept his own counsel
15   on his white, frozen lake,
the marble-topped table.
His breast was deep and white,
cold and caressable;
his eyes were red glass,
20   much to be desired.

"Come," said my mother,
"Come and say goodbye
to your little cousin Arthur."
I was lifted up and given
25   one lily of the valley
to put in Arthur's hand.

Arthur's coffin was
a little frosted cake,
and the red-eyed loon eyed it
30　from his white, frozen lake.

Arthur was very small.
He was all white, like a doll
that hadn't been painted yet.
Jack Frost had started to paint him
35　the way he always painted
The Maple Leaf (Forever).
He had just begun on his hair,
a few red strokes, and then
Jack Frost had dropped the brush
40　and left him white, forever.

The gracious royal couples
were warm in red and ermine;
their feet were well wrapped up
in the ladies' ermine trains.
45　They invited Arthur to be
the smallest page at court.
But how could Arthur go,
clutching his tiny lily,
with his eyes shut up so tight
50　and the roads deep in snow?

IRVING LAYTON

Song for Naomi

Who is that in the tall grasses singing
By herself, near the water?
I can not see her
But can it be her
5　Than whom the grasses so tall
Are taller,
My daughter,
My lovely daughter?

Who is that in the tall grasses running
10　Beside her, near the water?
She can not see there
Time that pursued her
In the deep grasses so fast
And faster
15　And caught her,
My foolish daughter.

What is the wind in the fair grass saying
Like a verse, near the water?
Saviours that over
20 All things have power
Make Time himself grow kind
And kinder
That sought her,
My little daughter.

25 Who is that at the close of the summer
Near the deep lake? Who wrought her
Comely and slender?
Time but attends and befriends her
Than whom the grasses though tall
30 Are not taller,
My daughter,
My gentle daughter.

Keine Lazarovitch[1]
1870–1959

When I saw my mother's head on the cold pillow,
Her white waterfalling hair in the cheeks' hollows,
I thought, quietly circling my grief, of how
She had loved God but cursed extravagantly his creatures.

For her final mouth was not water but a curse,
A small black hole, a black rent in the universe,
Which damned the green earth, stars and trees in its stillness
And the inescapable lousiness of growing old.

And I record she was comfortless, vituperative,
Ignorant, glad, and much else besides; I believe
She endlessly praised her black eyebrows, their thick weave,
Till plagiarizing Death leaned down and took them for his mould.

And spoiled a dignity I shall not again find,
And the fury of her stubborn limited mind;
Now none will shake her amber beads and call God blind,
Or wear them upon a breast so radiantly.

O fierce she was, mean and unaccommodating;
But I think now of the toss of her gold earrings,
Their proud carnal assertion, and her youngest sings,
While all the rivers of her red veins move into the sea.

---

1. Poet's mother who is identified here by the
family's Rumanian name.

DYLAN THOMAS

The Force that through the Green Fuse Drives the Flower

The force that through the green fuse drives the flower
Drives my green age; that blasts the roots of trees
Is my destroyer.
And I am dumb to tell the crooked rose
5   My youth is bent by the same wintry fever.

The force that drives the water through the rocks
Drives my red blood; that dries the mouthing streams
Turns mine to wax.
And I am dumb to mouth unto my veins
10   How at the mountain spring the same mouth sucks.

The hand that whirls the water in the pool
Stirs the quicksand; that ropes the blowing wind
Hauls my shroud sail.
And I am dumb to tell the hanging man
15   How of my clay is made the hangman's lime.

The lips of time leech to the fountain head;
Love drips and gathers, but the fallen blood
Shall calm her sores.
And I am dumb to tell a weather's wind
20   How time has ticked a heaven round the stars.

And I am dumb to tell the lover's tomb
How at my sheet goes the same crooked worm.

Fern Hill

Now as I was young and easy under the apple boughs
About the lilting house and happy as the grass was green,
    The night above the dingle starry,
        Time let me hail and climb
5   Golden in the heydays of his eyes,
And honoured among wagons I was prince of the apple towns
And once below a time I lordly had the trees and leaves
            Trail with daisies and barley
        Down the rivers of the windfall light.

10   And as I was green and carefree, famous among the barns
About the happy yard and singing as the farm was home,
        In the sun that is young once only,
            Time let me play and be
        Golden in the mercy of his means,

15 And green and golden I was huntsman and herdsman, the calves,
Sang to my horn, the foxes on the hills barked clear and cold,
    And the sabbath rang slowly
  In the pebbles of the holy streams.

All the sun long it was running, it was lovely, the hay-
20 Fields high as the house, the tunes from the chimneys, it was air
    And playing, lovely and watery
      And fire green as grass.
    And nightly under the simple stars
As I rode to sleep the owls were bearing the farm away,
25 All the moon long I heard, blessèd among stables, the night-jars
    Flying with the ricks, and the horses
      Flashing into the dark.

And then to awake, and the farm, like a wanderer white
With the dew, come back, the cock on his shoulder: it was all
30   Shining, it was Adam and maiden,
      The sky gathered again
    And the sun grew round that very day.
So it must have been after the birth of the simple light
In the first, spinning place, the spellbound horses walking warm
35   Out of the whinnying green stable
    On to the fields of praise.

And honoured among foxes and pheasants by the gay house
Under the new made clouds and happy as the heart was long,
    In the sun born over and over,
40   I ran my heedless ways,
    My wishes raced through the house-high hay
And nothing I cared, at my sky blue trades, that time allows
In all his tuneful turning so few and such morning songs
    Before the children green and golden
45   Follow him out of grace,

Nothing I cared, in the lamb white days, that time would take me
Up to the swallow thronged loft by the shadow of my hand,
    In the moon that is always rising,
    Nor that riding to sleep
50   I should hear him fly with the high fields
And wake to the farm forever fled from the childless land.
Oh as I was young and easy in the mercy of his means,
    Time held me green and dying
  Though I sang in my chains like the sea.

Do Not Go Gentle into That Good Night

Do not go gentle into that good night,
Old age should burn and rave at close of day;
Rage, rage against the dying of the light.

Though wise men at their end know dark is right,
Because their words have forked no lightning they
Do not go gentle into that good night.

Good men, the last wave by, crying how bright
Their frail deeds might have danced in a green bay,
Rage, rage against the dying of the light.

Wild men who caught and sang the sun in flight,
And learn, too late, they grieved it on its way,
Do not go gentle into that good night.

Grave men, near death, who see with blinding sight
Blind eyes could blaze like meteors and be gay,
Rage, rage against the dying of the light.

And you, my father, there on the sad height,
Curse, bless, me now with your fierce tears, I pray.
Do not go gentle into that good night.
Rage, rage against the dying of the light.

HENRY REED

Lessons of the War

Vixi duellis nuper idoneus
Et militavi non sine gloria[1]

I. Naming of Parts

Today we have naming of parts. Yesterday,
We had daily cleaning. And tomorrow morning,
We shall have what to do after firing. But today,
Today we have naming of parts. Japonica
5 Glistens like coral in all of the neighbouring gardens,
    And today we have naming of parts.

---

1. "Of late I have lived fit for the wars and have served as a soldier, even winning some glory" (Horace, *Odes* iii.26.1–2). Horace's text has "puellis" (girls) rather than "duellis" (wars), an ambiguity that Reed maintains.

This is the lower sling swivel. And this
Is the upper sling swivel, whose use you will see,
When you are given your slings. And this is the piling swivel
10   Which in your case you have not got. The branches
Hold in the gardens their silent, eloquent gestures,
     Which in our case we have not got.

This is the safety-catch, which is always released
With an easy flick of the thumb. And please do not let me
15   See anyone using his finger. You can do it quite easy
If you have any strength in your thumb. The blossoms
Are fragile and motionless, never letting anyone see
     Any of them using their finger.

And this you can see is the bolt. The purpose of this
20   Is to open the breech, as you see. We can slide it
Rapidly backwards and forwards: we call this
Easing the spring. And rapidly backwards and forwards
The early bees are assaulting and fumbling the flowers:
     They call it easing the Spring.

25   They call it easing the Spring: it is perfectly easy
If you have any strength in your thumb: like the bolt,
And the breech, and the cocking-piece, and the point of balance,
Which in our case we have not got; and the almond-blossom
Silent in all of the gardens and the bees going backwards and forwards,
30   For today we have naming of parts.

II. Judging Distances

Not only how far away, but the way that you say it
Is very important. Perhaps you may never get
The knack of judging a distance, but at least you know
How to report on a landscape: the central sector,
5   The right of arc and that, which we had last Tuesday,
     And at least you know

That maps are of time, not place, so far as the army
Happens to be concerned—the reason being,
Is one which need not delay us. Again, you know
10   There are three kinds of tree, three only, the fir and the poplar,
And those which have bushy tops to; and lastly
     That things only seem to be things.

A barn is not called a barn, to put it more plainly,
Or a field in the distance, where sheep may be safely grazing.
15   You must never be over-sure. You must say, when reporting:
At five o'clock in the central sector is a dozen
Of what appear to be animals; whatever you do,
     Don't call the bleeders *sheep*.

I am sure that's quite clear; and suppose, for the sake of example,
20 The one at the end, asleep, endeavours to tell us
What he sees over there to the west, and how far away,
After first having come to attention. There to the west,
On the fields of summer the sun and the shadows bestow
        Vestments of purple and gold.

25 The still white dwellings are like a mirage in the heat,
And under the swaying elms a man and a woman
Lie gently together. Which is, perhaps, only to say
That there is a row of houses to the left of arc,
And that under some poplars a pair of what appear to be humans
30   Appear to be loving.

Well that, for an answer, is what we might rightly call
Moderately satisfactory only, the reason being,
Is that two things have been omitted, and those are important.
The human beings, now: in what direction are they,
35 And how far away, would you say? And do not forget
        There may be dead ground in between.

There may be dead ground in between; and I may not have got
The knack of judging a distance; I will only venture
A guess that perhaps between me and the apparent lovers,
40 (Who, incidentally, appear by now to have finished,)
At seven o'clock from the houses, is roughly a distance
        Of about one year and a half.

RANDALL JARRELL

The Death of the Ball Turret Gunner[1]

From my mother's sleep I fell into the State,
And I hunched in its belly till my wet fur froze.
Six miles from earth, loosed from its dream of life,
I woke to black flak and the nightmare fighters.
When I died they washed me out of the turret with a hose.

1. "A ball turret was a plexiglass sphere set into the belly of a B-17 or B-24 and inhabited by two .50 caliber machine-guns and one man, a short, small man. When this gunner tracked with his machine-guns a fighter attacking his bomber from below, he revolved with the turret; hunched upside-down in his little sphere, he looked like the foetus in the womb. The fighters which attacked him were armed with cannon firing explosive shells. The hose was a steam hose" (Jarrell's note).

P. K. PAGE

The Stenographers

After the brief bivouac of Sunday,
their eyes, in the forced march of Monday to Saturday,
hoist the white flag, flutter in the snow-storm of paper,
haul it down and crack in the mid-sun of temper.

5   In the pause between the first draft and the carbon
they glimpse the smooth hours when they were children—
the ride in the ice-cart, the ice-man's name,
the end of the route and the long walk home;

remember the sea where floats at high tide
10   were sea marrows growing on the scatter-green vine
or spools of grey toffee, or wasps' nests on water;
remember the sand and the leaves of the country.

Bell rings and they go and the voice draws their pencil
like a sled across snow; when its runners are frozen
15   rope snaps and the voice then is pulling no burden
but runs like a dog on the winter of paper.

Their climates are winter and summer—no wind
for the kites of their hearts—no wind for a flight;
a breeze at the most, to tumble them over
20   and leave them like rubbish—the boy-friends of blood.

In the inch of the noon as they move they are stagnant.
The terrible calm of the noon is their anguish;
the lip of the counter, the shapes of the straws
like icicles breaking their tongues, are invaders.

25   Their beds are their oceans—salt water of weeping
the waves that they know—the tide before sleep;
and fighting to drown they assemble their sheep
in columns and watch them leap desks for their fences
and stare at them with their own mirror-worn faces.

30   In the felt of the morning the calico-minded,
sufficiently starched, insert papers, hit keys,
efficient and sure as their adding machines;
yet they weep in the vault, they are taut as net curtains
stretched upon frames. In their eyes I have seen
35   the pin men of madness in marathon trim
race round the track of the stadium pupil.

FRED COGSWELL

Watching These Two

Watching these two
flies on a pane
that clearly view
through glass between

5   but cannot touch,
I think how we
whose bodies clutch
sense unity

in our flesh are blind
10   to the dark core
of inner mind
that love should share

there are no keys
can penetrate
15   to it save these —
blunt words that grate

and wound the thin
nerved otherness
the deeper in
20   their edges press

though probing thus
might reach the best
each one of us
will shirk the test

25   each one will keep
half-tied, half-free
postponing deep
possibility

to easy peace
30   and partial love
an unrelease
where habits move

and bodies give
with no bliss or hurt
35   to minds that live
in rooms apart

where the noise of home
no deeper lies
than casual hum
40 of these two flies.

MIRIAM WADDINGTON

Advice to the Young

1
Keep bees and
grow asparagus,
watch the tides
and listen to the
5 wind instead of
the politicians
make up your own
stories and believe
them if you want to
10 live the good life.

2
All rituals
are instincts
never fully
trust them
15 study to im-
prove biology
with reason.

3
Digging trenches
for asparagus
20 is good for the
muscles and
waiting for the
plants to settle
teaches patience
25 to those who are
usually in too
much of a hurry.

4
There is morality
in bee-keeping
30 it teaches how
not to be afraid
of the bee swarm

Yet stop I did: in fact I often do,
20   And always end much at a loss like this,
Wondering what to look for; wondering, too,
When churches fall completely out of use
What we shall turn them into, if we shall keep
A few cathedrals chronically on show,
25   Their parchment, plate and pyx in locked cases,
And let the rest rent-free to rain and sheep.
Shall we avoid them as unlucky places?

Or, after dark, will dubious women come
To make their children touch a particular stone;
30   Pick simples for a cancer; or on some
Advised night see walking a dead one?
Power of some sort or other will go on
In games, in riddles, seemingly at random;
But superstition, like belief, must die,
35   And what remains when disbelief has gone?
Grass, weedy pavement, brambles, buttress, sky,

A shape less recognizable each week,
A purpose more obscure. I wonder who
Will be the last, the very last, to seek
40   This place for what it was; one of the crew
That tap and jot and know what rood-lofts were?
Some ruin-bibber, randy for antique,
Or Christmas-addict, counting on a whiff
Of gown-and-bands and organ-pipes and myrrh?
45   Or will he be my representative,

Bored, uninformed, knowing the ghostly silt
Dispersed, yet tending to this cross of ground
Through suburb scrub because it held unspilt
So long and equably what since is found
50   Only in separation—marriage, and birth,
And death, and thoughts of these—for whom was built
This special shell? For though I've no idea
What this accoutred frowsty barn is worth,
It pleases me to stand in silence here;

55   A serious house on serious earth it is,
In whose blent air all our compulsions meet,
Are recognized, and robed as destinies.
And that much never can be obsolete,
Since someone will forever be surprising
60   A hunger in himself to be more serious,
And gravitating with it to this ground,
Which, he once heard, was proper to grow wise in,
If only that so many dead lie round.

[handwritten: tone of mixed envy and contempt]

High Windows

When I see a couple of kids
And guess he's fucking her and she's
Taking pills or wearing a diaphragm,
I know this is paradise *[handwritten: → intensifies the dibs of ?]*

[handwritten: qualification of paradise]

Everyone old has dreamed of all their lives—
Bonds and gestures pushed to one side
Like an outdated combine harvester,
And everyone young going down the long slide

To happiness, endlessly. I wonder if
Anyone looked at me, forty years back,
And thought, *That'll be the life;*
No God any more, or sweating in the dark

About hell and that, or having to hide
What you think of the priest. He
And his lot will all go down the long slide
Like free bloody birds. And immediately

[handwritten: ⌐ contempt]

Rather than words comes the thought of high windows
The sun-comprehending glass,
And beyond it, the deep blue air, that shows
Nothing, and is nowhere, and is endless.

Ambulances *[handwritten: understand the grammar & prose sense.]*

Closed like confessionals, they thread
Loud noons of cities, giving back
None of the glances they absorb.
Light glossy grey, arms on a plaque,
5　They come to rest at any kerb:
All streets in time are visited.

Then children strewn on steps or road,
Or women coming from the shops
Past smells of different dinners, see
10　A wild white face that overtops
Red stretcher-blankets momently
As it is carried in and stowed,

And sense the solving emptiness
That lies just under all we do,
15　And for a second get it whole,

So permanent and blank and true.
The fastened doors recede. *Poor soul,*
They whisper at their own distress;

For borne away in deadened air
20 May go the sudden shut of loss
Round something nearly at an end, →*the end .*
And what cohered in it across
The years, the unique random blend
Of families and fashions, there

25 At last begin to loosen. Far
From the exchange of love to lie } *all subjects of "brings clos*
Unreachable inside a room
The traffic parts to let go by
Brings closer what is left to come,
30 And dulls to distance all we are.

ELI MANDEL

Houdini

I suspect he knew that trunks are metaphors,
could distinguish between the finest rhythms
unrolled on rope or singing in a chain
and knew the metrics of the deepest pools

I think of him listening to the words
spoken by manacles, cells, handcuffs,
chests, hampers, roll-top desks, vaults,
especially the deep words spoken by coffins

escape, escape: quaint Harry in his suit
his chains, his desk, attached to all attachments
how he'd sweat in that precise struggle
with those binding words, wrapped around him
like that mannered style, his formal suit

and spoken when? by whom? What thing first said
'there's no way out?'; so that he'd free himself,
leap, squirm, no matter how, to chain himself again,
once more jump out of the deep alive
with all his chains singing around his feet
like the bound crowds who sigh, who sigh.

MILTON ACORN

I've Tasted My Blood

If this brain's over-tempered
consider that the fire was want
and the hammers were fists.
I've tasted my blood too much
5   to love what I was born to.

But my mother's look
was a field of brown oats, soft-bearded;
her voice rain and air rich with lilacs:
and I loved her too much to like
10   how she dragged her days like a sled over gravel.

Playmates? I remember where their skulls roll!
One died hungry, gnawing grey perch-planks;
one fell, and landed so hard he splashed;
and many and many
15   come up atom by atom
in the worm-casts of Europe.

My deep prayer a curse.
My deep prayer the promise that this won't be.
My deep prayer my cunning,
20   my love, my anger,
and often even my forgiveness
that this won't be and be.
I've tasted my blood too much
to abide what I was born to.

JAMES REANEY

The Katzenjammer Kids[1]

With porcupine locks
And faces which, when
More closely examined,
Are composed of measle-pink specks,
5   These two dwarf imps,
The Katzenjammer Kids,

1. A popular American comic strip (1898–1913) that dramatized the adventures of the anarchic Katzenjammer twins, Hans and Fritz.

Flitter through their Desert Island world.
Sometimes they get so out of hand
That a blue Captain
10   With stiff whiskers of black wicker
And an orange Inspector
With a black telescope
Pursue them to spank them
All through that land
15   Where cannibals cut out of brown paper
In cardboard jungles feast and caper,
Where the sea's sharp waves continually
Waver against the shore faithfully
And the yellow sun above is thin and flat
20   With a collar of black spikes and spines
To tell the innocent childish heart that
It shines
And warms (see where she stands and stammers)
The dear fat mother of the Katzenjammers.
25   Oh, for years and years she has stood
At the window and kept fairly good
Guard over the fat pies that she bakes
For her two children, those dancing heartaches.
Oh, the blue skies of that funny paper weather!
30   The distant birds like two eyebrows close together!
And the rustling paper roar
Of the waves
Against the paper sands of the paper shore!

ANNE SEXTON

Cinderella

You always read about it:
the plumber with twelve children
who wins the Irish Sweepstakes.
From toilets to riches.
5   That story.

Or the nursemaid,
some luscious sweet from Denmark
who captures the oldest son's heart.
From diapers to Dior.
10   That story.

Or a milkman who serves the wealthy,
eggs, cream, butter, yogurt, milk,
the white truck like an ambulance

who goes into real estate
15   and makes a pile.
From homogenized to martinis at lunch.

Or the charwoman
who is on the bus when it cracks up
and collects enough from the insurance.
20   From mops to Bonwit Teller.
That story.

Once
the wife of a rich man was on her deathbed
and she said to her daughter Cinderella:
25   Be devout. Be good. Then I will smile
down from heaven in the seam of a cloud.
The man took another wife who had
two daughters, pretty enough
but with hearts like blackjacks.
30   Cinderella was their maid.
She slept on the sooty hearth each night
and walked around looking like Al Jolson.
Her father brought presents home from town,
jewels and gowns for the other women
35   but the twig of a tree for Cinderella.
She planted that twig on her mother's grave
and it grew to a tree where a white dove sat.
Whenever she wished for anything the dove
would drop it like an egg upon the ground.
40   The bird is important, my dears, so heed him.

Next came the ball, as you all know.
It was a marriage market.
The prince was looking for a wife.
All but Cinderella were preparing
45   and gussying up for the big event.
Cinderella begged to go too.
Her stepmother threw a dish of lentils
into the cinders and said: Pick them
up in an hour and you shall go.
50   The white dove brought all his friends;
all the warm wings of the fatherland came,
and picked up the lentils in a jiffy.
No, Cinderella, said the stepmother,
you have no clothes and cannot dance.
55   That's the way with stepmothers.

Cinderella went to the tree at the grave
and cried forth like a gospel singer:
Mama! Mama! My turtledove,
send me to the prince's ball!

60 The bird dropped down a golden dress
    and delicate little gold slippers.
    Rather a large package for a simple bird.
    So she went. Which is no surprise.
    Her stepmother and sisters didn't
65 recognize her without her cinder face
    and the prince took her hand on the spot
    and danced with no other the whole day.

    As nightfall came she thought she'd better
    get home. The prince walked her home
70 and she disappeared into the pigeon house
    and although the prince took an axe and broke
    it open she was gone. Back to her cinders.
    These events repeated themselves for three days.
    However on the third day the prince
75 covered the palace steps with cobbler's wax
    and Cinderella's gold shoe stuck upon it.

    Now he would find whom the shoe fit
    and find his strange dancing girl for keeps.
    He went to their house and the two sisters
80 were delighted because they had lovely feet.
    The eldest went into a room to try the slipper on
    but her big toe got in the way so she simply
    sliced it off and put on the slipper.
    The prince rode away with her until the white dove
85 told him to look at the blood pouring forth.
    That is the way with amputations.
    They don't just heal up like a wish.
    The other sister cut off her heel
    but the blood told as blood will.
90 The prince was getting tired.
    He began to feel like a shoe salesman.
    But he gave it one last try.
    This time Cinderella fit into the shoe
    like a love letter into its envelope.

95 At the wedding ceremony
    the two sisters came to curry favor
    and the white dove pecked their eyes out.
    Two hollow spots were left
    like soup spoons.

100 Cinderella and the prince
    lived, they say, happily ever after,
    like two dolls in a museum case
    never bothered by diapers or dust,
    never arguing over the timing of an egg,
105 never telling the same story twice,

never getting a middle-aged spread,
their darling smiles pasted on for eternity
Regular Bobbsey Twins.
That story.

ADRIENNE RICH — *american*
— divorce poem.

— farewell speech.

A Valediction Forbidding Mourning[1]

My swirling wants. Your frozen lips.
The grammar turned and attacked me.
Themes, written under duress.
Emptiness of the notations.

They gave me a drug that slowed the healing of wounds.

I want you to see this before I leave:
the experience of repetition as death
the failure of criticism to locate the pain
the poster in the bus that said:
my bleeding is under control.

A red plant in a cemetery of plastic wreaths.

A last attempt: the language is a dialect called metaphor.
These images go unglossed: hair, glacier, flashlight.
When I think of a landscape I am thinking of a time.
When I talk of taking a trip I mean forever.
I could say: those mountains have a meaning
but further than that I could not say.

To do something very common, in my own way.

— both ideas & images

THOM GUNN *— British born — narration*

— lives in america.

On the Move *— epigraph.* *— proposition about life*
"Man, you gotta Go."

The blue jay scuffling in the bushes follows
Some hidden purpose, and the gust of birds
That spurts across the field, the wheeling swallows,
Have nested in the trees and undergrowth.

1. See John Donne, "A Valediction Forbidding Mourning."

blue jays.

5   Seeking their instinct, or their poise, or both,
One moves with an uncertain violence
Under the dust thrown by a baffled sense
Or the dull thunder of approximate words.

On motorcycles, up the road, they come:
10   Small, black, as flies hanging in heat, the Boys,
Until the distance throws them forth, their hum
Bulges to thunder held by calf and thigh.
In goggles, donned impersonality,
In gleaming jackets trophied with the dust,
15   They strap in doubt — by hiding it, robust —
And almost hear a meaning in their noise.

thunder is under control.

Exact conclusion of their hardiness   *undeveloped.*
Has no shape yet, but from known whereabouts
They ride, direction where the tires press.
20   They scare a flight of birds across the field: *— first imagery.*
Much that is natural, to the will must yield.
Men manufacture both machine and soul,   *→ machines dwfs.*
And use what they imperfectly control   *soul.*
To dare a future from the taken routes.

25   It is a part solution, after all. *→ purpose of motorcyclists movement.*
One is not necessarily discord *only.*
On earth; or damned because, half animal,
One lacks direct instinct, because one wakes
Afloat on movement that divides and breaks.
30   One joins the movement in a <u>valueless world,</u> *pessimism (50's)*
Choosing it, till, both hurler and the hurled, *man must create*
One moves as well, always toward, toward. *value.*

A minute holds them, who have come to go:
The self-defined, astride the created will
35   They burst away; the towns they travel through
Are home for neither bird nor holiness,
For birds and saints complete their purposes.
At worst, one is in motion; and at best,
Reaching no absolute, in which to rest,
40   One is always nearer by <u>not keeping still.</u>

closure to reality

"Blackie, the Electric Rembrandt"

We watch through the shop-front while
Blackie draws stars — an equal

concentration on his and
the youngster's faces. The hand

is steady and accurate;
but the boy does not see it

for his eyes follow the point
that touches (quick, dark movement!)

a virginal arm beneath
his rolled sleeve: he holds his breath.

... Now that it is finished, he
hands a few bills to Blackie

and leaves with a bandage on
his arm, under which gleam ten

stars, hanging in a blue thick
cluster. Now he is starlike.

TED HUGHES —*Yorkshiremen*
— romantic tradition
— mystic
The Horses —*description*

I climbed through woods in the hour-before-dawn dark.
Evil air, a frost-making stillness,

Not a leaf, not a bird, —
A world cast in frost. I came out above the wood

5   Where my breath left tortuous statues in the iron light.
But the valleys were draining the darkness

Till the moorline — blackening dregs of the brightening grey —

Halved the sky ahead. And I saw the horses:

Huge in the dense grey — ten together —
10   Megalith-still. They breathed, making no move,

With draped manes and tilted hind-hooves,
Making no sound.

I passed: not one snorted or jerked its head.
Grey silent fragments

15   Of a grey silent world.

I listened in emptiness on the moor-ridge.
The curlew's tear turned its edge on the silence.

Slowly detail leafed from the darkness. Then the sun
Orange, red, red erupted

20 Silently, and splitting to its core tore and flung cloud,
Shook the gulf open, showed blue,

And the big planets hanging—.
I turned

Stumbling in the fever of a dream, down towards
25 The dark woods, from the kindling tops,

And came to the horses.
                    There, still they stood,
But now steaming and glistening under the flow of light,

Their draped stone manes, their tilted hind-hooves
Stirring under a thaw while all around them

30 The frost showed its fires. But still they made no sound.
Not one snorted or stamped,

Their hung heads patient as the horizons,
High over valleys, in the red levelling rays—

In din of the crowded streets, going among the years, the faces,
35 May I still meet my memory in so lonely a place

Between the streams and the red clouds, hearing curlews,
Hearing the horizons endure.

Wind

This house has been far out at sea all night,
The woods crashing through darkness, the booming hills,
Winds stampeding the fields under the window
Floundering black astride and blinding wet

5 Till day rose; then under an orange sky
The hills had new places, and wind wielded
Blade-light, luminous black and emerald,
Flexing like the lens of a mad eye.

10   At noon I scaled along the house-side as far as
     The coal-house door. Once I looked up—
     Through the brunt wind that dented the balls of my eyes
     The tent of the hills drummed and strained its guyrope,

     The fields quivering, the skyline a grimace,
     At any second to bang and vanish with a flap:
15   The wind flung a magpie away and a black-
     Back gull bent like an iron bar slowly. The house

     Rang like some fine green goblet in the note
     That any second would shatter it. Now deep
     In chairs, in front of the great fire, we grip
20   Our hearts and cannot entertain book, thought,

     Or each other. We watch the fire blazing,
     And feel the roots of the house move, but sit on,
     Seeing the window tremble to come in,
     Hearing the stones cry out under the horizons.

JAY MACPHERSON

The Fisherman

     The world was first a private park
     Until the angel, after dark,
     Scattered afar to wests and easts
     The lovers and the friendly beasts.

5   And later still a home-made boat
     Contained Creation set afloat,
     No rift nor leak that might betray
     The creatures to a hostile day.

     But now beside the midnight lake
10   One single fisher sits awake
     And casts and fights and hauls to land
     A myriad forms upon the sand.

     Old Adam on the naming-day
     Blessed each and let it slip away:
15   The fisher of the fallen mind
     Sees no occasion to be kind,

     But on his catch proceeds to sup;
     Then bends, and at one slurp sucks up
     The lake and all that therein is
20   To slake that hungry gut of his,

Then whistling makes for home and bed
As the last morning breaks in red;
But God the Lord with patient grin
Lets down his hook and hoicks him in.

SYLVIA PLATH — *American*

— waiting for poetic inspiration

Black Rook in Rainy Weather — *looking for a sign in nature that will supply it (her) with writing material*

On the stiff twig up there
Hunches a wet black rook
Arranging and rearranging its feathers in the rain.
I do not expect miracle
5   Or an accident

To set the sight on fire
In my eye, nor seek
Any more in the desultory weather some design,
But let spotted leaves fall as they fall,
10   Without ceremony, or portent.

Although, I admit, I desire,
Occasionally, some backtalk
From the mute sky, I can't honestly complain:
A certain minor light may still
15   Leap incandescent

Out of kitchen table or chair
As if a celestial burning took
Possession of the most obtuse objects now and then —
Thus hallowing an interval
20   Otherwise inconsequent

By bestowing largesse, honour,
One might say love. At any rate, I now walk
Wary (for it could happen
Even in this dull, ruinous landscape); sceptical,
25   Yet politic; ignorant

Of whatever angel may choose to flare
Suddenly at my elbow. I only know that a rook
Ordering its black feathers can so shine
As to seize my senses, haul
30   My eyelids up, and grant

A brief respite from fear
Of total neutrality. With luck,
Trekking stubborn through this season

Of fatigue, I shall
35   Patch together a content

Of sorts. Miracles occur,
If you care to call those spasmodic
Tricks of radiance miracles. The wait's begun again,
The long wait for the angel,
40   For that rare, random descent.

ALDEN NOWLAN – *maritime poet.*

Warren Pryor

When every pencil meant a sacrifice
his parents boarded him at school in town,
slaving to free him from the stony fields,
the meagre acreage that bore them down.

They blushed with pride when, at his graduation,
they watched him picking up the slender scroll,
his passport from the years of brutal toil
and lonely patience in a barren hole.

When he went in the Bank their cups ran over.
They marvelled how he wore a milk-white shirt
work days and jeans on Sundays. He was saved
from their thistle-strewn farm and its red dirt.

And he said nothing. Hard and serious
like a young bear inside his teller's cage,
his axe-hewn hands upon the paper bills
aching with empty strength and throttled rage.

The Bull Moose

Down from the purple mist of trees on the mountain,
lurching through forests of white spruce and cedar,
stumbling through tamarack swamps,
came the bull moose
5   to be stopped at last by a pole-fenced pasture.

Too tired to turn or, perhaps, aware
there was no place left to go, he stood with the cattle.
They, scenting the musk of death, seeing his great head
like the ritual mask of a blood god, moved to the other end
10   of the field and waited.

The neighbours heard of it, and by afternoon
cars lined the road. The children teased him
with alder switches and he gazed at them
like an old tolerant collie. The women asked
15   if he could have escaped from a Fair.

The oldest man in the parish remembered seeing
a gelded moose yoked with an ox for plowing.
The young men snickered and tried to pour beer
down his throat, while their girl friends
20   took their pictures.

And the bull moose let them stroke his tick-ravaged flanks,
let them pry open his jaws with bottles, let a giggling girl
plant a little purple cap
of thistles on his head.

25   When the wardens came, everyone agreed it was a shame
to shoot anything so shaggy and cuddlesome.
He looked like the kind of pet
women put to bed with their sons.

So they held their fire. But just as the sun dropped in the river
30   the bull moose gathered his strength
like a scaffolded king, straightened and lifted his horns
so that even the wardens backed away as they raised their rifles.
When he roared, people ran to their cars. All the young men
leaned on their automobile horns as he toppled.

The Execution

On the night of the execution
a man at the door
mistook me for the coroner.
"Press," I said.

5   But he didn't understand. He led me
into the wrong room
where the sheriff greeted me:
"You're late, Padre."

"You're wrong," I told him. "I'm Press."
10   "Yes, of course, Reverend Press."
We went down a stairway.

"Ah, Mr. Ellis," said the Deputy.
"Press!" I shouted. But he shoved me
through a black curtain.

15   The lights were so bright
I couldn't see the faces
of the men sitting
opposite. But, thank God, I thought
they can see me!

20   "Look!" I cried. "Look at my face!
Doesn't anybody know me?"

Then a hood covered my head.
"Don't make it harder for us," the hangman whispered.

GEORGE BOWERING

Grandfather

Grandfather
        Jabez Harry Bowering
strode across the Canadian prairie
hacking down trees

5   & building churches
delivering personal baptist sermons in them
leading Holy holy holy lord god almighty songs in them
red haired man squared off in the pulpit
reading Saul on the road to Damascus at them

10   Left home
           big walled Bristol town
at age eight
           to make a living
buried his stubby fingers in root snarled earth

15   for a suit of clothes & seven hundred gruelly meals a year
taking an anabaptist cane across the back every day
for four years till he was whipt out of England

Twelve years old
           & across the ocean alone

20   to apocalyptic Canada
           Ontario of bone bending labor
six years on the road to Damascus till his eyes were blinded
with the blast of Christ & he wandered west
to Brandon among wheat kings & heathen Saturday nights

25   young red haired Bristol boy shoveling coal
in the basement of Brandon college five in the morning

Then built his first wooden church & married
a sick girl who bore two live children & died
leaving several pitiful letters & the Manitoba night

30   He moved west with another wife & built children & churches
      Saskatchewan Alberta British Columbia Holy holy holy
      lord god almighty
                      struck his labored bones with pain
      & left him a postmaster prodding grandchildren with crutches
35   another dead wife & a glass bowl of photographs
      & holy books unopened save the bible by the bed

      Till he died the day before his eighty fifth birthday
      in a Catholic hospital of sheets white as his hair

MARGARET ATWOOD

This Is a Photograph of Me

      It was taken some time ago.
      At first it seems to be
      a smeared
      print: blurred lines and grey flecks
5   blended with the paper;

      then, as you scan
      it, you see in the left-hand corner
      a thing that is like a branch: part of a tree
      (balsam or spruce) emerging
10   and, to the right, halfway up
      what ought to be a gentle
      slope, a small frame house.

      In the background there is a lake,
      and beyond that, some low hills.

15   (The photograph was taken
      the day after I drowned.

      I am in the lake, in the centre
      of the picture, just under the surface.

      It is difficult to say where
20   precisely, or to say
      how large or small I am:
      the effect of water
      on light is a distortion

      but if you look long enough,
25   eventually
      you will be able to see me.)

The Animals in That Country *the old country*

In that country the animals
have the faces of people:

the ceremonial
cats possessing the streets

5   the fox run
politely to earth, the huntsmen
standing around him, fixed
in their tapestry of manners

the bull, embroidered
10   with blood and given
an elegant death, trumpets, his name
stamped on him, heraldic brand
because

(when he rolled
15   on the sand, sword in his heart, the teeth
in his blue mouth were human)

he is really a man

even the wolves, holding resonant
conversation in their
20   forests thickened with legend.

In this country the animals
have the faces of
animals.

Their eyes
25   flash once in car headlights
and are gone.

Their deaths are not elegant.

They have the faces of
no-one.

Brian the Still-Hunter

The man I saw in the forest
used to come to our house
every morning, never said anything;
I learned from the neighbours later
5   he once tried to cut his throat.

I found him at the end of the path
sitting on a fallen tree
cleaning his gun.

There was no wind;
10   around us the leaves rustled.

He said to me:
I kill because I have to

but every time I aim, I feel
my skin grow fur
15   my head heavy with antlers
and during the stretched instant
the bullet glides on its thread of speed
my soul runs innocent as hooves.

Is God just to his creatures?

20   I die more often than many.

He looked up and I saw
the white scar made by the hunting knife
around his neck.

When I woke
25   I remembered: he has been gone
twenty years and not heard from.

GWENDOLYN MACEWEN

Flight One

Good afternoon ladies and gentlemen
This is your Captain speaking.

We are flying at an unknown altitude
And an incalculable speed.
The temperature outside is beyond words.

If you look out your windows you will see
Many ruined cities and enduring seas
But if you wish to sleep please close the blinds.

My navigator has been ill for many years
And we are on Automatic Pilot; regrettably
I cannot foresee our ultimate destination.

Have a pleasant trip.
You may smoke, you may drink, you may dance
You may die.
We may even land oneday.

Introduction to Short Fiction

The short story, in the broad sense of a relatively brief fictional narrative in prose, is a very old literary form. One can go back to the ancient Egyptians for its origins and work up through Old Testament stories, Christ's parables, fables, folktales, sketches, and yarns. As a quite distinctive literary genre, however, the short story dates back only to the last half of the nineteenth century with practitioners such as Poe, Hawthorne, Maupassant, Chekhov, and E. T. A. Hoffman. The short story in this more closely defined sense is usually concerned with a single effect and often focuses on one character and/or episode. It often deals with a single moment of crisis or conflict in which the essence of character or some truth is revealed. The writing is characteristically intense and concentrated so that all aspects of the story—theme, character, tone, mood, and style—receive the stress of careful and considered crafting. It is an error, albeit a common one, to approach the short story as if it were a novel or, still worse, the novel's poor relation. The short story has quite separate formal characteristics and a generic life of its own. The short-story writers represented in this section are among some of the finest in the language, and it is our hope that their stories will demonstrate the considerable richness, breadth, and potency of this literary form.

We have included in this section some examples of the more ancient forms of prose narrative. Before the age of mass literacy, it was common for the story to be used as a vehicle for teaching or preaching a specific moral. Fables, in general, narrate an extremely simple story that exaggerates character and motive through the use of animal protagonists. They point to a highly specific moral that can usually be codified in a single sentence. The most widely known fables are traditionally ascribed to Aesop, a sixth-century B.C. Phrygian slave, but many of the fables usually ascribed to Aesop have been discovered on Egyptian papyri of nearly a thousand years earlier. These fables were retold many times by various writers, some of whom added their own original fables to the collection. A modern humorist, James Thurber, produced two volumes of fables that set out to parody the fable form while providing some sharp satirical comment. The parable, like the fable, is a simple narrative that points the reader towards a very specific interpretation of the story. Although its significance cannot always be codified in a single sentence, it none the less exists primarily as a "closed text" rather than one inviting a wide variety of readings.

The modern short story owes some of its origins to such early forms as the fable and the parable, but it came into being largely as a result of the rise of the popular literary magazine in the nineteenth century. The spread of literacy and an increasingly urban society created a wide audience for periodical literature. Short fiction was eminently suitable for a weekly or monthly publication and also proved popular with readers. Thus began an association between the short story and periodical publication that continues to the present day. The vast majority of short stories are still published first in journals. Although it is usually much longer than either a fable or a parable, the nineteenth-century short story bears a closer resemblance to such forms than does its later counterpart. For instance, the two nineteenth-century short stories in this selection, Hawthorne's "The Birthmark" and Sarah Orne Jewett's "A White Heron," point the reader towards rather clearer moral conclusions than any of the more recent stories reprinted here. Also popular with the nineteenth-century short-story reader and writer was a significant authorial presence in the narrative voice. The narrator of "The Birthmark" comments on the action, philosophizes, and moralizes in a manner that has now been all but abandoned. In addition, the nineteenth-century short-story reader and writer liked the story that had a sharp twist or reversal at its conclusion. In this respect, many writers were influenced by the works of Guy de Maupassant and Edgar Allan Poe—works that often concluded with a bitter or ironic twist.

Neither the unexpected ending, the pronounced authorial presence, nor the story with a clear-cut moral have remained very popular with more recent short-story writers. The great complexity of the modern short story derives largely from the writer's handling of point of view, or the view from which the writer presents the action of the story. An author's narrative technique must be understood before one can begin to suggest an adequate interpretation. Of the stories selected for inclusion here, five ("I Stand Here Ironing," "Material," "Initram," "The Boat," and "Report") use first-person narration. In each of these, the writer has invented a literary personage who speaks in character. These narrators have a limited point of view: they can tell readers only what they themselves know or what others tell them. A convincing use of this narrative technique requires the narrator to seem to belong wholly to the world of the story. One device for lending reality to a presentation by a character is to provide the reader with an ironic perspective. Generally the authors of the five first-person narrations included here develop some means whereby the narrator reveals himself or herself in ways that are not intended. Little inconsistencies, excessive self-justification, repetition, even trivial allusions to revealing details—all may point to a fundamental weakness of character that makes one aware that what one is told is a compound of reliable and unreliable reportage. Such a method certainly presents interesting challenges to the reader's powers of interpretation. More than that, it reinforces, in a moving way, our sense of the relativity and frailty of the human perception of ourselves and others.

An omniscient narrator is one who tells the story with a seemingly unlimited point of view or fund of knowledge about characters and their actions. Omniscient narrators sometimes speak in the third person, but they can speak in the first person as well. Often we are not aware of the omniscient narrator's presence at all. In "The Horse Dealer's Daughter" the point of view shifts so that at one moment the writer may be using an omniscient narrator while at another the events of the story, although still narrated in the third person, appear to be seen through the eyes of one of the characters, thus giving a limited point of view. Critics sometimes speak of such a story as having a central consciousness. In an increasing number of modern short stories, we are allowed only the characters' perspective on the action.

Short-story writers must develop, in addition to narrative technique, those devices that will work to suggest or say something quickly. There is virtually no room for weak spots, no space for even a flabby paragraph or two. Writers must be able to shape an incident or set of incidents into a memorable scene immediately, without the luxury of lengthy development. Often writers must depend on devices akin to those of poetry—figurative and rhythmical language. Crucial in all stories, both for dramatic impact and for psychological insight, are sharply observed details. Sometimes they are inserted unobtrusively, like the "snakelike little tongues of snow" in "The Painted Door." Often they are evocative prose images, like the cigarette butts in Alistair MacLeod's story. Characters can be sketched in a sentence with the right details. Polly, in Joyce's "The Boarding House," "had a habit of glancing upwards when she spoke with anyone, which made her look like a little perverse madonna." Often, of course, carefully observed details turn out to have some sort of symbolic import. The title of Alistair MacLeod's story, "The Boat," leads one to expect the boat to have more symbolic content than its description would at first suggest. Instead, the father's bed seems more symbolic.

Given the variety of its historical origins and the diversity of literary modes and techniques that can be employed in the short story, the reader is well-advised to approach the genre without fixed preconceptions or expectations. A story like "Report," for example, may upset preconceived notions about such a basic thing as plot. Similarly, stories like "The Horse Dealer's Daughter" or "Soldier's Home" may deliberately provoke a framework of reader expectations, only to demand a radical change in perception by the end of the story. In order to follow such subtle shifts to their conclusion the reader can only accept the story on its own terms, enjoying the drama, the resolution of problems, the human experience it embodies.

AESOP

The Wolf and the Dog

A (Literal Translation)

A dog who was very plump met with a wolf who began to question him: Where was he fed that he had become such a big dog and so well lined with fat? "A rich master feeds me," said the dog. "But your neck," asked the wolf, "how came the bare spot upon it?" "The flesh has been rubbed by the iron collar which my master forged and put upon me." The wolf laughed at him mockingly and said: "Away with that kind of luxury! It's not for me at the cost of having my neck frayed with an iron collar."

B (Sir John Mandeville's Version)

A wolf so piteous poor and thin
His very bones stuck through his skin,
(A sign the dogs were watchful) met
A sturdy Mastiff, sleek and fat.
Sir Wolf, revengeful on his foes
Had murder'd him,[1] as one of those
That hinder'd him from stealing cattle;
But was afraid of joining battle
With one, that look'd as if he could
Stand buff,[2] and make his party good.
And therefore in an humble way
He gives the Dog the time of day;
Talks mightly complaisant,[3] and vents
A wagon load of compliments
Upon his being in such a case—
His brawny flank and jolly face.
Sir Wolf, replies the Mastiff, you
May be as fat as any doe,
If you'll but follow my advice;
For Faith, I think you are unwise
To ramble up and down a wood
Where nothing's to be had, that's good,
No eleemosynary[4] meat,
Or e'er a bit that's good to eat,
But what is got by downright force,
For which at last you pay in course.
And thus yourselves, your hagged wives
And children lead by wretched lives;
Always in fear of being caught,
Till commonly y'are starved or shot.

---

1. Would have liked to kill him.
2. Stand his ground.
3. Courteously.
4. Given as an act of charity; gratuitous.

264

Quoth Wolf, show me a livelihood,
And then, the Devil take the wood:
I stand in need of better diet,
And would be glad to feed in quiet:
But pray, what's to be done, an't please ye?
Nothing, but what is very easy;
To bark at fellows that look poor,
Fright pilf'ring strollers from the door;
And then, which is the chiefest matter,
To wag your tail, to coax and flatter
Those of the family; for this
They'll give you hundred niceties,
As chicken bones, boiled loins of mutton,
As good as ever tooth was put in,
The licking of a greasy dish,
And all the dainties heart can wish;
Besides, the Master shall caress ye,
Spit in your mouth, and — Heaven bless ye.
Good Sir, let's go immediately,
Replied the Wolf, and wept for joy.
They went, and tho' they walked apace,
The Wolf spied here and there a place
About the neck of the Mastiff, where,
It seems, his Curship lost some hair,
And said, Pray Brother Dog, what's this?
Nothing. Nay, tell me what it is;
It looks like gall'd. Perhaps 'tis from
My collar. Then, I find, at home
They tie you. Yes. I'm not inclined to't,
Or goes it loose when y'have a mind to't?
Truly not always, but what's that?
What's that! quoth he, I smell a rat.
My liberty is such a treasure,
I'll change it for no Earthly pleasure.
At that his Wolfship fled, and so
Is flying still for ought I know.

BIBLE

The Burning Fiery Furnace (Daniel iii)

A (Authorized Version)

Neb-u-chad-nez'zar the king made an image of gold, whose height *was* threescore cubits, *and* the breadth thereof six cubits: he set it up in the plain of Du'ra, in the province of Bab'y-lon.

Then Neb-u-chad-nez'zar the king sent to gather together the princes, the governors, and the captains, the judges, the treasurers, the counsellors, the sheriffs, and all the rulers of the provinces, to come to the dedication of the image which Neb-u-chad-nez'zar the king had set up.

Then the princes, the governors, and captains, the judges, the treasurers, the counsellors, the sheriffs, and all the rulers of the provinces, were gathered together unto the dedication of the image that Neb-u-chad-nez'zar the king had set up; and they stood before the image that Neb-u-chad-nez'zar had set up.

Then an herald cried aloud, To you it is commanded, O people, nations, and languages.

That at what time ye hear the sound of the cornet, flute, harp, sackbut, psaltery, dulcimer, and all kinds of music, ye fall down and worship the golden image that Neb-u-chad-nez'zar the king hath set up:

And whoso falleth not down and worshippeth, shall the same hour be cast into the midst of a burning fiery furnace.

Therefore at that time, when all the people heard the sound of the cornet, flute, harp, sackbut, psaltery, and all kinds of music, all the people, the nations, and the languages, fell down *and* worshipped the golden image that Neb-u-chad-nez'zar the king had set up.

Wherefore at that time certain Chalde'ans came near, and accused the Jews.

They spake and said to the king Neb-u-chad-nez'zar, O king, live for ever.

Thou, O king, hast made a decree, that every man that shall hear the sound of the cornet, flute, harp, sackbut, psaltery, and dulcimer, and all kinds of music, shall fall down and worship the golden image:

And whoso falleth not down and worshippeth, *that* he should be cast into the midst of a burning fiery furnace.

There are certain Jews, whom thou hast set over the affairs of the province of Bab'y-lon, Sha'drach, Me'shach, and A-bed'ne-go; these men, O king, have not regarded thee; they serve not thy gods, nor worship the golden image which thou hast set up.

Then Neb-u-chad-nez'zar, in *his* rage and fury, commanded to bring Sha'drach, Me'shach, and A-bed'ne-go. Then they brought these men before the king.

Neb-u-chad-nez'zar spake and said unto them, *Is it* true, O Sha'drach, Me'shach, and A-bed'ne-go, do not ye serve my gods, nor worship the golden image which I have set up?

Now, if ye be ready, that at what time ye hear the sound of the cornet, flute, harp, sackbut, psaltery and dulcimer, and all kinds of music, ye fall down and worship the image which I have made, *well*: but if ye worship not, ye shall be cast the same hour into the midst of a burning fiery furnace: and who *is* that God that shall deliver you out of my hands?

Sha'drach, Me'shach, and A-bed'ne-go answered and said to the king, O Neb-u-chad-nez'zar, we *are* not careful to answer thee in this matter.

If it be *so*, our God, whom we serve, is able to deliver us from the burning fiery furnace; and he will deliver *us* out of thine hand, O king.

But if not, be it known unto thee, O king, that we will not serve thy gods, nor worship the golden image which thou hast set up.

Then was Neb-u-chad-nez'zar full of fury, and the form of his visage was changed against Sha'drach, Me'shach, and A-bed'ne-go: *therefore*, he spake, and commanded that they should heat the furnace one seven times more than it was wont to be heated.

And he commanded the most mighty men that *were* in his army to bind Sha'drach, Me'shach, and A-bed'ne-go; *and* to cast *them* into the burning fiery furnace.

Then these men were bound in their coats, their hosen, and their hats, and their *other* garments, and were cast into the midst of the burning fiery furnace.

Therefore because the king's commandment was urgent, and the furnace exceeding hot, the flame of the fire slew those men that took up Sha'drach, Me'shach, and A-bed'ne-go.

And these three men, Sha'drach, Me'shach, and A-bed'ne-go, fell down bound into the midst of the burning fiery furnace.

Then Neb-u-chad-nez'zar the king was astonished, and rose up in haste, *and* spake, and said unto his counsellors, Did not we cast three men bound into the midst of the fire? They answered and said unto the king, True, O king.

He answered and said, Lo, I see four men loose, walking in the midst of the fire, and they have no hurt; and the form of the fourth is like the Son of God.

Then Neb-u-chad-nez'zar came near to the mouth of the burning fiery furnace, *and* spake, and said, Sha'drach, Me'shach, and A-bed'ne-go, ye servants of the most high God, come forth, and come *hither*. Then Sha'drach, Me'shach, and A-bed'ne-go, came forth of the midst of the fire.

And the princes, governors, and captains, and the king's counsellors, being gathered together, saw these men, upon whose bodies the fire had no power, nor was an hair of their head singed, neither were their coats changed, nor the smell of fire had passed on them.

Then Neb-u-chad-nez'zar spake, and said, Blessed *be* the God of Sha'drach, Me'shach, and A-bed'ne-go, who hath sent his angel, and delivered his servants that trusted in him, and have changed the king's word, and yielded their bodies, that they might not serve nor worship any god except their own God.

Therefore I make a decree, That every people, nation, and language, which speak any thing amiss against the God of Shadrach, Me'shach, and A-bed'ne-go, shall be cut in pieces, and their houses shall be made a dunghill; because there is no other god that can deliver after this sort.

Then the king promoted, Sha'drach, Me'shach, and A-bed'ne-go, in the province of Bab'y-lon.

B (New English Bible Version)

King Nebuchadnezzar made an image of gold, ninety feet high and nine feet broad. He had it set up in the plain of Dura in the province of Babylon. Then he sent out a summons to assemble the satraps, prefects, viceroys, counsellors, treasurers, judges, chief constables, and all governors of provinces to attend the dedication of the image which he had set up. So they assembled — the satraps, prefects, viceroys, counsellors, treasurers, judges, chief constables, and all governors of provinces — for the dedication of the image which King Nebuchadnezzar had set up; and they stood before the image which Nebuchadnezzar had set up. Then the herald loudly proclaimed, 'O peoples and nations of every language, you are commanded, when you hear the sound of horn, pipe, zither, triangle, dulcimer, music, and singing of every kind, to prostrate yourselves and worship the golden image which King Nebuchadnezzar has set up. Whoever does not prostrate himself and worship shall forthwith be thrown into a blazing furnace.' Accordingly, no sooner did all the peoples hear the sound of horn, pipe, zither, triangle, dulcimer, music, and singing of every kind, than all the peoples and nations of every language prostrated themselves and worshipped the golden image which King Nebuchadnezzar had set up.

It was then that certain Chaldaeans came forward and brought a charge against the Jews. They said to King Nebuchadnezzar, 'Long live the king! Your majesty has issued an order that every man who hears the sound of horn, pipe, zither, triangle, dulcimer, music, and singing of every kind shall fall down and worship the image of gold. Whoever does not do so shall be thrown into a blazing furnace. There are certain Jews, Shadrach, Meshach and Abed-nego, whom you have put in charge of the administration of the province of Babylon. These men, your majesty, have taken no notice of your command; they do not serve your god, nor do they worship the golden image which you have set up.' Then in rage and fury Nebuchadnezzar ordered Shadrach, Meshach and Abed-nego to be fetched, and they were brought into the king's presence. Nebuchadnezzar said to them, 'Is it true, Shadrach, Meshach and Abed-nego, that you do not serve my god or worship the golden image which I have set up? If you are ready at once to prostrate yourselves when you hear the sound of horn, pipe, zither, triangle, dulcimer, music, and singing of every kind, and to worship the image that I have set up, well and good. But if you do not worship it, you shall forthwith be thrown into the blazing furnace; and what god is there that can save you from my power?' Shadrach, Meshach and Abed-nego said to King Nebuchadnezzar, 'We have no need to answer you on this matter. If there is a god who is able to save us from the blazing furnace, it is our God whom we serve, and he will save us from your power, O king; but if not, be it known to your majesty that we will neither serve your god nor worship the golden image that you have set up.'

Then Nebuchadnezzar flew into a rage with Shadrach, Meshach and

Abed-nego, and his face was distorted with anger. He gave orders that the furnace should be heated up to seven times its usual heat, and commanded some of the strongest men in his army to bind Shadrach, Meshach and Abed-nego and throw them into the blazing furnace. Then those men in their trousers, their shirts, and their hats and all their other clothes, were bound and thrown into the blazing furnace. Because the king's order was urgent and the furnace exceedingly hot, the men who were carrying Shadrach, Meshach and Abed-nego were killed by the flames that leapt out; and those three men, Shadrach, Meshach and Abed-nego, fell bound into the blazing furnace.

Then King Nebuchadnezzar was amazed and sprang to his feet in great trepidation. He said to his courtiers, 'Was it not three men whom we threw bound into the fire?' They answered the king, 'Assuredly, your majesty.' He answered, 'Yet I see four men walking about in the fire free and unharmed; and the fourth looks like a god.' Nebuchadnezzar approached the door of the blazing furnace and said to the men, 'Shadrach, Meshach and Abed-nego, servants of the Most High God, come out, come here.' Then Shadrach, Meshach and Abed-nego came out from the fire. And the satraps, prefects, viceroys, and the king's courtiers gathered round and saw how the fire had had no power to harm the bodies of these men; the hair of their heads had not been singed, their trousers were untouched, and no smell of fire lingered about them.

Then Nebuchadnezzar spoke out, 'Blessed is the God of Shadrach, Meshach and Abed-nego. He has sent his angel to save his servants who put their trust in him, who disobeyed the royal command and were willing to yield themselves to the fire rather than to serve or worship any god other than their own God. I therefore issue a decree that any man, to whatever people or nation he belongs, whatever his language, if he speaks blasphemy against the God of Shadrach, Meshach and Abed-nego, shall be torn to pieces and his house shall be forfeit; for there is no other god who can save men in this way.' Then the king advanced the fortunes of Shadrach, Meshach and Abed-nego in the province of Babylon.

The Parable of the Talents (Matthew xxv)

A (Authorized Version)

For *the kingdom of heaven is* as a man travelling into a far country, *who* called his own servants, and delivered unto them his goods.

And unto one he gave five talents, to another two, and to another one; to every man according to his several ability; and straightway took his journey.

Then he that had received the five talents went and traded with the same, and made *them* other five talents.

And likewise he that *had received* two, he also gained other two.

But he that had received one, went and digged in the earth, and hid his lord's money.

After a long time, the lord of those servants cometh, and reckoneth with them.

And so he that had received five talents came and brought other five talents, saying, Lord, thou deliveredst unto me five talents; behold, I have gained beside them five talents more.

His lord said unto him, Well done, *thou* good and faithful servant: thou hast been faithful over a few things, I will make thee ruler over many things: enter thou into the joy of thy lord.

He also that had received two talents came and said, Lord, thou deliveredst unto me two talents: behold, I have gained two other talents beside them.

His lord said unto him, Well done, good and faithful servant: thou hast been faithful over a few things, I will make thee ruler over many things: enter thou into the joy of thy lord.

Then he which had received the one talent came and said, Lord, I knew thee that thou art an hard man, reaping where thou hast not sown, and gathering where thou hast not strawed:

And I was afraid, and went, and hid thy talent in the earth: lo, *there* thou hast *that is* thine.

His lord answered and said unto him, *Thou* wicked and slothful servant, thou knewest that I reap where I sowed not, and gather where I have not strawed:

Thou oughtest therefore to have put my money to the exchangers and *then* at my coming I should have received mine own with usury.

Take therefore the talent from him, and give *it* unto him which hath ten talents.

For unto every one that hath shall be given, and he shall have abundance: but from him that hath not shall be taken away even that which he hath.

And cast ye the unprofitable servant into outer darkness: there shall be weeping and gnashing of teeth.

B (New English Bible Version)

'It is like a man going abroad, who called his servants and put his capital in their hands; to one he gave five bags of gold, to another two, to another one, each according to his capacity. Then he left the country. The man who had the five bags went at once and employed them in business, and made a profit of five bags, and the man who had the two bags made two. But the man who had been given one bag of gold went off and dug a hole in the ground, and hid his master's money. A long time afterwards their master returned, and proceeded to settle accounts with them. The man who had been given the five bags of gold came and produced the five he had made: "Master," he said, "you left five bags with me; look, I have made five more." "Well done, my good and trusty servant!" said the master. "You have proved trustworthy in a small way; I will now put you in charge of something big. Come and share your master's delight." The man with the two bags then came and said, "Master, you left two bags with me; look, I have made two more." "Well done, my good and trusty servant!" said the master. "You have proved trustworthy in a small way; I will now put you in charge of something big. Come and share your master's delight." Then the man who had been given one bag came and said, "Master, I knew you to be a hard man: you reap where you have not sown, you gather where you have not scattered; so I was afraid, and I went and hid your gold in the ground. Here it is—you have what belongs to you." "You lazy rascal!" said the master. "You knew that I reap where I have not sown, and gather where I have not scattered? Then you ought to have put my money on deposit, and on my return I should have got it back with interest. Take the bag of gold from him, and give it to the one with the ten bags. For the man who has will always be given more, till he has enough and to spare; and the man who has not will forfeit even what he has. Fling the useless servant out into the dark, the place of wailing and grinding of teeth!"

JAMES THURBER

The Bear Who Let It Alone

In the woods of the far west there once lived a brown bear who could take it or let it alone. He would go into a bar where they sold mead, a fermented drink made of honey, and he would have just two drinks. Then he would put some money on the bar and say, "See what the bears in the back room will have," and he would go home. But finally he took to drinking by himself most of the day. He would reel home at night, kick over the umbrella stand, knock down the bridge lamps, and ram his elbows through the windows. Then he would collapse on the floor and lie there until he went to sleep. His wife was greatly distressed and his children were very frightened.

At length the bear saw the error of his ways and began to reform. In the end he became a famous teetotaller and a persistent temperance lecturer. He would tell everybody that came to his house about the awful effects of drink, and he would boast about how strong and well he had become since he gave up touching the stuff. To demonstrate this, he would stand on his head and on his hands and he would turn cartwheels in the house, kicking over the umbrella stand, knocking down the bridge lamps, and ramming his elbows through the windows. Then he would lie down on the floor, tired by his healthful exercise, and go to sleep. His wife was greatly distressed and his children were very frightened.

Moral: You might as well fall flat on your face as lean over too far backward.

272

The Little Girl and the Wolf

One afternoon a big wolf waited in a dark forest for a little girl to come along carrying a basket of food to her grandmother. Finally a little girl did come along and she was carrying a basket of food. "Are you carrying that basket to your grandmother?" asked the wolf. The little girl said yes, she was. So the wolf asked her where her grandmother lived and the little girl told him and he disappeared into the wood.

When the little girl opened the door of her grandmother's house she saw that there was somebody in bed with a nightcap and nightgown on. She had approached no nearer than twenty-five feet from the bed when she saw that it was not her grandmother but the wolf, for even in a nightcap a wolf does not look any more like your grandmother than the Metro-Goldwyn lion looks like Calvin Coolidge. So the little girl took an automatic out of her basket and shot the wolf dead.

Moral: It is not so easy to fool little girls nowadays as it used to be.

The Unicorn in the Garden

Once upon a sunny morning a man who sat in a breakfast nook looked up from his scrambled eggs to see a white unicorn with a golden horn quietly cropping the roses in the garden. The man went up to the bedroom where his wife was still asleep and woke her. "There's a unicorn in the garden," he said. "Eating roses." She opened one unfriendly eye and looked at him. "The unicorn is a mythical beast," she said, and turned her back on him. The man walked slowly downstairs and out into the garden. The unicorn was still there; he was now browsing among the tulips. "Here, unicorn," said the man, and he pulled up a lily and gave it to him. The unicorn ate it gravely. With a high heart, because there was a unicorn in his garden, the man went upstairs and roused his wife again. "The unicorn," he said, "ate a lily." His wife sat up in bed and looked at him, coldly. "You are a booby," she said, "and I am going to have you put in the booby-hatch." The man, who had never liked the words "booby" and "booby-hatch," and who liked them even less on a shining morning when there was a unicorn in the garden, thought for a moment. "We'll see about that," he said. He walked over to the door. "He has a golden horn in the middle of his forehead," he told her. Then he went back to the garden to watch the unicorn; but the unicorn had gone away. The man sat down among the roses and went to sleep.

As soon as the husband had gone out of the house, the wife got up and dressed as fast as she could. She was very excited and there was a gloat in her eye. She telephoned the police and she telephoned a psychiatrist; she told them to hurry to her house and bring a strait-jacket. When the police and the psychiatrist arrived they sat down in chairs and looked at her, with great interest. "My husband," she said, "saw a unicorn this morning." The police looked at the psychiatrist and the psychiatrist looked at the police. "He told me it ate a lily," she said. The psychiatrist looked at the police and the police looked at the psychiatrist. "He told me it had a golden horn in the middle of its forehead," she said. At a solemn signal from the psychiatrist, the police leaped from their chairs and seized the wife. They had a hard time subduing her, for she put up a terrific struggle, but they finally subdued her. Just as they got her into the strait-jacket, the husband came back into the house.

"Did you tell your wife you saw a unicorn?" asked the police. "Of course not," said the husband. "The unicorn is a mythical beast." "That's all I wanted to know," said the psychiatrist. "Take her away. I'm sorry, sir, but your wife is as crazy as a jay bird." So they took her away, cursing and screaming, and shut her up in an institution. The husband lived happily ever after.

Moral: Don't count your boobies until they are hatched.

NATHANIEL HAWTHORNE

The Birthmark

In the latter part of the last century there lived a man of science, an eminent proficient in every branch of natural philosophy, who not long before our story opens had made experience of a spiritual affinity more attractive than any chemical one. He had left his laboratory to the care of an assistant, cleared his fine countenance from the furnace smoke, washed the stain of acids from his fingers, and persuaded a beautiful woman to become his wife. In those days, when the comparatively recent discovery of electricity and other kindred mysteries of Nature seemed to open paths into the region of miracle, it was not unusual for the love of science to rival the love of woman in its depth and absorbing energy. The higher intellect, the imagination, the spirit, and even the heart might all find their congenial aliment in pursuits which, as some of their ardent votaries believed, would ascend from one step of powerful intelligence to another, until the philosopher should lay his hand on the secret of creative force and perhaps make new worlds for himself. We know not whether Aylmer possessed this degree of faith in man's ultimate control over Nature. He had devoted himself, however, too unreservedly to scientific studies ever to be weaned from them by any second passion. His love for his young wife might prove the stronger of the two; but it could only be by intertwining itself with his love of science and uniting the strength of the latter to his own.

Such a union accordingly took place, and was attended with truly remarkable consequences and a deeply impressive moral. One day, very soon after their marriage, Aylmer sat gazing at his wife with a trouble in his countenance that grew stronger until he spoke.

"Georgiana," said he, "has it never occurred to you that the mark upon your cheek might be removed?"

"No, indeed," said she, smiling; but, perceiving the seriousness of his manner, she blushed deeply. "To tell you the truth, it has been so often called a charm that I was simple enough to imagine it might be so."

"Ah, upon another face perhaps it might," replied her husband; "but never on yours. No, dearest Georgiana, you came so nearly perfect from the hand of Nature that this slightest possible defect, which we hesitate whether to term a defect or a beauty, shocks me, as being the visible mark of earthly imperfection."

"Shocks you, my husband!" cried Georgiana, deeply hurt; at first reddening with momentary anger, but then bursting into tears. "Then why did you take me from my mother's side? You cannot love what shocks you!"

To explain this conversation it must be mentioned that in the centre of Georgiana's left cheek there was a singular mark, deeply interwoven, as it were, with the texture and substance of her face. In the usual state of her complexion—a healthy though delicate bloom—the mark wore a tint of deeper crimson, which imperfectly defined its shape amid the surrounding rosiness. When she blushed it gradually became more indistinct, and finally vanished amid the triumphant rush of blood that bathed the whole cheek with its brilliant glow. But if any shifting motion caused her to turn pale there was the mark again, a crimson stain upon the snow, in what Aylmer sometimes deemed an almost fearful distinctness. Its shape bore not a little similarity to the human hand, though of the smallest pygmy size. Georgiana's lovers were wont to say that some fairy at birth hour had laid her tiny hand upon the infant's cheek, and left this impress there in token of the magic endowments that were to give her such sway over all hearts. Many a desperate swain would have risked life for the privilege of pressing his lips to the mysterious hand. It must not be concealed, however, that the impression wrought by this fairy sign manual varied exceedingly, according to the difference of temperament in the beholders. Some fastidious persons—but they were exclusively of her own sex—affirmed that the bloody hand, as they chose to call it, quite destroyed the effect of Georgiana's beauty, and rendered her countenance even hideous. But it would be as reasonable to say that one of those small blue stains which sometimes occur in the purest statuary marble would convert the Eve of Powers[1] to a monster. Masculine observers, if the birthmark did not heighten their admiration, contented themselves with wishing it away, that the world might possess one living specimen of ideal loveliness without the semblance of a flaw. After his marriage,—for he thought little or nothing of the matter before,—Aylmer discovered that this was the case with himself.

Had she been less beautiful,—if Envy's self could have found aught else to sneer at,—he might have felt his affection heightened by the prettiness of this mimic hand, now vaguely portrayed, now lost, now stealing forth again and glimmering to and fro with every pulse of emotion that throbbed within her heart; but seeing her otherwise so perfect, he found this one defect grow more and more intolerable with every moment of their united lives. It was the fatal flaw of humanity which Nature, in one shape or another, stamps ineffaceably on all her productions, either to imply that they are temporary and finite, or that their perfection must be wrought by toil and pain. The crimson hand expressed the ineludible gripe in which mortality clutches the highest and purest of earthly mould, degrading them into kindred with the lowest, and even with the very brutes, like whom their visible frames return to dust. In this manner, selecting it as the symbol of his wife's liability to sin, sorrow, decay, and death, Aylmer's sombre imagination was not long in rendering the birthmark a frightful object, causing him more trouble and horror than ever Georgiana's beauty, whether of soul or sense, had given him delight.

At all the seasons which should have been their happiest he invariably, and without intending it, nay, in spite of a purpose to the contrary, reverted to this one disastrous topic. Trifling as it at first appeared, it so connected itself with innumerable trains of thought and modes of feeling that it became the central point of all. With the morning twilight Aylmer opened his eyes upon his wife's face and recognized the symbol of imperfection; and when they sat together at the evening hearth his eyes wandered stealthily to her cheek, and beheld, flickering with the blaze of the wood fire, the spectral hand that wrote mortality where he would fain have

1. Hiram Powers (1805–73) was an American sculptor.

worshipped. Georgiana soon learned to shudder at his gaze. It needed but a glance with the peculiar expression that his face often wore to change the roses of her cheek into a deathlike paleness, amid which the crimson hand was brought strongly out, like a bas-relief of ruby on the whitest marble.

Late one night, when the lights were growing dim so as hardly to betray the stain on the poor wife's cheek, she herself, for the first time, voluntarily took up the subject.

"Do you remember, my dear Aylmer," said she, with a feeble attempt at a smile, "have you any recollection, of a dream last night about this odious hand?"

"None! none whatever!" replied Aylmer, starting; but then he added, in a dry, cold tone, affected for the sake of concealing the real depth of his emotion, "I might well dream of it; for, before I fell asleep, it had taken a pretty firm hold of my fancy."

"And you did dream of it?" continued Georgiana, hastily; for she dreaded lest a gush of tears should interrupt what she had to say. "A terrible dream! I wonder that you can forget it. Is it possible to forget this one expression? — 'It is in her heart now; we must have it out!' Reflect, my husband; for by all means I would have you recall that dream."

The mind is in a sad state when Sleep, the all-involving, cannot confine her spectres within the dim region of her sway, but suffers them to break forth, affrighting this actual life with secrets that perchance belong to a deeper one. Aylmer now remembered his dream. He had fancied himself with his servant Aminadab, attempting an operation for the removal of the birthmark; but the deeper went the knife, the deeper sank the hand, until at length its tiny grasp appeared to have caught hold of Georgiana's heart; whence, however, her husband was inexorably resolved to cut or wrench it away.

When the dream had shaped itself perfectly in his memory, Aylmer sat in his wife's presence with a guilty feeling. Truth often finds its way to the mind close muffled in robes of sleep, and then speaks with uncompromising directness, of matters in regard to which we practise an unconscious self-deception during our waking moments. Until now he had not been aware of the tyrannizing influence acquired by one idea over his mind, and of the lengths which he might find in his heart to go for the sake of giving himself peace.

"Aylmer," resumed Georgiana, solemnly, "I know not what may be the cost to both of us to rid me of this fatal birthmark. Perhaps its removal may cause cureless deformity; or it may be the stain goes as deep as life itself. Again: do we know that there is a possibility, on any terms, of unclasping the firm gripe of this little hand which was laid upon me before I came into the world?"

"Dearest Georgiana, I have spent much thought upon the subject," hastily interrupted Aylmer. "I am convinced of the perfect practicability of its removal."

"If there be the remotest possibility of it," continued Georgiana, "let the attempt be made at whatever risk. Danger is nothing to me; for life, while this hateful mark makes me the object of your horror and disgust, — life is a burden which I would fling down with joy. Either remove this dreadful hand, or take my wretched life! You have deep science. All the world bears witness of it. You have achieved great wonders. Cannot you remove this little, little mark, which I cover with the tips of two small fingers? Is this beyond your power, for the sake of your own peace, and to save your poor wife from madness?"

"Noblest, dearest, tenderest wife," cried Aylmer, rapturously, "doubt not my power. I have already given this matter the deepest thought—thought which might almost have enlightened me to create a being less perfect than yourself. Georgiana, you have led me deeper than ever into the heart of science. I feel myself fully competent to render this dear cheek as faultless as its fellow; and then, most beloved, what will be my triumph when I shall have corrected what Nature left imperfect in her fairest work! Even Pygmalion, when his sculptured woman assumed life, felt not greater ecstasy than mine will be."

"It is resolved, then," said Georgiana, faintly smiling. "And, Aylmer, spare me not, though you should find the birthmark take refuge in my heart at last."

Her husband tenderly kissed her cheek—her right cheek—not that which bore the impress of the crimson hand.

The next day Aylmer apprised his wife of a plan that he had formed whereby he might have opportunity for the intense thought and constant watchfulness which the proposed operation would require; while Georgiana, likewise, would enjoy the perfect repose essential to its success. They were to seclude themselves in the extensive apartments occupied by Aylmer as a laboratory, and where, during his toilsome youth, he had made discoveries in the elemental powers of Nature that had roused the admiration of all the learned societies in Europe. Seated calmly in this laboratory, the pale philosopher had investigated the secrets of the highest cloud region and of the profoundest mines; he had satisfied himself of the causes that kindled and kept alive the fires of the volcano; and had explained the mystery of fountains, and how it is that they gush forth, some so bright and pure, and others with such rich medicinal virtues, from the dark bosom of the earth. Here, too, at an earlier period, he had studied the wonders of the human frame, and attempted to fathom the very process by which Nature assimilates all her precious influences from earth and air, and from the spiritual world, to create and foster man, her masterpiece. The latter pursuit, however, Aylmer had long laid aside in unwilling recognition of the truth—against which all seekers sooner or later stumble—that our great creative Mother, while she amuses us with apparently working in the broadest sunshine, is yet severely careful to keep her own secrets, and, in spite of her pretended openness, shows us nothing but results. She permits us, indeed, to mar, but seldom to mend, and, like a jealous patentee, on no account to make. Now, however, Aylmer resumed these half-forgotten investigations; not, of course, with such hopes or wishes as first suggested them; but because they involved much physiological truth and lay in the path of his proposed scheme for the treatment of Georgiana.

As he led her over the threshold of the laboratory, Georgiana was cold and tremulous. Aylmer looked cheerfully into her face, with intent to reassure her, but was so startled with the intense glow of the birthmark upon the whiteness of her cheek that he could not restrain a strong convulsive shudder. His wife fainted.

"Aminadab! Aminadab!" shouted Aylmer, stamping violently on the floor.

Forthwith there issued from an inner apartment a man of low stature, but bulky frame, with shaggy hair hanging about his visage, which was grimed with the vapors of the furnace. This personage had been Aylmer's underworker during his whole scientific career, and was admirably fitted for that office by his great mechanical readiness, and the skill with which, while incapable of comprehending a single principle, he executed all the details of his master's experiments. With his vast strength, his shaggy hair, his smoky aspect, and the indescribable earthiness that incrusted him, he seemed to represent man's physical nature; while Aylmer's slender figure, and pale, intellectual face, were no less apt a type of the spiritual element.

"Throw open the door of the boudoir, Aminadab," said Aylmer, "and burn a pastil."

"Yes, master," answered Aminadab, looking intently at the lifeless form of Georgiana; and then he muttered to himself, "If she were my wife, I'd never part with that birthmark."

When Georgiana recovered consciousness she found herself breathing an atmosphere of penetrating fragrance, the gentle potency of which had recalled her from her deathlike faintness. The scene around her looked like enchantment. Aylmer had converted those smoky, dingy, sombre rooms, where he had spent his brightest years in recondite pursuits, into a series of beautiful apartments not unfit to be the secluded abode of a lovely woman. The walls were hung with gorgeous curtains, which imparted the combination of grandeur and grace that no other species of adornment can achieve; and as they fell from the ceiling to the floor, their rich and ponderous folds, concealing all angles and straight lines, appeared to shut in the scene from infinite space. For aught Georgiana knew, it might be a pavilion among the clouds. And Aylmer, excluding the sunshine, which would have interfered with his chemical processes, had supplied its place with perfumed lamps, emitting flames of various hue, but all uniting in a soft, impurpled radiance. He now knelt by his wife's side, watching her earnestly, but without alarm; for he was confident in his science, and felt that he could draw a magic circle round her within which no evil might intrude.

"Where am I? Ah, I remember," said Georgiana, faintly; and she placed her hand over her cheek to hide the terrible mark from her husband's eyes.

"Fear not, dearest!" exclaimed he. "Do not shrink from me! Believe me, Georgiana, I even rejoice in this single imperfection, since it will be such a rapture to remove it."

"Oh, spare me!" sadly replied his wife. "Pray do not look at it again. I can never forget that convulsive shudder."

In order to soothe Georgiana, and, as it were, to release her mind from the burden of actual things, Aylmer now put in practice some of the light and playful secrets which science had taught him among its profounder lore. Airy figures, absolutely bodiless ideas, and forms of unsubstantial beauty came and danced before her, imprinting their momentary footsteps on beams of light. Though she had some indistinct idea of the method of these optical phenomena, still the illusion was almost perfect enough to warrant the belief that her husband possessed sway over the spiritual world. Then again, when she felt a wish to look forth from her seclusion, immediately, as if her thoughts were answered, the procession of external existence flitted across a screen. The scenery and the figures of actual life were perfectly represented, but with that bewitching yet indescribable difference which always makes a picture, an image, or a shadow so much more attractive than the original. When wearied of this, Aylmer bade her cast her eyes upon a vessel containing a quantity of earth. She did so, with little interest at first; but was soon startled to perceive the germ of a plant shooting upward from the soil. Then came the slender stalk; the leaves gradually unfolded themselves; and amid them was a perfect and lovely flower.

"It is magical!" cried Georgiana. "I dare not touch it."

"Nay, pluck it," answered Aylmer,—"pluck it, and inhale its brief perfume while you may. The flower will wither in a few moments and leave nothing save its brown seed vessels; but thence may be perpetuated with a race as ephemeral as itself."

But Georgiana had no sooner touched the flower than the whole plant suffered a blight, its leaves turning coal-black as if by the agency of fire.

"There was too powerful a stimulus," said Aylmer, thoughtfully.

To make up for this abortive experiment, he proposed to take her portrait by a scientific process of his own invention. It was to be effected by rays of light striking upon a polished plate of metal. Georgiana assented; but, on looking at the result, was affrighted to find the features of the portrait blurred and indefinable; while the minute figure of a hand appeared where the cheek should have been. Aylmer snatched the metallic plate and threw it into a jar of corrosive acid.

Soon, however, he forgot these mortifying failures. In the intervals of study and chemical experiment he came to her flushed and exhausted, but seemed invigorated by her presence, and spoke in glowing language of the resources of his art. He gave a history of the long dynasty of the alchemists, who spent so many ages in quest of the universal solvent by which the golden principle might be elicited from all things vile and base. Aylmer appeared to believe that, by the plainest scientific logic, it was altogether within the limits of possibility to discover this long-sought medium; "but," he added, "a philosopher who should go deep enough to acquire the power would attain too lofty a wisdom to stoop to the exercise of it." Not less singular were his opinions in regard to the elixir vitae. He more than intimated that it was at his option to concoct a liquid that should prolong life for years, perhaps interminably; but that it would produce a discord in Nature which all the world, and chiefly the quaffer of the immortal nostrum, would find cause to curse.

"Aylmer, are you in earnest?" asked Georgiana, looking at him with amazement and fear. "It is terrible to possess such power, or even to dream of possessing it."

"O, do not tremble, my love," said her husband. "I would not wrong either you or myself by working such inharmonious effects upon our lives; but I would have you consider how trifling, in comparison, is the skill requisite to remove this little hand."

At the mention of the birthmark, Georgiana, as usual, shrank as if a red-hot iron had touched her cheek.

Again Aylmer applied himself to his labors. She could hear his voice in the distant furnace room giving directions to Aminadab, whose harsh, uncouth, misshapen tones were audible in response, more like the grunt or growl of a brute than human speech. After hours of absence, Aylmer reappeared and proposed that she should now examine his cabinet of chemical products and natural treasures of the earth. Among the former he showed her a small vial, in which, he remarked, was contained a gentle yet most powerful fragrance, capable of impregnating all the breezes that blow across a kingdom. They were of inestimable value, the contents of that little vial; and, as he said so, he threw some of the perfume into the air and filled the room with piercing and invigorating delight.

"And what is this?" asked Georgiana, pointing to a small crystal globe containing a gold-colored liquid. "It is so beautiful to the eye that I could imagine it the elixir of life."

"In one sense it is," replied Aylmer; "or rather, the elixir of immortality. It is the most precious poison that ever was concocted in this world. By its aid I could apportion the lifetime of any mortal at whom you might point your finger. The strength of the dose would determine whether he were to linger out years, or drop dead in the midst of a breath. No king on his guarded throne could keep his life if I, in my private station, should deem the welfare of millions justified me in depriving him of it."

"Why do you keep such a terrific drug?" inquired Georgiana in horror.

"Do not mistrust me, dearest," said her husband, smiling; "its virtuous potency is yet greater than its harmful one. But see! here is a powerful cosmetic. With a few drops of this in a vase of water, freckles may be washed away as easily as the hands are cleansed. A stronger infusion would take the blood out of the cheek, and leave the rosiest beauty a pale ghost."

"Is it with this lotion that you intend to bathe my cheek?" asked Georgiana, anxiously.

"Oh, no," hastily replied her husband; "this is merely superficial. Your case demands a remedy that shall go deeper."

In his interviews with Georgiana, Aylmer generally made minute inquiries as to her sensations, and whether the confinement of the rooms and the temperature of the atmosphere agreed with her. These questions had such a particular drift that Georgiana began to conjecture that she was already subjected to certain physical influences, either breathed in with the fragrant air or taken with her food. She fancied likewise, but it might be altogether fancy, that there was a stirring up of her system—a strange, indefinite sensation creeping through her veins, and tingling, half painfully, half pleasurably, at her heart. Still, whenever she dared to look into the mirror, there she beheld herself pale as a white rose and with the crimson birthmark stamped upon her cheek. Not even Aylmer now hated it so much as she.

To dispel the tedium of the hours which her husband found it necessary to devote to the processes of combination and analysis, Georgiana turned over the volumes of his scientific library. In many dark old tomes she met with chapters full of romance and poetry. They were the works of the philosophers of the middle ages, such as Albertus Magnus, Cornelius Agrippa, Paracelsus, and the famous friar[2] who created the prophetic Brazen Head.[3] All these antique naturalists stood in advance of their centuries, yet were imbued with some of their credulity, and therefore were believed, and perhaps imagined themselves to have acquired from the investigation of Nature a power above Nature, and from physics a sway over the spiritual world. Hardly less curious and imaginative were the early volumes of the Transactions of the Royal Society,[4] in which the members, knowing little of the limits of natural possibility, were continually recording wonders or proposing methods whereby wonders might be wrought.

But to Georgiana, the most engrossing volume was a large folio from her husband's own hand, in which he had recorded every experiment of his scientific career, its original aim, the methods adopted for its development, and its final success or failure, with the circumstances to which either event was attributable. The book, in truth, was both the history and emblem of his ardent, ambitious, imaginative, yet practical and laborious life. He handled physical details as if there were nothing beyond them; yet spiritualized them all and redeemed himself from materialism by his strong and eager aspiration towards the infinite. In his grasp the veriest clod of earth assumed a soul. Georgiana, as she read, reverenced Aylmer and loved him more profoundly than ever, but with a less entire dependence on his judgment than heretofore. Much as he had accomplished, she could not but observe that his most splendid successes were almost invariably failures, if compared with the ideal at which he aimed. His brightest diamonds were the merest pebbles, and felt to be so by himself, in comparison with the inestimable gems which lay hidden beyond his reach. The volume, rich with achievements that had won renown for its author, was yet as melancholy a record as ever mortal hand had penned. It was the sad confession and continual exemplification of the shortcomings of the composite man, the spirit burdened with clay and working in matter, and of the despair that assails the higher nature at finding itself so miserably thwarted by the earthly part. Perhaps every man of genius, in whatever sphere, might recognize the image of his own experience in Aylmer's journal.

So deeply did these reflections affect Georgiana that she laid her face upon the open volume and burst into tears. In this situation she was found by her husband.

"It is dangerous to read in a sorcerer's books," said he with a smile, though his countenance was uneasy and displeased. "Georgiana, there are pages in that volume which I can scarcely glance over and keep my senses. Take heed lest it prove detrimental to you."

"It has made me worship you more than ever," said she.

"Ah, wait for this one success," rejoined he, "then worship me if you will. I shall deem myself hardly unworthy of it. But come, I have sought you for the luxury of your voice. Sing to me, dearest."

---

2. Roger Bacon (c. 1214–94?) was an English scholastic philosopher and scientist.
3. The Brazen Head, an alchemical statue that prophesies the future, appears in Robert Greene's play *Friar Bacon and Friar Bungay*.

4. The Royal Society, founded in 1660, is the oldest scientific organization in Great Britain and one of the oldest in Europe. Its activities include the publication of its *Proceedings* and of *The Philosophical Transactions*.

So she poured out the liquid music of her voice to quench the thirst of his spirit. He then took his leave with a boyish exuberance of gayety, assuring her that her seclusion would endure but a little longer, and that the result was already certain. Scarcely had he departed when Georgiana felt irresistibly impelled to follow him. She had forgotten to inform Aylmer of a symptom which for two or three hours past had begun to excite her attention. It was a sensation in the fatal birthmark, not painful, but which induced a restlessness throughout her system. Hastening after her husband, she intruded for the first time into the laboratory.

The first thing that struck her eye was the furnace, that hot and feverish worker, with the intense glow of its fire, which by the quantities of soot clustered above it seemed to have been burning for ages. There was a distilling apparatus in full operation. Around the room were retorts, tubes, cylinders, crucibles, and other apparatus of chemical research. An electrical machine stood ready for immediate use. The atmosphere felt oppressively close, and was tainted with gaseous odors which had been tormented forth by the processes of science. The severe and homely simplicity of the apartment, with its naked walls and brick pavement, looked strange, accustomed as Georgiana had become to the fantastic elegance of her boudoir. But what chiefly, indeed almost solely, drew her attention, was the aspect of Aylmer himself.

He was pale as death, anxious and absorbed, and hung over the furnace as if it depended upon his utmost watchfulness whether the liquid which it was distilling should be the draught of immortal happiness or misery. How different from the sanguine and joyous mien that he had assumed for Georgiana's encouragement!

"Carefully now, Aminadab; carefully, thou human machine, carefully, thou man of clay," muttered Aylmer, more to himself than his assistant. "Now, if there be a thought too much or too little, it is all over."

"Ho! ho!" mumbled Aminadab. "Look, master! look!"

Aylmer raised his eyes hastily, and at first reddened, then grew paler than ever, on beholding Georgiana. He rushed towards her and seized her arm with a gripe that left the print of his fingers upon it.

"Why do you come hither? Have you no trust in your husband?" cried he, impetuously. "Would you throw the blight of that fatal birthmark over my labors? It is not well done. Go, prying woman! go!"

"Nay, Aylmer," said Georgiana with the firmness of which she possessed no stinted endowment, "it is not you that have a right to complain. You mistrust your wife; you have concealed the anxiety with which you watch the development of this experiment. Think not so unworthily of me, my husband. Tell me all the risk we run, and fear not that I shall shrink; for my share in it is far less than your own."

"No, no, Georgiana!" said Aylmer, impatiently; "it must not be."

"I submit," replied she, calmly. "And, Aylmer, I shall quaff whatever draught you bring me; but it will be on the same principle that would induce me to take a dose of poison if offered by your hand."

"My noble wife," said Aylmer, deeply moved, "I knew not the height and depth of your nature until now. Nothing shall be concealed. Know, then, that this crimson hand, superficial as it seems, has clutched its grasp into your being with a strength of which I had no previous conception. I have already administered agents powerful enough to do aught except to change your entire physical system. Only one thing remains to be tried. If that fail us we are ruined."

"Why did you hesitate to tell me this?" asked she.

"Because, Georgiana," said Aylmer, in a low voice, "there is danger."

"Danger? There is but one danger—that this horrible stigma shall be left upon my cheek!" cried Georgiana. "Remove it, remove it, whatever be the cost, or we shall both go mad!"

"Heaven knows your words are too true," said Aylmer, sadly. "And now, dearest, return to your boudoir. In a little while all will be tested."

He conducted her back and took leave of her with a solemn tenderness which spoke far more than his words how much was now at stake. After his departure Georgiana became rapt in musings. She considered the character of Aylmer and did it completer justice than at any previous moment. Her heart exulted, while it trembled, at his honorable love—so pure and lofty that it would accept nothing less than perfection nor miserably make itself contented with an earthlier nature than he had dreamed of. She felt how much more precious was such a sentiment than that meaner kind which would have borne with the imperfection for her sake, and have been guilty of treason to holy love by degrading its perfect idea to the level of the actual; and with her whole spirit she prayed that, for a single moment, she might satisfy his highest and deepest conception. Longer than one moment she well knew it could not be; for his spirit was ever on the march, ever ascending, and each instant required something that was beyond the scope of the instant before.

The sound of her husband's footsteps aroused her. He bore a crystal goblet containing a liquor colorless as water, but bright enough to be the draught of immortality. Aylmer was pale; but it seemed rather the consequence of a highly-wrought state of mind and tension of spirit than of fear or doubt.

"The concoction of the draught has been perfect," said he, in answer to Georgiana's look. "Unless all my science have deceived me, it cannot fail."

"Save on your account, my dearest Aylmer," observed his wife, "I might wish to put off this birthmark of mortality by relinquishing mortality itself in preference to any other mode. Life is but a sad possession to those who have attained precisely the degree of moral advancement at which I stand. Were I weaker and blinder, it might be happiness. Were I stronger, it might be endured hopefully. But, being what I find myself, methinks I am of all mortals the most fit to die."

"You are fit for heaven without tasting death!" replied her husband. "But why do we speak of dying? The draught cannot fail. Behold its effect upon this plant."

On the window seat there stood a geranium diseased with yellow blotches which had overspread all its leaves. Aylmer poured a small quantity of the liquid upon the soil in which it grew. In a little time, when the roots of the plant had taken up the moisture, the unsightly blotches began to be extinguished in a living verdure.

"There needed no proof," said Georgiana, quietly. "Give me the goblet. I joyfully stake all upon your word."

"Drink, then, thou lofty creature!" exclaimed Aylmer, with fervid admiration. "There is no taint of imperfection on thy spirit. Thy sensible frame, too, shall soon be all perfect."

She quaffed the liquid and returned the goblet to his hand.

"It is grateful," said she, with a placid smile. "Methinks it is like water from a heavenly fountain; for it contains I know not what of unobtrusive fragrance and deliciousness. It allays a feverish thirst that had parched me for many days. Now, dearest, let me sleep. My earthly senses are closing over my spirit like the leaves around the heart of a rose at sunset."

She spoke the last words with a gentle reluctance, as if it required almost more energy than she could command to pronounce the faint and lingering syllables. Scarcely had they loitered through her lips ere she was lost in slumber. Aylmer sat by her side, watching her aspect with the emotions proper to a man the whole value of whose existence was involved in the process now to be tested. Mingled with this mood, however, was the philosophic investigation characteristic of the man of science. Not the minutest symptom escaped him. A heightened flush of the cheek, a slight irregularity of breath, a quiver of the eyelid, a hardly perceptible tremor through the frame, — such were the details which, as the moments passed, he wrote down in his folio volume. Intense thought had set its stamp upon every previous page of that volume; but the thoughts of years were all concentrated upon the last.

While thus employed, he failed not to gaze often at the fatal hand, and not without a shudder. Yet once, by a strange and unaccountable impulse, he pressed it with his lips. His spirit recoiled, however, in the very act; and Georgiana, out of the midst of her deep sleep, moved uneasily and murmured as if in remonstrance. Again Aylmer resumed his watch. Nor was it without avail. The crimson hand, which at first had been strongly visible upon the marble paleness of Georgiana's cheek, now grew more faintly outlined. She remained not less pale than ever; but the birthmark, with every breath that came and went lost somewhat of its former distinctness. Its presence had been awful; its departure was more awful still. Watch the stain of the rainbow fading out of the sky, and you will know how that mysterious symbol passed away.

"By Heaven! it is well nigh gone!" said Aylmer to himself, in almost irrepressible ecstasy. "I can scarcely trace it now. Success! success! And now it is like the faintest rose color. The lightest flush of blood across her cheek would overcome it. But she is so pale!"

He drew aside the window curtain and suffered the light of natural day to fall into the room and rest upon her cheek. At the same time he heard a gross, hoarse chuckle, which he had long known as his servant Aminadab's expression of delight.

"Ah, clod! ah, earthly mass!" cried Aylmer, laughing in a sort of frenzy, "you have served me well! Matter and spirit — earth and heaven — have both done their part in this! Laugh, thing of the senses! You have earned the right to laugh."

These exclamations broke Georgiana's sleep. She slowly unclosed her eyes and gazed into the mirror which her husband had arranged for that purpose. A faint smile flitted over her lips when she recognized how barely perceptible was now that crimson hand which had once blazed forth with such disastrous brilliancy as to scare away all their happiness. But then her eyes sought Aylmer's face with a trouble and anxiety that he could by no means account for.

"My poor Aylmer!" murmured she.

"Poor? Nay, richest, happiest, most favored!" exclaimed he. "My peerless bride, it is successful! You are perfect!"

"My poor Aylmer," she repeated, with a more than human tenderness, "you have aimed loftily; you have done nobly. Do not repent that, with so high and pure a feeling, you have rejected the best the earth could offer. Aylmer, dearest Aylmer, I am dying!"

Alas! it was too true! The fatal hand had grappled with the mystery of life, and was the bond by which an angelic spirit kept itself in union with a mortal frame. As the last crimson tint of the birthmark—that sole token of human imperfection—faded from her cheek, the parting breath of the now perfect woman passed into the atmosphere, and her soul, lingering a moment near her husband, took its heavenward flight. Then a hoarse, chuckling laugh was heard again! Thus ever does the gross fatality of earth exult in its invariable triumph over the immortal essence which, in this dim sphere of half development, demands the completeness of a higher state. Yet, had Aylmer reached a profounder wisdom, he need not thus have flung away the happiness which would have woven his mortal life of the selfsame texture with the celestial. The momentary circumstance was too strong for him; he failed to look beyond the shadowy scope of time, and, living once for all in eternity, to find the perfect future in the present.

SARAH ORNE JEWETT

A White Heron

1

The woods were already filled with shadows one June evening, just before eight o'clock, though a bright sunset still glimmered faintly among the trunks of the trees. A little girl was driving home her cow, a plodding, dilatory, provoking creature in her behavior, but a valued companion for all that. They were going away from the western light, and striking deep into the dark woods, but their feet were familiar with the path, and it was no matter whether their eyes could see it or not.

There was hardly a night the summer through when the old cow could be found waiting at the pasture bars; on the contrary, it was her greatest pleasure to hide herself away among the high huckleberry bushes, and though she wore a loud bell she had made the discovery that if one stood perfectly still it would not ring. So Sylvia had to hunt for her until she found her, and call Co'! Co'! with never an answering Moo, until her childish patience was quite spent. If the creature had not given good milk and plenty of it, the case would have seemed very different to her owners. Besides, Sylvia had all the time there was, and very little use to make of it. Sometimes in pleasant weather it was a consolation to look upon the cow's pranks as an intelligent attempt to play hide and seek, and as the child had no playmates she lent herself to this amusement with a good deal of zest. Though this chase had been so long that the wary animal herself had given an unusual signal of her whereabouts, Sylvia had only laughed when she came upon Mistress Moolly at the swamp-side, and urged her affectionately homeward with a twig of birch leaves. The old cow was not inclined to wander farther, she even turned in the right direction for once as they left the pasture, and stepped along the road at a good pace. She was quite ready to be milked now, and seldom stopped to browse. Sylvia wondered what her grandmother would say because they were so late. It was a great while since she had left home at half past five o'clock, but everybody knew the difficulty of making this errand a short one. Mrs. Tilley had chased the hornéd torment too many summer evenings herself to blame any one else for lingering, and was only thankful as she waited that she had Sylvia, nowadays, to give such valuable assistance. The good woman suspected that Sylvia loitered occasionally on her own account; there never was such a child for straying about out-of-doors since the world was made! Everybody said that it was a good change for a little maid who had tried to grow for eight years in a crowded manufacturing town, but, as for Sylvia herself, it seemed as if she never had been alive at all before she came to live at the farm. She thought often with wistful compassion of a wretched dry geranium that belonged to a town neighbor.

"'Afraid of folks,'" old Mrs. Tilley said to herself, with a smile, after she had made the unlikely choice of Sylvia from her daughter's houseful of children, and was returning to the farm. "'Afraid of folks,' they said! I guess she won't be troubled no great with 'em up to the old place!" When they reached the door of the lonely house and stopped to unlock it, and the cat came to purr loudly, and rub against them, a deserted pussy, indeed, but fat with young robins, Sylvia whispered that this was a beautiful place to live in, and she never should wish to go home.

The companions followed the shady woodroad, the cow taking slow steps, and the child very fast ones. The cow stopped long at the brook to drink, as if the pasture were not half swamp, and Sylvia stood still and waited, letting her bare feet cool themselves in the shoal water, while the great twilight moths struck softly against her. She waded on through the brook as the cow moved away, and listened to the thrushes with a heart that beat fast with pleasure. There was a stirring in the great boughs overhead. They were full of little birds and beasts that seemed to be wide-awake, and going about their world, or else saying goodnight to each other in sleepy twitters. Sylvia herself felt sleepy as she walked along. However, it was not much farther to the house, and the air was soft and sweet. She was not often in the woods so late as this, and it made her feel as if she were a part of the gray shadows and the moving leaves. She was just thinking how long it seemed since she first came to the farm a year ago, and wondering if everything went on in the noisy town just the same as when she was there; the thought of the great red-faced boy who used to chase and frighten her made her hurry along the path to escape from the shadow of the trees.

Suddenly this little woods-girl is horror-stricken to hear a clear whistle not very far away. Not a bird's whistle, which would have a sort of friendliness, but a boy's whistle, determined, and somewhat aggressive. Sylvia left the cow to whatever sad fate might await her, and stepped discreetly aside into the bushes, but she was just too late. The enemy had discovered her, and called out in a very cheerful and persuasive tone, "Halloa, little girl, how far is it to the road?" and trembling Sylvia answered almost inaudibly, "A good ways."

She did not dare to look boldly at the tall young man, who carried a gun over his shoulder, but she came out of her bush and again followed the cow, while he walked alongside.

"I have been hunting for some birds," the stranger said kindly, "and I have lost my way, and need a friend very much. Don't be afraid," he added gallantly. "Speak up and tell me what your name is, and whether you think I can spend the night at your house, and go out gunning early in the morning."

Sylvia was more alarmed than before. Would not her grandmother consider her much to blame? But who could have foreseen such an accident as this? It did not appear to be her fault, and she hung her head as if the stem of it were broken, but managed to answer "Sylvy," with much effort when her companion again asked her name.

Mrs. Tilley was standing in the doorway when the trio came into view. The cow gave a loud moo by way of explanation.

"Yes, you'd better speak up for yourself, you old trial! Where'd she tuck herself away this time, Sylvy?" Sylvia kept an awed silence; she knew by instinct that her grandmother did not comprehend the gravity of the situation. She must be mistaking the stranger for one of the farmer-lads of the region.

The young man stood his gun beside the door, and dropped a heavy game-bag beside it; then he bade Mrs. Tilley good-evening, and repeated his wayfarer's story, and asked if he could have a night's lodging.

"Put me anywhere you like," he said. "I must be off early in the morning, before day; but I am very hungry, indeed. You can give me some milk at any rate, that's plain."

"Dear sakes, yes," responded the hostess, whose long slumbering hospitality seemed to be easily awakened. "You might fare better if you went out on the main road a mile or so, but you're welcome to what we've got. I'll milk right off, and you make yourself at home. You can sleep on husks or feathers," she proffered graciously. "I raised them all myself. There's good pasturing for geese just below here towards the ma'sh. Now step round and set a plate for the gentleman, Sylvy!" And Sylvia promptly stepped. She was glad to have something to do, and she was hungry herself.

It was a surprise to find so clean and comfortable a little dwelling in this New England wilderness. The young man had known the horrors of its most primitive housekeeping, and the dreary squalor of that level of society which does not rebel at the companionship of hens. This was the best thrift of an old-fashioned farmstead, though on such a small scale that it seemed like a hermitage. He listened eagerly to the old woman's quaint talk, he watched Sylvia's pale face and shining gray eyes with ever growing enthusiasm, and insisted that this was the best supper he had eaten for a month; then, afterward, the new-made friends sat down in the doorway together while the moon came up.

Soon it would be berry-time, and Sylvia was a great help at picking. The cow was a good milker, through a plaguy thing to keep track of, the hostess gossiped frankly, adding presently that she had buried four children, so that Sylvia's mother, and a son (who might be dead) in California were all the children she had left. "Dan, my boy, was a great hand to go gunning," she explained sadly, "I never wanted for pa'tridges or gray squer'ls while he was to home. He's been a great wand'rer, I expect, and he's no hand to write letters. There, I don't blame him, I'd ha' seen the world myself if it had been so I could.

"Sylvia takes after him," the grandmother continued affectionately, after a minute's pause. "There ain't a foot o' ground she don't know her way over, and the wild creatur's counts her one o' themselves. Squer'ls she'll tame to come an' feed right out o' her hands, and all sorts o' birds. Last winter she got the jay-birds to bangeing here, and I believe she'd 'a' scanted herself of her own meals to have plenty to throw out amongst 'em, if I hadn't kep' watch. Anything but crows, I tell her, I'm willin' to help support, — though Dan he went an' tamed one o' them that did seem to have reason same as folks. It was round here a good spell after he went away. Dan an' his father they didn't hitch, — but he never held up his head ag'in after Dan dared him an' gone off."

The guest did not notice this hint of family sorrows in his eager interest in something else.

"So Sylvy knows all about birds, does she?" he exclaimed, as he looked round at the little girl who sat, very demure but increasingly sleepy, in the moonlight. "I am making a collection of birds myself. I have been at it ever since I was a boy." (Mrs. Tilley smiled.) "There are two or three very rare ones I have been hunting for these five years. I mean to get them on my own ground if they can be found."

"Do you cage 'em up?" asked Mrs. Tilley doubtfully, in response to this enthusiastic announcement.

"Oh, no, they're stuffed and preserved, dozens and dozens of them," said the ornithologist, "and I have shot or snared every one myself. I caught a glimpse of a white heron three miles from here on Saturday, and I have followed it in this direction. They have never been found in this district at all. The little white heron, it is," and he turned again to look at Sylvia with the hope of discovering that the rare bird was one of her acquaintances.

But Sylvia was watching a hop-toad in the narrow footpath.

"You would know the heron if you saw it," the stranger continued eagerly. "A queer tall white bird with soft feathers and long thin legs. And it would have a nest perhaps in the top of a high tree, made of sticks, something like a hawk's nest."

Sylvia's heart gave a wild beat; she knew that strange white bird, and had once stolen softly near where it stood in some bright green swamp grass, away over at the other side of the woods. There was an open place where the sunshine always seemed strangely yellow and hot, where tall, nodding rushes grew, and her grandmother had warned her that she might sink in the soft black mud underneath and never be heard of more. Not far beyond were the salt marshes and beyond those was the sea, the sea which Sylvia wondered and dreamed about, but never had looked upon, though its great voice could often be heard above the noise of the woods on stormy nights.

"I can't think of anything I should like so much as to find that heron's nest," the handsome stranger was saying. "I would give ten dollars to anybody who could show it to me," he added desperately, "and I mean to spend my whole vacation hunting for it if need be. Perhaps it was only migrating, or had been chased out of its own region by some bird of prey."

Mrs. Tilley gave amazed attention to all this, but Sylvia still watched the toad, not divining, as she might have done at some calmer time, that the creature wished to get to its hole under the doorstep, and was much hindered by the unusual spectators at that hour of the evening. No amount of thought, that night, could decide how many wished-for treasures the ten dollars, so lightly spoken of, would buy.

The next day the young sportsman hovered about the woods, and Sylvia kept him company, having lost her first fear of the friendly lad, who proved to be most kind and sympathetic. He told her many things about the birds and what they knew and where they lived and what they did with themselves. And he gave her a jack-knife, which she thought as great a treasure as if she were a desert-islander. All day long he did not once make her troubled or afraid except when he brought down some unsuspecting singing creature from its bough. Sylvia would have liked him vastly better without his gun; she could not understand why he killed the very birds he seemed to like so much. But as the day waned, Sylvia still watched the young man with loving admiration. She had never seen anybody so charming and delightful; the woman's heart, asleep in the child, was vaguely thrilled by a dream of love. Some premonition of that great power stirred and swayed these young foresters who traversed the solemn woodlands with soft-footed silent care. They stopped to listen to a bird's song; they pressed forward again eagerly, parting the branches, — speaking to each other rarely and in whispers; the young man going first and Sylvia following, fascinated, a few steps behind, with her gray eyes dark with excitement.

She grieved because the longed-for white heron was elusive, but she did not lead the guest, she only followed, and there was no such thing as speaking first. The sound of her own unquestioned voice would have terrified her, — it was hard enough to answer yes or no when there was need of that. At last evening began to fall, and they drove the cow home together, and Sylvia smiled with pleasure when they came to the place where she heard the whistle and was afraid only the night before.

2

Half a mile from home, at the farther edge of the woods, where the land was highest, a great pine-tree stood, the last of its generation. Whether it was left for a boundary mark, or for what reason, no one could say; the woodchoppers who had felled its mates were dead and gone long ago, and a whole forest of sturdy trees, pines and oaks and maples, had grown again. But the stately head of this old pine towered above them all and made a landmark for sea and shore miles and miles away. Sylvia knew it well. She had always believed that whoever climbed to the top of it could see the ocean; and the little girl had often laid her hand on the great rough trunk and looked up wistfully at those dark boughs that the wind always stirred, no matter how hot and still the air might be below. Now she thought of the tree with a new excitement, for why, if one climbed it at break of day, could not one see all the world, and easily discover whence the white heron flew, and mark the place and find the hidden nest?

What a spirit of adventure, what wild ambition! What fancied triumph and delight and glory for the later morning when she could make known the secret! It was almost too real and too great for the childish heart to bear.

All night the door of the little house stood open, and the whippoorwills came and sang upon the very step. The young sportsman and his old hostess were sound asleep, but Sylvia's great design kept her broad awake and watching. She forgot to think of sleep. The short summer night seemed as long as the winter darkness, and at last when the whippoorwills ceased, and she was afraid the morning would after all come too soon, she stole out of the house and followed the pasture path through the woods, hastening toward the open ground beyond, listening with a sense of comfort and companionshp to the drowsy twitter of a half-awakened bird, whose perch she had jarred in passing. Alas, if the great wave of human interest which flooded for the first time this dull little life should sweep away the satisfactions of an existence heart to heart with nature and the dumb life of the forest!

There was the huge tree asleep yet in the paling moonlight, and small and hopeful Sylvia began with utmost bravery to mount to the top of it, with tingling, eager blood coursing the channels of her whole frame, with her bare feet and fingers, that pinched and held like bird's claws to the monstrous ladder reaching up, up, almost to the sky itself. First she must mount the white oak tree that grew alongside, where she was almost lost among the dark branches and the green leaves heavy and wet with dew; a bird fluttered off its nest, and a red squirrel ran to and fro and scolded pettishly at the harmless housebreaker. Sylvia felt her way easily. She had often climbed there, and knew that higher still one of the oak's upper branches chafed against the pine trunk, just where its lower boughs were set close together. There, when she made the dangerous pass from one tree to the other, the great enterprise would really begin.

She crept out along the swaying oak limb at last, and took the daring step across into the old pine-tree. The way was harder than she thought; she must reach far and hold fast, the sharp dry twigs caught and held her and scratched her like angry talons, the pitch made her thin little fingers clumsy and stiff as she went round and round the tree's great stem, higher and higher upward. The sparrows and robins in the woods below were beginning to wake and twitter to the dawn, yet it seemed much lighter there aloft in the pine-tree, and the child knew that she must hurry if her project were to be of any use.

The tree seemed to lengthen itself out as she went up, and to reach farther and farther upward. It was like a great main-mast to the voyaging earth; it must truly have been amazed that morning through all its ponderous frame as it felt this determined spark of human spirit creeping and climbing from higher branch to branch. Who knows how steadily the least twigs held themselves to advantage this light, weak creature on her way! The old pine must have loved his new dependent. More than all the hawks, and bats, and moths, and even the sweet-voiced thrushes, was the brave, beating heart of the solitary gray-eyed child. And the tree stood still and held away the winds that June morning while the dawn grew bright in the east.

Sylvia's face was like a pale star, if one had seen it from the ground, when the last thorny bough was past, and she stood trembling and tired but wholly triumphant, high in the tree-top. Yes, there was the sea with the dawning sun making a golden dazzle over it, and toward that glorious east flew two hawks with slow-moving pinions. How low they looked in the air from that height when before one had only seen them far up, and dark against the blue sky. Their gray feathers were soft as moths; they seemed only a little way from the tree, and Sylvia felt as if she too could go flying away among the clouds. Westward, the woodlands and farms reached miles and miles into the distance; here and there were church steeples, and white villages; truly it was a vast and awesome world.

The birds sang louder and louder. At last the sun came up bewilderingly bright. Sylvia could see the white sails of ships out at sea, and the clouds that were purple and rose-colored and yellow at first began to fade away. Where was the white heron's nest in the sea of green branches, and was this wonderful sight and pageant of the world the only reward for having climbed to such a giddy height? Now look down again, Sylvia, where the green marsh is set among the shining birches and dark hemlocks; there where you saw the white heron once you will see him again; look, look! a white spot of him like a single floating feather comes up from the dead hemlock and grows larger, and rises, and comes close at last, and goes by the landmark pine with steady sweep of wing and outstretched slender neck and crested head. And wait! wait! do not move a foot or a finger, little girl, do not send an arrow of light and consciousness from your two eager eyes, for the heron has perched on a pine bough not far beyond yours, and cries back to his mate on the nest, and plumes his feathers for the new day!

The child gives a long sigh a minute later when a company of shouting cat-birds comes also to the tree, and vexed by their fluttering and law-lessness the solemn heron goes away. She knows his secret now, the wild, light, slender bird that floats and wavers, and goes back like an arrow presently to his home in the green world beneath. Then Sylvia, well satisfied, makes her perilous way down again, not daring to look far below the branch she stands on, ready to cry sometimes because her fingers ache and her lamed feet slip. Wondering over and over again what the stranger would say to her, and what he would think when she told him how to find his way straight to the heron's nest.

"Sylvy, Sylvy!" called the busy old grandmother again and again, but nobody answered, and the small husk bed was empty, and Sylvia had disappeared.

The guest waked from a dream, and remembering his day's pleasure hurried to dress himself that it might sooner begin. He was sure from the way the shy little girl looked once or twice yesterday that she had at least seen the white heron, and now she must really be persuaded to tell. Here she comes now, paler than ever, and her worn old frock is torn and tattered, and smeared with pine pitch. The grandmother and the sportsman stand in the door together and question her, and the splendid moment has come to speak of the dead hemlock-tree by the green marsh.

But Sylvia does not speak after all, though the old grandmother fretfully rebukes her, and the young man's kind appealing eyes are looking straight in her own. He can make them rich with money; he has promised it, and they are poor now. He is so well worth making happy, and he waits to hear the story she can tell.

No, she must keep silence! What is it that suddenly forbids her and makes her dumb? Has she been nine years growing, and now, when the great world for the first time puts out a hand to her, must she thrust it aside for a bird's sake? The murmur of the pine's green branches is in her ears, she remembers how the white heron came flying through the golden air and how they watched the sea and the morning together, and Sylvia cannot speak; she cannot tell the heron's secret and give its life away.

Dear loyalty, that suffered a sharp pang as the guest went away disap-pointed later in the day, that could have served and followed him and loved him as a dog loves! Many a night Sylvia heard the echo of his whistle haunting the pasture path as she came home with the loitering cow. She forgot even her sorrow at the sharp report of his gun and the piteous sight of thrushes and sparrows dropping silent to the ground, their songs hushed and their pretty feathers stained and wet with blood. Were the birds better friends than their hunter might have been, — who can tell? What-ever treasures were lost to her, woodlands and summer-time, remember! Bring your gifts and graces and tell your secrets to this lonely country child!

JAMES JOYCE

The Boarding House[1]

Mrs. Mooney was a butcher's daughter. She was a woman who was quite able to keep things to herself: a determined woman. She had married her father's foreman, and opened a butcher's shop near Spring Gardens. But as soon as his father-in-law was dead Mr. Mooney began to go to the devil. He drank, plundered the till, ran headlong into debt. It was no use making him take the pledge: he was sure to break out again a few days after. By fighting his wife in the presence of customers and by buying bad meat he ruined his business. One night he went for his wife with the cleaver, and she had to sleep in a neighbour's house.

After that they lived apart. She went to the priest and got a separation from him, with care of the children. She would give him neither money nor food nor house-room; and so he was obliged to enlist himself as a sheriff's man. He was a shabby stooped little drunkard with a white face and a white moustache and white eyebrows, pencilled above his little eyes, which were pink-veined and raw; and all day long he sat in the bailiff's room, waiting to be put on a job. Mrs. Mooney, who had taken what remained of her money out of the butcher business and set up a boarding house in Hardwicke Street, was a big imposing woman. Her house had a floating population made up of tourists from Liverpool and the Isle of Man and, occasionally, *artistes* from the music halls. Its resident population was made up of clerks from the city. She governed the house cunningly and firmly, knew when to give credit, when to be stern and when to let things pass. All the resident young men spoke of her as *The Madam*.

Mrs. Mooney's young men paid fifteen shillings a week for board and lodgings (beer or stout at dinner excluded). They shared in common tastes and occupations and for this reason they were very chummy with one another. They discussed with one another the chances of favourites and outsiders. Jack Mooney, the Madam's son, who was clerk to a commission agent in Fleet Street, had the reputation of being a hard case. He was fond of using soldiers' obscenities: usually he came home in the small hours. When he met his friends he had always a good one to tell them and he was always sure to be on to a good thing—that is to say, a likely horse or a likely *artiste*. He was also handy with the mits and sang comic songs. On Sunday nights there would often be a reunion in Mrs. Mooney's front drawing-room. The music-hall *artistes* would oblige; and Sheridan played waltzes and polkas and vamped accompaniments. Polly Mooney, the Madam's daughter, would also sing. She sang:

> *I'm a . . . naughty girl.*
> *You needn't sham:*
> *You know I am.*

---

1. From a collection of stories, *Dubliners*.
Place names mainly refer to the city of Dublin,
Ireland.

Polly was a slim girl of nineteen; she had light soft hair and a small full mouth. Her eyes, which were grey with a shade of green through them, had a habit of glancing upwards when she spoke with anyone, which made her look like a little perverse madonna. Mrs. Mooney had first sent her daughter to be a typist in a corn-factor's[2] office, but as a disreputable sheriff's man used to come every other day to the office, asking to be allowed to say a word to his daughter, she had taken her daughter home again and set her to do housework. As Polly was very lively, the intention was to give her the run of the young men. Besides, young men like to feel that there is a young woman not very far away. Polly, of course, flirted with the young men, but Mrs. Mooney, who was a shrewd judge, knew that the young men were only passing the time away: none of them meant business. Things went on so for a long time, and Mrs. Mooney began to think of sending Polly back to typewriting, when she noticed that something was going on between Polly and one of the young men. She watched the pair and kept her own counsel.

Polly knew that she was being watched, but still her mother's persistent silence could not be misunderstood. There had been no open complicity between mother and daughter, no open understanding, but though people in the house began to talk of the affair, still Mrs. Mooney did not intervene. Polly began to grow a little strange in her manner and the young man was evidently perturbed. At last, when she judged it to be the right moment, Mrs. Mooney intervened. She dealt with moral problems as a cleaver deals with meat: and in this case she had made up her mind.

It was a bright Sunday morning of early summer, promising heat, but with a fresh breeze blowing. All the windows of the boarding house were open and the lace curtains ballooned gently towards the street beneath the raised sashes. The belfry of George's Church sent out constant peals and worshippers, singly or in groups, traversed the little circus before the church, revealing their purpose by their self-contained demeanour no less than by the little volumes in their gloved hands. Breakfast was over in the boarding house, and the table of the breakfast-room was covered with plates on which lay yellow streaks of eggs with morsels of bacon-fat and bacon-rind. Mrs. Mooney sat in the straw arm-chair and watched the servant Mary remove the breakfast things. She made Mary collect the crusts and pieces of broken bread to help to make Tuesday's bread-pudding. When the table was cleared, the broken bread collected, the sugar and butter safe under lock and key, she began to reconstruct the interview which she had had the night before with Polly. Things were as she had suspected: she had been frank in her questions and Polly had been frank in her answers. Both had been somewhat awkward, of course. She had been made awkward by her not wishing to receive the news in too cavalier a fashion or to seem to have connived, and Polly had been made awkward not merely because allusions of that kind always made her awkward, but also because she did not wish it to be thought that in her wise innocence she had divined the intention behind her mother's tolerance.

Mrs. Mooney glanced instinctively at the little gilt clock on the mantelpiece as soon as she had become aware through her reverie that the bells of

---

2. Corn-merchant.

George's Church had stopped ringing. It was seventeen minutes past eleven: she would have lots of time to have the matter out with Mr. Doran and then catch short twelve at Marlborough Street. She was sure she would win. To begin with, she had all the weight of social opinion on her side: she was an outraged mother. She had allowed him to live beneath her roof, assuming that he was a man of honour, and he had simply abused her hospitality. He was thirty-four or thirty-five years of age, so that youth could not be pleaded as his excuse; nor could ignorance be his excuse, since he was a man who had seen something of the world. He had simply taken advantage of Polly's youth and inexperience: that was evident. The question was: What reparation would he make?

There must be reparation made in such case. It is all very well for the man: he can go his ways as if nothing had happened, having had his moment of pleasure, but the girl has to bear the brunt. Some mothers would be content to patch up such an affair for a sum of money; she had known cases of it. But she would not do so. For her only one reparation could make up for the loss of her daughter's honour: marriage.

She counted all her cards again before sending Mary up to Mr. Doran's room to say that she wished to speak with him. She felt sure she would win. He was a serious young man, not rakish or loud-voiced like the others. If it had been Mr. Sheridan or Mr. Meade or Bantam Lyons, her task would have been much harder. She did not think he would face publicity. All the lodgers in the house knew something of the affair; details had been invented by some. Besides, he had been employed for thirteen years in a great Catholic wine-merchant's office, and publicity would mean for him, perhaps, the loss of his sit. Whereas if he agreed all might be well. She knew he had a good screw[3] for one thing, and she suspected he had a bit of stuff put by.

Nearly the half-hour! She stood up and surveyed herself in the pier-glass. The decisive expression of her great florid face satisfied her, and she thought of some mothers she knew who could not get their daughters off their hands.

Mr. Doran was very anxious indeed this Sunday morning. He had made two attempts to shave, but his hand had been so unsteady that he had been obliged to desist. Three days' reddish beard fringed his jaws, and every two or three minutes a mist gathered on his glasses so that he had to take them off and polish them with his pocket-handkerchief. The recollection of his confession of the night before was a cause of acute pain to him; the priest had drawn out every ridiculous detail of the affair, and in the end had so magnified his sin that he was almost thankful at being afforded a loophole of reparation. The harm was done. What could he do now but marry her or run away? He could not brazen it out. The affair would be sure to be talked of, and his employer would be certain to hear of it. Dublin is such a small city: everyone knows everyone else's business. He felt his heart leap warmly in his throat as he heard in his excited imagination old Mr. Leonard calling out in his rasping voice: *'Send Mr. Doran here, please.'*

All his long years of service gone for nothing! All his industry and

3. Salary.

diligence thrown away! As a young man he had sown his wild oats, of course; he had boasted of his free-thinking and denied the existence of God to his companions in public-houses. But that was all passed and done with... nearly. He still bought a copy of *Reynolds Newspaper*[4] every week, but he attended to his religious duties, and for nine-tenths of the year lived a regular life. He had money enough to settle down on; it was not that. But the family would look down on her. First of all there was her disreputable father, and then her mother's boarding house was beginning to get a certain fame. He had a notion that he was being had. He could imagine his friends talking of the affair and laughing. She *was* a little vulgar; sometimes she said '*I seen*' and '*If I had've known*'. But what would grammar matter if he really loved her? He could not make his mind whether to like her or depise her for what she had done. Of course he had done it too. His instinct urged him to remain free, not to marry. Once you are married you are done for, it said.

While he was sitting helplessly on the side of the bed in shirt and trousers, she tapped lightly at his door and entered. She told him all, that she had made a clean breast of it to her mother and that her mother would speak with him that morning. She cried and threw her arms round his neck, saying:

'O Bob! Bob! What am I to do? What am I to do at all?'

She would put an end to herself, she said.

He comforted her feebly, telling her not to cry, that it would be all right, never fear. He felt against his shirt the agitation of her bosom.

It was not altogether his fault that it had happened. He remembered well, with the curious patient memory of the celibate, the first casual caresses her dress, her breath, her fingers had given him. Then late one night as he was undressing for bed she had tapped at his door, timidly. She wanted to relight her candle at his, for hers had been blown out by a gust. It was her bath night. She wore a loose open combing-jacket of printed flannel. Her white instep shone in the opening of her furry slippers and the blood glowed warmly behind her perfumed skin. From her hands and wrists too as she lit and steadied her candle a faint perfume arose.

On nights when he came in very late it was she who warmed up his dinner. He scarcely knew what he was eating feeling her beside him alone, at night, in the sleeping house. And her thoughtfulness! If the night was anyway cold or wet or windy there was sure to be a little tumbler of punch ready for him. Perhaps they could be happy together. . . .

They used to go upstairs together on tiptoe, each with a candle, and on the third landing exchange reluctant good nights. They used to kiss. He remembered well her eyes, the touch of her hand and his delirium. . . .

But delirium passes. He echoed her phrase, applying it to himself: '*What am I to do?*' The instinct of the celibate warned him to hold back. But the sin was there; even his sense of honour told him that reparation must be made for such a sin.

While he was sitting with her on the side of the bed Mary came to the door and said that the missus wanted to see him in the parlour. He stood up

4. A popular newspaper regarded as somewhat sensational.

to put on his coat and waistcoat, more helpless than ever. When he was dressed he went over to her to comfort her. It would be all right, never fear. He left her crying on the bed and moaning softly: '*O my God!*'

Going down the stairs his glasses became so dimmed with moisture that he had to take them off and polish them. He longed to ascend through the roof and fly away to another country where he would never hear again of his trouble, and yet a force pushed him downstairs step by step. The implacable faces of his employer and of the Madam stared upon his discomfiture. On the last flight of stairs he passed Jack Mooney, who was coming up from the pantry nursing two bottles of *Bass*.[5] They saluted coldly; and the lover's eyes rested for a second or two on a thick bulldog face and a pair of thick short arms. When he reached the foot of the staircase he glanced up and saw Jack regarding him from the door of the return-room.

Suddenly he remembered the night when one of the music-hall *artistes*, a little blond Londoner, had made a rather free allusion to Polly. The reunion had been almost broken up on account of Jack's violence. Everyone tried to quiet him. The music-hall *artiste*, a little paler than usual, kept smiling and saying that there was no harm meant; but Jack kept shouting at him that if any fellow tried that sort of a game on with his sister he'd bloody well put his teeth down his throat, so he would.

Polly sat for a little time on the side of the bed, crying. Then she dried her eyes and went over to the looking-glass. She dipped the end of the towel in the water-jug and refreshed her eyes with the cool water. She looked at herself in profile and readjusted a hairpin above her ear. Then she went back to the bed again and sat at the foot. She regarded the pillows for a long time, and the sight of them awakened in her mind secret, amiable memories. She rested the nape of her neck against the cool iron bed-rail and fell into a reverie. There was no longer any perturbation visible on her face.

She waited on patiently, almost cheerfully, without alarm, her memories gradually giving place to hopes and visions of the future. Her hopes and visions were so intricate that she no longer saw the white pillows on which her gaze was fixed, or remembered that she was waiting for anything.

At last she heard her mother calling. She started to her feet and ran to the banisters.

'Polly! Polly!'

'Yes, mamma?'

'Come down, dear. Mr. Doran wants to speak to you.'

Then she remembered what she had been waiting for.

5. A brand of beer.

KATHERINE MANSFIELD

The Garden-Party

And after all the weather was ideal. They could not have had a more perfect day for a garden-party if they had ordered it. Windless, warm, the sky without a cloud. Only the blue was veiled with a haze of light gold, as it is sometimes in early summer. The gardener had been up since dawn, mowing the lawns and sweeping them, until the grass and the dark flat rosettes where the daisy plants had been seemed to shine. As for the roses, you could not help feeling they understood that roses are the only flowers that impress people at garden-parties; the only flowers that everybody is certain of knowing. Hundreds, yes, literally hundreds, had come out in a single night; the green bushes bowed down as though they had been visited by archangels.

Breakfast was not yet over before the men came to put up the marquee.

"Where do you want the marquee put, mother?"

"My dear child, it's no use asking me. I'm determined to leave everything to you children this year. Forget I am your mother. Treat me as an honoured guest."

But Meg could not possibly go and supervise the men. She had washed her hair before breakfast, and she sat drinking her coffee in a green turban, with a dark wet curl stamped on each cheek. Jose, the butterfly, always came down in a silk petticoat and a kimono jacket.

"You'll have to go, Laura; you're the artistic one."

Away Laura flew, still holding her piece of bread-and-butter. It's so delicious to have an excuse for eating out of doors and, besides, she loved having to arrange things; she always felt she could do it so much better than anybody else.

Four men in their shirt-sleeves stood grouped together on the garden path. They carried staves covered with rolls of canvas and they had big tool-bags slung on their backs. They looked impressive. Laura wished now that she was not holding that piece of bread-and-butter, but there was nowhere to put it and she couldn't possibly throw it away. She blushed and tried to look severe and even a little bit short-sighted as she came up to them.

"Good morning," she said, copying her mother's voice. But that sounded so fearfully affected that she was ashamed, and stammered like a little girl, "Oh—er—have you come—is it about the marquee?"

"That's right, miss," said the tallest of the men, a lanky, freckled fellow, and he shifted his tool-bag, knocked back his straw hat and smiled down at her. "That's about it."

His smile was so easy, so friendly, that Laura recovered. What nice eyes he had, small, but such a dark blue! And now she looked at the others, they were smiling too. "Cheer up, we won't bite," their smile seemed to say. How very nice workmen were! And what a beautiful morning! She mustn't mention the morning; she must be business-like. The marquee.

"Well, what about the lily-lawn? Would that do?"

And she pointed to the lily-lawn with the hand that didn't hold the bread-and-butter. They turned, they stared in the direction. A little fat chap thrust out his underlip and the tall fellow frowned.

"I don't fancy it," said he. "Not conspicuous enough. You see, with a thing like a marquee" — and he turned to Laura in his easy way — "you want to put it somewhere where it'll give you a bang slap in the eye, if you follow me."

Laura's upbringing made her wonder for a moment whether it was quite respectful of a workman to talk to her of bangs slap in the eye. But she did quite follow him.

"A corner of the tennis-court," she suggested. "But the band's going to be in one corner."

"H'm, going to have a band, are you?" said another of the workmen. He was pale. He had a haggard look as his dark eyes scanned the tennis-court. What was he thinking?

"Only a very small band," said Laura gently. Perhaps he wouldn't mind so much if the band was quite small. But the tall fellow interrupted.

"Look here, miss, that's the place. Against those trees. Over there. That'll do fine."

Against the karakas. Then the karaka trees would be hidden. And they were so lovely, with their broad, gleaming leaves, and their clusters of yellow fruit. They were like trees you imagined growing on a desert island, proud, solitary, lifting their leaves and fruits to the sun in a kind of silent splendour. Must they be hidden by a marquee?

They must. Already the men had shouldered their staves and were making for the place. Only the tall fellow was left. He bent down, pinched a sprig of lavender, put his thumb and forefinger to his nose and snuffed up the smell. When Laura saw that gesture she forgot all about the karakas in her wonder at him caring for things like that — caring for the smell of lavender. How many men that she knew would have done such a thing. Oh, how extraordinarily nice workmen were, she thought. Why couldn't she have workmen for friends rather than the silly boys she danced with and who came to Sunday night supper? She would get on much better with men like these.

It's all the fault, she decided, as the tall fellow drew something on the back of an envelope, something that was to be looped up or left to hang, of these absurd class distinctions. Well, for her part, she didn't feel them. Not a bit, not an atom. . . . And now there came the chock-chock of wooden hammers. Someone whistled, someone sang out, "Are you right there, matey?" "Matey!" The friendliness of it, the — the — Just to prove how happy she was, just to show the tall fellow how at home she felt, and how she despised stupid conventions, Laura took a big bite of her bread-and-butter as she stared at the little drawing. She felt just like a work-girl.

"Laura, Laura, where are you? Telephone, Laura!" a voice cried from the house.

"Coming!" Away she skimmed, over the lawn, up the path, up the steps, across the veranda and into the porch. In the hall her father and Laurie were brushing their hats ready to go to the office.

"I say, Laura," said Laurie very fast, "you might just give a squiz at my coat before this afternoon. See if it wants pressing."

"I will," said she. Suddenly she couldn't stop herself. She ran at Laurie and gave him a small, quick squeeze. "Oh, I do love parties, don't you?" gasped Laura.

"Ra-ther," said Laurie's warm, boyish voice, and he squeezed his sister too and gave her a gentle push. "Dash off to the telephone, old girl."

The telephone. "Yes, yes; oh yes. Kitty? Good morning, dear. Come to lunch? Do, dear. Delighted, of course. It will only be a very scratch meal — just the sandwich crusts and broken meringue-shells and what's left over. Yes, isn't it a perfect morning? Your white? Oh, I certainly should. One moment—hold the line. Mother's calling." And Laura sat back. "What, mother? Can't hear."

Mrs. Sheridan's voice floated down the stairs. "Tell her to wear that sweet hat she had on last Sunday."

"Mother says you're to wear that *sweet* hat you had on last Sunday. Good. One o'clock. Bye-bye."

Laura put back the receiver, flung her arms over her head, took a deep breath, stretched and let them fall. "Huh," she sighed, and the moment after the sigh she sat up quickly. She was still, listening. All the doors in the house seemed to be open. The house was alive with soft, quick steps and running voices. The green baize door that led to the kitchen regions swung open and shut with a muffled thud. And now there came a long, chuckling absurd sound. It was the heavy piano being moved on its stiff castors. But the air! If you stopped to notice, was the air always like this? Little faint winds were playing chase in at the tops of the windows, out at the doors. And there were two tiny spots of sun, one on the inkpot, one on a silver photograph frame, playing too. Darling little spots. Especially the one on the inkpot lid. It was quite warm. A warm little silver star. She could have kissed it.

The front door bell pealed and there sounded the rustle of Sadie's print skirt on the stairs. A man's voice murmured; Sadie answered, careless, "I'm sure I don't know. Wait. I'll ask Mrs. Sheridan."

"What is it, Sadie?" Laura came into the hall.

"It's the florist, Miss Laura."

It was, indeed. There, just inside the door, stood a wide, shallow tray full of pots of pink lilies. No other kind. Nothing but lilies—canna lilies, big pink flowers, wide open, radiant, almost frighteningly alive on bright crimson stems.

"O-oh, Sadie!" said Laura, and the sound was like a little moan. She crouched down as if to warm herself at that blaze of lilies; she felt they were in her fingers, on her lips, growing in her breast.

"It's some mistake," she said faintly. "Nobody ever ordered so many. Sadie, go and find mother."

But at that moment Mrs. Sheridan joined them.

"It's quite right," she said calmly. "Yes, I ordered them. Aren't they lovely?" She pressed Laura's arm. "I was passing the shop yesterday, and I saw them in the window. And I suddenly thought for once in my life I shall have enough canna lilies. The garden-party will be a good excuse."

"But I thought you said you didn't mean to interfere," said Laura. Sadie had gone. The florist's man was still outside at his van. She put her arm round her mother's neck and gently, very gently, she bit her mother's ear.

"My darling child, you wouldn't like a logical mother, would you? Don't do that. Here's the man."

He carried more lilies still, another whole tray.

"Bank them up, just inside the door, on both sides of the porch, please," said Mrs. Sheridan. "Don't you agree, Laura?"

"Oh, I *do*, mother."

In the drawing-room Meg, Jose and good little Hans had at last succeeded in moving the piano.

"Now, if we put this chesterfield against the wall and move everything out of the room except the chairs, don't you think?"

"Quite."

"Hans, move these tables into the smoking-room, and bring a sweeper to take these marks off the carpet and — one moment, Hans — " Jose loved giving orders to the servants and they loved obeying her. She always made them feel they were taking part in some drama. "Tell mother and Miss Laura to come here at once."

"Very good, Miss Jose."

She turned to Meg. "I want to hear what the piano sounds like, just in case I'm asked to sing this afternoon. Let's try over 'This Life is Weary.'"

Pom! Ta-ta-ta *Tee*-ta! The piano burst out so passionately that Jose's face changed. She clasped her hands. She looked mournfully and enigmatically at her mother and Laura as they came in.

> This Life is *Wee*-ary,
> A Tear — a Sigh.
> A Love that *Chan*-ges,
>   This Life is *Wee*-ary,
> A Tear — a Sigh.
> A Love that *Chan*-ges,
> And then... Good-bye!

But at the word "Good-bye," and although the piano sounded more desperate than ever, her face broke into a brilliant, dreadfully unsympathetic smile.

"Aren't I in good voice, mummy?" she beamed.

> This Life is *Wee*-ary,
> Hope comes to Die.
> A Dream — a *Wa*-kening.

But now Sadie interrupted them. "What is it, Sadie?"

"If you please, m'm, cook says have you got the flags for the sandwiches?"

"The flags for the sandwiches, Sadie?" echoed Mrs. Sheridan dreamily. And the children knew by her face that she hadn't got them. "Let me see." And she said to Sadie firmly, "Tell cook I'll let her have them in ten minutes."

Sadie went.

"Now, Laura," said her mother quickly, "come with me into the smoking-room. I've got the names somewhere on the back of an envelope.

You'll have to write them out for me. Meg, go upstairs this minute and take that wet thing off your head. Jose, run and finish dressing this instant. Do you hear me, children, or shall I have to tell your father when he comes home to-night? And—and, Jose, pacify cook if you do go into the kitchen, will you? I'm terrified of her this morning."

The envelope was found at last behind the dining-room clock, though how it had got there Mrs. Sheridan could not imagine.

"One of you children must have stolen it out of my bag, because I remember vividly—cream-cheese and lemon-curd. Have you done that?"

"Yes."

"Egg and—" Mrs. Sheridan held the envelope away from her. "It looks like mice. It can't be mice, can it?"

"Olive, pet," said Laura, looking over her shoulder.

"Yes, of course, olive. What a horrible combination it sounds. Egg and olive."

They were finished at last, and Laura took them off to the kitchen. She found Jose there pacifying the cook, who did not look at all terrifying.

"I have never seen such exquisite sandwiches," said Jose's rapturous voice. "How many kinds did you say there were, cook? Fifteen?"

"Fifteen, Miss Jose."

"Well, cook, I congratulate you."

Cook swept up crusts with the long sandwich knife, and smiled broadly.

"Godber's has come," announced Sadie, issuing out of the pantry. She had seen the man pass the window.

That meant the cream puffs had come. Godber's were famous for their cream puffs. Nobody ever thought of making them at home.

"Bring them in and put them on the table, my girl," ordered cook.

Sadie brought them in and went back to the door. Of course Laura and Jose were far too grown-up to really care about such things. All the same, they couldn't help agreeing that the puffs looked very attractive. Very. Cook began arranging them, shaking off the extra icing sugar.

"Don't they carry one back to all one's parties?" said Laura.

"I suppose they do," said practical Jose, who never liked to be carried back. "They look beautifully light and feathery, I must say."

"Have one each, my dears," said cook in her comfortable voice. "Yer ma won't know."

Oh, impossible. Fancy cream puffs so soon after breakfast. The very idea made one shudder. All the same, two minutes later Jose and Laura were licking their fingers with that absorbed inward look that only comes from whipped cream.

"Let's go into the garden, out by the back way," suggested Laura. "I want to see how the men are getting on with the marquee. They're such awfully nice men."

But the back door was blocked by cook, Sadie, Godber's man and Hans.

Something had happened.

"Tuk-tuk-tuk," clucked cook like an agitated hen. Sadie had her hand clapped to her cheek as though she had a toothache. Hans' face was screwed up in the effort to understand. Only Godber's man seemed to be enjoying himself; it was his story.

"What's the matter? What's happened?"

"There's been a horrible accident," said cook. "A man killed."

"A man killed! Where? How? When?"

But Godber's man wasn't going to have his story snatched from under his very nose.

"Know those little cottages just below here, miss?" Know them? Of course she knew them. "Well, there's a young chap living there, name of Scott, a carter. His horse shied at a traction-engine, corner of Hawke Street this morning, and he was thrown out on the back of his head. Killed."

"Dead!" Laura stared at Godber's man.

"Dead when they picked him up." said Godber's man with relish. "They were taking the body home as I come up here." And he said to the cook, "He's left a wife and five little ones."

"Jose, come here." Laura caught hold of her sister's sleeve and dragged her through the kitchen to the other side of the green baize door. There she paused and leaned against it. "Jose!" she said, horrified, "however are we going to stop everything?"

"Stop everything, Laura!" cried Jose in astonishment. "What do you mean?"

"Stop the garden-party, of course." Why did Jose pretend?

But Jose was still more amazed. "Stop the garden-party? My dear Laura, don't be so absurd. Of course we can't do anything of the kind. Nobody expects us to. Don't be so extravagant."

"But we can't possibly have a garden-party with a man dead just outside the front gate."

That really was extravagant, for the little cottages were in a lane to themselves at the very bottom of a steep rise that led up to the house. A broad road ran between. True, they were far too near. They were the greatest possible eyesore and they had no right to be in that neighbourhood at all. They were little mean dwellings painted a chocolate brown. In the garden patches there was nothing but cabbage stalks, sick hens and tomato cans. The very smoke coming out of their chimneys was poverty-stricken. Little rags and shreds of smoke, so unlike the great silvery plumes that uncurled from the Sheridans' chimneys. Washerwomen lived in the lane and sweeps and a cobbler and a man whose house-front was studded all over with minute bird-cages. Children swarmed. When the Sheridans were little they were forbidden to set foot there because of the revolting language and of what they might catch. But since they were grown up Laura and Laurie on their prowls sometimes walked through. It was disgusting and sordid. They came out with a shudder. But still one must go everywhere; one must see everything. So through they went.

"And just think of what the band would sound like to that poor woman," said Laura.

"Oh, Laura!" Jose began to be seriously annoyed. "If you're going to stop a band playing every time someone has an accident, you'll lead a very strenuous life. I'm every bit as sorry about it as you. I feel just as sympathetic." Her eyes hardened. She looked at her sister just as she used to when they were little and fighting together. "You won't bring a drunken workman back to life by being sentimental," she said softly.

"Drunk! Who said he was drunk?" Laura turned furiously on Jose. She said just as they had used to say on those occasions, "I'm going straight up to tell mother."

"Do, dear," cooed Jose.

"Mother, can I come into your room?" Laura turned the big glass door-knob.

"Of course, child. Why, what's the matter? What's given you such a colour?" And Mrs. Sheridan turned round from her dressing-table. She was trying on a new hat.

"Mother, a man's been killed," began Laura.

"*Not* in the garden?" interrupted her mother.

"No, no!"

"Oh, what a fright you gave me!" Mrs. Sheridan sighed with relief and took off the big hat and held it on her knees.

"But listen, mother," said Laura. Breathless, half choking, she told the dreadful story. "Of course, we can't have our party, can we?" she pleaded. "The band and everybody arriving. They'd hear us, mother; they're nearly neighbours!"

To Laura's astonishment her mother behaved just like Jose; it was harder to bear because she seemed amused. She refused to take Laura seriously.

"But, my dear child, use your common sense. It's only by accident we've heard of it. If someone had died there normally—and I can't understand how they keep alive in those poky little holes—we should still be having our party, shouldn't we?"

Laura had to say "yes" to that, but she felt it was all wrong. She sat down on her mother's sofa and pinched the cushion frill.

"Mother, isn't it really terribly heartless of us?" she asked.

"Darling!" Mrs. Sheridan got up and came over to her, carrying the hat. Before Laura could stop her she had popped it on. "My child!" said her mother, "the hat is yours. It's made for you. It's much too young for me. I have never seen you look such a picture. Look at yourself!" And she held up her hand-mirror.

"But, mother," Laura began again. She couldn't look at herself; she turned aside.

This time Mrs. Sheridan lost patience just as Jose had done.

"You are being very absurd, Laura," she said coldly. "People like that don't expect sacrifices from us. And it's not very sympathetic to spoil everybody's enjoyment as you're doing now."

"I don't understand," said Laura, and she walked quickly out of the room into her own bedroom. There, quite by chance, the first thing she saw was this charming girl in the mirror, in her black hat trimmed with gold daisies and a long black velvet ribbon. Never had she imagined she could look like that. Is mother right? she thought. And now she hoped her mother was right. Am I being extravagant? Perhaps it was extravagant. Just for a moment she had another glimpse of that poor woman and those little children and the body being carried into the house. But it all seemed blurred, unreal, like a picture in the newspaper. I'll remember it again after the party's over, she decided. And somehow that seemed quite the best plan. . . .

Lunch was over by half-past one. By half-past two they were all ready for the fray. The green-coated band had arrived and was established in a corner of the tennis-court.

"My dear!" trilled Kitty Maitland, "aren't they too like frogs for words? You ought to have arranged them round the pond with the conductor in the middle on a leaf."

Laurie arrived and hailed them on his way to dress. At the sight of him Laura remembered the accident again. She wanted to tell him. If Laurie agreed with the others, then it was bound to be all right. And she followed him into the hall.

"Laurie!"

"Hallo!" He was half-way upstairs, but when he turned round and saw Laura he suddenly puffed out his cheeks and goggled his eyes at her. "My word, Laura! You do look stunning," said Laurie. "What an absolutely topping hat!"

Laura said faintly, "Is it?" and smiled up at Laurie and didn't tell him after all.

Soon after that people began coming in streams. The band struck up; the hired waiters ran from the house to the marquee. Wherever you looked there were couples strolling, bending to the flowers, greeting, moving on over the lawn. They were like bright birds that had alighted in the Sheridans' garden for this one afternoon, on their way to—where? Ah, what happiness it is to be with people who all are happy, to press hands, press cheeks, smile into eyes.

"Darling Laura, how well you look!"

"What a becoming hat, child!"

"Laura, you look quite Spanish. I've never seen you look so striking."

And Laura, glowing, answered softly, "Have you had tea? Won't you have an ice? The passion-fruit ices really are rather special." She ran to her father and begged him: "Daddy darling, can't the band have something to drink?"

And the perfect afternoon slowly ripened, slowly faded, slowly its petals closed.

"Never a more delightful garden-party . . ." "The greatest success . . ." "Quite the most . . ."

Laura helped her mother with the good-byes. They stood side by side in the porch till it was all over.

"All over, all over, thank heaven," said Mrs. Sheridan. "Round up the others, Laura. Let's go and have some fresh coffee. I'm exhausted. Yes, it's been very successful. But oh, these parties, these parties! Why will you children insist on giving parties!" And they all of them sat down in the deserted marquee.

"Have a sandwich, daddy dear. I wrote the flag."

"Thanks." Mr. Sheridan took a bite and the sandwich was gone. He took another. "I suppose you didn't hear of a beastly accident that happened to-day?" he said.

"My dear," said Mrs. Sheridan, holding up her hand, "we did. It nearly ruined the party. Laura insisted we should put if off."

"Oh, mother!" Laura didn't want to be teased about it.

"It was a horrible affair all the same," said Mr. Sheridan. "The chap was married too. Lived just below in the lane, and leaves a wife and half a dozen kiddies, so they say."

An awkward little silence fell. Mrs. Sheridan fidgeted with her cup. Really, it was very tactless of father. . . .

Suddenly she looked up. There on the table were all those sandwiches, cakes, puffs, all uneaten, all going to be wasted. She had one of her brilliant ideas.

"I know," she said. "Let's make up a basket. Let's send that poor creature some of this perfectly good food. At any rate, it will be the greatest treat for the children. Don't you agree? And she's sure to have neighbours calling in and so on. What a point to have it all ready prepared. Laura!" She jumped up. "Get me the big basket out of the stairs cupboard."

"But, mother, do you really think it's a good idea?" said Laura.

Again, how curious, she seemed to be different from them all. To take scraps from their party. Would the poor woman really like that?

"Of course! What's the matter with you to-day? An hour or two ago you were insisting on us being sympathetic."

Oh well! Laura ran for the basket. It was filled, it was now heaped by her mother.

"Take it yourself, darling," said she. "Run down just as you are. No, wait, take the arum lilies too. People of that class are so impressed by arum lilies."

"The stems will ruin her lace frock," said practical Jose.

So they would. Just in time. "Only the basket, then. And, Laura!"—her mother followed her out of the marquee—"don't on any account—"

"What, mother?"

No, better not put such ideas into the child's head! "Nothing! Run along."

It was just growing dusky as Laura shut their garden gates. A big dog ran by like a shadow. The road gleamed white, and down below in the hollow the little cottages were in deep shade. How quiet it seemed after the afternoon. Here she was going down the hill to somewhere where a man lay dead, and she couldn't realise it. Why couldn't she? She stopped a minute. And it seemed to her that kisses, voices, tinkling spoons, laughter, the smell of crushed grass were somehow inside her. She had no room for anything else. How strange! She looked up at the pale sky, and all she thought was, "Yes, it was the most successful party."

Now the broad road was crossed. The lane began, smoky and dark. Women in shawls and men's tweed caps hurried by. Men hung over the palings; the children played in the doorways. A low hum came from the mean little cottages. In some of them there was a flicker of light, and a shadow, crab-like, moved across the window. Laura bent her head and hurried on. She wished now she had put on a coat. How her frock shone! And the big hat with the velvet streamer—if only it was another hat! Were the people looking at her? They must be. It was a mistake to have come; she knew all along it was a mistake. Should she go back even now?

No, too late. This was the house. It must be. A dark knot of people stood outside. Beside the gate an old, old woman with a crutch sat in a chair, watching. She had her feet on a newspaper. The voices stopped as Laura drew near. The group parted. It was as though she was expected, as though they had known she was coming here.

Laura was terribly nervous. Tossing the velvet ribbon over her shoulder, she said to a woman standing by, "Is this Mrs. Scott's house?" and the woman, smiling queerly, said, "It is, my lass."

Oh, to be away from this! She actually said, "Help me, God," as she walked up the tiny path and knocked. To be away from those staring eyes, or to be covered up in anything, one of those women's shawls even. I'll just leave the basket and go, she decided. I shan't even wait for it to be emptied.

Then the door opened. A little woman in black showed in the gloom.

Laura said, "Are you Mrs. Scott?" But to her horror the woman answered, "Walk in, please, miss," and she was shut in the passage.

"No," said Laura, "I don't want to come in. I only want to leave this basket. Mother sent—"

The little woman in the gloomy passage seemed not to have heard her. "Step this way, please, miss," she said in an oily voice, and Laura followed her.

She found herself in a wretched little low kitchen, lighted by a smoky lamp. There was a woman sitting before the fire.

"Em," said the little creature who had let her in. "Em! It's a young lady." She turned to Laura. She said meaningly, "I'm 'er sister, miss. You'll excuse 'er, won't you?"

"Oh, but of course!" said Laura. "Please, please don't disturb her. I—I only want to leave—"

But at that moment the woman at the fire turned around. Her face, puffed up, red, with swollen eyes and swollen lips, looked terrible. She seemed as though she couldn't understand why Laura was there. What did it mean? Why was this stranger standing in the kitchen with a basket? What was it all about? And the poor face puckered up again.

"All right, my dear," said the other. "I'll thenk the young lady."

And again she began, "You'll excuse her, miss, I'm sure," and her face, swollen too, tried an oily smile.

Laura only wanted to get out, to get away. She was back in the passage. The door opened. She walked straight through into the bedroom, where the dead man was lying.

"You'd like a look at 'im, wouldn't you?" said Em's sister, and she brushed past Laura over to the bed. "Don't be afraid, my lass"—and now her voice sounded fond and sly, and fondly she drew down the sheet—"'e looks a picture. There's nothing to show. Come along, my dear."

Laura came.

There lay a young man, fast asleep—sleeping so soundly, so deeply, that he was far, far away from them both. Oh, so remote, so peaceful. He was dreaming. Never wake him up again. His head was sunk in the pillow, his eyes were closed; they were blind under the closed eyelids. He was given up to his dream. What did garden-parties and baskets and lace frocks matter to him? He was far from all those things. He was wonderful, beautiful. While they were laughing and while the band was playing, this marvel had come to the lane. Happy . . . happy. . . . All is well, said that sleeping face. This is just as it should be. I am content.

But all the same you had to cry, and she couldn't go out of the room without saying something to him. Laura gave a loud childish sob.

"Forgive my hat," she said.

And this time she didn't wait for Em's sister. She found her way out of the door, down the path past all those dark people. At the corner of the lane she met Laurie.

He stepped out of the shadow. "Is that you, Laura?"

"Yes."

"Mother was getting anxious. Was it all right?"

"Yes, quite, Oh, Laurie!" She took his arm, she pressed up against him.

"I say, you're not crying, are you?" asked her brother.

Laura shook her head. She was.

Laurie put his arm round her shoulder. "Don't cry," he said in his warm, loving voice. "Was it awful?"

"No," sobbed Laura. "It was simply marvellous. But, Laurie—" She stopped, she looked at her brother. "Isn't life," she stammered, "isn't life —" But what life was she couldn't explain. No matter. He quite understood.

"*Isn't* it, darling?" said Laurie.

D. H. LAWRENCE

The Horse Dealer's Daughter

"Well, Mabel, and what are you going to do with yourself?" asked Joe, with foolish flippancy. He felt quite safe himself. Without listening for an answer, he turned aside, worked a grain of tobacco to the tip of his tongue, and spat it out. He did not care about anything, since he felt safe himself.

The three brothers and the sister sat round the desolate breakfast-table, attempting some sort of desultory consultation. The morning's post had given the final tap to the family fortunes, and all was over. The dreary dining-room itself, with its heavy mahogany furniture, looked as if it were waiting to be done away with.

But the consultation amounted to nothing. There was a strange air of ineffectuality about the three men, as they sprawled at table, smoking and reflecting vaguely on their own condition. The girl was alone, a rather short, sullen-looking young woman of twenty-seven. She did not share the same life as her brothers. She would have been good-looking, save for the impressive fixity of her face, 'bull-dog', as her brothers called it.

There was a confused tramping of horses' feet outside. The three men all sprawled round in their chairs to watch. Beyond the dark holly bushes that separated the strip of lawn from the high-road, they could see a cavalcade of shire horses swinging out of their own yard, being taken for exercise. This was the last time. These were the last horses that would go through their hands. The young men watched with critical, callous look. They were all frightened at the collapse of their lives, and the sense of disaster in which they were involved left them no inner freedom.

Yet they were three fine, well-set fellows enough. Joe, the eldest, was a man of thirty-three, broad and handsome in a hot, flushed way. His face was red, he twisted his black moustache over a thick finger, his eyes were shallow and restless. He had a sensual way of uncovering his teeth when he laughed, and his bearing was stupid. Now he watched the horses with a glazed look of helplessness in his eyes, a certain stupor of downfall.

The great draught-horses swung past. They were tied head to tail, four of them, and they heaved along to where a lane branched off from the high-road, planting their great hoofs floutingly in the fine black mud, swinging their great rounded haunches sumptuously, and trotting a few sudden steps as they were led into the lane, round the corner. Every movement showed a massive, slumbrous strength, and a stupidity which held them in subjection. The groom at the head looked back, jerking the leading rope. And the cavalcade moved out of sight up the lane, the tail of the last horse, bobbed up tight and stiff, held out taut from the swinging great haunches as they rocked behind the hedges in a motion like sleep.

Joe watched with glazed hopeless eyes. The horses were almost like his own body to him. He felt he was done for now. Luckily he was engaged to a woman as old as himself, and therefore her father, who was steward of a neighbouring estate, would provide him with a job. He would marry and go into harness. His life was over, he would be a subject animal now.

He turned uneasily aside, the retreating steps of the horses echoing in his ears. Then, with foolish restlessness, he reached for the scraps of bacon-rind from the plates, and making a faint whistling sound, flung them to the terrier that lay against the fender. He watched the dog swallow them, and waited till the creature looked into his eyes. Then a faint grin came on his face, and in a high, foolish voice he said:

"You won't get much more bacon, shall you, you little b———?"

The dog faintly and dismally wagged its tail, then lowered its haunches, circled round, and lay down again.

There was another helpless silence at the table. Joe sprawled uneasily in his seat, not willing to go till the family conclave was dissolved. Fred Henry, the second brother, was erect, clean-limbed, alert. He had watched the passing of the horses with more *sang-froid*.[1] If he was an animal, like Joe, he was an animal which controls, not one which is controlled. He was master of any horse, and he carried himself with a well-tempered air of mastery. But he was not master of the situations of life. He pushed his coarse brown moustache upwards, off his lip, and glanced irritably at his sister, who sat impassive and inscrutable.

"You'll go and stop with Lucy for a bit, shan't you?" he asked. The girl did not answer.

"I don't see what else you can do," persisted Fred Henry.

"Go as a skivvy," Joe interpolated laconically.

The girl did not move a muscle.

"If I was her, I should go in for training for a nurse," said Malcolm, the youngest of them all. He was the baby of the family, a young man of twenty-two, with a fresh, jaunty *museau*.[2]

But Mabel did not take any notice of him. They had talked at her and round her for so many years, that she hardly heard them at all.

The marble clock on the mantelpiece softly chimed the half-hour, the dog rose uneasily from the hearth-rug and looked at the party at the breakfast-table. But still they sat on in ineffectual conclave.

"Oh, all right," said Joe suddenly, apropos of nothing. "I'll get a move on."

He pushed back his chair, straddled his knees with a downward jerk, to get them free, in horsey fashion, and went to the fire. Still he did not go out of the room; he was curious to know what the others would do or say. He began to charge his pipe, looking down at the dog and saying in a high, affected voice:

"Going wi' me? Going wi' me are ter? Tha'rt goin' further than tha counts on just now, dost hear?"

The dog faintly wagged its tail, the man stuck out his jaw and covered his pipe with his hands, and puffed intently, losing himself in the tobacco, looking down all the while at the dog with an absent brown eye. The dog looked up at him in mournful distrust. Joe stood with his knees stuck out, in real horsey fashion.

"Have you had a letter from Lucy?" Fred Henry asked of his sister.

"Last week," came the neutral reply.

"And what does she say?"

1. Nonchalance.
2. Face, mug.

There was no answer.

"Does she *ask* you to go and stop there?" persisted Fred Henry.

"She says I can if I like."

"Well, then, you'd better. Tell her you'll come on Monday."

This was received in silence.

"That's what you'll do then, is it?" said Fred Henry, in some exasperation.

But she made no answer. There was a silence of futility and irritation in the room. Malcolm grinned fatuously.

"You'll have to make up your mind between now and next Wednesday," said Joe loudly, "or else find yourself lodgings on the kerbstone."

The face of the young woman darkened, but she sat on immutable.

"Here's Jack Fergusson!" exclaimed Malcolm, who was looking aimlessly out of the window.

"Where?" exclaimed Joe loudly.

"Just gone past."

"Coming in?"

Malcolm craned his neck to see the gate.

"Yes," he said.

There was a silence. Mabel sat on like one condemned, at the head of the table. Then a whistle was heard from the kitchen. The dog got up and barked sharply. Joe opened the door and shouted:

"Come on."

After a moment a young man entered. He was muffled up in overcoat and a purple woollen scarf, and his tweed cap, which he did not remove, was pulled down on his head. He was of medium height, his face was rather long and pale, his eyes looked tired.

"Hello, Jack! Well, Jack!" exclaimed Malcolm and Joe. Fred Henry merely said: "Jack."

"What's doing?" asked the newcomer, evidently addressing Fred Henry.

"Same. We've got to be out by Wednesday. Got a cold?"

"I have—got it bad, too."

"Why don't you stop in?"

"*Me* stop in? When I can't stand on my legs, perhaps I shall have a chance." The young man spoke huskily. He had a slight Scotch accent.

"It's a knock-out, isn't it," said Joe, boisterously, "if a doctor goes round croaking with a cold. Looks bad for the patients, doesn't it?"

The young doctor looked at him slowly.

"Anything the matter with *you*, then?" he asked sarcastically.

"Not as I know of. Damn your eyes, I hope not. Why?"

"I thought you were very concerned about the patients, wondered if you might be one yourself."

"Damn it, no, I've never been patient to no flaming doctor, and hope I never shall be," returned Joe.

At this point Mabel rose from the table, and they all seemed to become aware of her existence. She began putting the dishes together. The young doctor looked at her, but did not address her. He had not greeted her. She went out of the room with the tray, her face impassive and unchanged.

"When are you off then, all of you?" asked the doctor.

"I'm catching the eleven-forty," replied Malcolm. "Are you goin' down wi' th' trap, Joe?"

"Yes, I've told you I'm going down wi' th' trap, haven't I?"

"We'd better be getting her in then. So long, Jack, if I don't see you before I go," said Malcolm, shaking hands.

He went out, followed by Joe, who seemed to have his tail between his legs.

"Well, this is the devil's own," exclaimed the doctor, when he was left alone with Fred Henry. "Going before Wednesday, are you?"

"That's the orders," replied the other.

"Where, to Northampton?"

"That's it."

"The devil!" exclaimed Fergusson, with quiet chagrin.

And there was silence between the two.

"And settled up, are you?" asked Fergusson.

"About."

There was another pause.

"Well, I shall miss yer, Freddy, boy," said the young doctor.

"And I shall miss thee, Jack," returned the other.

"Miss you like hell," mused the doctor.

Fred Henry turned aside. There was nothing to say. Mabel came in again, to finish clearing the table.

"What are *you* going to do, then, Miss Pervin?" asked Fergusson. "Going to your sister's, are you?"

Mabel looked at him with her steady, dangerous eyes, that always made him uncomfortable, unsettling his superficial ease.

"No," she said.

"Well, what in the name of fortune *are* you going to do? Say what you mean to do," cried Fred Henry, with futile intensity.

But she only averted her head, and continued her work. She folded the white table-cloth, and put on the chenille cloth.

"The sulkiest bitch that ever trod!" muttered her brother.

But she finished her task with perfectly impassive face, the young doctor watching her interestedly all the while. Then she went out.

Fred Henry stared after her, clenching his lips, his blue eyes fixing in sharp antagonism, as he made a grimace of sour exasperation.

"You could bray her into bits, and that's all you'd get out of her," he said, in a small, narrowed tone.

The doctor smiled faintly.

"What's she *going* to do, then?" he asked.

"Strike me if *I* know!" returned the other.

There was a pause. Then the doctor stirred.

"I'll be seeing you to-night, shall I?" he said to his friend.

"Ay—where's it to be? Are we going over to Jessdale?"

"I don't know. I've got such a cold on me. I'll come round to the 'Moon and Stars', anyway."

"Let Lizzie and May miss their night for once, eh?"

"That's it—if I feel as I do now."

"All's one—"

The two young men went through the passage and down to the back door together. The house was large, but it was servantless now, and desolate. At the back was a small bricked house-yard and beyond that a big square, gravelled fine and red, and having stables on two sides. Sloping, dank, winter-dark fields stretched away on the open sides.

But the stables were empty. Joseph Pervin, the father of the family, had been a man of no education, who had become a fairly large horse dealer. The stables had been full of horses, there was a great turmoil and come-and-go of horses and of dealers and grooms. Then the kitchen was full of servants. But of late things had declined. The old man had married a second time, to retrieve his fortunes. Now he was dead and everything was gone to the dogs, there was nothing but debt and threatening.

For months, Mabel had been servantless in the big house, keeping the home together in penury for her ineffectual brothers. She had kept house for ten years. But previously it was with unstinted means. Then, however brutal and coarse everything was, the sense of money had kept her proud, confident. The men might be foul-mouthed, the women in the kitchen might have bad reputations, her brothers might have illegitimate children. But so long as there was money, the girl felt herself established, and brutally proud, reserved.

No company came to the house, save dealers and coarse men. Mabel had no associates of her own sex, after her sister went away. But she did not mind. She went regularly to church, she attended to her father. And she lived in the memory of her mother, who had died when she was fourteen, and whom she had loved. She had loved her father, too, in a different way, depending upon him, and feeling secure in him, until at the age of fifty-four he married again. And then she had set hard against him. Now he had died and left them all hopelessly in debt.

She had suffered badly during the period of poverty. Nothing, however, could shake the curious, sullen, animal pride that dominated each member of the family. Now, for Mabel, the end had come. Still she would not cast about her. She would follow her own way just the same. She would always hold the keys of her own situation. Mindless and persistent, she endured from day to day. Why should she think? Why should she answer anybody? It was enough that this was the end, and there was no way out. She need not pass any more darkly along the main street of the small town, avoiding every eye. She need not demean herself any more, going into the shops and buying the cheapest food. This was at an end. She thought of nobody, not even of herself. Mindless and persistent, she seemed in a sort of ecstasy to be coming nearer to her fulfilment, her own glorification, approaching her dead mother, who was glorified.

In the afternoon she took a little bag, with shears and sponge and a small scrubbing-brush, and went out. It was a grey, wintry day, with saddened, dark green fields and an atmosphere blackened by the smoke of foundries not far off. She went quickly, darkly along the causeway, heeding nobody, through the town to the churchyard.

There she always felt secure, as if no one could see her, although as a matter of fact she was exposed to the stare of everyone who passed along under the churchyard wall. Nevertheless, once under the shadow of the great looming church, among the graves, she felt immune from the world, reserved within the thick churchyard wall as in another country.

Carefully she clipped the grass from the grave, and arranged the pinky white, small chrysanthemums in the tin cross. When this was done, she took an empty jar from a neighbouring grave, brought water, and carefully, most scrupulously sponged the marble headstone and the coping-stone.

It gave her sincere satisfaction to do this. She felt in immediate contact with the world of her mother. She took minute pains, went through the park in a state bordering on pure happiness, as if in performing this task she came into a subtle, intimate connection with her mother. For the life she followed here in the world was far less real than the world of death she inherited from her mother.

The doctor's house was just by the church. Fergusson, being a mere hired assistant, was slave to the country-side. As he hurried now to attend to the out-patients in the surgery, glancing across the graveyard with his quick eye, he saw the girl at her task at the grave. She seemed so intent and remote, it was like looking into another world. Some mystical element was touched in him. He slowed down as he walked, watching her as if spellbound.

She lifted her eyes, feeling him looking. Their eyes met. And each looked again at once, each feeling, in some way, found out by the other. He lifted his cap and passed on down the road. There remained distinct in his consciousness, like a vision, the memory of her face, lifted from the tombstone in the churchyard, and looking at him with slow, large, portentous eyes. It *was* portentous, her face. It seemed to mesmerise him. There was a heavy power in her eyes which laid hold of his whole being, as if he had drunk some powerful drug. He had been feeling weak and done before. Now the life came back into him, he felt delivered from his own fretted, daily self.

He finished his duties at the surgery as quickly as might be, hastily filling up the bottles of the waiting people with cheap drugs. Then, in perpetual haste, he set off again to visit several cases in another part of his round, before tea-time. At all times he preferred to walk if he could, but particularly when he was not well. He fancied the motion restored him.

The afternoon was falling. It was grey, deadened, and wintry, with a slow, moist, heavy coldness sinking in and deadening all the faculties. But why should he think or notice? He hastily climbed the hill and turned across the dark green fields, following the black cinder-track. In the distance, across a shallow dip in the country, the small town was clustered like smouldering ash, a tower, a spire, a heap of low, raw, extinct houses. And on the nearest fringe of the town, sloping into the dip, was Oldmeadow, the Pervins' house. He could see the stables and the outbuildings distinctly, as they lay towards him on the slope. Well, he would not go there many more times! Another resource would be lost to him, another place gone: the only company he cared for in the alien, ugly little town he was losing. Nothing but work, drudgery, constant hastening from dwelling to dwelling among the colliers and the iron-workers. It wore him out, but at the same time he had a craving for it. It was a stimulant to him to be in the homes of the working people, moving, as it were, through the innermost body of their life. His nerves were excited and gratified. He could come so near, into the very lives of the rough, inarticulate, powerfully emotional men and women. He grumbled, he said he hated the hellish hole. But as a matter of fact it excited him, the contact with the rough, strongly-feeling people was a stimulant applied direct to his nerves.

Below Oldmeadow, in the green, shallow, soddened hollow of fields, lay a square, deep pond. Roving across the landscape, the doctor's quick eye detected a figure in black passing through the gate of the field, down towards the pond. He looked again. It would be Mabel Pervin. His mind suddenly became alive and attentive.

Why was she going down there? He pulled up on the path on the slope above, and stood staring. He could just make sure of the small black figure moving in the hollow of the failing day. He seemed to see her in the midst of such obscurity, that he was like a clairvoyant, seeing rather with the mind's eye than with ordinary sight. Yet he could see her positively enough, whilst he kept his eye attentive. He felt, if he looked away from her, in the thick, ugly falling dusk, he would lose her altogether.

He followed her minutely as she moved, direct and intent, like something transmitted rather than stirring in voluntary activity, straight down the field towards the pond. There she stood on the bank for a moment. She never raised her head. Then she waded slowly into the water.

He stood motionless as the small black figure walked slowly and deliberately towards the centre of the pond, very slowly, gradually moving deeper into the motionless water, and still moving forward as the water got up to her breast. Then he could see her no more in the dusk of the dead afternoon.

"There!" he exclaimed. "Would you believe it?"

And he hastened straight down, running over the wet, soddened fields, pushing through the hedges, down into the depression of callous wintry obscurity. It took him several minutes to come to the pond. He stood on the bank, breathing heavily. He could see nothing. His eyes seemed to penetrate the dead water. Yes, perhaps that was the dark shadow of her black clothing beneath the surface of the water.

He slowly ventured into the pond. The bottom was deep, soft clay, he sank in, and the water clasped dead cold round his legs. As he stirred he could smell the cold, rotten clay that fouled up into the water. It was objectionable in his lungs. Still, repelled and yet not heeding, he moved deeper into the pond. The cold water rose over his thighs, over his loins, upon his abdomen. The lower part of his body was all sunk in the hideous cold element. And the bottom was so deeply soft and uncertain, he was afraid of pitching with his mouth underneath. He could not swim, and was afraid.

He crouched a little, spreading his hands under the water and moving them round, trying to feel for her. The dead cold pond swayed upon his chest. He moved again, a little deeper, and again, with his hands underneath, he felt all around under the water. And he touched her clothing. But it evaded his fingers. He made a desperate effort to grasp it.

And so doing he lost his balance and went under, horribly, suffocating in the foul earthy water, struggling madly for a few moments. At last, after what seemed an eternity, he got his footing, rose again into the air and looked around. He gasped, and knew he was in the world. Then he looked at the water. She had risen near him. He grasped her clothing, and drawing her nearer, turned to take his way to land again.

He went very slowly, carefully, absorbed in the slow progress. He rose higher, climbing out of the pond. The water was now only about his legs; he was thankful, full of relief to be out of the clutches of the pond. He lifted her and staggered on to the bank, out of the horror of wet, grey clay.

He laid her down on the bank. She was quite unconscious and running with water. He made the water come from her mouth, he worked to restore her. He did not have to work very long before he could feel the breathing begin again in her; she was breathing naturally. He worked a little longer. He could feel her live beneath his hands; she was coming back. He wiped her face, wrapped her in his overcoat, looked round into the dim, dark grey world, then lifted her and staggered down the bank and across the fields.

It seemed an unthinkably long way, and his burden so heavy he felt he would never get to the house. But at last he was in the stable-yard, and then in the house-yard. He opened the door and went into the house. In the kitchen he laid her down on the hearth-rug and called. The house was empty. But the fire was burning in the grate.

Then again he kneeled to attend to her. She was breathing regularly, her eyes were wide open and as if conscious, but there seemed something missing in her look. She was conscious in herself, but unconscious of her surroundings.

He ran upstairs, took blankets from a bed, and put them before the fire to warm. Then he removed her saturated, earthy-smelling clothing, rubbed her dry with a towel, and wrapped her naked in the blankets. Then he went into the dining-room, to look for spirits. There was a little whisky. He drank a gulp himself, and put some into her mouth.

The effect was instantaneous. She looked full into his face, as if she had been seeing him for some time, and yet had only just become conscious of him.

"Dr. Fergusson?" she said.

"What?" he answered.

He was divesting himself of his coat, intending to find some dry clothing upstairs. He could not bear the smell of the dead, clayey water, and he was mortally afraid for his own health.

"What did I do?" she asked.

"Walked into the pond," he replied. He had begun to shudder like one sick, and could hardly attend to her. Her eyes remained full on him, he seemed to be going dark in his mind, looking back at her helplessly. The shuddering became quieter in him, his life came back to him, dark and unknowing, but strong again.

"Was I out of my mind?" she asked, while her eyes were fixed on him all the time.

"Maybe, for the moment," he replied. He felt quiet, because his strength had come back. The strange fretful strain had left him.

"Am I out of my mind now?" she asked.

"Are you?" he reflected a moment. "No," he answered truthfully, "I don't see that you are." He turned his face aside. He was afraid now, because he felt dazed, and felt dimly that her power was stronger than his, in this issue. And she continued to look at him fixedly all the time. "Can you tell me where I shall find some dry things to put on?" he asked.

"Did you dive into the pond for me?" she asked.

"No," he answered. "I walked in. But I went in overhead as well."

There was silence for a moment. He hesitated. He very much wanted to go upstairs to get into dry clothing. But there was another desire in him. And she seemed to hold him. His will seemed to have gone to sleep, and left him, standing there slack before her. But he felt warm inside himself. He did not shudder at all, though his clothes were sodden on him.

"Why did you?" she asked.

"Because I didn't want you to do such a foolish thing," he said.

"It wasn't foolish," she said, still gazing at him as she lay on the floor, with a sofa cushion under her head. "It was the right thing to do. *I* knew best, then."

"I'll go and shift these wet things," he said. But still he had not the power to move out of her presence, until she sent him. It was as if she had the life of his body in her hands, and he could not extricate himself. Or perhaps he did not want to.

Suddenly she sat up. Then she became aware of her own immediate condition. She felt the blankets about her, she knew her own limbs. For a moment it seemed as if her reason were going. She looked round, with wild eye, as if seeking something. He stood still with fear. She saw her clothing lying scattered.

"Who undressed me?" she asked, her eyes resting full and inevitable on his face.

"I did," he replied, "to bring you round."

For some moments she sat and gazed at him awfully, her lips parted.

"Do you love me, then?" she asked.

He only stood and stared at her, fascinated. His soul seemed to melt.

She shuffled forward on her knees, and put her arms round him, round his legs, as he stood there, pressing her breasts against his knees and thighs, clutching him with strange, convulsive certainty, pressing his thighs against her, drawing him to her face, her throat, as she looked up at him with flaring, humble eyes of transfiguration, triumphant in first possession.

"You love me," she murmured, in strange transport, yearning and triumphant and confident. "You love me. I know you love me, I know."

And she was passionately kissing his knees, through the wet clothing, passionately and indiscriminately kissing his knees, his legs, as if unaware of everything.

He looked down at the tangled wet hair, the wild, bare, animal shoulders. He was amazed, bewildered, and afraid. He had never thought of loving her. He had never wanted to love her. When he rescued and restored her, he was a doctor, and she was a patient. He had had no single personal thought of her. Nay, this introduction of the personal element was very distasteful to him, a violation of his professional honour. It was horrible to have her there embracing his knees. It was horrible. He revolted from it, violently. And yet—and yet—he had not the power to break away.

She looked at him again, with the same supplication of powerful love, and that same transcendent, frightening light of triumph. In view of the delicate flame which seemed to come from her face like a light, he was powerless. And yet he had never intended to love her. He had never intended. And something stubborn in him could not give way.

"You love me," she repeated, in a murmur of deep, rhapsodic assurance. "You love me."

Her hands were drawing him, drawing him down to her. He was afraid, even a little horrified. For he had, really, no intention of loving her. Yet her hands were drawing him towards her. He put out his hand quickly to steady himself, and grasped her bare shoulder. A flame seemed to burn the hand that grasped her soft shoulder. He had no intention of loving her: his whole will was against his yielding. It was horrible. And yet wonderful was the touch of her shoulders, beautiful the shining of her face. Was she perhaps mad? He had a horror of yielding to her. Yet something in him ached also.

He had been staring away at the door, away from her. But his hand remained on her shoulder. She had gone suddenly very still. He looked down at her. Her eyes were now wide with fear, with doubt, the light was dying from her face, a shadow of terrible greyness was returning. He could not bear the touch of her eyes' question upon him, and the look of death behind the question.

With an inward groan he gave way, and let his heart yield towards her. A sudden gentle smile came on his face. And her eyes, which never left his face, slowly, slowly filled with tears. He watched the strange water rise in her eyes, like some slow fountain coming up. And his heart seemed to burn and melt away in his breast.

He could not bear to look at her any more. He dropped on his knees and caught her head with his arms and pressed her face against his throat. She was very still. His heart, which seemed to have broken, was burning with a kind of agony in his breast. And he felt her slow, hot tears wetting his throat. But he could not move.

He felt the hot tears wet his neck and the hollows of his neck, and he remained motionless, suspended through one of man's eternities. Only now it had become indispensable to him to have her face pressed close to him; he could never let her go again. He could never let her head go away from the close clutch of his arm. He wanted to remain like that for ever, with his heart hurting him in a pain that was also life to him. Without knowing, he was looking down on her damp, soft brown hair.

Then, as it were suddenly, he smelt the horrid stagnant smell of that water. And at the same moment she drew away from him and looked at him. Her eyes were wistful and unfathomable. He was afraid of them, and he fell to kissing her, not knowing what he was doing. He wanted her eyes not to have that terrible, wistful, unfathomable look.

When she turned her face to him again, a faint delicate flush was glowing, and there was again dawning that terrible shining of joy in her eyes, which really terrified him, and yet which he now wanted to see, because he feared the look of doubt still more.

"You love me?" she said, rather faltering.

"Yes." The word cost him a painful effort. Not because it wasn't true. But because it was too newly true, the *saying* seemed to tear open again his newly-torn heart. And he hardly wanted it to be true, even now.

She lifted her face to him, and he bent forward and kissed her on the mouth, gently, with the one kiss that is an eternal pledge. And as he kissed her his heart strained again in his breast. He never intended to love her. But now it was over. He had crossed over the gulf to her, and all that he had left behind had shrivelled and become void.

After the kiss, her eyes again slowly filled with tears. She sat still, away from him, with her face drooped aside, and her hands folded in her lap. The tears fell very slowly. There was complete silence. He too sat there motionless and silent on the hearth-rug. The strange pain of his heart that was broken seemed to consume him. That he should love her? That this was love! That he should be ripped open in this way! Him, a doctor! How they would all jeer if they knew! It was agony to him to think they might know.

In the curious naked pain of the thought he looked again to her. She was sitting there drooped into a muse. He saw a tear fall, and his heart flared hot. He saw for the first time that one of her shoulders was quite uncovered, one arm bare, he could see one of her small breasts; dimly, because it had become almost dark in the room.

"Why are you crying?" he asked, in an altered voice.

She looked up at him, and behind her tears the consciousness of her situation for the first time brought a dark look of shame to her eyes.

"I'm not crying, really," she said, watching him, half frightened.

He reached his hand, and softly closed it on her bare arm.

"I love you! I love you!" he said in a soft, low vibrating voice, unlike himself.

She shrank, and dropped her head. The soft, penetrating grip of his hand on her arm distressed her. She looked up at him.

"I want to go," she said. "I want to go and get you some dry things."

"Why?" he said. "I'm all right."

"But I want to go," she said. "And I want you to change your things."

He released her arm, and she wrapped herself in the blanket, looking at him rather frightened. And still she did not rise.

"Kiss me," she said wistfully.

He kissed her, but briefly, half in anger.

Then, after a second, she rose nervously, all mixed up in the blanket. He watched her in her confusion as she tried to extricate herself and wrap herself up so that she could walk. He watched her relentlessly, as she knew. And as she went, the blanket trailing, and as he saw a glimpse of her feet and her white leg, he tried to remember her as she was when he had wrapped her in the blanket. But then he didn't want to remember, because she had been nothing to him then, and his nature revolted from remembering her as she was when she was nothing to him.

A tumbling, muffled noise from within the dark house startled him. Then he heard her voice: "There are clothes." He rose and went to the foot of the stairs, and gathered up the garments she had thrown down. Then he came back to the fire, to rub himself down and dress. He grinned at his own appearance when he had finished.

The fire was sinking, so he put on coal. The house was now quite dark, save for the light of a street-lamp that shone in faintly from beyond the holly trees. He lit the gas with matches he found on the mantelpiece. Then he emptied the pockets of his own clothes, and threw all his wet things in a heap into the scullery. After which he gathered up her sodden clothes, gently, and put them in a separate heap on the copper-top in the scullery.

It was six o'clock on the clock. His own watch had stopped. He ought to go back to the surgery. He waited, and still she did not come down. So he went to the foot of the stairs and called:

"I shall have to go."

Almost immediately he heard her coming down. She had on her best dress of black voile, and her hair was tidy, but still damp. She looked at him —and in spite of herself, smiled.

"I don't like you in those clothes," she said.

"Do I look a sight?" he answered.

They were shy of one another.

"I'll make you some tea," she said.

"No, I must go."

"Must you?" And she looked at him again with the wide, strained, doubtful eyes. And again, from the pain of his breast, he knew how he loved her. He went and bent to kiss her, gently, passionately, with his heart's painful kiss.

"And my hair smells so horrible," she murmured in distraction. "And I'm so awful, I'm so awful! Oh no, I'm too awful." And she broke into bitter, heart-broken sobbing. "You can't want to love me, I'm horrible."

"Don't be silly, don't be silly," he said, trying to comfort her, kissing her, holding her in his arms. "I want you, I want to marry you, we're going to be married, quickly, quickly—to-morrow if I can."

But she only sobbed terribly, and cried:

"I feel awful. I feel awful. I feel I'm horrible to you."

"No, I want you, I want you," was all he answered, blindly, with that terrible intonation which frightened her almost more than her horror lest he should *not* want her.

ERNEST HEMINGWAY

Soldier's Home

Krebs went to the war from a Methodist college in Kansas. There is a picture which shows him among his fraternity brothers, all of them wearing exactly the same height and style collar. He enlisted in the Marines in 1917 and did not return to the United States until the second division returned from the Rhine in the summer of 1919.

There is a picture which shows him on the Rhine with two German girls and another corporal. Krebs and the corporal look too big for their uniforms. The German girls are not beautiful. The Rhine does not show in the picture. *[handwritten note: irony]*

By the time Krebs returned to his home town in Oklahoma the greeting of heroes was over. He came back much too late. The men from the town who had been drafted had all been welcomed elaborately on their return. There had been a great deal of hysteria. Now the reaction had set in. People seemed to think it was rather ridiculous for Krebs to be getting back so late, years after the war was over.

At first Krebs, who had been at Belleau Wood, Soissons, the Champagne, St. Mihiel and in the Argonne[1] did not want to talk about the war at all. Later he felt the need to talk but no one wanted to hear about it. His town had heard too many atrocity stories to be thrilled by actualities. Krebs found that to be listened to at all he had to lie, and after he had done this twice he, too, had a reaction against the war and against talking about it. A distaste for everything that had happened to him in the war set in because of the lies he had told. All of the times that had been able to make him feel cool and clear inside himself when he thought of them; the times so long back when he had done the one thing, the only thing for a man to do, easily and naturally, when he might have done something else, now lost their cool, valuable quality and then were lost themselves.

His lies were quite unimportant lies and consisted in attributing to himself things other men had seen, done or heard of, and stating as facts certain apocryphal incidents familiar to all soldiers. Even his lies were not sensational at the pool room. His acquaintances, who had heard detailed accounts of German women found chained to machine guns in the Argonne forest and who could not comprehend, or were barred by their patriotism from interest in, any German machine gunners who were not chained, were not thrilled by his stories.

Krebs acquired the nausea in regard to experience that is the result of untruth or exaggeration, and when he occasionally met another man who had really been a soldier and they talked a few minutes in the dressing room at a dance he fell into the easy pose of the old soldier among other

1. French battlefields during the First World War (1914–18). Belleau Wood, a forested area in northern France, was the scene of a victory over the Germans after hard fighting (6–25 June 1918) involving chiefly U.S. troops. It was dedicated in 1923 as a permanent memorial to the American war dead. St. Mihiel was recovered from the Germans in September 1918 in the first battle of the war in which American forces fought independently. In the Allied victory drive (September to November 1918), the Meuse-Argonne sector was carried by the Americans, who entered the war in 1917.

soldiers: that he had been badly, sickeningly frightened all the time. In this way he lost everything.

During this time, it was late summer, he was sleeping late in bed, getting up to walk down town to the library to get a book, eating lunch at home, reading on the front porch until he became bored and then walking down through the town to spend the hottest hours of the day in the cool dark of the pool room. He loved to play pool.

In the evening he practiced on his clarinet, strolled down town, read and went to bed. He was still a hero to his two young sisters. His mother would have given him breakfast in bed if he had wanted it. She often came in when he was in bed and asked him to tell her about the war, but her attention always wandered. His father was non-committal.

Before Krebs went away to the war he had never been allowed to drive the family motor car. His father was in the real estate business and always wanted the car to be at his command when he required it to take clients out into the country to show them a piece of farm property. The car always stood outside the First National Bank building where his father had an office on the second floor. Now, after the war, it was still the same car.

Nothing was changed in the town except that the young girls had grown up. But they lived in such a complicated world of already defined alliances and shifting feuds that Krebs did not feel the energy or the courage to break into it. He liked to look at them, though. There were so many good-looking young girls. Most of them had their hair cut short. When he went away only little girls wore their hair like that or girls that were fast. They all wore sweaters and shirt waists with round Dutch collars. It was a pattern. He liked to look at them from the front porch as they walked on the other side of the street. He liked to watch them walking under the shade of the trees. He liked the round Dutch collars above their sweaters. He liked their silk stockings and flat shoes. He liked their bobbed hair and the way they walked.

When he was in town their appeal to him was not very strong. He did not like them when he saw them in the Greek's ice cream parlor. He did not want them themselves really. They were too complicated. There was something else. Vaguely he wanted a girl but he did not want to have to work to get her. He would have liked to have a girl but he did not want to have to spend a long time getting her. He did not want to get into the intrigue and the politics. He did not want to have to do any courting. He did not want to tell any more lies. It wasn't worth it.

He did not want any consequences. He did not want any consequences ever again. He wanted to live along without consequences. Besides he did not really need a girl. The army had taught him that. It was all right to pose as though you had to have a girl. Nearly everybody did that. But it wasn't true. You did not need a girl. That was the funny thing. First a fellow boasted how girls mean nothing to him, that he never thought of them, that they could not touch him. Then a fellow boasted that he could not get along without girls, that he had to have them all the time, that he could not go to sleep without them.

That was all a lie. It was all a lie both ways. You did not need a girl unless you thought about them. He learned that in the army. Then sooner or later you always got one. When you were really ripe for a girl you always got one. You did not have to think about it. Sooner or later it would come. He had learned that in the army.

Now he would have liked a girl if she had come to him and not wanted to talk. But here at home it was all too complicated. He knew he could never get through it all again. It was not worth the trouble. That was the thing about French girls and German girls. There was not all this talking. You couldn't talk much and you did not need to talk. It was simple and you were friends. He thought about France and then he began to think about Germany. On the whole he had liked Germany better. He did not want to leave Germany. He did not want to come home. Still, he had come home. He sat on the front porch.

He liked the girls that were walking along the other side of the street. He liked the look of them much better than the French girls or the German girls. But the world they were in was not the world he was in. He would like to have one of them. But it was not worth it. They were such a nice pattern. He liked the pattern. It was exciting. But he would not go through all the talking. He did not want one badly enough. He liked to look at them all, though. It was not worth it. Not now when things were getting good again.

He sat there on the porch reading a book on the war. It was a history and he was reading about all the engagements he had been in. It was the most interesting reading he had ever done. He wished there were more maps. He looked forward with a good feeling to reading all the really good histories when they would come out with good detail maps. Now he was really learning about the war. He had been a good soldier. That made a difference.

One morning after he had been home about a month his mother came into his bedroom and sat on the bed. She smoothed her apron.

"I had a talk with your father last night, Harold," she said, "and he is willing for you to take the car out in the evenings."

"Yeah?" said Krebs, who was not fully awake. "Take the car out? Yeah?"

"Yes. Your father has felt for some time that you should be able to take the car out in the evenings whenever you wished but we only talked it over last night."

"I'll bet you made him," Krebs said.

"No. It was your father's suggestion that we talk the matter over."

"Yeah. I'll bet you made him," Krebs sat up in bed.

"Will you come down to breakfast, Harold?" his mother said.

"As soon as I get my clothes on," Krebs said.

His mother went out of the room and he could hear her frying something downstairs while he washed, shaved and dressed to go down into the dining-room for breakfast. While he was eating breakfast his sister brought in the mail.

"Well, Hare," she said. "You old sleepyhead. What do you ever get up for?"

Krebs looked at her. He liked her. She was his best sister.

"Have you got the paper?" he asked.

She handed him the Kansas City *Star* and he shucked off its brown wrapper and opened it to the sporting page. He folded the *Star* open and

propped it against the water pitcher with his cereal dish to steady it, so he
could read while he ate.

"Harold," his mother stood in the kitchen doorway, "Harold, please.
don't muss up the paper. Your father can't read his *Star* if it's been
mussed."

"I won't muss it," Krebs said.

His sister sat down at the table and watched him while he read.

"We're playing indoor over at school this afternoon," she said. "I'm
going to pitch."

"Good," said Krebs. "How's the old wing?"

"I can pitch better than lots of the boys. I tell them all you taught me.
The other girls aren't much good."

"Yeah?" said Krebs.

"I tell them all you're my beau. Aren't you my beau, Hare?"

"You bet."

"Couldn't your brother really be your beau just because he's your
brother?"

"I don't know."

"Sure you know. Couldn't you be my beau, Hare, if I was old enough
and if you wanted to?"

"Sure. You're my girl now."

"Am I really your girl?"

"Sure."

"Do you love me?"

"Uh, huh."

"Will you love me always?"

"Sure."

"Will you come over and watch me play indoor?"

"Maybe."

"Aw, Hare, you don't love me. If you loved me, you'd want to come
over and watch me play indoor."

Krebs' mother came into the dining-room from the kitchen. She carried a plate with two fried eggs and some crisp bacon on it and a plate of
buckwheat cakes.

"You run along, Helen," she said. "I want to talk to Harold."

She put the eggs and bacon down in front of him and brought in a jug of
maple syrup for the buckwheat cakes. Then she sat down across the table
from Krebs.

"I wish you'd put down the paper a minute, Harold," she said.

Krebs took down the paper and folded it.

"Have you decided what you are going to do yet, Harold?" his mother
said, taking off her glasses.

"No," said Krebs.

"Don't you think it's about time?" His mother did not say this in a mean
way. She seemed worried.

"I hadn't thought about it," Krebs said.

"God has some work for everyone to do," his mother said. "There can
be no idle hands in His Kingdom."

"I'm not in His Kingdom," Krebs said.

"We are all of us in His Kingdom."

Krebs felt embarrassed and resentful as always.

"I've worried about you so much, Harold," his mother went on. "I know the temptations you must have been exposed to. I know how weak men are. I know what your own dear grandfather, my own father, told us about the Civil War and I have prayed for you. I pray for you all day long, Harold."

Krebs looked at the bacon fat hardening on his plate.

"Your father is worried, too," his mother went on. "He thinks you have lost your ambition, that you haven't got a definite aim in life. Charley Simmons, who is just your age, has a good job and is going to be married. The boys are all settling down; they're all determined to get somewhere; you can see that boys like Charley Simmons are on their way to being really a credit to the community."

Krebs said nothing.

"Don't look that way, Harold," his mother said. "You know we love you and I want to tell you for your own good how matters stand. Your father does not want to hamper your freedom. He thinks you should be allowed to drive the car. If you want to take some of the nice girls out riding with you, we are only too pleased. We want you to enjoy yourself. But you are going to have to settle down to work, Harold. Your father doesn't care what you start in at. All work is honorable as he says. But you've got to make a start at something. He asked me to speak to you this morning and then you can stop in and see him at his office."

"Is that all?" Krebs said.

"Yes. Don't you love your mother, dear boy?"

"No," Krebs said.

His mother looked at him across the table. Her eyes were shiny. She started crying.

"I don't love anybody," Krebs said.

It wasn't any good. He couldn't tell her, he couldn't make her see it. It was silly to have said it. He had only hurt her. He went over and took hold of her arm. She was crying with her head in her hands.

"I didn't mean it," he said. "I was just angry at something. I didn't mean I didn't love you."

His mother went on crying. Krebs put his arm on her shoulder.

"Can't you believe me, mother?"

His mother shook her head.

"Please, please, mother. Please believe me."

"All right," his mother said chokily. She looked up at him. "I believe you, Harold."

Krebs kissed her hair. She put her face up to him.

"I'm your mother," she said. "I held you next to my heart when you were a tiny baby."

Krebs felt sick and vaguely nauseated.

"I know, Mummy," he said. "I'll try and be a good boy for you."

"Would you kneel and pray with me, Harold?" his mother asked.

They knelt down beside the dining-room table and Krebs's mother prayed.

"Now, you pray, Harold," she said.

"I can't," Krebs said.

"Try, Harold."

"I can't."

"Do you want me to pray for you?"

"Yes."

So his mother prayed for him and then they stood up and Krebs kissed his mother and went out of the house. He had tried so to keep his life from being complicated. Still, none of it had touched him. He had felt sorry for his mother and she had made him lie. He would go to Kansas City and get a job and she would feel all right about it. There would be one more scene maybe before he got away. He would not go down to his father's office. He would miss that one. He wanted his life to go smoothly. It had just gotten going that way. Well, that was all over now, anyway. He would go over to the schoolyard and watch Helen play indoor baseball.

GRAHAM GREENE

The Destructors

1

It was on the eve of August Bank Holiday that the latest recruit became the leader of the Wormsley Common Gang. No one was surprised except Mike, but Mike at the age of nine was surprised by everything. 'If you don't shut your mouth,' somebody once said to him, 'you'll get a frog down it.' After that Mike kept his teeth tightly clamped except when the surprise was too great.

The new recruit had been with the gang since the beginning of the summer holidays, and there were possibilities about his brooding silence that all recognized. He never wasted a word even to tell his name until that was required of him by the rules. When he said 'Trevor' it was a statement of fact, not as it would have been with the others a statement of shame or defiance. Nor did anyone laugh except Mike, who finding himself without support and meeting the dark gaze of the newcomer opened his mouth and was quiet again. There was every reason why T., as he was afterwards referred to, should have been an object of mockery—there was his name (and they substituted the initial because otherwise they had no excuse not to laugh at it), the fact that his father, a former architect and present clerk, had 'come down in the world' and that his mother considered herself better than the neighbours. What but an odd quality of danger, of the unpredictable, established him in the gang without any ignoble ceremony of initiation?

The gang met every morning in an impromptu car-park, the site of the last bomb of the first blitz. The leader, who was known as Blackie, claimed to have heard it fall, and no one was precise enough in his dates to point out that he would have been one year old and fast asleep on the down platform of Wormsley Common Underground Station. On one side of the car-park leant the first occupied house, No. 3, of the shattered Northwood Terrace —literally leant, for it had suffered from the blast of the bomb and the side walls were supported on wooden struts. A smaller bomb and some incendiaries had fallen beyond, so that the house stuck up like a jagged tooth and carried on the further wall relics of its neighbour, a dado, the remains of a fireplace. T., whose words were almost confined to voting 'Yes' or 'No' to the plan of operations proposed each day by Blackie, once startled the whole gang by saying broodingly, 'Wren built that house, father says.'

'Who's Wren?'[1]

'The man who built St Paul's.'

'Who cares?' Blackie said. 'It's only Old Misery's.'

Old Misery—whose real name was Thomas—had once been a builder and decorator. He lived alone in the crippled house, doing for himself: once

---

1. Sir Christopher Wren (1632–1723), the most famous English architect, designed St. Paul's Cathedral and more than fifty churches as well as other buildings, many of them built in the City of London, in the late seventeenth century.

a week you could see him coming back across the common with bread and vegetables, and once as the boys played in the car-park he put his head over the smashed wall of his garden and looked at them.

'Been to the lav,' one of the boys said, for it was common knowledge that since the bombs fell something had gone wrong with the pipes of the house and Old Misery was too mean to spend money on the property. He could do the redecorating himself at cost price, but he had never learnt plumbing. The lav was a wooden shed at the bottom of the narrow garden with a star-shaped hole in the door: it had escaped the blast which had smashed the house next door and sucked out the window-frames of No. 3.

The next time the gang became aware of Mr Thomas was more surprising. Blackie, Mike and a thin yellow boy, who for some reason was called by his surname Summers, met him on the common coming back from the market. Mr Thomas stopped them. He said glumly, 'You belong to the lot that play in the car-park?'

Mike was about to answer when Blackie stopped him. As the leader he had responsibilities. 'Suppose we are?' he said ambiguously.

'I got some chocolates,' Mr Thomas said. 'Don't like 'em myself. Here you are. Not enough to go round, I don't suppose. There never is,' he added with sombre conviction. He handed over three packets of Smarties.

The gang was puzzled and perturbed by this action and tried to explain it away. 'Bet someone dropped them and he picked 'em up,' somebody suggested.

'Pinched 'em and then got in a bleeding funk,' another thought aloud.

'It's a bribe,' Summers said. 'He wants us to stop bouncing balls on his wall.'

'We'll show him we don't take bribes,' Blackie said, and they sacrificed the whole morning to the game of bouncing that only Mike was young enough to enjoy. There was no sign from Mr Thomas.

Next day T. astonished them all. He was late at the rendezvous, and the voting for that day's exploit took place without him. At Blackie's suggestion the gang was to disperse in pairs, take buses at random and see how many free rides could be snatched from unwary conductors (the operation was to be carried out in pairs to avoid cheating). They were drawing lots for their companions when T. arrived.

'Where you been, T.?' Blackie asked. 'You can't vote now. You know the rules.'

'I've been *there*,' T. said. He looked at the ground, as though he had thoughts to hide.

'Where?'

'At Old Misery's.' Mike's mouth opened and then hurriedly closed again with a click. He had remembered the frog.

'At Old Misery's?' Blackie said. There was nothing in the rules against it, but he had a sensation that T. was treading on dangerous ground. He asked hopefully, 'Did you break in?'

'No. I rang the bell.'

'And what did you say?'

'I said I wanted to see his house.'

'What did he do?'

'He showed it me.'

'Pinch anything?'

'No.'

'What did you do it for then?'

The gang had gathered round: it was as though an impromptu court were about to form and try some case of deviation. T. said, 'It's a beautiful house,' and still watching the ground, meeting no one's eyes, he licked his lips first one way, then the other.

'What do you mean, a beautiful house?' Blackie asked with scorn.

'It's got a staircase two hundred years old like a corkscrew. Nothing holds it up.'

'What do you mean, nothing holds it up. Does it float?'

'It's to do with opposite forces, Old Misery said.'

'What else?'

'There's panelling.'

'Like in the Blue Boar?'

'Two hundred years old.'

'Is Old Misery two hundred years old?'

Mike laughed suddenly and then was quiet again. The meeting was in a serious mood. For the first time since T. had strolled into the car-park on the first day of the holidays his position was in danger. It only needed a single use of his real name and the gang would be at his heels.

'What did you do it for?' Blackie asked. He was just, he had no jealousy, he was anxious to retain T. in the gang if he could. It was the word 'beautiful' that worried him—that belonged to a class world that you could still see parodied at the Wormsley Common Empire by a man wearing a top hat and a monocle, with a haw-haw accent. He was tempted to say, 'My dear Trevor, old chap,' and unleash his hell hounds. 'If you'd broken in,' he said sadly—that indeed would have been an exploit worthy of the gang.

'This was better,' T. said. 'I found out things.' He continued to stare at his feet, not meeting anybody's eye, as though he were absorbed in some dream he was unwilling—or ashamed—to share.

'What things?'

'Old Misery's going to be away all tomorrow and Bank Holiday.'

Blackie said with relief, 'You mean we could break in?'

'And pinch things?' somebody asked.

Blackie said, 'Nobody's going to pinch things. Breaking in—that's good enough, isn't it? We don't want any court stuff.'

'I don't want to pinch anything,' T. said. 'I've got a better idea.'

'What is it?'

T. raised eyes, as grey and disturbed as the drab August day. 'We'll pull it down,' he said. 'We'll destroy it.'

Blackie gave a single hoot of laughter and then, like Mike, fell quiet, daunted by the serious implacable gaze. 'What'd the police be doing all the time?' he said.

'They'd never know. We'd do it from inside. I've found a way in.' He said with a sort of intensity, 'We'd be like worms, don't you see, in an apple. When we came out again there'd be nothing there, no staircase, no panels, nothing but just walls, and then we'd make the walls fall down — somehow.'

'We'd go to jug,'[2] Blackie said.

'Who's to prove? and anyway we wouldn't have pinched anything.' He added without the smallest flicker of glee, 'There wouldn't be anything to pinch after we'd finished.'

'I've never heard of going to prison for breaking things,' Summers said.

'There wouldn't be time,' Blackie said. 'I've seen housebreakers at work.'

'There are twelve of us,' T. said. 'We'd organize.'

'None of us know how . . .'

'I know,' T. said. He looked across at Blackie. 'Have you got a better plan?'

'Today,' Mike said tactlessly, 'we're pinching free rides . . .'

'Free rides,' T. said. 'Kid stuff. You can stand down, Blackie, if you'd rather . . .'

'The gang's got to vote.'

'Put it up then.'

Blackie said uneasily, 'It's proposed that tomorrow and Monday we destroy Old Misery's house.'

'Here, here,' said a fat boy called Joe.

'Who's in favour?'

T. said, 'It's carried.'

'How do we start?' Summers asked.

'He'll tell you,' Blackie said. It was the end of his leadership. He went away to the back of the car-park and began to kick a stone, dribbling it this way and that. There was only one old Morris in the park, for few cars were left there except lorries: without an attendant there was no safety. He took a flying kick at the car and scraped a little paint off the rear mudguard. Beyond, paying no more attention to him than to a stranger, the gang had gathered round T.; Blackie was dimly aware of the fickleness of favour. He thought of going home, of never returning, of letting them all discover the hollowness of T.'s leadership, but suppose after all what T. proposed was possible — nothing like it had ever been done before. The fame of the Wormsley Common car-park gang would surely reach around London. There would be headlines in the papers. Even the grown-up gangs who ran the betting at the all-in wrestling and the barrow-boys would hear with respect of how Old Misery's house had been destroyed. Driven by the pure, simple and altruistic ambition of fame for the gang, Blackie came back to where T. stood in the shadow of old Misery's wall.

T. was giving his orders with decision: it was as though this plan had been with him all his life, pondered through the seasons, now in his fifteenth year crystallized with the pain of puberty. 'You,' he said to Mike, 'bring some big nails, the biggest you can find, and a hammer. Anybody who can better bring a hammer and a screwdriver. We'll need plenty of them. Chisels too. We can't have too many chisels. Can anybody bring a saw?

'I can,' Mike said.

2. Jail.

'Not a child's saw,' T. said. 'A real saw.'

Blackie realized he had raised his hand like any ordinary member of the gang.

'Right, you bring one, Blackie. But now there's a difficulty. We want a hacksaw.'

'What's a hacksaw?' someone asked.

'You can get 'em at Woolworth's,' Summers said.

The fat boy called Joe said gloomily, 'I knew it would end in a collection.'

'I'll get one myself,' T. said. 'I don't want your money. But I can't buy a sledge-hammer.'

Blackie said, 'They are working on No. 15. I know where they'll leave their stuff for Bank Holiday.'

'Then that's all,' T. said. 'We meet here at nine sharp.'

'I've got to go to church,' Mike said.

'Come over the wall and whistle. We'll let you in.'

2

On Sunday morning all were punctual except Blackie, even Mike. Mike had a stroke of luck. His mother felt ill, his father was tired after Saturday night, and he was told to go to church alone with many warnings of what would happen if he strayed. Blackie had difficulty in smuggling out the saw, and then in finding the sledge-hammer at the back of No. 15. He approached the house from a lane at the rear of the garden, for fear of the policeman's beat along the main road. The tired evergreens kept off a stormy sun: another wet Bank Holiday was being prepared over the Atlantic, beginning in swirls of dust under the trees. Blackie climbed the wall into Misery's garden.

There was no sign of anybody anywhere. The lav stood like a tomb in a neglected graveyard. The curtains were drawn. The house slept. Blackie lumbered nearer with the saw and the sledge-hammer. Perhaps after all nobody had turned up: the plan had been a wild invention: they had woken wiser. But when he came close to the back door he could hear a confusion of sound hardly louder than a hive in swarm: a clickety-clack, a bang bang, a scraping, a creaking, a sudden painful crack. He thought: it's true, and whistled.

They opened the back door to him and he came in. He had at once the impression of organization, very different from the old happy-go-lucky ways under his leadership. For a while he wandered up and down stairs looking for T. Nobody addressed him: he had a sense of great urgency, and already he could begin to see the plan. The interior of the house was being carefully demolished without touching the outer walls. Summers with hammer and chisel was ripping out the skirting-boards in the ground floor dining-room: he had already smashed the panels of the door. In the same room Joe was heaving up the parquet blocks, exposing the soft wood floor-boards over the cellar. Coils of wire came out of the damaged skirting and Mike sat happily on the floor clipping the wires.

On the curved stairs two of the gang were working hard with an inadequate child's saw on the banisters—when they saw Blackie's big saw they signalled for it wordlessly. When he next saw them a quarter of the banisters had been dropped into the hall. He found T. at last in the bathroom—he sat moodily in the least cared-for room in the house, listening to the sounds coming up from below.

'You've really done it,' Blackie said with awe. 'What's going to happen?'

'We've only just begun,' T. said. He looked at the sledge-hammer and gave his instructions. 'You stay here and break the bath and the wash-basin. Don't bother about the pipes. They come later.'

Mike appeared at the door. 'I've finished the wires, T.,' he said.

'Good. You've just got to go wandering round now. The kitchen's in the basement. Smash all the china and glass and bottles you can lay hold of. Don't turn on the taps—we don't want a flood—yet. Then go into all the rooms and turn out drawers. If they are locked get one of the others to break them open. Tear up any papers you find and smash all the ornaments. Better take a carving-knife with you from the kitchen. The bedroom's opposite here. Open the pillows and tear up the sheets. That's enough for the moment. And you, Blackie, when you've finished in here crack the plaster in the passage up with your sledge-hammer.'

'What are you going to do?' Blackie asked.

'I'm looking for something special,' T. said.

It was nearly lunch-time before Blackie had finished and went in search of T. Chaos had advanced. The kitchen was a shambles of broken glass and china. The dining-room was stripped of parquet, the skirting was up, the door had been taken off its hinges, and the destroyers had moved up a floor. Streaks of light came in through the closed shutters where they worked with the seriousness of creators—and destruction after all is a form of creation. A kind of imagination had seen this house as it had now become.

Mike said, 'I've got to go home for dinner.'

'Who else?' T. asked, but all the others on one excuse or another had brought provisions with them.

They squatted in the ruins of the room and swapped unwanted sandwiches. Half an hour for lunch and they were at work again. By the time Mike returned they were on the top floor, and by six the superficial damage was completed. The doors were all off, all the skirtings raised, the furniture pillaged and ripped and smashed—no one could have slept in the house except on a bed of broken plaster. T. gave his orders—eight o'clock next morning, and to escape notice they climbed singly over the garden wall, into the car-park. Only Blackie and T. were left: the light had nearly gone, and when they touched a switch, nothing worked—Mike had done his job thoroughly.

'Did you find anything special?' Blackie asked.

T. nodded. 'Come over here,' he said, 'and look.' Out of both pockets he drew bundles of pound notes. 'Old Misery's savings,' he said. 'Mike ripped out the mattress, but he missed them.'

'What are you going to do? Share them?'

'We aren't thieves,' T. said. 'Nobody's going to steal anything from this house. I kept these for you and me—a celebration.' He knelt down on the floor and counted them out—there were seventy in all. 'We'll burn them,' he said, 'one by one,' and taking it in turns they held a note upwards and lit the top corner, so that the flame burnt slowly towards their fingers. The grey ash floated above them and fell on their heads like age. 'I'd like to see Old Misery's face when we are through,' T. said.

'You hate him a lot?' Blackie asked.

'Of course I don't hate him,' T. said. 'There'd be no fun if I hated him.' The last burning note illuminated his brooding face. 'All this hate and love,' he said, 'it's soft, it's hooey. There's only things, Blackie,' and he looked round the room crowded with the unfamiliar shadows of half things, broken things, former things. 'I'll race you home, Blackie,' he said.

3

Next morning the serious destruction started. Two were missing—Mike and another boy whose parents were off to Southend and Brighton in spite of the slow warm drops that had begun to fall and the rumble of thunder in the estuary like the first guns of the old blitz. 'We've got to hurry,' T. said.

Summers was restive. 'Haven't we done enough?' he asked. 'I've been given a bob[3] for slot machines. This is like work.'

'We've hardly started,' T. said. 'Why, there's all the floors left, and the stairs. We haven't taken out a single window. You voted like the others. We are going to *destroy* this house. There won't be anything left when we've finished.'

They began again on the first floor picking up the top floor-boards next the outer wall, leaving the joists exposed. Then they sawed through the joists and retreated into the hall, as what was left of the floor heeled and sank. They had learnt with practice, and the second floor collapsed more easily. By the evening an odd exhilaration seized them as they looked down the great hollow of the house. They ran risks and made mistakes: when they thought of the windows it was too late to reach them. 'Cor,' Joe said, and dropped a penny down into the dry rubble-filled well. It cracked and span amongst the broken glass.

'Why did we start this?' Summers asked with astonishment; T. was already on the ground, digging at the rubble, clearing a space along the outer wall. 'Turn on the taps,' he said. 'It's too dark for anyone to see now, and in the morning it won't matter.' The water overtook them on the stairs and fell through the floorless rooms.

It was then they heard Mike's whistle at the back. 'Something's wrong,' Blackie said. They could hear his urgent breathing as they unlocked the door.

'The bogies?'[4] Summers asked.

'Old Misery,' Mike said. 'He's on his way.' He put his head between his knees and retched. 'Ran all the way,' he said with pride.

'But why?' T. said. 'He told me...' He protested with the fury of the child he had never been, 'It isn't fair.'

'He was down at Southend,' Mike said, 'and he was on the train coming back. Said it was too cold and wet.' He paused and gazed at the water. 'My, you've had a storm here. Is the roof leaking?'

'How long will he be?'

3. Shilling.
4. Police.

'Five minutes. I gave Ma the slip and ran.'

'We better clear,' Summers said. 'We've done enough, anyway.'

'Oh no, we haven't. Anybody could do this—' 'this' was the shattered hollowed house with nothing left but the walls. Yet walls could be preserved. Façades were valuable. They could build inside again more beautifully than before. This could again be a home. He said angrily, 'We've got to finish. Don't move. Let me think.'

'There's no time,' a boy said.

'There's got to be a way,' T. said. 'We couldn't have got this far . . .'

'We've done a lot,' Blackie said.

'No. No, we haven't. Somebody watch the front.'

'We can't do any more.'

'He may come in at the back.'

'Watch the back too.' T. began to plead. 'Just give me a minute and I'll fix it. I swear I'll fix it.' But his authority had gone with his ambiguity. He was only one of the gang. 'Please,' he said.

'Please,' Summers mimicked him, and then suddenly struck home with the fatal name. 'Run along home, Trevor.'

T. stood with his back to the rubble like a boxer knocked groggy against the ropes. He had no words as his dreams shook and slid. Then Blackie acted before the gang had time to laugh, pushing Summers backward. 'I'll watch the front, T.,' he said, and cautiously he opened the shutters of the hall. The grey wet common stretched ahead, and the lamps gleamed in the puddles. 'Someone's coming, T. No, it's not him. What's your plan, T.?'

'Tell Mike to go out to the lav and hide close beside it. When he hears me whistle he's got to count ten and start to shout.'

'Shout what?'

'Oh, "Help", anything.'

'You hear, Mike,' Blackie said. He was the leader again. He took a quick look between the shutters. 'He's coming, T.'

'Quick, Mike. The lav. Stay here, Blackie, all of you, till I yell.'

'Where are you going, T.?'

'Don't worry. I'll see to this. I said I would, didn't I?'

Old Misery came limping off the common. He had mud on his shoes and he stopped to scrape them on the pavement's edge. He didn't want to soil his house, which stood jagged and dark between the bomb-sites, saved so narrowly, as he believed, from destruction. Even the fan-light had been left unbroken by the bomb's blast. Somewhere somebody whistled. Old Misery looked sharply round. He didn't trust whistles. A child was shouting: it seemed to come from his own garden. Then a boy ran into the road from the car-park. 'Mr Thomas,' he called, 'Mr Thomas.'

'What is it?'

'I'm terribly sorry, Mr Thomas. One of us got taken short, and we thought you wouldn't mind, and now he can't get out.'

'What do you mean, boy?'

'He's got stuck in your lav.'

'He'd no business. . . . Haven't I seen you before?'

'You showed me your house.'

'So I did. So I did. That doesn't give you the right to . . .'

'Do hurry, Mr Thomas. He'll suffocate.'

'Nonsense. He can't suffocate. Wait till I put my bag in.'

'I'll carry your bag.'

'Oh no, you don't. I carry my own.'

'This way, Mr Thomas.'

'I can't get in the garden that way. I've got to go through the house.'

'But you *can* get in the garden this way, Mr Thomas. We often do.'

'You often do?' He followed the boy with a scandalized fascination. 'When? What right...?'

'Do you see...? the wall's low.'

'I'm not going to climb walls into my own garden. It's absurd.'

'This is how we do it. One foot here, one foot there, and over.' The boy's face peered down, an arm shot out, and Mr Thomas found his bag taken and deposited on the other side of the wall.

'Give me back my bag,' Mr Thomas said. From the loo a boy yelled and yelled. 'I'll call the police.'

'Your bag's all right, Mr Thomas. Look. One foot there. On your right. Now just above. To your left.' Mr Thomas climbed over his own garden wall. 'Here's your bag, Mr Thomas.'

'I'll have the wall built up,' Mr Thomas said, 'I'll not have you boys coming over here, using my loo.' He stumbled on the path, but the boy caught his elbow and supported him. 'Thank you, thank you, my boy,' he murmured automatically. Somebody shouted again through the dark. 'I'm coming, I'm coming,' Mr Thomas called. He said to the boy beside him, 'I'm not unreasonable. Been a boy myself. As long as things are done regular. I don't mind you playing round the place Saturday mornings. Sometimes I like company. Only it's got to be regular. One of you asks leave and I say Yes. Sometimes I'll say No. Won't feel like it. And you come in at the front door and out at the back. No garden walls.'

'Do get him out, Mr Thomas.'

'He won't come to any harm in my loo,' Mr Thomas said, stumbling slowly down the garden. 'Oh, my rheumatics,' he said. 'Always get 'em on Bank Holiday. I've got to go careful. There's loose stones here. Give me your hand. Do you know what my horoscope said yesterday? "Abstain from any dealings in first half of week. Danger of serious crash." That might be on this path,' Mr Thomas said. 'They speak in parables and double meanings.' He paused at the door of the loo. 'What's the matter in there?' he called. There was no reply.

'Perhaps he's fainted,' the boy said.

'Not in my loo. Here, you, come out,' Mr Thomas said, and giving a great jerk at the door he nearly fell on his back when it swung easily open. A hand first supported him and then pushed him hard. His head hit the opposite wall and he sat heavily down. His bag hit his feet. A hand whipped the key out of the lock and the door slammed. 'Let me out,' he called, and heard the key turn in the lock. 'A serious crash,' he thought, and felt dithery and confused and old.

A voice spoke to him softly through the star-shaped hole in the door. 'Don't worry, Mr Thomas,' it said, 'we won't hurt you, not if you stay quiet.'

Mr Thomas put his head between his hands and pondered. He had noticed that there was only one lorry in the car-park, and he felt certain that the driver would not come for it before the morning. Nobody could hear him from the road in front, and the lane at the back was seldom used. Anyone who passed there would be hurrying home and would not pause for what they would certainly take to be drunken cries. And if he did call 'Help', who, on a lonely Bank Holiday evening, would have the courage to investigate? Mr Thomas sat on the loo and pondered with the wisdom of age.

After a while it seemed to him that there were sounds in the silence — they were faint and came from the direction of his house. He stood up and peered through the ventilation-hole — between the cracks in one of the shutters he saw a light, not the light of a lamp, but the wavering light that a candle might give. Then he thought he heard the sound of hammering and scraping and chipping. He thought of burglars — perhaps they had employed the boy as a scout, but why should burglars engage in what sounded more and more like a stealthy form of carpentry? Mr Thomas let out an experimental yell, but nobody answered. The noise could not even have reached his enemies.

4

Mike had gone home to bed, but the rest stayed. The question of leadership no longer concerned the gang. With nails, chisels, screwdrivers, anything that was sharp and penetrating, they moved around the inner walls worrying at the mortar between the bricks. They started too high, and it was Blackie who hit on the damp course and realized the work could be halved if they weakened the joints immediately above. It was a long, tiring, unamusing job, but at last it was finished. The gutted house stood there balanced on a few inches of mortar between the damp course and the bricks.

There remained the most dangerous task of all, out in the open at the edge of the bomb-site. Summers was sent to watch the road for passers-by, and Mr Thomas, sitting on the loo, heard clearly now the sound of sawing. It no longer came from his house, and that a little reassured him. He felt less concerned. Perhaps the other noises too had no significance.

A voice spoke to him through the hole. 'Mr Thomas.'

'Let me out,' Mr Thomas said sternly.

'Here's a blanket,' the voice said, and a long grey sausage was worked through the hole and fell in swathes over Mr Thomas's head.

'There's nothing personal,' the voice said. 'We want you to be comfortable tonight.'

'Tonight,' Mr Thomas repeated incredulously.

'Catch,' the voice said. 'Penny buns — we've buttered them, and sausage-rolls. We don't want you to starve, Mr Thomas.'

Mr Thomas pleaded desperately. 'A joke's a joke, boy. Let me out and I won't say a thing. I've got rheumatics. I got to sleep comfortable.'

'You wouldn't be comfortable, not in your house, you wouldn't. Not now.'

'What do you mean, boy?' But the footsteps receded. There was only the silence of night: no sound of sawing. Mr Thomas tried one more yell, but he was daunted and rebuked by the silence — a long way off an owl hooted and made away again on its muffled flight through the soundless world.

At seven next morning the driver came to fetch his lorry. He climbed into the seat and tried to start the engine. He was vaguely aware of a voice shouting, but it didn't concern him. At last the engine responded and he backed the lorry until it touched the great wooden shore that supported Mr Thomas's house. That way he could drive right out and down the street without reversing. The lorry moved forward, was momentarily checked as though something were pulling it from behind, and then went on to the sound of a long rumbling crash. The driver was astonished to see bricks bouncing ahead of him, while stones hit the roof of his cab. He put on his brakes. When he climbed out the whole landscape had suddenly altered. There was no house beside the car-park, only a hill of rubble. He went round and examined the back of his lorry for damage, and found a rope tied there that was still twisted at the other end round part of a wooden strut.

The driver again became aware of somebody shouting. It came from the wooden erection which was the nearest thing to a house in that desolation of broken brick. The driver climbed the smashed wall and unlocked the door. Mr Thomas came out of the loo. He was wearing a grey blanket to which flakes of pastry adhered. He gave a sobbing cry. 'My house,' he said. 'Where's my house?'

'Search me,' the driver said. His eye lit on the remains of a bath and what had once been a dresser and he began to laugh. There wasn't anything left anywhere.

'How dare you laugh,' Mr Thomas said. 'It was my house. My house.'

'I'm sorry,' the driver said, making heroic efforts, but when he remembered the sudden check to his lorry, the crash of bricks falling, he became convulsed again. One moment the house had stood there with such dignity between the bomb-sites like a man in a top hat, and then, bang, crash, there wasn't anything left—not anything. He said, 'I'm sorry. I can't help it, Mr Thomas. There's nothing personal, but you got to admit it's funny.'

SINCLAIR ROSS

The Painted Door

Straight across the hills it was five miles from John's farm to his father's. But in winter, with the roads impassable, a team had to make a wide detour and skirt the hills, so that from five the distance was more than trebled to seventeen.

"I think I'll walk," John said at breakfast to his wife. "The drifts in the hills wouldn't hold a horse, but they'll carry me all right. If I leave early I can spend a few hours helping him with his chores, and still be back by suppertime."

She went to the window, and thawing a clear place in the frost with her breath, stood looking across the snowswept farmyard to the huddle of stables and sheds. "There was a double wheel around the moon last night," she countered presently. "You said yourself we could expect a storm. It isn't right to leave me here alone. Surely I'm as important as your father."

He glanced up uneasily, then drinking off his coffee tried to reassure her. "But there's nothing to be afraid of—even supposing it does start to storm. You won't need to go near the stable. Everything's fed and watered now to last till night. I'll be back at the latest by seven or eight."

She went on blowing against the frosted pane, carefully elongating the clear place until it was oval-shaped and symmetrical. He watched her a moment or two longer, then more insistently repeated, "I say you won't need to go near the stable. Everything's fed and watered, and I'll see that there's plenty of wood in. That will be all right, won't it?"

"Yes—of course—I heard you—" It was a curiously cold voice now, as if the words were chilled by their contact with the frosted pane. "Plenty to eat—plenty of wood to keep me warm—what more could a woman ask for?"

"But he's an old man—living there all alone. What is it, Ann? You're not like yourself this morning."

She shook her head without turning. "Pay no attention to me. Seven years a farmer's wife—it's time I was used to staying alone."

Slowly the clear place on the glass enlarged: oval, then round, then oval again. The sun was risen above the frost mists now, so keen and hard a glitter on the snow that instead of warmth its rays seemed shedding cold. One of the two-year-old colts that had cantered away when John turned the horses out for water stood covered with rime at the stable door again, head down and body hunched, each breath a little plume of steam against the frosty air. She shivered, but did not turn. In the clear, bitter light the long white miles of prairie landscape seemed a region alien to life. Even the distant farmsteads she could see served only to intensify a sense of isolation. Scattered across the face of so vast and bleak a wilderness it was difficult to conceive them as a testimony of human hardihood and endurance. Rather they seemed futile, lost, to cower before the implacability of snow-swept earth and clear pale sun-chilled sky.

And when at last she turned from the window there was a brooding stillness in her face as if she had recognized this mastery of snow and cold.

340

It troubled John. "If you're really afraid," he yielded, "I won't go today. Lately it's been so cold, that's all. I just wanted to make sure he's all right in case we do have a storm."

"I know — I'm not really afraid." She was putting in a fire now, and he could no longer see her face. "Pay no attention. It's ten miles there and back, so you'd better get started."

"You ought to know by now I wouldn't stay away," he tried to brighten her. "No matter how it stormed. Before we were married — remember? Twice a week I never missed and we had some bad blizzards that winter too."

He was a slow, unambitious man, content with his farm and cattle, naïvely proud of Ann. He had been bewildered by it once, her caring for a dull-witted fellow like him; then assured at last of her affection he had relaxed against it gratefully, unsuspecting it might ever be less constant than his own. Even now, listening to the restless brooding in her voice, he felt only a quick, unformulated kind of pride that after seven years his absence for a day should still concern her. While she, his trust and earnestness controlling her again:

"I know. It's just that sometimes when you're away I get lonely. . . . There's a long cold tramp in front of you. You'll let me fix a scarf around your face."

He nodded. "And on my way I'll drop in at Steven's place. Maybe he'll come over tonight for a game of cards. You haven't seen anybody but me for the last two weeks."

She glanced up sharply, then busied herself clearing the table. "It will mean another two miles if you do. You're going to be cold and tired enough as it is. When you're gone I think I'll paint the kitchen woodwork. White this time — you remember we got the paint last fall. It's going to make the room a lot lighter. I'll be too busy to find the day long."

"I will though," he insisted, "and if a storm gets up you'll feel safer, knowing that he's coming. That's what you need, maybe — someone to talk to besides me."

She stood at the stove motionless a moment, then turned to him uneasily. "Will you shave then, John — now — before you go?"

He glanced at her questioningly, and avoiding his eyes she tried to explain, "I mean — he may be here before you're back — and you won't have a chance then."

"But it's only Steven — we're not going anywhere."

"He'll be shaved, though — that's what I mean — and I'd like you too to spend a little time on yourself."

He stood up, stroking the heavy stubble on his chin. "Maybe I should — only it softens up the skin too much. Especially when I've got to face the wind."

She nodded and began to help him dress, bringing heavy socks and a big woollen sweater from the bedroom, wrapping a scarf around his face and forehead. "I'll tell Steven to come early," he said, as he went out. "In time for supper. Likely there'll be chores for me to do, so if I'm not back by six don't wait."

From the bedroom window she watched him nearly a mile along the road. The fire had gone down when at last she turned away, and already through the house there was an encroaching chill. A blaze sprang up again when the draughts were opened, but as she went on clearing the table her movements were furtive and constrained. It was the silence weighing upon her—the frozen silence of the bitter fields and sun-chilled sky—lurking outside as if alive, relentlessly in wait, mile-deep between her now and John. She listened to it, suddenly tense, motionless. The fire crackled and the clock ticked. Always it was there. "I'm a fool," she whispered, rattling the dishes in defiance, going back to the stove to put in another fire. "Warm and safe—I'm a fool. It's a good chance when he's away to paint. The day will go quickly. I won't have time to brood."

Since November now the paint had been waiting warmer weather. The frost in the walls on a day like this would crack and peel it as it dried, but she needed something to keep her hands occupied, something to stave off the gathering cold and loneliness. "First of all," she said aloud, opening the paint and mixing it with a little turpentine, "I must get the house warmer. Fill up the stove and open the oven door so that all the heat comes out. Wad something along the window sills to keep out the draughts. Then I'll feel brighter. It's the cold that depresses."

She moved briskly, performing each little task with careful and exaggerated absorption, binding her thoughts to it, making it a screen between herself and the surrounding snow and silence. But when the stove was filled and the windows sealed it was more difficult again. Above the quiet, steady swishing of her brush against the bedroom door the clock began to tick. Suddenly her movements became precise, deliberate, her posture self-conscious, as if someone had entered the room and were watching her. It was the silence again, aggressive, hovering. The fire spit and crackled at it. Still it was there. "I'm a fool," she repeated. "All farmers' wives have to stay alone. I mustn't give in this way. I mustn't brood. A few hours now and they'll be here."

The sound of her voice reassured her. She went on: "I'll get them a good supper—and for coffee after cards bake some of the little cakes with raisins that he likes. . . . Just three of us, so I'll watch, and let John play. It's better with four, but at least we can talk. That's all I need—someone to talk to. John never talks. He's stronger—doesn't need to. But he likes Steven—no matter what the neighbours say. Maybe he'll have him come again, and some other young people too. It's what we need, both of us, to help keep young ourselves. . . . And then before we know it we'll be into March. It's cold still in March sometimes, but you never mind the same. At least you're beginning to think about spring."

She began to think about it now. Thoughts that outstripped her words, that left her alone again with herself and the ever-lurking silence. Eager and hopeful first, then clenched, rebellious, lonely. Windows open, sun and thawing earth again, the urge of growing, living things. Then the days that began in the morning at half-past four and lasted till ten at night; the meals at which John gulped his food and scarcely spoke a word; the brute-tired stupid eyes he turned on her if ever she mentioned town or visiting.

For spring was drudgery again. John never hired a man to help him. He wanted a mortgage-free farm; then a new house and pretty clothes for her. Sometimes, because with the best of crops it was going to take so long to pay off anyway, she wondered whether they mightn't better let the mortgage wait a little. Before they were worn out, before their best years were gone. It was something of life she wanted, not just a house and furniture; something of John, not pretty clothes when she would be too old to wear them. But John of course couldn't understand. To him it seemed only right that she should have the clothes—only right that he, fit for nothing else, should slave away fifteen hours a day to give them to her. There was in his devotion a baffling, insurmountable humility that made him feel the need of sacrifice. And when his muscles ached, when his feet dragged stolidly with weariness, then it seemed that in some measure at least he was making amends for his big hulking body and simple mind. Year after year their lives went on in the same little groove. He drove his horses in the field; she milked the cows and hoed potatoes. By dint of his drudgery he saved a few months' wages, added a few dollars more each fall to his payments on the mortgage; but the only real difference that it all made was to deprive her of his companionship, to make him a little duller, older, uglier than he might otherwise have been. He never saw their lives objectively. To him it was not what he actually accomplished by means of the sacrifice that mattered, but the sacrifice itself, the gesture—something done for her sake.

And she, understanding, kept her silence. In such a gesture, however futile, there was a graciousness not to be shattered lightly. "John," she would begin sometimes, "you're doing too much. Get a man to help you—just for a month—" but smiling down at her he would answer simply, "I don't mind. Look at the hands on me. They're made for work." While in his voice there would be a stalwart ring to tell her that by her thoughtfulness she had made him only the more resolved to serve her, to prove his devotion and fidelity.

They were useless, such thoughts. She knew. It was his very devotion that made them useless, that forbade her to rebel. Yet over and over, sometimes hunched still before their bleakness, sometimes her brush making swift sharp strokes to pace the chafe and rancour that they brought, she persisted in them.

This now, the winter, was their slack season. She could sleep sometimes till eight, and John till seven. They could linger over their meals a little, read, play cards, go visiting the neighbours. It was the time to relax, to indulge and enjoy themselves; but instead, fretful and impatient, they kept on waiting for the spring. They were compelled now, not by labour, but by the spirit of labour. A spirit that pervaded their lives and brought with idleness a sense of guilt. Sometimes they did sleep late, sometimes they did play cards, but always uneasily, always reproached by the thought of more important things that might be done. When John got up at five to attend to the fire he wanted to stay up and go out to the stable. When he sat down to a meal he hurried his food and pushed his chair away again, from habit, from sheer work-instinct, even though it was only to put more wood in the stove, or go down cellar to cut up beets and turnips for the cows.

And anyway, sometimes she asked herself, why sit trying to talk with a man who never talked? Why talk when there was nothing to talk about but crops and cattle, the weather and the neighbours? The neighbours, too

—why go visiting them when still it was the same—crops and cattle, the weather and the other neighbours? Why go to the dances in the schoolhouse to sit among the older women, one of them now, married seven years, or to waltz with the work-bent, tired old farmers to a squeaky fiddle tune? Once she had danced with Steven six or seven times in the evening, and they had talked about it for as many months. It was easier to stay at home. John never danced or enjoyed himself. He was always uncomfortable in his good suit and shoes. He didn't like shaving in the cold weather oftener than once or twice a week. It was easier to stay at home, to stand at the window staring out across the bitter fields, to count the days and look forward to another spring.

But now, alone with herself in the winter silence, she saw the spring for what it really was. This spring—next spring—all the springs and summers still to come. While they grew old, while their bodies warped, while their minds kept shrivelling dry and empty like their lives. "I mustn't," she said aloud again. "I married him—and he's a good man. I mustn't keep on this way. It will be noon before long, and then time to think about supper.... Maybe he'll come early—and as soon as John is finished at the stable we can all play cards."

It was getting cold again, and she left her painting to put in more wood. But this time the warmth spread slowly. She pushed a mat up to the outside door, and went back to the window to pat down the woollen shirt that was wadded along the sill. Then she paced a few times round the room, then poked the fire and rattled the stove lids, then paced again. The fire crackled, the clock ticked. The silence now seemed more intense than ever, seemed to have reached a pitch where it faintly moaned. She began to pace on tiptoe, listening, her shoulders drawn together, not realising for a while that it was the wind she heard, thin-strained and whimpering through the eaves.

Then she wheeled to the window, and with quick short breaths thawed the frost to see again. The glitter was gone. Across the drifts sped swift and snakelike little tongues of snow. She could not follow them, where they sprang from, or where they disappeared. It was as if all across the yard the snow were shivering awake—roused by the warnings of the wind to hold itself in readiness for the impending storm. The sky had become a sombre, whitish grey. It, too, as if in readiness, had shifted and lay close to earth. Before her as she watched a mane of powdery snow reared up breast-high against the darker background of the stable, tossed for a moment angrily, and then subsided again as if whipped down to obedience and restraint. But another followed, more reckless and impatient than the first. Another reeled and dashed itself against the window where she watched. Then ominously for a while there were only the angry little snakes of snow. The wind rose, creaking the troughs that were wired beneath the eaves. In the distance, sky and prairie now were merged into one another linelessly. All round her it was gathering; already in its press and whimpering there strummed a boding of eventual fury. Again she saw a mane of snow spring up, so dense and high this time that all the sheds and stables were obscured. Then others followed, whirling fiercely out of hand; and, when at last they cleared, the stables seemed in dimmer outline than before. It was the snow beginning, long lancet shafts of it, straight from the north, borne almost level by the straining wind. "He'll be there soon," she whispered, "and coming home it will be in his back. He'll leave again right away. He saw the double wheel—he knows the kind of storm there'll be."

She went back to her painting. For a while it was easier, all her thoughts half-anxious ones of John in the blizzard, struggling his way across the hills; but petulantly again she soon began, "I knew we were going to have a storm—I told him so—but it doesn't matter what I say. Big stubborn fool—he goes his own way anyway. It doesn't matter what becomes of me. In a storm like this he'll never get home. He won't even try. And while he sits keeping his father company I can look after his stable for him, go ploughing through snowdrifts up to my knees—nearly frozen—"

Not that she meant or believed her words. It was just an effort to convince herself that she did have a grievance, to justify her rebellious thoughts, to prove John responsible for her unhappiness. She was young still, eager for excitement and distractions; and John's steadfastness rebuked her vanity, made her complaints seem weak and trivial. She went on, fretfully, "If he'd listen to me sometimes and not be so stubborn we wouldn't still be living in a house like this. Seven years in two rooms—seven years and never a new stick of furniture. . . . There—as if another coat of paint could make it different anyway."

She cleaned her brush, filled up the stove again, and went back to the window. There was a void white moment that she thought must be frost formed on the window pane; then, like a fitful shadow through the whirling snow, she recognized the stable roof. It was incredible. The sudden, maniac raging of the storm struck from her face all its pettishness. Her eyes glazed with fear a little; her lips blanched. "If he starts for home now," she whispered silently—"But he won't—he knows I'm safe—he knows Steven's coming. Across the hills he would never dare."

She turned to the stove, holding out her hands to the warmth. Around her now there seemed a constant sway and tremor, as if the air were vibrating with the shudderings of the walls. She stood quite still, listening. Sometimes the wind struck with sharp, savage blows. Sometimes it bore down in a sustained, minute-long blast, silent with effort and intensity; then with a foiled shriek of threat wheeled away to gather and assault again. Always the eave-troughs creaked and sawed. She stared towards the window again, then detecting the morbid trend of her thoughts, prepared fresh coffee and forced herself to drink a few mouthfuls. "He would never dare," she whispered again. "He wouldn't leave the old man anyway in such a storm. Safe in here—there's nothing for me to keep worrying about. It's after one already. I'll do my baking now, and then it will be time to get supper ready for Steven."

Soon, however, she began to doubt whether Steven would come. In such a storm even a mile was enough to make a man hesitate. Especially Steven, who was hardly the one to face a blizzard for the sake of someone else's chores. He had a stable of his own to look after anyway. It would be only natural for him to think that when the storm blew up John had turned again for home. Another man would have—would have put his wife first.

But she felt little dread or uneasiness at the prospect of spending the night alone. It was the first time she had been left like this on her own resources, and her reaction, now that she could face and appraise her situation calmly, was gradually to feel it a kind of adventure and responsibility. It stimulated her. Before nightfall she must go to the stable and feed everything. Wrap up in some of John's clothes — take a ball of string in her hand, one end tied to the door, so that no matter how blinding the storm she could at least find her way back to the house. She had heard of people having to do that. It appealed to her now because suddenly it made life dramatic. She had not felt the storm yet, only watched it for a minute through the window.

It took nearly an hour to find enough string, to choose the right socks and sweaters. Long before it was time to start out she tried on John's clothes, changing and rechanging, striding around the room to make sure there would be play enough for pitching hay and struggling over snowdrifts; then she took them off again, and for a while busied herself baking the little cakes with raisins that he liked.

Night came early. Just for a moment on the doorstep she shrank back, uncertain. The slow dimming of the light clutched her with an illogical sense of abandonment. It was like the covert withdrawal of an ally, leaving the alien miles unleashed and unrestrained. Watching the hurricane of writhing snow rage past the little house she forced herself, "They'll never stand the night unless I get them fed. It's nearly dark already, and I've work to last an hour."

Timidly, unwinding a little of the string, she crept out from the shelter of the doorway. A gust of wind spun her forward a few yards, then plunged her headlong against a drift that in the dense white whirl lay invisible across her path. For nearly a minute she huddled still, breathless and dazed. The snow was in her mouth and nostrils, inside her scarf and up her sleeves. As she tried to straighten a smothering scud flung itself against her face, cutting off her breath a second time. The wind struck from all sides, blustering and furious. It was as if the storm had discovered her, as if all its forces were concentrated upon her extinction. Seized with panic suddenly she threshed out a moment with her arms, then stumbled back and sprawled her length across the drift.

But this time she regained her feet quickly, roused by the whip and batter of the storm to retaliative anger. For a moment her impulse was to face the wind and strike back blow for blow; then, as suddenly as it had come, her frantic strength gave way to limpness and exhaustion. Suddenly, a comprehension so clear and terrifying that it struck all thoughts of the stable from her mind, she realized in such a storm her puniness. And the realization gave her new strength, stilled this time to a desperate persistence. Just for a moment the wind held her, numb and swaying in its vise; then slowly, buckled far forward, she groped her way again towards the house.

Inside, leaning against the door, she stood tense and still a while. It was almost dark now. The top of the stove glowed a deep, dull red. Heedless of the storm, self-absorbed and self-satisfied, the clock ticked on like a glib little idiot. "He shouldn't have gone," she whispered silently. "He saw the double wheel — he knew. He shouldn't have left me here alone."

For so fierce now, so insane and dominant did the blizzard seem, that she could not credit the safety of the house. The warmth and lull around her was not real yet, not to be relied upon. She was still at the mercy of the storm. Only her body pressing hard like this against the door was staving it off. She didn't dare move. She didn't dare ease the ache and strain. "He shouldn't have gone," she repeated, thinking of the stable again, reproached by her helplessness. "They'll freeze in their stalls—and I can't reach them. He'll say it's all my fault. He won't believe I tried."

Then Steven came. Quickly, startled to quietness and control, she let him in and lit the lamp. He stared at her a moment, then flinging off his cap crossed to where she stood by the table and seized her arms. "You're so white—what's wrong? Look at me—" It was like him in such little situations to be masterful. "You should have known better—for a while I thought I wasn't going to make it here myself—"

"I was afraid you wouldn't come—John left early, and there was the stable—"

But the storm had unnerved her, and suddenly at the assurance of his touch and voice the fear that had been gripping her gave way to an hysteria of relief. Scarcely aware of herself she seized his arm and sobbed against it. He remained still a moment unyielding, then slipped his other arm around her shoulder. It was comforting and she relaxed against it, hushed by a sudden sense of lull and safety. Her shoulders trembled with the easing of the strain, then fell limp and still. "You're shivering,"—he drew her gently towards the stove. "It's all right—nothing to be afraid of. I'm going to see to the stable."

It was a quiet, sympathetic voice, yet with an undertone of insolence, a kind of mockery even, that made her draw away quickly and busy herself putting in a fire. With his lips drawn in a little smile he watched her till she looked at him again. The smile too was insolent, but at the same time companionable; Steven's smile, and therefore difficult to reprove. It lit up his lean, still-boyish face with a peculiar kind of arrogance: features and smile that were different from John's, from other men's—wilful and derisive, yet naïvely so—as if it were less the difference itself he was conscious of, than the long-accustomed privilege that thereby fell his due. He was erect, tall, square-shouldered. His hair was dark and trim, his lips curved soft and full. While John, she made the comparison swiftly, was thickset, heavy-jowled, and stooped. He always stood before her helpless, a kind of humility and wonderment in his attitude. And Steven now smiled on her appraisingly with the worldly-wise assurance of one for whom a woman holds neither mystery nor illusion.

"It was good of you to come, Steven," she responded, the words running into a sudden, empty laugh. "Such a storm to face—I suppose I should feel flattered."

For his presumption, his misunderstanding of what had been only a momentary weakness, instead of angering quickened her, roused from latency and long disuse all the instincts and resources of her femininity. She felt eager, challenged. Something was at hand that hitherto had always eluded her, even in the early days with John, something vital, beckoning, meaningful. She didn't understand, but she knew. The texture of the moment was satisfyingly dreamlike: an incredibility perceived as such, yet acquiesced in. She was John's wife—she knew—but also she knew that Steven standing here was different from John. There was no thought or motive, no understanding of herself as the knowledge persisted. Wary and poised round a sudden little core of blind excitement she evaded him, "But it's nearly dark—hadn't you better hurry if you're going to do the chores? Don't trouble—I can get them off myself—"

An hour later when he returned from the stable she was in another dress, hair rearranged, a little flush of colour in her face. Pouring warm water for him from the kettle into the basin she said evenly, "By the time you're washed supper will be ready. John said we weren't to wait for him."

He looked at her a moment, "You don't mean you're expecting John tonight? The way it's blowing—"

"Of course." As she spoke she could feel the colour deepening in her face. "We're going to play cards. He was the one that suggested it."

He went on washing, and then as they took their places at the table, resumed, "So John's coming. When are you expecting him?"

"He said it might be seven o'clock—or a little later." Conversation with Steven at other times had always been brisk and natural, but now all at once she found it strained. "He may have work to do for his father. That's what he said when he left. Why do you ask, Steven?"

"I was just wondering—it's a rough night."

"You don't know John. It would take more than a storm to stop him."

She glanced up again and he was smiling at her. The same insolence, the same little twist of mockery and appraisal. It made her flinch, and ask herself why she was pretending to expect John—why there should be this instinct of defence to force her. This time, instead of poise and excitement, it brought a reminder that she had changed her dress and rearranged her hair. It crushed in a sudden silence, through which she heard the whistling wind again, and the creaking saw of the eaves. Neither spoke now. There was something strange, almost frightening, about this Steven and his quiet, unrelenting smile; but strangest of all was the familiarity: the Steven she had never seen or encountered, and yet had always known, always expected, always waited for. It was less Steven himself that she felt than his inevitability. Just as she had felt the snow, the silence and the storm. She kept her eyes lowered, on the window past his shoulder, on the stove, but his smile now seemed to exist apart from him, to merge and hover with the silence. She clinked a cup—listened to the whistle of the storm—always it was there. He began to speak, but her mind missed the meaning of his words. Swiftly she was making comparisons again; his face so different to John's, so handsome and young and clean-shaven. Swiftly, helplessly, feeling the imperceptible and relentless ascendancy that thereby he was gaining over her, sensing sudden menace in this new, more vital life, even as she felt drawn towards it.

The lamp between them flickered as an onslaught of the storm sent shudderings through the room. She rose to build up the fire again and he followed her. For a long time they stood close to the stove, their arms almost touching. Once as the blizzard creaked the house she spun around sharply, fancying it was John at the door; but quietly he intercepted her. "Not tonight—you might as well make up your mind to it. Across the hills in a storm like this—it would be suicide to try."

Her lips trembled suddenly in an effort to answer, to parry the certainty in his voice, then set thin and bloodless. She was afraid now.

Afraid of his face so different from John's — of his smile, of her own helplessness to rebuke it. Afraid of the storm, isolating her here alone with him. They tried to play cards, but she kept starting up at every creak and shiver of the walls. "It's too rough a night," he repeated. "Even for John. Just relax a few minutes — stop worrying and pay a little attention to me."

But in his tone there was a contradiction to his words. For it implied that she was not worrying — that her only concern was lest it really might be John at the door.

And the implication persisted. He filled up the stove for her, shuffled the cards — won — shuffled — still it was there. She tried to respond to his conversation, to think of the game, but helplessly into her cards instead she began to ask, Was he right? Was that why he smiled? Why he seemed to wait, expectant and assured?

The clock ticked, the fire crackled. Always it was there. Furtively for a moment she watched him as he deliberated over his hand. John, even in the days before they were married, had never looked like that. Only this morning she had asked him to shave. Because Steven was coming — because she had been afraid to see them side by side — because deep within herself she had known even then. The same knowledge, furtive and forbidden, that was flaunted now in Steven's smile. "You look cold," he said at last, dropping his cards and rising from the table. "We're not playing, anyway. Come over to the stove for a few minutes and get warm."

"But first I think we'll hang blankets over the door. When there's a blizzard like this we always do." It seemed that in sane, commonplace activity there might be release, a moment or two in which to recover herself. "John has nails to put them on. They keep out a little of the draught."

He stood on a chair for her, and hung the blankets that she carried from the bedroom. Then for a moment they stood silent, watching the blankets sway and tremble before the blade of wind that spurted around the jamb. "I forgot," she said at last, "that I painted the bedroom door. At the top there, see — I've smeared the blankets."

He glanced at her curiously, and went back to the stove. She followed him, trying to imagine the hills in such a storm, wondering whether John would come. "A man couldn't live in it," suddenly he answered her thoughts, lowering the oven door and drawing up their chairs one on each side of it. "He knows you're safe. It isn't likely that he'd leave his father, anyway."

"The wind will be in his back," she persisted. "The winter before we were married — all the blizzards that we had that year — and he never missed —"

"Blizzards like this one? Up in the hills he wouldn't be able to keep his direction for a hundred yards. Listen to it a minute and ask yourself."

His voice seemed softer, kindlier now. She met his smile a moment, its assured little twist of appraisal, then for a long time sat silent, tense, careful again to avoid his eyes.

Everything now seemed to depend on this. It was the same as a few hours ago when she braced the door against the storm. He was watching her, smiling. She dared not move, unclench her hands, or raise her eyes. The flames crackled, the clock ticked. The storm wrenched the walls as if to make them buckle in. So rigid and desperate were all her muscles set, withstanding, that the room around her seemed to swim and reel. So rigid and strained that for relief at last, despite herself, she raised her head and met his eyes again.

Intending that it should be for only an instant, just to breathe again, to ease the tension that had grown unbearable — but in his smile now, instead of the insolent appraisal that she feared, there seemed a kind of warmth and sympathy. An understanding that quickened and encouraged her — that made her wonder why but a moment ago she had been afraid. It was as if the storm had lulled, as if she had suddenly found calm and shelter.

Or perhaps, the thought seized her, perhaps instead of his smile it was she who had changed. She who, in the long, wind-creaked silence, had emerged from the increment of codes and loyalties to her real, unfettered self. She who now felt his air of appraisal as nothing more than an understanding of the unfulfilled woman that until this moment had lain within her brooding and unadmitted, reproved out of consciousness by the insistence of an outgrown, routine fidelity.

For there had always been Steven. She understood now. Seven years — almost as long as John — ever since the night they first danced together.

The lamp was burning dry, and through the dimming light, isolated in the fastness of silence and storm, they watched each other. Her face was white and struggling still. His was handsome, clean-shaven, young. Her eyes were fanatic, believing desperately, fixed upon him as if to exclude all else, as if to find justification. His were cool, bland, drooped a little with expectancy. The light kept dimming, gathering the shadows round them, hushed, conspiratorial. He was smiling still. Her hands again were clenched up white and hard.

"But he always came," she persisted. "The wildest, coldest nights — even such a night as this. There was never a storm —"

"Never a storm like this one." There was a quietness in his smile now, a kind of simplicity almost, as if to reassure her. "You were out in it yourself for a few minutes. He'd have it for five miles, across the hills. . . . I'd think twice myself, on such a night before risking even one."

Long after he was asleep she lay listening to the storm. As a check on the draught up the chimney they had left one of the stovelids partly off, and through the open bedroom door she could see the flickerings of flame and shadow on the kitchen wall. They leaped and sank fantastically. The longer she watched the more alive they seemed to be. There was one great shadow that struggled towards her threateningly, massive and black and engulfing all the room. Again and again it advanced, about to spring, but each time a little whip of light subdued it to its place among the others on the wall. Yet though it never reached her still she cowered, feeling that gathered there was all the frozen wilderness, its heart of terror and invincibility.

Then she dozed a while, and the shadow was John. Interminably he advanced. The whips of light still flickered and coiled, but now suddenly they were the swift little snakes that this afternoon she had watched twist and shiver across the snow. And they too were advancing. They writhed and vanished and came again. She lay still, paralysed. He was over her now, so close that she could have touched him. Already it seemed that a deadly tightening hand was on her throat. She tried to scream but her lips were locked. Steven beside her slept on heedlessly.

Until suddenly as she lay staring up at him a gleam of light revealed his face. And in it was not a trace of threat or anger—only calm, and stonelike hopelessness.

That was like John. He began to withdraw, and frantically she tried to call him back. "It isn't true—not really true—listen, John—" but the words clung frozen to her lips. Already there was only the shriek of wind again, the sawing eaves, the leap and twist of shadow on the wall.

She sat up, startled now and awake. And so real had he seemed there, standing close to her, so vivid the sudden age and sorrow in his face, that at first she could not make herself understand she had been only dreaming. Against the conviction of his presence in the room it was necessary to insist over and over that he must still be with his father on the other side of the hills. Watching the shadows she had fallen asleep. It was only her mind, her imagination, distorted to a nightmare by the illogical and unadmitted dread of his return. But he wouldn't come. Steven was right. In such a storm he would never try. They were safe, alone. No one would ever know. It was only fear, morbid and irrational; only the sense of guilt that even her new-found and challenged womanhood could not entirely quell.

She knew now. She had not let herself understand or acknowledge it as guilt before, but gradually through the wind-torn silence of the night his face compelled her. The face that had watched her from the darkness with its stonelike sorrow—the face that was really John—John more than his features of mere flesh and bone could ever be.

She wept silently. The fitful gleam of light began to sink. On the ceiling and wall at last there was only a faint dull flickering glow. The little house shuddered and quailed, and a chill crept in again. Without wakening Steven she slipped out to build up the fire. It was burned to a few spent embers now, and the wood she put on seemed a long time catching light. The wind swirled through the blankets they had hung around the door, and then, hollow and moaning, roared up the chimney again, as if against its will drawn back to serve still longer with the onrush of the storm.

For a long time she crouched over the stove, listening. Earlier in the evening, with the lamp lit and the fire crackling, the house had seemed a stand against the wilderness, a refuge of feeble walls wherein persisted the elements of human meaning and survival. Now, in the cold, creaking darkness, it was strangely extinct, looted by the storm and abandoned again. She lifted the stove lid and fanned the embers till at last a swift little tongue of flame began to lick around the wood. Then she replaced the lid, extended her hands, and as if frozen in that attitude stood waiting.

It was not long now. After a few minutes she closed the draughts, and as the flames whirled back upon each other, beating against the top of the stove and sending out flickers of light again, a warmth surged up to relax her stiffened limbs. But shivering and numb it had been easier. The bodily well-being that the warmth induced gave play again to an ever more insistent mental suffering. She remembered the shadow that was John. She saw him bent towards her, then retreating, his features pale and overcast with unaccusing grief. She re-lived their seven years together and, in retrospect, found them to be years of worth and dignity. Until crushed by it all at last, seized by a sudden need to suffer and atone, she crossed to where the draught was bitter, and for a long time stood unflinching on the icy floor.

The storm was close here. Even through the blankets she could feel a sift of snow against her face. The eaves sawed, the walls creaked, and the wind was like a wolf in howling flight.

And yet, suddenly she asked herself, hadn't there been other storms, other blizzards? And through the worst of them hadn't he always reached her?

Clutched by the thought she stood rooted a minute. It was hard now to understand how she could have so deceived herself—how a moment of passion could have quieted within her not only conscience, but reason and discretion too. John always came. There could never be a storm to stop him. He was strong, inured to the cold. He had crossed the hills since his boyhood, knew every creek-bed and gully. It was madness to go on like this—to wait. While there was still time she must waken Steven, and hurry him away.

But in the bedroom again, standing at Steven's side, she hesitated. In his detachment from it all, in his quiet, even breathing, there was such sanity, such realism. For him nothing had happened; nothing would. If she wakened him he would only laugh and tell her to listen to the storm. Already it was long past midnight; either John had lost his way or not set out at all. And she knew that in his devotion there was nothing foolhardy. He would never risk a storm beyond his endurance, never permit himself a sacrifice likely to endanger her lot or future. They were both safe. No one would ever know. She must control herself—be sane like Steven.

For comfort she let her hand rest a while on Steven's shoulder. It would be easier were he awake now, with her, sharing her guilt; but gradually as she watched his handsome face in the glimmering light she came to understand that for him no guilt existed. Just as there had been no passion, no conflict. Nothing but the sane appraisal of their situation, nothing but the expectant little smile, and the arrogance of features that were different from John's. She winced deeply, remembering how she had fixed her eyes on those features, how she had tried to believe that so handsome and young, so different from John's, they must in themselves be her justification.

In the flickering light they were still young, still handsome. No longer her justification—she knew now—John was the man—but wistfully still, wondering sharply at their power and tyranny, she touched them a moment with her fingertips again.

She could not blame him. There had been no passion, no guilt; therefore there could be no responsibility. Looking down at him as he slept, half-smiling still, his lips relaxed in the conscienceless complacency of his achievement, she understood that thus he was revealed in his entirety—all there ever was or ever could be. John was the man. With him lay all the future. For tonight, slowly and contritely through the day and years to come, she would try to make amends.

Then she stole back to the kitchen, and without thought, impelled by overwhelming need again, returned to the door where the draught was bitter still. Gradually towards morning the storm began to spend itself. Its terror blast became a feeble, worn-out moan. The leap of light and shadow sank, and a chill crept in again. Always the eaves creaked, tortured with wordless prophecy. Heedless of it all the clock ticked on in idiot content.

They found him the next day, less than a mile from home. Drifting with the storm he had run against his own pasture fence and overcome had frozen there, erect still, both hands clasping fast the wire.

"He was south of here," they said wonderingly when she told them how he had come across the hills. "Straight south—you'd wonder how he could have missed the buildings. It was the wind last night, coming every way at once. He shouldn't have tried. There was a double wheel around the moon."

She looked past them a moment, then as if to herself said simply, "If you knew him, though—John would try."

It was later, when they had left her a while to be alone with him, that she knelt and touched his hand. Her eyes dimmed, it was still such a strong and patient hand; then, transfixed, they suddenly grew wide and clear. On the palm, white even against its frozen whiteness, was a little smear of paint.

TILLIE OLSEN

I Stand Here Ironing

I stand here ironing, and what you asked me moves tormented back and forth with the iron.

"I wish you would manage the time to come in and talk with me about your daughter. I'm sure you can help me understand her. She's a youngster who needs help and whom I'm deeply interested in helping."

"Who needs help." Even if I came, what good would it do? You think because I am her mother I have a key, or that in some way you could use me as a key? She has lived for nineteen years. There is all that life that has happened outside of me, beyond me.

And when is there time to remember, to sift, to weigh, to estimate, to total? I will start and there will be an interruption and I will have to gather it all together again. Or I will become engulfed with all I did or did not do, with what should have been and what cannot be helped.

She was a beautiful baby. The first and only one of our five that was beautiful at birth. You do not guess how new and uneasy her tenancy in her now-loveliness. You did not know her all those years she was thought homely, or see her poring over her baby pictures, making me tell her over and over how beautiful she had been—and would be, I would tell her—and was now, to the seeing eye. But the seeing eyes were few or nonexistent. Including mine.

I nursed her. They feel that's important nowadays. I nursed all the children, but with her, with all the fierce rigidity of first motherhood, I did like the books then said. Though her cries battered me to trembling and my breasts ached with swollenness, I waited till the clock decreed.

Why do I put that first? I do not even know if it matters, or if it explains anything.

She was a beautiful baby. She blew shining bubbles of sound. She loved motion, loved light, loved color and music and textures. She would lie on the floor in her blue overalls patting the surface so hard in ecstasy her hands and feet would blur. She was a miracle to me, but when she was eight months old I had to leave her daytimes with the woman downstairs to whom she was no miracle at all, for I worked or looked for work and for Emily's father, who "could no longer endure" (he wrote in his good-bye note) "sharing want with us."

I was nineteen. It was the pre-relief, pre-WPA[1] world of the depression. I would start running as soon as I got off the streetcar, running up the stairs, the place smelling sour, and awake or asleep to startle awake, when she saw me she would break into a clogged weeping that could not be comforted, a weeping I can hear yet.

After a while I found a job hashing at night so I could be with her days,

1. Works Progress Administration. An agency created during the Great Depression in the U.S. to make work for the unemployed.

and it was better. But it came to where I had to bring her to his family and leave her.

It took a long time to raise the money for her fare back. Then she got chicken pox and I had to wait longer. When she finally came, I hardly knew her, walking quick and nervous like her father, looking like her father, thin, and dressed in a shoddy red that yellowed her skin and glared at the pockmarks. All the baby loveliness gone.

She was two. Old enough for nursery school they said, and I did not know then what I know now—the fatigue of the long day, and the lacerations of group life in nurseries that are only parking places for children.

Except that it would have made no difference if I had known. It was the only place there was. It was the only way we could be together, the only way I could hold a job.

And even without knowing, I knew. I knew the teacher that was evil because all these years it has curdled into my memory, the little boy hunched in the corner, her rasp, "why aren't you outside, because Alvin hits you? that's no reason, go out, scaredy." I knew Emily hated it even if she did not clutch and implore "don't go Mommy" like the other children, mornings.

She always had a reason why we should stay home. Momma, you look sick, Momma. I feel sick. Momma, the teachers aren't there today, they're sick. Momma, we can't go, there was a fire there last night. Momma, it's a holiday today, no school, they told me.

But never a direct protest, never rebellion. I think of our others in their three-, four-year-oldness—the explosions, the tempers, the denunciations, the demands—and I feel suddenly ill. I put the iron down. What in me demanded that goodness in her? And what was the cost, the cost to her of such goodness?

The old man living in the back once said in his gentle way: "You should smile at Emily more when you look at her." What *was* in my face when I looked at her? I loved her. There were all the acts of love.

It was only with the others I remembered what he said, and it was the face of joy, and not of care or tightness or worry I turned to them—too late for Emily. She does not smile easily, let alone almost always as her brothers and sisters do. Her face is closed and sombre, but when she wants, how fluid. You must have seen it in her pantomimes, you spoke of her rare gift for comedy on the stage that rouses a laughter out of the audience so dear they applaud and applaud and do not want to let her go.

Where does it come from, that comedy? There was none of it in her when she came back to me that second time, after I had had to send her away again. She had a new daddy now to learn to love, and I think perhaps it was a better time.

Except when we left her alone nights, telling ourselves she was old enough.

"Can't you go some other time, Mommy, like tomorrow?" she would ask. "Will it be just a little while you'll be gone? Do you promise?"

The time we came back, the front door open, the clock on the floor in the hall. She rigid awake. "It wasn't just a little while. I didn't cry. Three times I called you, just three times, and then I ran downstairs to open the door so you could come faster. The clock talked loud. I threw it away, it scared me what it talked."

She said the clock talked loud again that night I went to the hospital to have Susan. She was delirious with the fever that comes before red measles, but she was fully conscious all the week I was gone and the week after we were home when she could not come near the new baby or me.

She did not get well. She stayed skeleton thin, not wanting to eat, and night after night she had nightmares. She would call for me, and I would rouse from exhaustion to sleepily call back: "You're all right, darling, go to sleep, it's just a dream," and if she still called, in a sterner voice, "now go to sleep, Emily, there's nothing to hurt you." Twice, only twice, when I had to get up for Susan anyhow, I went in to sit with her.

Now when it is too late (as if she would let me hold and comfort her like I do the others) I get up and go to her at once at her moan or restless stirring. "Are you awake, Emily? Can I get you something?" And the answer is always the same: "No, I'm all right, go back to sleep, Mother."

They persuaded me at the clinic to send her away to a convalescent home in the country where "she can have the kind of food and care you can't manage for her, and you'll be free to concentrate on the new baby." They still send children to that place. I see pictures on the society page of sleek young women planning affairs to raise money for it, or dancing at the affairs, or decorating Easter eggs or filling Christmas stockings for the children.

They never have a picture of the children so I do not know if the girls still wear those gigantic red bows and the ravaged looks on the every other Sunday when parents can come to visit "unless otherwise notified" — as we were notified the first six weeks.

Oh it is a handsome place, green lawns and tall trees and fluted flower beds. High up on the balconies of each cottage the children stand, the girls in their red bows and white dresses, the boys in white suits and giant red ties. The parents stand below shrieking up to be heard and the children shriek down to be heard, and between them the invisible wall "Not To Be Contaminated by Parental Germs or Physical Affection."

There was a tiny girl who always stood hand in hand with Emily. Her parents never came. One visit she was gone. "They moved her to Rose College," Emily shouted in explanation. "They don't like you to love anybody here."

She wrote once a week, the labored writing of a seven-year-old. "I am fine. How is the baby. If I write my leter nicly I will have a star. Love." There never was a star. We wrote every other day, letters she could never hold or keep but only hear read once. "We simply do not have room for children to keep any personal possessions," they patiently explained when we pieced one Sunday's shrieking together to plead how much it would mean to Emily, who loved so to keep things, to be allowed to keep her letters and cards.

Each visit she looked frailer. "She isn't eating," they told us.

(They had runny eggs for breakfast or mush with lumps, Emily said later, I'd hold it in my mouth and not swallow. Nothing ever tasted good, just when they had chicken.)

It took us eight months to get her released home, and only the fact that she gained back so little of her seven lost pounds convinced the social worker.

I used to try to hold and love her after she came back, but her body would stay stiff, and after a while she'd push away. She ate little. Food sickened her, and I think much of life too. Oh she had physical lightness and brightness, twinkling by on skates, bouncing like a ball up and down up and down over the jump rope, skimming over the hill; but these were momentary.

She fretted about her appearance, thin and dark and foreign-looking at a time when every little girl was supposed to look or thought she should look a chubby blonde replica of Shirley Temple. The doorbell sometimes rang for her, but no one seemed to come and play in the house or be a best friend. Maybe because we moved so much.

There was a boy she loved painfully through two school semesters. Months later she told me how she had taken pennies from my purse to buy him candy. "Licorice was his favorite and I brought him some every day, but he still liked Jennifer better'n me. Why, Mommy?" The kind of question for which there is no answer.

School was a worry to her. She was not glib or quick in a world where glibness and quickness were easily confused with ability to learn. To her overworked and exasperated teachers she was an overconscientious "slow learner" who kept trying to catch up and was absent entirely too often.

I let her be absent, though sometimes the illness was imaginary. How different from my now-strictness about attendance with the others. I wasn't working. We had a new baby, I was home anyhow. Sometimes, after Susan grew old enough, I would keep her home from school, too, to have them all together.

Mostly Emily had asthma, and her breathing, harsh and labored, would fill the house with a curiously tranquil sound. I would bring the two old dresser mirrors and her boxes of collections to her bed. She would select beads and single earrings, bottle tops and shells, dried flowers and pebbles, old postcards and scraps, all sorts of oddments; then she and Susan would play Kingdom, setting up landscapes and furniture, peopling them with action.

Those were the only times of peaceful companionship between her and Susan. I have edged away from it, that poisonous feeling between them, that terrible balancing of hurts and needs I had to do between the two, and did so badly, those earlier years.

Oh there are conflicts between the others too, each one human, needing, demanding, hurting, taking—but only between Emily and Susan, no, Emily toward Susan that corroding resentment. It seems so obvious on the surface, yet it is not obvious. Susan, the second child, Susan, golden- and curly-haired and chubby, quick and articulate and assured, everything in appearance and manner Emily was not; Susan, not able to resist Emily's precious things, losing or sometimes clumsily breaking them; Susan telling jokes and riddles to company for applause while Emily sat silent (to say to me later: that was *my* riddle, Mother, I told it to Susan); Susan, who for all the five years' difference in age was just a year behind Emily in developing physically.

I am glad for that slow physical development that widened the differ-

358 *Tillie Olsen*

ence between her and her contemporaries, though she suffered over it. She was too vulnerable for that terrible world of youthful competition, of preening and parading, of constant measuring of yourself against every other, of envy, "If I had that copper hair," "If I had that skin...." She tormented herself enough about not looking like the others, there was enough of the unsureness, the having to be conscious of words before you speak, the constant caring—what are they thinking of me? without having it all magnified by the merciless physical drives.

Ronnie is calling. He is wet and I change him. It is rare there is such a cry now. That time of motherhood is almost behind me when the ear is not one's own but must always be racked and listening for the child cry, the child call. We sit for a while and I hold him, looking out over the city spread in charcoal with its soft aisles of light. "*Shoogily*," he breathes and curls closer. I carry him back to bed, asleep. *Shoogily*. A funny word, a family word, inherited from Emily, invented by her to say: *comfort*.

In this and other ways she leaves her seal, I say aloud. And startle at my saying it. What do I mean? What did I start to gather together, to try and make coherent? I was at the terrible, growing years. War years. I do not remember them well. I was working, there were four smaller ones now, there was not time for her. She had to help be a mother, a housekeeper, and shopper. She had to set her seal. Mornings of crisis and near hysteria trying to get lunches packed, hair combed, coats and shoes found, everyone to school or Child Care on time, the baby ready for transportation. And always the paper scribbled on by a smaller one, the book looked at by Susan then mislaid, the homework not done. Running out to that huge school where she was one, she was lost, she was a drop; suffering over the unpreparedness, stammering and unsure in her classes.

There was so little time left at night after the kids were bedded down. She would struggle over books, always eating (it was in those years she developed her enormous appetite that is legendary in our family) and I would be ironing, or preparing food for the next day, or writing V-mail[2] to Bill, or tending the baby. Sometimes, to make me laugh, or out of her despair, she would imitate happenings or types at school.

I think I said once: "Why don't you do something like this in the school amateur show?" One morning she phoned me at work, hardly understandable through the weeping: "Mother, I did it. I won, I won; they gave me first prize; they clapped and clapped and wouldn't let me go."

Now suddenly she was Somebody, and as imprisoned in her difference as she had been in anonymity.

She began to be asked to perform at other high schools, even in colleges, then at city and statewide affairs. The first one we went to, I only recognized her that first moment when thin, shy, she almost drowned herself into the curtains. Then: Was this Emily? The control, the command, the convulsing and deadly clowning, the spell, then the roaring, stamping audience, unwilling to let this rare and precious laughter out of their lives.

Afterwards: You ought to do something about her with a gift like that

2. Mail to U.S. troops overseas during the Second World War.

—but without money or knowing how, what does one do? We have left it all to her, and the gift has as often eddied inside, clogged and clotted, as been used and growing.

She is coming. She runs up the stairs two at a time with her light graceful step, and I know she is happy tonight. Whatever it was that occasioned your call did not happen today.

"Aren't you ever going to finish the ironing, Mother? Whistler painted his mother in a rocker. I'd have to paint mine standing over an ironing board." This is one of her communicative nights and she tells me everything and nothing as she fixes herself a plate of food out of the icebox.

She is so lovely. Why did you want me to come in at all? Why were you concerned? She will find her way.

She starts up the stairs to bed. "Don't get me up with the rest in the morning." "But I thought you were having midterms." "Oh, those," she comes back in, kisses me, and says quite lightly, "in a couple of years when we'll all be atom-dead they won't matter a bit."

She has said it before. She *believes* it. But because I have been dredging the past, and all that compounds a human being is so heavy and meaningful in me, I cannot endure it tonight.

I will never total it all. I will never come in to say: She was a child seldom smiled at. Her father left me before she was a year old. I had to work her first six years when there was work, or I sent her home and to his relatives. There were years she had care she hated. She was dark and thin and foreign-looking in a world where the prestige went to blondeness and curly hair and dimples, she was slow where glibness was prized. She was a child of anxious, not proud, love. We were poor and could not afford for her the soil of easy growth. I was a young mother, I was a distracted mother. There were the other children pushing up, demanding. Her younger sister seemed all that she was not. There were years she did not want me to touch her. She kept too much in herself, her life was such she had to keep too much in herself. My wisdom came too late. She has much to her and probably nothing will come of it. She is a child of her age, of depression, of war, of fear.

Let her be. So all that is in her will not bloom—but in how many does it? There is still enough left to live by. Only help her to know—help make it so there is cause for her to know—that she is more than this dress on the ironing board, helpless before the iron.

BERNARD MALAMUD

Naked Nude

Fidelman listlessly doodled all over a sheet of yellow paper. Odd indecipherable designs, ink-spotted blotched words, esoteric ideographs, tormented figures in a steaming sulfurous lake, including a stylish nude rising
newborn from the water. Not bad at all, though more mannequin than
Knidean Aphrodite.[1] Scarpio, sharp-nosed on the former art student's
gaunt left, looking up from his cards inspected her with his good eye.

"Not bad, who is she?"

"Nobody I really know."

"You must be hard up."

"It happens in art."

"Quiet," rumbled Angelo, the padrone, on Fidelman's fat right, his
two-chinned face molded in lard. He flipped the top card.

Scarpio then turned up a deuce, making eight and a half and out. He
cursed his Sainted Mother, Angelo wheezing. Fidelman showed four and
his last hundred lire. He picked a cautious ace and sighed. Angelo, with
seven showing, chose that passionate moment to get up and relieve himself.

"Wait for me," he ordered. "Watch the money, Scarpio."

"Who's that hanging?" Scarpio pointed to a long-coated figure loosely
dangling from a gallows rope amid Fidelman's other drawings.

Who but Susskind, surely, a figure out of the far-off past.

"Just a friend."

"Which one?"

"Nobody you know."

"It better not be."

Scarpio picked up the yellow paper for a closer squint.

"But whose head?" he asked with interest. A long-nosed severed head
bounced down the steps of the guillotine platform.

A man's head or his sex? Fidelman wondered. In either case a terrible
wound.

"Looks a little like mine," he confessed. "At least the long jaw."

Scarpio pointed to a street scene. In front of American Express here's
this starving white Negro pursued by a hooting mob of cowboys on horses.

Embarrassed by the recent past Fidelman blushed.

It was long after midnight. They sat motionless in Angelo's stuffy
office, a small lit bulb hanging down over a square wooden table on which
lay a pack of puffy cards, Fidelman's naked hundred lire note, and a green
bottle of Munich beer that the padrone of the Hotel du Ville, Milano,
swilled from, between hands or games. Scarpio, his major domo and
secretary-lover, sipped an espresso, and Fidelman only watched, being
without privileges. Each night they played sette e mezzo,[2] jeenrummy or

---

1. Most famous statue of Praxiteles, Athenian
sculptor of the mid-fourth century B.C. The
goddess was shown nude, one hand in front of
her, the other holding a drapery.
2. Seven and a half.

baccarat and Fidelman lost the day's earnings, the few meager tips he had garnered from the whores for little services rendered. Angelo said nothing and took all.

Scarpio, snickering, understood the street scene. Fidelman, adrift penniless in the stony gray Milanese streets, had picked his first pocket, of an American tourist staring into a store window. The Texan, feeling the tug, and missing his wallet, had bellowed murder. A carabiniere[3] looked wildly at Fidelman, who broke into a run, another well-dressed carabiniere on a horse clattering after him down the street, waving his sword. Angelo, cleaning his fingernails with his penknife in front of his hotel, saw Fidelman coming and ducked him around a corner, through a cellar door, into the Hotel du Ville, a joint for prostitutes who split their fees with the padrone for the use of a room. Angelo registered the former art student, gave him a tiny dark room, and pointing a gun, relieved him of his passport, recently renewed, and the contents of the Texan's wallet. He warned him that if he so much as peeped to anybody, he would at once report him to the questura,[4] where his brother presided, as a dangerous alien thief. The former art student, desperate to escape, needed money to travel, so he sneaked into Angelo's room one morning and from the strapped suitcase under the bed, extracted fistfuls of lire, stuffing all his pockets. Scarpio, happening in, caught him at it and held a pointed dagger to Fidelman's ribs — who fruitlessly pleaded they could both make a living from the suitcase — until the padrone appeared.

"A hunchback is straight only in the grave." Angelo slapped Fidelman's face first with one fat hand, then with the other, till it turned red and the tears freely flowed. He chained him to the bed in his room for a week. When Fidelman promised to behave he was released and appointed "mastro delle latrine,"[5] having to clean thirty toilets every day with a stiff brush, for room and board. He also assisted Teresa, the asthmatic, hairy-legged chambermaid, and ran errands for the whores. The former art student hoped to escape but the portiere or his assistant was at the door twenty-four hours a day. And thanks to the card games and his impassioned gambling Fidelman was without sufficient funds to go anywhere, if there was anywhere to go. And without passport, so he stayed put.

Scarpio secretly felt Fidelman's thigh.

"Let go or I'll tell the padrone."

Angelo returned and flipped up a card. Queen. Seven and a half on the button. He pocketed Fidelman's last hundred lire.

"Go to bed," Angelo commanded. "It's a long day tomorrow."

Fidelman climbed up to his room on the fifth floor and stared out the window into the dark street to see how far down was death. Too far, so he undressed for bed. He looked every night and sometimes during the day. Teresa, screaming, had once held onto both his legs as Fidelman dangled half out of the window until one of the girls' naked customers, a barrel-chested man, rushed into the room and dragged him back in. Sometimes Fidelman wept in his sleep.

---

3. Policeman.
4. Police station.
5. Master of the latrine.

He awoke, cringing. Angelo and Scarpio had entered his room but nobody hit him.

"Search anywhere," he offered, "you won't find anything except maybe half a stale pastry."

"Shut up," said Angelo. "We came to make a proposition."

Fidelman slowly sat up. Scarpio produced the yellow sheet he had doodled on. "We notice you draw." He pointed a dirty fingernail at the nude figure.

"After a fashion," Fidelman said modestly. "I doodle and see what happens."

"Could you copy a painting?"

"What sort of painting?"

"A nude. Tiziano's 'Venus of Urbino.'[6] The one after Giorgione.'"[7]

"That one," said Fidelman, thinking. "I doubt that I could."

"Any fool can."

"Shut up, Scarpio," Angelo said. He sat his bulk at the foot of Fidelman's narrow bed. Scarpio, with his good eye, moodily inspected the cheerless view from the window.

"On Isola[8] Bella in Lago[9] Maggiore, about an hour from here," said Angelo, "there's a small castello[10] full of lousy paintings, except for one which is a genuine Tiziano, authenticated by three art experts, including a brother-in-law of mine. It's worth half a million dollars but the owner is richer than Olivetti and won't sell though an American museum is breaking its head to get it."

"Very interesting," Fidelman said.

"Exactly," said Angelo. "Anyway, it's insured for at least $400,000. Of course if anyone stole it it would be impossible to sell."

"Then why bother?"

"Bother what?"

"Whatever it is," Fidelman said lamely.

"You'll learn more by listening," Angelo said. "Suppose it was stolen and held for ransom. What do you think of that?"

"Ransom?" said Fidelman.

"Ransom," Scarpio said from the window.

"At least $300,000," said Angelo. "It would be a bargain for the insurance company. They'd save a hundred thousand on the deal."

He outlined a plan. They had photographed the Titian on both sides, from all angles and several distances and had collected from art books the best color plates. They also had the exact measurements of the canvas and every figure on it. If Fidelman could make a decent copy they would duplicate the frame and on a dark night sneak the reproduction into the castello gallery and exit with the original. The guards were stupid, and the advantage of the plan—instead of just slitting the canvas out of its frame— was that nobody would recognize the substitution for days, possibly

---

6. Titian (c. 1477–1576) was the leading master of the Venetian school of painting. His famous *Venus of Urbino* was executed in 1538.
7. Italian painter (1475–1510) associated with Titian. Titian's *Venus* seems to be derived from Giorgione's *The Sleeping Venus*. There is some speculation that Titian finished this particular painting by Giorgione.
8. Island.
9. Lake.
10. Castle.

longer. In the meantime they would row the picture across the lake and truck it out of the country down to the French Riviera. The Italian police had fantastic luck in recovering stolen paintings; one had a better chance in France. Once the picture was securely hidden, Angelo back at the hotel, Scarpio would get in touch with the insurance company. Imagine the sensation! Recognizing the brilliance of the execution, the company would have to kick in with the ransom money.

"If you make a good copy, you'll get yours," said Angelo.

"Mine? What would that be?" Fidelman asked.

"Your passport," Angelo said cagily. "Plus two hundred dollars in cash and a quick goodbye."

"Five hundred dollars," said Fidelman.

"Scarpio," said the padrone patiently, "show him what you have in your pants."

Scarpio unbuttoned his jacket and drew a long mean-looking dagger from a sheath under his belt. Fidelman without trying, could feel the cold blade sinking into his ribs.

"Three fifty," he said. "I'll need plane fare."

"Three fifty," said Angelo. "Payable when you deliver the finished reproduction."

"And you pay for all supplies?"

"I pay all expenses within reason. But if you try any monkey tricks — snitch or double cross you'll wake up with your head gone, or something worse."

"Tell me," Fidelman asked after a minute of contemplation, "what if I turn down the proposition? I mean in a friendly way?"

Angelo rose sternly from the creaking bed. "Then you'll stay here for the rest of your life. When you leave you leave in a coffin, very cheap wood."

"I see," said Fidelman.

"What do you say?"

"What more can I say?"

"Then it's settled," said Angelo.

"Take the morning off," said Scarpio.

"Thanks," Fidelman said.

Angelo glared. "First finish the toilet bowls."

Am I worthy? Fidelman thought. Can I do it? Do I dare? He had these and other doubts, felt melancholy, and wasted time.

Angelo one morning called him into his office. "Have a Munich beer."

"No, thanks."

"Cordial?"

"Nothing now."

"What's the matter with you? You look like you buried your mother."

Fidelman set down his mop and pail with a sigh and said nothing.

"Why don't you put those things away and get started?" the padrone asked. "I've had the portiere move six trunks and some broken furniture out of the storeroom where you have two big windows. Scarpio wheeled in an easel and he's bought you brushes, colors and whatever else you need."

"It's west light, not very even."

Angelo shrugged. "It's the best I can do. This is our season and I can't spare any rooms. If you'd rather work at night we can set up some lamps. It's a waste of electricity but I'll make that concession to your temperament if you work fast and produce the goods."

"What's more I don't know the first thing about forging paintings," Fidelman said. "All I might do is just about copy the picture."

"That's all we ask. Leave the technical business to us. First do a decent drawing. When you're ready to paint I'll get you a piece of sixteenth-century Belgian linen that's been scraped clean of a former picture. You prime it with white lead and when it's dry you sketch. Once you finish the nude, Scarpio and I will bake it, put in the cracks, and age them with soot. We'll even stipple in fly spots before we varnish and glue. We'll do what's necessary. There are books on this subject and Scarpio reads like a demon. It isn't as complicated as you think."

"What about the truth of the colors?"

"I'll mix them for you. I've made a life study of Tiziano's work."

"Really?"

"Of course."

But Fidelman's eyes still looked unhappy.

"What's eating you now?" the padrone asked.

"It's stealing another painter's ideas and work."

The padrone wheezed. "Tiziano will forgive you. Didn't he steal the figure of the Urbino from Giorgione? Didn't Rubens steal the Andrian nude[11] from Tiziano? Art steals and so does everybody. You stole a wallet and tried to steal my lire. It's the way of the world. We're only human."

"Isn't it sort of a desecration?"

"Everybody desecrates. We live off the dead and they live off us. Take for instance religion."

"I don't think I can do it without seeing the original," Fidelman said. "The color plates you gave me aren't true."

"Neither is the original any more. You don't think Rembrandt painted in those sfumato browns? As for painting the Venus, you'll have to do the job here. If you copied it in the castello gallery one of those cretin guards might remember your face and the next thing you know you'd have trouble. So would we, probably, and we naturally wouldn't want that."

"I still ought to see it," Fidelman said obstinately.

The padrone then reluctantly consented to a one-day excursion to Isola Bella, assigning Scarpio to closely accompany the copyist.

On the vaporetto[12] to the island, Scarpio, wearing dark glasses and a light straw hat, turned to Fidelman.

"In all confidence, what do you think of Angelo?"

"He's all right, I guess."

"Do you think he's handsome?"

"I haven't given it a thought. Possibly he was, once."

"You have many fine insights," said Scarpio. He pointed in the dis-

---

11. Titian's painting *Bacchanal of the And-*
rians (1518–19) was copied by Rubens.
12. Steam launch.

tance where the long blue lake disappeared amid towering Alps. "Locarno, sixty kilometers."

"You don't say." At the thought of Switzerland so close by, freedom swelled in Fidelman's heart but he did nothing about it. Scarpio clung to him like a long-lost brother and sixty kilometers was a long swim with a knife in your back.

"That's the castello over there," the major domo said. "It looks like a joint."

The castello was pink on a high terraced hill amid tall trees in formal gardens. It was full of tourists and bad paintings. But in the last gallery, "infinite riches in a little room"[13] hung the "Venus of Urbino" alone.

What a miracle, thought Fidelman.

The golden brown-haired Venus, a woman of the real world, lay on her couch in serene beauty, her hand lightly touching her intimate mystery, the other holding red flowers, her nude body her truest accomplishment.

"I would have painted somebody in bed with her," Scarpio said.

"Shut up," said Fidelman.

Scarpio, hurt, left the gallery.

Fidelman, alone with Venus, worshipped the painting. What magnificent tones, what extraordinary flesh that can turn the body into spirit.

While Scarpio was out talking to the guard, the copyist hastily sketched the Venus, and with a Leica Angelo had borrowed from a friend for the purpose, took several new color shots.

Afterwards he approached the picture and kissed the lady's hands, thighs, and breasts, but as he was murmuring, "I love you," a guard struck him hard on the head with both fists.

That night as they returned on the rapido to Milano, Scarpio fell asleep, snoring. He awoke in a hurry, tugging at his dagger, but Fidelman hadn't moved.

2

The copyist threw himself into his work with passion. He had swallowed lightning and hoped it would strike whatever he touched. Yet he had nagging doubts he could do the job right and feared he would never escape alive from the Hotel du Ville. He tried at once to paint the Titian directly on canvas but hurriedly scraped it clean when he saw what a garish mess he had made. The Venus was insanely disproportionate and the maids in the background foreshortened into dwarfs. He then took Angelo's advice and made several drawings on paper to master the composition before committing it again to canvas.

Angelo and Scarpio came up every night and shook their heads over the drawings.

"Not even close," said the padrone.

"Far from it," said Scarpio.

"I'm trying," Fidelman said, anguished.

"Try harder," Angelo said grimly.

---

13. Christopher Marlowe, *The Jew of Malta*, I.i.37.

Fidelman had a sudden insight. "What happened to the last guy who tried?"

"He's still floating," Scarpio said.

"I'll need some practice," the copyist coughed. "My vision seems tight and the arm tires easily. I'd better go back to some exercises to loosen up."

"What kind of exercises?" Scarpio inquired.

"Nothing physical, just some warm-up nudes to get me going."

"Don't overdo it," Angelo said. "You've got about a month, not much more. There's a certain advantage in making the exchange of pictures during the tourist season."

"Only a month?"

The padrone nodded.

"Maybe you'd better trace it," Scarpio said.

"No."

"I'll tell you what," said Angelo. "I could get you an old reclining nude you could paint over. You might get the form of this one by altering the form of another."

"No."

"Why not?"

"It's not honest. I mean to myself."

Everyone tittered.

"Well, it's your headache," Angelo said.

Fidelman, unwilling to ask what happened if he failed, after they had left, feverishly drew faster.

Things went badly for the copyist. Working all day and often into the very early morning hours, he tried everything he could think of. Since he always distorted the figure of Venus, though he carried it perfect in his mind, he went back to a study of Greek statuary with ruler and compass to compute the mathematical proportions of the ideal nude. Scarpio accompanied him to one or two museums. Fidelman also worked with the Vetruvian square[14] in the circle, experimented with Dürer's intersecting circles and triangles[15] and studied Leonardo's schematic heads and bodies.[16] Nothing doing. He drew paper dolls, not women, certainly not Venus. He drew girls who would not grow up. He then tried sketching every nude he could lay eyes on in the art books Scarpio brought him from the library, from the Esquiline goddess[17] to "Les Demoiselles d'Avignon."[18] Fidelman copied not badly many figures from classical statuary and modern painting, but when he returned to his Venus, with something of a laugh she eluded him. What am I, bewitched, the copyist asked himself, and if so by what? It's

14. Vitruvius was a late first century B.C. and early first century A.D. Roman writer on architecture and an engineer and architect. His theories were much used by Renaissance artists. Squares, circles, and triangles were used as units of measurement.

15. Dürer (1471–1528) was a German painter, engraver, and theoretician. Influenced by Vitruvius and Leonardo, he is known for superbly proportioned figures. He developed a highly rational system of perspective and bodily proportions.

16. Leonardo da Vinci (1452–1519) was an Italian painter, sculptor, architect, musician, engineer, and scientist. Like Vitruvius and Dürer, Leonardo was interested in proportion, or measurement, and he executed intricate anatomical studies of people.

17. Statue of Aphrodite called the *Esquiline Venus*. Roman copy of Greek statue, first half of first century B.C.

18. Painting by Picasso (1907).

only a copy job so what's taking so long? He couldn't even guess until he happened to see a naked whore cross the hall and enter a friend's room. Maybe the ideal is cold and I like it hot? Nature over art? Inspiration—the live model? Fidelman knocked on the door and tried to persuade the girl to pose for him but she wouldn't for economic reasons. Neither would any of the others—there were four girls in the room.

A red-head among them called out to Fidelman, "Shame on you, Arturo, are you too good to bring up pizzas and coffee any more?"

"I'm busy on a job for Angelo."

The girls laughed.

"Painting a picture, that is. A business proposition."

They laughed louder.

Their laughter further depressed his spirits. No inspiration from whores. Maybe too many naked women around made it impossible to draw a nude. Still he'd better try a live model, having tried everything else and failed.

In desperation, practically on the verge of panic because time was going so fast, he thought of Teresa, the chambermaid. She was a poor specimen of feminine beauty but the imagination could enhance anything. Fidelman asked her to pose for him, and Teresa, after a shy laugh, consented.

"I will if you promise not to tell anybody."

Fidelman promised.

She got undressed, a meager, bony girl, breathing heavily, and he drew her with flat chest, distended belly, thin hips and hairy legs, unable to alter a single detail. Van Eyck[19] would have loved her. When Teresa saw the drawing she wept profusely.

"I thought you would make me beautiful."

"I had that in mind."

"Then why didn't you?"

"It's hard to say," said Fidelman.

"I'm not in the least bit sexy," she wept.

Considering her body with half-open eyes, Fidelman told her to go borrow a long slip.

"Get one from one of the girls and I'll draw you sexy."

She returned in a frilly white slip and looked so attractive that instead of painting her, Fidelman, with a lump in his throat, got her to lie down with him on a dusty mattress in the room. Clasping her slip-encased form, the copyist shut both eyes and concentrated on his elusive Venus. He felt about to recapture a rapturous experience and was looking forward to it but at the last minute it turned into a limerick he didn't know he knew:

"Whilst Titian was mixing rose madder,
His model was crouched on a ladder;
Her position to Titian suggested coition,
So he stopped mixing madder and had 'er."

Angelo entering the storeroom just then, let out a furious bellow. He

19. Jan Van Eyck, a fifteenth-century
Flemish painter.

fired Teresa on her naked knees pleading with him not to, and Fidelman had to go back to latrine duty the rest of the day.

"You might just as well keep me doing this permanently," Fidelman, disheartened, told the padrone in his office afterward. "I'll never finish that cursed picture."

"Why not? What's eating you? I've treated you like a son."

"I'm blocked, that's what."

"Get to work, you'll feel better."

"I just can't paint."

"For what reason?"

"I don't know."

"Because you've had it too good here." Angelo angrily struck Fidelman across the face. When the copyist wept, he booted him hard in the rear.

That night Fidelman went on a hunger strike but the padrone, hearing of it, threatened force feeding.

After midnight Fidelman stole some clothes from a sleeping whore, dressed quickly, tied on a kerchief, made up his eyes and lips, and walked out the door past Scarpio sitting on a bar stool, enjoying the night breeze. Having gone a block, fearing he would be chased, Fidelman broke into a high-heeled run but it was too late. Scarpio had recognized him in aftermath and called the portiere. Fidelman kicked off his slippers and ran furiously but the skirt impeded him. The major domo and portiere caught up with him and dragged him, kicking and struggling, back to the hotel. A carabiniere, hearing the commotion, appeared on the scene, but seeing how Fidelman was dressed, would do nothing for him. In the cellar Angelo hit him with a short rubber hose until he collapsed.

Fidelman lay in bed three days, refusing to eat or get up.

"What'll we do now?" Angelo, worried, whispered. "How about a fortune teller? Either that or let's bury him."

"Astrology is better," Scarpio advised. "I'll check his planets. If that doesn't work we'll try psychology."

"Well, make it fast," said Angelo.

The next morning Scarpio entered Fidelman's room with an American breakfast on a tray and two thick books under his arm. Fidelman was still in bed, smoking a butt. He wouldn't eat.

Scarpio set down his books and took a chair close to the bed.

"What's your birthday, Arturo?" he asked gently, feeling Fidelman's pulse.

Fidelman told him, also the hour of birth and the place: Bronx, New York.

Scarpio, consulting the zodiacal tables, drew up Fidelman's horoscope on a sheet of paper and studied it thoroughly with his good eye. After a few minutes he shook his head. "It's no wonder."

"What's wrong?" Fidelman sat up weakly.

"Your Uranus and Venus are both in bad shape."

"My Venus?"

"She rules your fate." He studied the chart. "Taurus ascending, Venus afflicted. That's why you're blocked."

"Afflicted by what?"

"Sh," said Scarpio, "I'm checking your Mercury."

"Concentrate on Venus, when will she be better?"

Scarpio consulted the tables, jotted down some numbers and signs and slowly turned pale. He searched through a few more pages of tables, then got up and stared out the dirty window.

"It's hard to tell. Do you believe in psychoanalysis?"

"Sort of."

"Maybe we'd better try that. Don't get up."

Fidelman's head fell back on the pillow.

Scarpio opened a thick book to its first chapter. "The thing to do is associate freely."

"If I don't get out of this whorehouse soon I'll surely die," said Fidelman.

"Do you have any memories of your mother?" Scarpio asked. "For instance, did you ever see her naked?"

"She died at my birth," Fidelman answered, on the verge of tears. "I was raised by my sister Bessie."

"Go on, I'm listening," said Scarpio.

"I can't. My mind goes blank."

Scarpio turned to the next chapter, flipped through several pages, then rose with a sigh.

"It might be a medical matter. Take a physic tonight."

"I already have."

The major domo shrugged. "Life is complicated. Anyway, keep track of your dreams. Write them down as soon as you have them."

Fidelman puffed his butt.

That night he dreamed of Bessie about to bathe. He was peeking at her through the bathroom keyhole as she was preparing her bath. Open-mouthed he watched her remove her robe and step into the tub. Her hefty well-proportioned body then was young and full in the right places; and in the dream Fidelman, then fourteen, looked at her with longing that amounted to anguish. The older Fidelman, the dreamer, considered doing a "La Baigneuse"[20] right then and there, but when Bessie began to soap herself with Ivory soap, the boy slipped away into her room, opened her poor purse, filched fifty cents for the movies, and went on tiptoes down the stairs.

He was shutting the vestibule door with great relief when Arthur Fidelman woke with a headache. As he was scribbling down this dream he suddenly remembered what Angelo had said: "Everybody steals. We're all human."

A stupendous thought occurred to him: Suppose he personally were to steal the picture?

A marvelous idea all around. Fidelman heartily ate that morning's breakfast.

---

20. The "bather" was a popular subject for the post-impressionist painters of the late nineteenth century. This is possibly a refer-ence to a specific *La Baigneuse* by Cézanne (1839–1906), who painted a number of bathers.

370 *Bernard Malamud*

To steal the picture he had to paint one. Within another day the copyist successfully sketched Titian's painting and then began to work in oils on an old piece of Flemish linen that Angelo had hastily supplied him with after seeing the successful drawing. Fidelman underpainted the canvas and after it was dry began the figure of Venus as the conspirators looked on sucking their breaths.

"Stay relaxed," begged Angelo, sweating. "Don't spoil it now. Remember you're painting the appearance of a picture. The original has already been painted. Give us a decent copy and we'll do the rest with chemistry."

"I'm worried about the brush strokes."

"Nobody will notice them. Just keep in your mind that Tiziano painted resolutely with few strokes, his brush loaded with color. In the end he would paint with his fingers. Don't worry about that. We don't ask for perfection, just a good copy."

He rubbed his fat hands nervously.

But Fidelman painted as though he were painting the original. He worked alone late at night, when the conspirators were snoring, and he painted with what was left of his heart. He had caught the figure of the Venus but when it came to her flesh, her thighs and breasts, he never thought he would make it. As he painted he seemed to remember every nude that had ever been done, Fidelman satyr, with Silenus[21] beard and goatlegs dancing among them, piping and peeking at backside, frontside, or both, at the "Rokeby Venus," "Bathsheba," "Suzanna," "Venus Anadyomene," "Olympia," at picnickers in dress or undress, bathers ditto, Vanitas or Truth, Niobe or Leda, in chase or embrace, hausfrau or whore, amorous ladies modest or brazen, single or in the crowds at the Turkish bath, in every conceivable shape or position, while he sported or disported until a trio of maenads[22] pulled his curly beard and he galloped after them through the dusky woods. He was at the same time choked by remembered lust for all the women he had ever desired, from Bessie to Annamaria Oliovino, and for their garters, underpants, slips or half slips, brassieres and stockings. Although thus tormented, Fidelman felt himself falling in love with the one he painted, every inch of her, including the ring on her pinky, bracelet on arm, the flowers she touched with her fingers, and the bright green earring that dangled from her eatable ear. He would have prayed her alive if he weren't certain she would fall in love, not with her famished creator, but surely the first Apollo Belvedere[23] she laid eyes on. Is there, Fidelman asked himself, a world where love endures and is always satisfying? He answered in the negative. Still she was his as he painted, so he went on painting, planning never to finish, to be happy as he was in loving her, thus forever happy.

21. In Greek mythology, the foster father and tutor of Bacchus and leader of the satyrs. Traditionally pictured as a fat, drunken, lecherous, jovial old man with pointed ears and goat's legs.
22. In Greek and Roman mythology, female devotees of Dionysus. When they danced they worked themselves into an ecstatic frenzy.
23. Roman marble copy probably of a Greek original of the late fourth (or first) century B.C. This statue was tremendously popular in the eighteenth and nineteenth centuries, and many plaster casts or reproductions of it exist today.

But he finished the picture on Saturday night, Angelo's gun pressed to his head. Then the Venus was taken from him and Scarpio and Angelo baked, smoked, stippled and varnished, stretched and framed Fidelman's masterwork as the artist lay on his bed in his room in a state of collapse.

"The Venus of Urbino, c'est moi."

3

"What about my three hundred and fifty?" Fidelman asked Angelo during a card game in the padrone's stuffy office several days later. After completing the painting the copyist was again back on janitorial duty.

"You'll collect when we've got the Tiziano."

"I did my part."

"Don't question decisions."

"What about my passport?"

"Give it to him, Scarpio."

Scarpio handed him the passport. Fidelman flipped through the booklet and saw all the pages were intact.

"If you skidoo now," Angelo warned him, "You'll get spit."

"Who's skidooing?"

"So the plan is this: You and Scarpio will row out to the castello after midnight. The caretaker is an old man and half deaf. You hang our picture and breeze off with the other."

"If you wish," Fidelman suggested, "I'll gladly do the job myself. Alone, that is."

"Why alone?" said Scarpio suspiciously.

"Don't be foolish," Angelo said. "With the frame it weighs half a ton. Now listen to directions and don't give any. One reason I detest Americans is they never know their place."

Fidelman apologized.

"I'll follow in the putt-putt and wait for you halfway between Isola Bella and Stresa in case we need a little extra speed at the last minute."

"Do you expect trouble?"

"Not a bit. If there's any trouble it'll be your fault. In that case watch out."

"Off with his head," said Scarpio. He played a deuce and took the pot.

Fidelman laughed politely.

The next night, Scarpio rowed a huge weatherbeaten rowboat, both oars muffled. It was a moonless night with touches of Alpine lightning in the distant sky. Fidelman sat on the stern, holding with both hands and balancing against his knees the large framed painting, heavily wrapped in monk's cloth and cellophane, and tied around with rope.

At the island the major domo docked the boat and secured it. Fidelman, peering around in the dark, tried to memorize where they were. They carried the picture up two hundred steps, both puffing when they got to the formal gardens on top.

The castello was black except for a square of yellow light from the caretaker's turret window high above. As Scarpio snapped the lock of an embossed heavy wooden door with a strip of celluloid, the yellow window slowly opened and an old man peered down. They froze against the wall until the window was drawn shut.

"Fast," Scarpio hissed. "If anyone sees us they'll wake the whole island."

Pushing open the creaking door, they quickly carried the painting, growing heavier as they hurried, through an enormous room cluttered with cheap statuary, and by the light of the major domo's flashlight, ascended a narrow flight of spiral stairs. They hastened in sneakers down a deep-shadowed, tapestried hall into the picture gallery, Fidelman stopping in his tracks when he beheld the Venus, the true and magnificent image of his counterfeit creation.

"Let's get to work." Scarpio quickly unknotted the rope and they unwrapped Fidelman's painting and leaned it against the wall. They were taking down the Titian when footsteps sounded unmistakably in the hall. Scarpio's flashlight went out.

"Sh, it's the caretaker. If he comes in I'll have to conk him."

"That'll destroy Angelo's plan—deceit, not force."

"I'll think of that when we're out of here."

They pressed their backs to the wall, Fidelman's clammy, as the old man's steps drew nearer. The copyist had anguished visions of losing the picture and made helter-skelter plans somehow to reclaim it. Then the footsteps faltered, came to a stop, and after a moment of intense hesitation, moved in another direction. A door slammed and the sound was gone.

It took Fidelman several seconds to breathe. They waited in the dark without moving until Scarpio shone his light. Both Venuses were resting against the same wall. The major domo closely inspected each canvas with one eye shut, then signaled the painting on the left. "That's the one, let's wrap it up."

Fidelman broke into profuse sweat.

"Are you crazy? That's mine. Don't you know a work of art when you see it?" He pointed to the other picture.

"Art?" said Scarpio, removing his hat and turning pale. "Are you sure?" He peered at the painting.

"Without a doubt."

"Don't try to confuse me." He tapped the dagger under his coat.

"The lighter one is the Titian," Fidelman said through a dry throat. "You smoked mine a shade darker."

"I could have sworn yours was the lighter."

"No, Titian's. He used light varnishes. It's a historical fact."

"Of course." Scarpio mopped his brow with a soiled handkerchief. "The trouble is with my eyes. One is in bad shape and I overuse the other."

"Tst-tst," clucked Fidelman.

"Anyway, hurry up. Angelo's waiting on the lake. Remember, if there's any mistake he'll cut your throat first."

They hung the darker painting on the wall, quickly wrapped the lighter and hastily carried it through the long hall and down the stairs, Fidelman leading the way with Scarpio's light.

At the dock the major domo nervously turned to Fidelman. "Are you absolutely sure we have the right one?"

"I give you my word."

"I accept it but under the circumstances I'd better have another look. Shine the flashlight through your fingers."

Scarpio knelt to undo the wrapping once more, and Fidelman, trembling, brought the flashlight down hard on Scarpio's straw hat, the light shattering in his hand. The major domo, pulling at his dagger, collapsed.

Fidelman had trouble loading the painting into the rowboat but finally got it in and settled, and quickly took off. In ten minutes he had rowed out of sight of the dark castled island. Not long afterward he thought he heard Angelo's putt-putt behind him, and his heart beat erratically, but the padrone did not appear. He rowed as the waves deepened.

Locarno, sixty kilometers.

A wavering flash of lightning pierced the broken sky, lighting the agitated lake all the way to the Alps, as a dreadful thought assailed Fidelman: had he the right painting, after all? After a minute he pulled in his oars, listened once more for Angelo, and hearing nothing, stepped to the stern of the rowboat, letting it drift as he frantically unwrapped the Venus.

In the pitch black, on the lake's choppy waters, he saw she was indeed his, and by the light of numerous matches adored his handiwork.

W. D. VALGARDSON

Hunting

In his prime, Sonny Brum had been 280 pounds of muscle that angled sharply from broad, straight shoulders to a narrow waist, but years of sitting around a display room drinking coffee and eating jelly busters as he waited for customers had thickened him. The muscle had diminished but his appetite had not and a heavy roll of flesh sagged over his belt. His head was square, his skin swarthy and his nose, which was large and hooked, had been broken so many times that it was permanently bent to the left. A white scar curved like a third eyebrow in the middle of his forehead. When he walked, he did so with a hesitating limp.

If he had been older, he could have been a casualty of some foreign war, one of those who put on blue blazers and lay wreaths once a year, but he was not. His facial scars had been gathered in the vicious struggles of semi-pro football and his knee-cap had been smashed during the first game he played for the Winnipeg Blue Bombers. Although his first game as a pro had been his last, he had, on the wall of his office, a 24-by-18-inch photograph of himself in uniform with the rest of the team and he always carried a wallet-size duplicate along with his birth certificate and his driver's licence.

Although it was only seven o'clock, he had been awake since five. First, he lay in bed and worried. Then, when he couldn't stand to be inactive any longer, he dressed and paced through the cold rooms of the house. Because it was Sunday and there was no hunting, he was afraid that Buzz Anderson and Roger Charleston, having nothing to keep them entertained, would want to return home. Not having got their deer right away had made them discontented. Even though they hadn't complained, he could tell that it wouldn't take much for them to decide to leave. Since he was unable to think of anything else to keep them happy, he had decided to take them to the bootlegger's.

They had meant to use the entire house but they couldn't get the furnace to work so they had moved three cots into the kitchen and were heating the room with a catalytic heater.

Sonny swung open the kitchen door and let it bang closed behind him. Roger sat up and dug the knuckles of his index fingers into his eyes. He kicked himself free of his blankets and swung his feet over the edge of the cot. His legs, like the rest of him, were pale and flat looking. All he had on were jockey shorts as he sauntered over to the counter and bent down to peer outside.

"We're going to get some snow," he said.

The sky was dull grey and the distant sun was small and pale. On the horizon there was a ridge of pewter cloud.

"Good," Sonny replied. "That'll make tracking easier. You wound a deer and he'll leave a trail nobody can miss. Blood on the snow's the best thing you can have."

Roger stood on one leg, then the other, to pull on his pants. "We've got to see them before we shoot them." His voice carried a hint of irritation. He tucked in his shirt, then went back to standing on one leg to pull on his white coveralls.

"Hey, Buzz, what do you want for breakfast?" Sonny lit the Coleman stove and put on the coffee-pot.

Buzz groaned and sat up. He had on an orange toque and a matching scarf. He was constantly afraid of catching a cold or getting laryngitis and not being able to host his morning radio show for housewives. "Bacon, eggs, coffee, whisky," he said. "In that order." With a sigh, he dropped back onto the bed.

The kitchen smelled stale. The house was solid and large, with five bedrooms upstairs, four rooms downstairs and a full basement, but it had been empty for so long that the front yard was overgrown with young poplars.

After breakfast, when Sonny led the way outside, the air was sharp. The Russian thistle, touched by frost, drooped blackly. In the muted light the branches of the trees were stark and brittle looking. Huddled together on the porch, the three of them studied the dark edge of the forest that gaped toward them, then turned to study the yellows and browns of the fields that staggered toward the horizon.

"See there!" Sonny called out, punching his large red fist in the air. His two companions squinted and strained to see what had excited him, but there was nothing except the trees and weeds.

Keeping his left leg stiff, he awkwardly descended the stairs and with his massive arms moving before him in a breast stroke, swept the saplings out of his way. The other two followed him uncertainly. He snapped off the stem of a poplar and held it out for their inspection. The top had been bitten off and the tender outer bark nibbled away.

"Look at that," he said. "There were deer in here last night. Tomorrow morning we can get up early and shoot one or two from the doorway."

Buzz and Roger's interest had risen sharply and, for the moment, Sonny's worry eased. Their goodwill was crucial to him. After recuperating from a series of operations on his knee, he had become a salesman with a Ford dealership next to the stadium. He hated every minute of his fifteen years of working for someone else but by saving every cent possible, and buying and selling used cars out of his backyard, he finally managed to gather enough for a down payment on a dealership. At the same time, he moved his wife and daughter into a new house in a good neighbourhood. Then, a series of small reverses combined with too little capital squeezed him into a position where he had to have more money or lose his business.

During his two years in his new neighbourhood, he had assiduously cultivated his neighbours in the hope of turning them into customers. Now, pressed for cash, and unable to obtain further credit, he had invited Roger and Buzz on a hunting trip.

Neither of them had been deer hunting before but both had said they would like to go hunting. That, and the fact that they both had steered customers his way in return for a bottle of whisky or a pair of football tickets, made him choose them. As well, he knew from a credit check he had had run on them, that they had a fair amount of money salted away.

What he intended to do was wait until they both had a deer and a few drinks and then offer to make them silent partners. He already had the papers made up.

Buzz quit studying the chewed stems and started for the car. His low, gentle voice drew women to his program in large numbers but he never allowed himself to be photographed if he could help it. He was barely five feet tall and his face — round and smooth, with slightly bulging eyes, a small, nearly bridgeless nose, red hair and freckles — made him look like a mildly retarded child.

They set off in Buzz's car, a maroon Cadillac he had bought for $200. It wasn't much to look at. The left rear door was caved in, its window held together with a black spider-web of electrician's tape. The fenders were so rusted that their edges resembled brown lace, but the motor ran well and the tires still had half a penny's width of rubber. Its major fault was that the steering was so loose that Buzz had a hard time keeping it under control.

The area they were driving through had, at one time, been the bottom of a lake. Now, a series of gravel ridges marked the successive shorelines. In the hollows, swamp grass that was the same pale brown as a red squirrel's ruff rose as high as the car windows and willow clustered in dark, impenetrable thickets. The crests were crowded with scrub oak, hazel and black poplar.

It was on the crest of a ridge that they saw a buck standing in a hazel thicket.

"Lookit that!" Roger hollered, startling Buzz so badly that he jammed on the brakes. Sonny was sitting in the back. The sudden stop nearly pitched him into the front seat.

"Look at that rack," Buzz sighed, thinking of the family room in his basement. "He's got seven points."

"I told you," Sonny said jubilantly. "I told you the way it was."

"We don't have our rifles," Roger reminded them. He had a long tubular face and the minute he was unhappy he looked like an undertaker. He pressed as close as possible to the windshield.

"I put my .22 into the trunk, remember," Sonny answered. "Give me the keys."

Buzz handed him the keys and Sonny slipped outside. Without taking his eyes off the buck, he crept to the rear of the car. Easing the trunk up slowly, he reached past the spare wheel and lifted out a rifle wound in burlap. He unwrapped it, raised it to his shoulder and squeezed the trigger. There was a sharp click.

Cursing under his breath, he tip-toed along the driver's side of the car. "Bullets," he whispered urgently. "I left them in the glove compartment."

The buck was so close that Sonny could have hit it with a rock. It stood at an angle to them, shoulder-deep in brush, its head turned sideways. The curving antlers looked polished.

"Here," Buzz said, shoving the box out of the window upside down. As Sonny snatched the box, the lid popped open and the cartridges cascaded to the ground. Sonny stood stupefied, then flung the empty box aside and scooped up a handful of cartridges and gravel. Before he could get a bullet into the chamber, the buck trotted across the road and disappeared with a bound.

Sonny fumbled a moment longer, then bitterly snapped, "Son-of-a-bitch!" He restrained an impulse to smash the car window.

As Roger and Buzz joined him, Sonny handed Roger the rifle. Then he and Buzz picked up the spilled cartridges.

"I couldn't get a bullet into the gun," Sonny explained defensively. The incident had shaken him. The buck seemed symbolic. Everything, his house, his business, his independence, seemed ready to slip away while he stood and watched helplessly.

"It was Sunday anyway," Buzz replied.

"Mounties," Roger warned. A black car had topped the adjacent ridge and was racing toward them. As Buzz and Sonny ran to the side of the road, Roger stood stupefied, then, as his long legs scissored beneath him, carrying him to safety, he flung the rifle into the bush.

Seconds later, a black Ford rocketed past, spraying them with gravel. The driver was an old woman with a green, wide-brimmed hat jammed over her ears.

With a sigh of relief, Buzz sat on a tree stump. Dramatically, he felt his heart. "You shouldn't do that, Roger. If my sponsors ever found out that I had been arrested for hunting illegally. . . . " He left the rest unsaid.

"Where's my rifle?" Sonny asked.

Wordlessly, Roger scurried into the bush and began flailing about like a wounded duck. When he found the rifle, he waved it over his head.

To be certain the rifle was not damaged, Sonny loaded it, then fired three times. A hundred feet away, on the edge of the road, gravel flew into the air and a tin can jumped and spun on its rim before falling back. With a grunt of satisfaction, he rewrapped the rifle and stuffed it under the front seat.

Buzz brought back the can. It was pitted with rust but the edges of the bullet holes were bright and shiny. Where a hollow-nosed slug had entered, the hole was smaller than the end of a little finger. Where it exited, the hole was larger than a nickel and the edges were bent back like the sepals of a rose after the petals have fallen.

As they drove, they passed some farmhouses that, except for the television aerials on the roofs, looked abandoned. Frequently, they saw people working among the roadside bushes. Buzz slowed down.

"What are they doing?" he asked.

"Collecting hazelnuts," Sonny answered. "They husk them and sell them to the wholesale in Winnipeg."

A man and woman were working close to the road. Each held a gunny sack. The man wore rubber boots, overalls, a brown jacket and cap. The woman wore a red *babushka*, a brown jacket and a faded dress with men's pants underneath. Two boys, dressed exactly like their father, emerged to stare at the car. Like their parents, they might have been part of the weathered landscape. From a short distance, they were nearly indistinguishable from the trees.

Buzz pulled away. "They can't get much for their work."

"They don't." Sonny was glad they were moving again. The sight of the children had been like a thrust of pain. He had been like that once. Suddenly, he could feel the weight of the scoop shovel. The stink of manure clogged his nostrils and the car seemed filled with the restless shifting of cattle.

Every morning from the time he was eight he had shovelled out the barn. In the evenings and on weekends, he hauled or pitched hay or cut wood or staggered behind the stone boat, drunk with tiredness, as he attempted the hopeless task of trying to clear the fields of their yearly crop of stone.

"What keeps people here?" Roger asked.

"Stupidity. They don't know nothing and they don't want to know nothing."

On either side, the ditches were clogged with bulrushes. Behind the ditches were hay fields, then thin lines of trees marking the edges of the fields and more trees.

"Slow down," Sonny said. "It should be along here." He was puzzled, apologetic. He had Buzz turn at the next crossroads but, after 200 yards, the road trailed away to a grassy path.

A farmhouse with the wreckage of three cars littering its front yard appeared on their right. Someone had tarpapered the outside walls and tacked on laths and chicken wire but had never put on stucco. Tattered plastic from the previous winter clung to the window-frames. The yard was adrift with chickens.

Sonny could hear the steady one-stroke beat of a small engine so he braved a black mongrel that rushed up to bare his teeth and glare malevolently from pus-stained eyes.

Behind the house, a rawboned woman in a grey shapeless dress that came to her ankles was washing clothes in a gasoline washing machine. She looked no friendlier than her dog but, when Sonny motioned to her, she moved close enough to hear what he had to say. Her face was haggard, her eyes sunken and suspicious and her hair was pinned in an untidy bun at the back of her neck. Sonny forced a smile while he tried to keep an eye on the dog, which constantly twisted out of sight.

"We've got lost. We're looking for Joe Luprypa's place," he explained.

"Down the road one mile, then turn west." Her teeth were rotted to brown stumps.

He hadn't recognized her face but he remembered her voice. He looked at her more carefully. In the lined, coarse skin there was nothing to guide him but then she said, thinking he hadn't understood. "It's that way. See. Go down to the mile road."

Annie, sprang into his mind.

He nodded and said, "Thank you. Thank you," as he backed away. Except for the voice, he was unable to see any resemblance between the girl who had sat in front of him at school and the woman with the ravaged face and raw, rough hands folded across drooping breasts.

As Sonny opened the car door, the dog lunged for his ankle but he was ready and caught it in the ribs with his foot. Joe Luprypa's driveway was deeply rutted and only wide enough for one car. It twisted down a gentle slope through a meadow of uncut hay and disappeared into a dense grove of poplars. The trees stopped at the beginning of a marsh. The car, caught by the twin ruts, was locked as securely to its path as any train. As a joke, Buzz took both hands from the wheel and clasped them behind his head. As the car bumped and rocked along the grooves in the dark earth, the wheel seemed to take on a life of its own.

In the center of the grove there was a large patch of rutted dirt. They bounced toward a small house covered in plastic panelling that was supposed to look like natural stone. At the back of the house there was a summer kitchen painted bright purple. Permanently marching across the brown grass of the side yard to their diamond mine were plywood cutouts of the seven dwarves. An elderly blue pick-up was parked to one side.

"No-one's home," Buzz said. He sounded relieved. He could listen for hours to someone else's escapades, but when he became involved in one his enthusiasm quickly cooled. "We might as well go." He studied the house apprehensively.

Sonny shoved open his door and stepped away from the car. "They're just waiting to see who we are."

The back door cracked open but they couldn't see who had opened it. Then the door was flung back and a short, fat man in charcoal-grey suit pants, a white shirt and a red flowered tie, waddled over, threw his arms around Sonny and beat him on the back. "Sonny! Long time no see. I wouldn't have recognized you except for that nose. It's still travelling in a different direction."

"We've come for a drink." Sonny waved his arm in a half-circle. "I thought there'd be no place to park."

Joe was studying Buzz and Roger closely.

"It's okay," Sonny reassured him. "They're next-door neighbours. Roger's in medicine and Buzz is in communications. Have you anything to drink?"

Joe nodded. Each time he ducked his head, he accumulated three more chins. "A little." He waved them inside. "Go in," he urged. "What do you want? Government or homebrew? My brother, Alec, made the homebrew."

"Homebrew," Sonny replied. "I haven't had any for years."

The house smelled strongly of cabbage. Joe's wife, a dried-out woman with a disapproving look frozen to her face, cleared the table and set out three beer glasses.

The kitchen was smaller and shabbier than Sonny remembered it. It was painted bright yellow. Flowers and birds cut from magazines had been glued to the cupboards and shellacked. The windows were crammed with geraniums in red clay pots. Over the doorway to the living-room there was a plaster crucifix. The blood on it had been brightened with purple paint. From his place at the kitchen table, all Sonny could see of the living-room was a high-backed brown chesterfield layered with scalloped pink and orange doilies. Above the chesterfied in an ornate gilt frame was a paint-by-number picture of a collie.

Joe scraped his feet and locked the door behind him. "We've just come from church," he explained. He was carrying a 26-ounce bottle that was smeared with mud and grass. He held the bottle to the light and grimaced with distaste.

"We sterilize our bottles. But on the outside it's like this because of the mounties' dogs. I have to tie the bottles with a string and throw them to into the marsh." He made a pulling motion with his hands. "Then I go fishing."

He rinsed the bottle under the tap. "Five dollars for this. 65 cents for tomato juice." After he pocketed Sonny's $6, Joe handed over the bottle and punched holes in a can. The tomato juice and homebrew swirled together like oil and water.

The homebrew was as raw as the cheapest bourbon. Joe brought a glass to the table and half filled it with tomato juice but his wife said, "No. His liver's bad. He's just home from the hospital," when Sonny went to add liquor.

Joe laughed to cover his embarrassment. "It must be great to be in the city. I heard you on radio once, in a football game. Since then I heard you're doing good at cars. It's a good business. Everybody needs cars."

"It's a great business," Sonny enthusiastically agreed. He watched Roger and Buzz. "You can make a lot of money. Right now I'm ready to expand. Profits are going to be even bigger. For $10,000 I'd make someone a one-quarter partner."

Joe shook his head. "That's big money."

"It's a good investment," Sonny added. "Anybody buys in and from then on they collect while I work. No headaches, no problems, just profits."

Joe raised his glass at Roger. "Doctors always make lots of money. Somebody's always sick. That's the deal for your retirement fund."

Roger laughed off the suggestion. "Not me," he protested. "I like to put it in a nice safe bank."

"Me, too," Buzz agreed. "No risk." He gently felt this throat. "You never know when a delicate instrument might lose its tone."

Quickly, Sonny asked, "How's business for you, Joe?"

"Not good. The mounties are a problem."

"The mounties were always a problem."

Joe was downcast. He made rings on the table with the bottom of his glass. "Not like now. On weekends, in good weather, they park at the end of my driveway and sit all day. Nobody dares come. Last time, the judge said no more fines. From now on, jail. I'm too old for that."

As Joe complained, Sonny could see how much he had changed. It was not just the new lines on his face or his thinning hair. He looked worn. At one time he had been prosperous. On weekends, fifty, a hundred people came and he dispensed homebrew from a water pitcher. Then, Joe's was a place to get drunk, pick a fight or pick up a woman.

They drank steadily. At noon, Joe's wife made them roast-pork sandwiches with lots of salt and thick slices of Spanish onion. Sonny bought another bottle. By two o'clock, Roger and Buzz were very drunk. Their conversation had become so loud they were nearly shouting.

Sonny kept his glass full of tomato juice. He wanted to stay sober so that he could lead the conversation back to his dealership when the time was right. He tried to follow the conversation but couldn't because Annie kept forcing her way into his thoughts. Once he had had a crush on her. She had been pretty, with large dark eyes and a soft mouth. Now, his wife, with her trips to the health spa and the clothing stores and beauty parlour, looked like an adolescent compared to Annie. Poverty had done that. It could still do it to his wife and daughter. If he lost his dealership, the ballet, music and figure-skating lessons would be the first to go. Then the house. He was 41 and no-one would want him when they could get college kids fresh out of school.

The more he brooded about it, the worse his situation seemed. The others were so involved in their story-telling that they ignored him. Then Roger started to tell Joe about the deer. As Roger demonstrated how he got rid of the rifle, his glass slipped and crashed into the cupboard. Joe brought him a new one.

"Shooting a deer on Sunday." Joe frowned. "That's bad."

Buzz laughed and slopped his drink down the front of his coveralls. "Never mind. Sonny couldn't have hit it anyway." He stumbled from his chair and began scrambling around in a circle as he imitated Sonny's attempts to pick up the cartridges. Roger and Joe were shouting with laughter. As he turned faster and faster, like a dog chasing its tail, he shouted, "A deer. Bullets. Help. A deer."

Sonny was offended. He could see the story being told back home. Angrily, he said, "You think I can't hunt? Come on, I'll show you." He grabbed the bottle by the neck and marched outside. "I'll get a deer the way we used to."

Buzz and Roger staggered after him. A heavy, wet snow was starting to fall. Buzz drove the car to the main road. Sonny crouched in the back with the rifle sticking out the window.

"I'll show you some shooting," he said.

They swerved wildly on the slick clay. The first thing Sonny shot was a stop sign. They halted to inspect it.

"See that," he said, jabbing at the hole with his finger. "Roger couldn't do that."

"Sure, I could. Give me that rifle." Roger grabbed the barrel.

"You're in no condition." Sonny held onto the butt.

"I said give it to me." Roger's voice was belligerent. He jerked the rifle out of Sonny's hands.

The snow was beginning to fall so heavily that the countryside was blurred. They started up again and Buzz had even more difficulty controlling the car. Roger leaned so far out the car window that he looked like he was going to fall out.

"Turn left," Sonny ordered. "That's the best way. There's always deer there."

The road was so slick that they were reduced to a crawl. The snow covered the back window and clogged the windshield wipers.

"Turn here," Sonny directed. "We'll try along here."

They followed the road for over a mile, then Buzz said excitedly, "A deer."

Roger emptied the rifle as Buzz skidded to a stop.

"Did you see it?" Buzz asked. Both he and Roger started down the road. Both had difficulty keeping their balance and they walked with exaggerated care, their legs stiffly spread. With a yelp, Buzz slipped backwards and sat down in the mud. Sonny stayed in the car.

"Sonny!" Roger screamed in a high, frightened voice. "Sonny!"

When Buzz and Sonny reached Roger, he was kneeling beside a middle-aged woman in a faded brown coat with a fur collar. A man's felt cap was tied under her chin and her face was lined and shrunken. It looked like a small, dark leaf. She was an average-sized woman but lying on the ground, her legs drawn up so that only the toes of her black rubbers showed, she seemed a grotesque dwarf. Tightly gripped in her left hand was a gunny sack.

Sonny shook Roger's shoulder. "Do something. You're a doctor."

"No, I'm not," Roger replied. "I'm an optometrist."

The woman was lying on her side and a red stain was spreading over the snow at her back. The stain was as scarlet as lipstick.

"You shot her," Buzz accused him.

"You said it was a deer." Roger's voice trembled.

The woman's slack mouth tightened, then, as her lips drew back over her teeth, she gave a low, harsh cry.

"Maybe she isn't hurt bad," Roger said.

Behind them, Buzz gagged and threw up. Roger began to cry. "Lady," he said, his face stricken. "I didn't mean it."

"You shot her," Buzz repeated.

Sonny turned to him. "Shut up," he ordered. "You said she was a deer."

Snow was gathering along the woman's nose and in the folds of her coat. Except for her harsh breathing and the muted throbbing of the car's exhaust, there was no sound. They stayed absolutely still, watching the blood spread outward, becoming pink at its edge.

Just then, the woman's eyes, which had been nearly shut, opened wide and fixed fiercely upon them. Her body tensed and, for a moment, it seemed as if she would rise and strike them. Instead, her body was shaken with a violent convulsion and she rolled onto her back. After that, she was still.

"It was an accident," Roger mumbled.

"Manslaughter," Sonny replied harshly. "You were both drunk."

"We've got to get her out of here." As Buzz spoke, he began to back away. Roger hesitated, then he rose. Together, they rushed for the car. Buzz tried to open the front door on the passenger's side but his hands were trembling so violently he couldn't control them. Sonny yanked open the rear door and shoved Buzz, then Roger, inside.

The snow was falling heavily. The nearby woods were dark and endless. The air was filled with an impenetrable whiteness that isolated them in a landscape without familiar landmarks. There were no signs, not even the sun, by which to take their bearing.

"Joe," Buzz said. "He'll know."

"Joe," Sonny replied, "won't know anything. He doesn't want to go to jail." He put the car into gear.

In the back seat, Roger and Buzz stared through the windows but there was nothing except the endless whiteness. The world was blurred and indistinct and as dangerous as an uncharted coast in dense fog. Even the road was gradually disappearing.

"Where are we going?" Roger cried, his hands gripping the back seat. Buzz, his arms wrapped tightly around himself, sat hunched and mute.

Expertly, Sonny steered the car to the crest of the ridge. Roger repeated his plaintive question but Sonny, having already started them down the side of the ridge into the next hollow, was too busy to reply.

DONALD BARTHELME

Report

Our group is against the war. But the war goes on. I was sent to Cleveland to talk to the engineers. The engineers were meeting in Cleveland. I was supposed to persuade them not to do what they are going to do. I took United's 4:45 from LaGuardia arriving in Cleveland at 6:13. Cleveland is dark blue at that hour. I went directly to the motel, where the engineers were meeting. Hundreds of engineers attended the Cleveland meeting. I noticed many fractures among the engineers, bandages, traction. I noticed what appeared to be fracture of the carpal scraphoid in six examples. I noticed numerous fractures of the humeral shaft, of the os calcis, of the pelvic girdle. I noticed a high incidence of clay-shoveller's fracture. I could not account for these fractures. The engineers were making calculations, taking measurements, sketching on the blackboard, drinking beer, throwing bread, buttonholing employers, hurling glasses into the fireplace. They were friendly.

They were friendly. They were full of love and information. The chief engineer wore shades. Patella in Monk's traction, clamshell fracture by the look of it. He was standing in a slum of beer bottles and microphone cable. "Have some of this chicken à la Isambard Kingdom Brunel the Great Ingineer," he said. "And declare who you are and what we can do for you. What is your line, distinguished guest?"

"Software," I said. "In every sense. I am here representing a small group of interested parties. We are interested in your thing, which seems to be functioning. In the midst of so much dysfunction, function is interesting. Other people's things don't seem to be working. The State Department's thing doesn't seem to be working. The U.N.'s thing doesn't seem to be working. The democratic left's thing doesn't seem to be working. Buddha's thing—"

"Ask us anything about our thing, which seems to be working," the chief engineer said. "We will open our hearts and heads to you, Software Man, because we want to be understood and loved by the great lay public, and have our marvels appreciated by that public, for which we daily unsung produce tons of new marvels each more life-enhancing than the last. Ask us anything. Do you want to know about evaporated thin-film metallurgy? Monolithic and hybrid integrated-circuit processes? The algebra of inequalities? Optimization theory? Complex high-speed micro-miniature closed and open loop systems? Fixed variable mathematical cost searches? Expitaxial deposition of semi-conductor materials? Gross inter-faced space gropes? We also have specialists in the cuckooflower, the doctorfish, and the dumdum bullet as these relate to aspects of today's expanding technology, and they do in the damnedest ways."

I spoke to him then about the war. I said the same things people always say when they speak against the war. I said that the war was wrong. I said that large countries should not burn down small countries. I said that the government had made a series of errors. I said that these errors once small and forgivable were now immense and unforgivable. I said that the government was attempting to conceal its original errors under layers of new errors. I said that the government was sick with error, giddy with it. I said that ten thousand of our soldiers had already been killed in pursuit of the government's errors. I said that tens of thousands of the enemy's soldiers and civilians had been killed because of various errors, ours and theirs. I said that we are responsible for errors made in our name. I said that the government should not be allowed to make additional errors.

"Yes, yes," the chief engineer said, "there is doubtless much truth in what you say, but we can't possibly *lose* the war, can we? And stopping is losing, isn't it? The war regarded as a process, stopping regarded as an abort? We don't know *how* to lose a war. That skill is not among our skills. Our array smashes their array, that is what we know. That is the process. That is what is.

"But let's not have any more of this dispiriting downbeat counter-productive talk. I have a few new marvels here I'd like to discuss with you just briefly. A few new marvels that are just about ready to be gaped at by the admiring layman. Consider for instance the area of real-time online computer-controlled wish evaporation. Wish evaporation is going to be crucial in meeting the rising expectations of the world's peoples, which are as you know rising entirely too fast."

I noticed then distributed about the room a great many transverse fractures of the ulna. "The development of the pseudo-ruminant stomach for underdeveloped peoples," he went on, "is one of our interesting things you should be interested in. With the pseudo-ruminant stomach they can chew cuds, that is to say, eat grass. Blue is the most popular color worldwide and for that reason we are working with certain strains of your native Kentucky *Poa pratensis*, or bluegrass, as the staple input for the p/r stomach cycle, which would also give a shot in the arm to our balance-of-payments thing don't you know. . . ." I noticed about me then a great number of metatarsal fractures in banjo splints. "The kangaroo initiative . . . eight hundred thousand harvested last year . . . highest percentage of edible protein of any herbivore yet studied. . . ."

"Have new kangaroos been planted?"

The engineer looked at me.

"I intuit your hatred and jealousy of our thing," he said. "The ineffectual always hate our thing and speak of it as anti-human, which is not at all a meaningful way to speak of our thing. Nothing mechanical is alien to me," he said (amber spots making bursts of light in his shades), "because I am human, in a sense, and if I think it up, then 'it' is human too, whatever 'it' may be. Let me tell you, Software Man, we have been damned forbearing in the matter of this little war you declare yourself to be interested in. Function is the cry, and our thing is functioning like crazy. There are things we could do that we have not done. Steps we could take that we have not taken. These steps are, regarded in a certain light, the light of our enlightened self-interest, quite justifiable steps. We could, of course, get irritated. We could, of course, *lose patience*.

"We could, of course, release thousands upon thousands of self-powered crawling-along-the-ground lengths of titanium wire eighteen inches long with a diameter of .0005 centimetres (that is to say, invisible) which, scenting an enemy, climb up his trouser leg and wrap themselves around his neck. We have developed those. They are within our capabilities. We could, of course, release in the arena of the upper air our new improved pufferfish toxin which precipitates an identity crisis. No special technical problems there. That is almost laughably easy. We could, of course, place up to two million maggots in the their rice within twenty-four hours. The maggots are ready, massed in secret staging areas in Alabama. We have hypodermic darts capable of piebalding the enemy's pigmentation. We have rots, blights, and rusts capable of attacking his alphabet. Those are dandies. We have a hut-shrinking chemical which penetrates the fibres of the bamboo, causing it, the hut, to strangle its occupants. This operates only after 10 P.M., when people are sleeping. Their mathematics are at the mercy of a suppurating surd we have invented. We have a family of fishes trained to attack their fishes. We have the deadly testicle-destroying telegram. The cable-companies are co-operating. We have a green substance that, well, I'd rather not talk about. We have a secret word that, if pronounced, produces multiple fractures in all living things in an area the size of four football fields."

"That's why—"

"Yes. Some damned fool couldn't keep his mouth shut. The point is that the whole structure of enemy life is within our power to *rend*, *vitiate*, *devour*, and *crush*. But that's not the interesting thing."

"You recount these possiblities with uncommon relish."

"Yes I realize that there is too much relish here. But *you* must realize that these capabilities represent in and of themselves highly technical and complex and interesting problems and hurdles on which our boys have expended many thousands of hours of hard work and brilliance. And that the effects are often grossly exaggerated by irresponsible victims. And that the whole thing represents a fantastic series of triumphs for the multi-disciplined problem-solving team concept."

"I appreciate that."

"We *could* unleash all this technology at once. You can imagine what would happen then. But that's not the interesting thing."

"What is the interesting thing?"

"The interesting thing is that we have a *moral sense*. It is on punched cards, perhaps the most advanced and sensitive moral sense the world has ever known."

"Because it is on punched cards?"

"It considers all considerations in endless and subtle detail," he said. "It even quibbles. With this great new moral tool, how can we go wrong? I confidently predict that, although we *could* employ all this splendid new weaponry I've been telling you about, *we're not going to do it*."

"We're not going to do it?"

I took United's 5:44 from Cleveland arriving at Newark at 7:19. New Jersey is bright pink at that hour. Living things move about the surface of New Jersey at that hour molesting each other only in traditional ways. I made my report to the group. I stressed the friendliness of the engineers. I said, It's all right. I said, We have a moral sense. I said, *We're not going to do it*. They didn't believe me.

ALICE MUNRO

Material

I don't keep up with Hugo's writing. Sometimes I see his name, in the library, on the cover of some literary journal that I don't open — I haven't opened a literary journal in a dozen years, praise God. Or I read in the paper or see on a poster — this would be in the library, too, or in a bookstore — an announcement of a panel discussion at the University, with Hugo flown in to discuss the state of the novel today, or the contemporary short story, or the new nationalism in our literature. Then I think, will people really go, will people who could be swimming or drinking or going for a walk really take themselves out to the campus to find the room and sit in rows listening to those vain quarrelsome men? Bloated, opinionated, untidy men, that is how I see them, cosseted by the academic life, the literary life, by women. People will go to hear them say that such and such a writer is not worth reading any more, and that some writer must be read; to hear them dismiss and glorify and argue and chuckle and shock. People, I say, but I mean women, middle-aged women like me, alert and trembling, hoping to ask intelligent questions and not be ridiculous; soft-haired young girls awash in adoration, hoping to lock eyes with one of the men on the platform. Girls, and women too, fall in love with such men, they imagine there is power in them.

The wives of the men on the platform are not in that audience. They are buying groceries or cleaning up messes or having a drink. Their lives are concerned with food and mess and houses and cars and money. They have to remember to get the snow tires on and go to the bank and take back the beer bottles, because their husbands are such brilliant, such talented incapable men, who must be looked after for the sake of the words that will come from them. The women in the audience are married to engineers or doctors or businessmen. I know them, they are my friends. Some of them have turned to literature frivolously, it is true, but most come shyly, and with enormous transitory hope. They absorb the contempt of the men on the platform as if they deserved it; they half-believe they do deserve it, because of their houses and expensive shoes, and their husbands who read Arthur Hailey.

I am married to an engineer myself. His name is Gabriel, but he prefers the name Gabe. In this country he prefers the name Gabe. He was born in Romania, he lived there until the end of the war, when he was sixteen. He has forgotten how to speak Romanian. How can you forget, how can you forget the language of your childhood? I used to think he was pretending to forget, because the things he had seen and lived through when he spoke that language were too terrible to remember. He told me this was not so. He told me his experience of the war was not so bad. He described the holiday uproar at school when the air raid sirens sounded. I did not quite believe him. I required him to be an ambassador from bad times as well as distant countries. Then I thought he might not be Romanian at all, but an imposter.

386

This was before we were married, when he used to come and see me in the apartment on Clark Road where I lived with my little daughter, Clea. Hugo's daughter too, of course, but he had to let go of her. Hugo had grants, he traveled, he married again, and his wife had three children; he divorced and married again and his next wife, who had been his student, had three more children, the first born to her while he was still living with his second wife. In such circumstances a man can't hang onto everything. Gabriel used to stay all night sometimes on the pull-out couch I had for a bed in this tiny, shabby apartment; and I would look at him sleeping and think that for all I knew he might be a German or a Russian or even of all things a Canadian faking a past and an accent to make himself interesting. He was mysterious to me. Long after he became my lover and after he became my husband he remained, remains, mysterious to me. In spite of all the things I know about him, daily and physical things. His face curves out smoothly and his eyes, set shallowly in his head, curve out too under the smooth pink lids. The wrinkles he has are traced on top of this smoothness, this impenetrable surface; they are of no consequence. His body is substantial, calm. He used to be a fine, rather lazy-looking, skater. I cannot describe him without a familiar sense of capitulation. I cannot describe him. I could describe Hugo, if anybody asked me, in great detail— Hugo as he was eighteen, twenty years ago, crew-cut and skinny, with the bones of his body and even of his skull casually, precariously, joined and knitted together, so that there was something uncoordinated, unexpected about the shifting planes of his face as well as the movements, often dangerous, of his limbs. He's held together by nerves, a friend of mine at college said when I first brought him around, and it was true; after that I could almost see the fiery strings.

Gabriel told me when I first knew him that he enjoyed life. He did not say that he believed in enjoying it; he said that he did. I was embarrassed for him. I never believed people who said such things and anyway, I associated this statement with gross, self-advertising, secretly unpleasantly restless men. But it seems to be the truth. He is not curious. He is able to take pleasure and give off smiles and caresses and say softly, "Why do you worry about that? It is not a problem of yours." He has forgotten the language of his childhood. His lovemaking was strange to me at first, because it was lacking in desperation. He made love without emphasis, so to speak, with no memory of sin or hope of depravity. He does not watch himself. He will never write a poem about it, never, and indeed may have forgotten it in half an hour. Such men are commonplace, perhaps. It was only that I had not known any. I used to wonder if I would have fallen in love with him if his accent and his forgotten, nearly forgotten, past had been taken away; if he had been, say, an engineering student in my own year at college. I don't know, I can't tell. What holds anybody in a man or a woman may be something as flimsy as a Romanian accent or the calm curve of an eyelid, some half-fraudulent mystery.

No mystery of this sort about Hugo. I did not miss it, did not know about it, maybe would not have believed in it. I believed in something else, then. Not that I knew him, all the way through, but the part I knew was in my blood and from time to time would give me a poison rash. None of that with Gabriel, he does not disturb me, any more than he is disturbed himself.

It was Gabriel who found me Hugo's story. We were in a bookstore, and he came to me with a large, expensive paperback, a collection of short stories. There was Hugo's name on the cover. I wondered how Gabriel had found it, what he had been doing in the fiction section of the store anyway, he never reads fiction. I wondered if he sometimes went and looked for things by Hugo. He is interested in Hugo's career as he would be interested in the career of a magician or popular singer or politician with whom he had, through me, a plausible connection, a proof of reality. I think it is because he does such anonymous work himself, work intelligible only to his own kind. He is fascinated by people who work daringly out in the public eye, without the protection of any special discipline—it must seem so, to an engineer—just trying to trust themselves, and elaborating their bag of tricks, and hoping to catch on.

"Buy it for Clea," he said.

"Isn't it a lot of money for a paperback?"

He smiled.

"There's your father's picture, your real father, and he has written this story you might like to read," I said to Clea, who was in the kitchen making toast. She is seventeen. Some days she eats toast and honey and peanut butter and Oreos and creamed cheese and chicken sandwiches and fried potatoes. If anybody comments on what she is eating or not eating, she may run upstairs and slam the door of her room.

"He looks overweight," said Clea and put the book down. "You always said he was skinny." Her interest in her father is all from the point of view of heredity, and what genes he might have passed on to herself. Did he have a bad complexion, did he have a high I.Q., did the women in his family have big breasts?

"He was when I knew him," I said. "How was I to know what had happened to him since?"

He looked, however, very much as I would have thought he would look by now. When I saw his name in the newspaper or on a poster I had pictured somebody much like this; I had foreseen the ways in which time and his life would have changed him. It did not surprise me that he had got fat but not bald, that he had let his hair grow wild and had grown a full, curly beard. Pouches under his eyes, a dragged-down look to the cheeks even when he is laughing. He is laughing, into the camera. His teeth have gone from bad to worse. He hated dentists, said his father died of a heart attack in the dentist's chair. A lie, like so much else, or at least an exaggeration. He used to smile crookedly for photographs to hide the right top incisor, dead since somebody at high school pushed him into a drinking fountain. Now he doesn't care, he laughs, he bares those rotting stumps. He looks, at the same time, woebegone and cheerful. A Rabelaisian writer. Checked wool shirt open at the top to show his undershirt, he didn't use to wear one. Do you wash, Hugo? Do you have bad breath, with those teeth? Do you call your girl students fond exasperated dirty names, are there phone calls from insulted parents, does the Dean or somebody have to explain that no harm is meant, that writers are not as other men are? Probably not, probably no one minds. Outrageous writers may bounce from one blessing to another nowadays, bewildered, as permissively reared children are said to be, by excess of approval.

I have no proof. I construct somebody from this one smudgy picture, I am content with such clichés. I have not the imagination or good will to proceed differently; and I have noticed anyway, everybody must have noticed as we go further into middle age, how shopworn and simple, really, are the disguises, the identities if you like, that people take up. In fiction, in Hugo's business, such disguises would not do, but in life they are all we seem to want, all anybody can manage. Look at Hugo's picture, look at the undershirt, listen to what it says about him.

> Hugo Johnson was born and semi-educated in the bush, and in the mining and lumbering towns of Northern Ontario. He has worked as a lumberjack, beer-slinger, counterman, telephone lineman and sawmill foreman, and has been sporadically affiliated with various academic communities. He lives now most of the time on the side of a mountain above Vancouver, with his wife and six children.

The student wife, it seems, got stuck with all the children. What happened to Mary Frances, did she die, is she liberated, did he drive her crazy? But listen to the lies, the half-lies, the absurdities. *He lives on the side of a mountain above Vancouver.* It sounds as if he lives in a wilderness cabin, and all it means, I'm willing to bet, is that he lives in an ordinary comfortable house in North or West Vancouver, which now stretch far up the mountain. He has been *sporadically affiliated with various academic communities.* What does that mean? If it means he has taught for years, most of his adult life, at universities, that teaching at universities has been the only steady well-paid job he has ever had, why doesn't it say so? You would think he came out of the bush now and then to fling them scraps of wisdom, to give them a demonstration of what a real male *writer,* a creative *artist,* is like; you would never think he was a practicing *academic.* I don't know if he was a lumberjack or a beer-slinger or a counterman, but I do know that he was not a telephone lineman. He had a job painting telephone poles. He quit that job in the middle of the second week because the heat and the climbing made him sick. It was a broiling June, just after we had both graduated. Fair enough. The sun really did make him sick, twice he came home and vomited. I have quit jobs myself that I could not stand. The same summer I quit my job folding bandages at Victoria Hospital, because I was going mad with boredom. But if I was a writer, and was listing all my varied and colorful occupations, I don't think I would put down *bandage folder,* I don't think I would find that entirely honest.

After he quit, Hugo found a job marking Grade Twelve examination papers. Why didn't he put that down? Examination marker. He liked marking examination papers better than he liked climbing telephone poles, and probably better than he liked lumberjacking or beer-slinging or any of those other things if he ever did them; why couldn't he put it down? *Examination marker.*

Nor has he, to my knowledge, ever been the foreman in a sawmill. He worked in his uncle's mill the summer before I met him. What he did all day was load lumber and get sworn at by the real foreman, who didn't like him because of his uncle being the boss. In the evenings, if he was not too tired, he used to walk half a mile to a little creek and play his recorder. Black flies bothered him, but he did it anyway. He could play "Morning", from *Peer Gynt*, and some Elizabethan airs whose names I have forgotten. Except for one: "Wolsey's Wilde". I learned to play it on the piano so we could play a duet. Was that meant for Cardinal Wolsey, and what was a *wilde*, a dance? Put that down, Hugo. *Recorder player.* That would be quite all right, quite in fashion now; as I understand things, recorder playing and such fey activities are not out of favor now, quite the contrary. Indeed, they may be more acceptable than all that lumberjacking and beer-slinging. Look at you, Hugo, your image is not only fake but out-of-date. You should have said you'd meditated for a year in the mountains of Uttar Pradesh; you should have said you'd taught Creative Drama to autistic children; you should have shaved your head, shaved your beard, put on a monk's cowl; you should have shut up, Hugo.

When I was pregnant with Clea we lived in a house on Argyle Street in Vancouver. It was such a sad gray stucco house on the outside, in the rainy winter, that we painted the inside, all the rooms, vivid ill-chosen colors. Three walls of the bedroom were Wedgwood blue, one was a magenta. We said it was an experiment to see if color could drive anybody mad. The bathroom was a deep orange-yellow. "It's like being inside a cheese," Hugo said when we finished it. "That's right, it is," I said. "That's very good, phrase-maker." He was pleased but not as pleased as if he'd written it. After that he said, every time he showed anybody the bathroom, "See the color? It's like being inside a cheese." Or, "It's like peeing inside a cheese." Not that I didn't do the same thing, save things up and say them over and over. Maybe I said that about peeing inside a cheese. We had many phrases in common. We both called the landlady the Green Hornet, because she had worn, the only time we had seen her, a poison-green outfit with bits of rat fur and a clutch of violets, and had given off a venomous sort of buzz. She was over seventy and she ran a downtown boardinghouse for men. Her daughter Dotty we called the harlot-in-residence. I wonder why we chose to say *harlot*; that was not, is not, a word in general use. I suppose it had a classy sound, a classy depraved sound, contrasting ironically—we were strong on irony—with Dotty herself.

She lived in a two-room apartment in the basement of the house. She was supposed to pay her mother forty-five dollars monthly rent and she told me she meant to try to make the money baby-sitting.

"I can't go out to work," she said, "on account of my nerves. My last husband, I had him six months dying down at Mother's, dying with his kidney disease, and I owe her three hundred dollars board still on that. She made me make him his eggnog with skim milk. I'm broke every day of my life. They say it's all right not having wealth if you got health, but what if you never had either one? Bronchial pneumonia from the time I was three years old. Rheumatic fever at twelve. Sixteen I married my first husband, he was killed in a logging accident. Three miscarriages. My womb is in shreds. I use up three packs of Kotex every month. I married a dairy farmer out in the Valley and his herd got the fever. Wiped us out. That was the one who died with his kidneys. No wonder. No wonder my nerves are shot."

I am condensing. This came out at greater length and by no means dolefully, indeed with some amazement and pride, at Dotty's table. She asked me down for cups of tea, then for beer. This is life, I thought, fresh from books, classes, essays, discussions. Unlike her mother, Dotty was flat-faced, soft, doughy, fashioned for defeat, the kind of colorless puzzled woman you see carrying a shopping bag, waiting for the bus. In fact, I had seen her once on a bus downtown, and not recognized her at first in her dull blue winter coat. Her rooms were full of heavy furniture salvaged from her marriage—an upright piano, overstuffed chesterfield and chairs, walnut veneer china cabinet and dining room table, where we sat. In the middle of the table was a tremendous lamp, with a painted china base and a pleated, dark red silk shade, held out at an extravagant angle, like a hoop skirt.

I described it to Hugo. "That is a whorehouse lamp," I said. Afterwards I wanted to be congratulated on the accuracy of this description. I told Hugo he ought to pay more attention to Dotty if he wanted to be a writer. I told him about her husbands and her womb and her collection of souvenir spoons, and he said I was welcome to look at them all by myself. He was writing a verse play.

Once when I went down to put coal on the furnace, I found Dotty in her pink chenille dressing gown saying good-bye to a man in a uniform, some sort of delivery man or gas station attendant. It was the middle of the afternoon. She and this man were not parting in any way that suggested either lechery or affection and I would not have understood anything about it, I would probably have thought he was some relative, if she had not begun at once a long complicated slightly drunk story about how she had got wet in the rain and had to leave her clothes at her mother's house and worn home her mother's dress which was too tight and that was why she was now in her dressing gown. She said that first Larry had caught her in it delivering some sewing he wanted her to do for his wife, and now me, and she didn't know what we would think of her. This was strange, as I had seen her in her dressing gown many times before. In the middle of her laughing and explaining, the man, who had not looked at me, not smiled or said a word or in any way backed up her story, simply ducked out the door.

"Dotty has a lover," I said to Hugo.

"You don't get out enough. You're trying to make life interesting."

The next week I watched to see if this man came back. He did not. But three other men came, and one of them came twice. They walked with their heads down, quickly, and did not have to wait at the basement door. Hugo couldn't deny it. He said it was life imitating art again, it was bound to happen, after all the fat varicose-veined whores he'd met in books. It was then we named her the harlot-in-residence and began to brag about her to our friends. They stood behind the curtains to catch a glimpse of her going in and out.

"That's not her!" they said. "Is that her? Isn't she disappointing? Doesn't she have any professional clothes?"

"Don't be so naive," we said. "Did you think they all wore spangles and boas?"

Everybody hushed to hear her play the piano. She sang or hummed along with her playing, not steadily, but loudly, in the rather defiant, self-parodying voice people use when they are alone, or think they are alone. She sang "Yellow Rose of Texas", and "You Can't Be True, Dear".

"Whores should sing hymns."

"We'll get her to learn some."

"You're all such voyeurs. You're all so mean," said a girl named Mary Frances Shrecker, a big-boned, calm-faced girl with black braids down her back. She was married to a former mathematical prodigy, Elsworth Shrecker, who had had a breakdown. She worked as a dietician. Hugo said he could not look at her without thinking of the word *lumpen*,[1] but he supposed she might be nourishing, like oatmeal porridge. She became his second wife. I thought she was the right wife for him, I thought she would stay forever, nourishing him, but the student evicted her.

The piano-playing was an entertainment for our friends, but disastrous on the days when Hugo was home trying to work. He was supposed to be working on his thesis but he really was writing his play. He worked in our bedroom, at a card table in front of the window, facing a board fence. When Dotty had been playing for a bit, he might come out to the kitchen and stick his face into mine and say in low, even tones of self-consciously controlled rage, "You go down and tell her to cut that out."

"You go."

"Bloody hell. She's your friend. You cultivate her. You encourage her."

"I never told her to play the piano."

"I arranged so that I could have this afternoon free. That did not just happen. I arranged it. I am at a crucial point, I am at the point where this play *lives or dies*. If I go down there I'm afraid I might strangle her."

"Well don't look at *me*. Don't strangle *me*. Excuse my breathing and everything."

I always did go down to the basement, of course, and knock on Dotty's door and ask her if she would mind not playing the piano now, because my husband was at home and was trying to work. I never said the word *write*, Hugo had trained me not to, that word was like a bare wire to us. Dotty apologized every time, she was scared of Hugo and respectful of his work and his intelligence. She left off playing but the trouble was she might forget, she might start again in an hour, half an hour. The possibility made me nervous and miserable. Because I was pregnant I always wanted to eat, and I would sit at the kitchen table greedily, unhappily, eating something like a warmed-up plateful of Spanish rice. Hugo felt the world was hostile to his writing, he felt not only all its human inhabitants but its noises and diversions and ordinary clutter were linked against him, maliciously, purposefully, diabolically thwarting and maiming him and keeping him from his work. And I, whose business it was to throw myself between him and the world, was failing to do so, by choice perhaps as much as ineptitude for the job. I did not believe in him. I had not understood how it would be necessary to believe in him. I believed that he was clever and talented, whatever that might mean, but I was not sure he would turn out to be a writer. He did not have the authority I thought a writer should have. He was too nervous, too touchy with everybody, too much of a showoff. I believed that writers were calm, sad people, knowing too much.

1. Ragged, shabby.

I believed that there was a difference about them, some hard and shining, rare intimidating quality they had from the beginning, and Hugo didn't have it. I thought that someday he would recognize this. Meanwhile, he lived in a world whose rewards and punishments were as strange, as hidden from me, as if he had been a lunatic. He would sit at supper, pale and disgusted; he would clench himself over the typewriter in furious paralysis when I had to get something from the bedroom, or he would leap around the living room asking me what he was (a rhinoceros who thinks he is a gazelle, Chairman Mao dancing a war dance in a dream dreamt by John Foster Dulles)[2] and then kiss me all over the neck and throat with hungry gobbling noises. I was cut off from the source of these glad or bad moods, I did not affect them. I teased him sourly:

"Suppose after we have the baby the house is on fire and the baby and the play are both in there, which would you save?"

"Both."

"But supposing you can just save one? Never mind the baby, suppose *I* am in there, no, suppose I am drowning *here* and you are *here* and cannot possibly reach us both—"

"You're making it tough for me."

"I know I am. I know I am. Don't you hate me?"

"Of course I hate you." After this we might go to bed, playful, squealing, mock-fighting, excited. All our life together, the successful part of our life together, was games. We made up conversations to startle people on the bus. Once we sat in a beer parlor and he berated me for going out with other men and leaving the children alone while he was off in the bush working to support us. He pleaded with me to remember my duty as a wife and as a mother. I blew smoke in his face. People around us were looking stern and gratified. When we got outside we laughed till we had to hold each other up, against the wall. We played in bed that I was Lady Chatterley and he was Mellors.[3]

"Where be that little rascal John Thomas?" he said thickly. "I canna find John Thomas!"

"Frightfully sorry, I think I must have swallowed him," I said, ladylike.

There was a water pump in the basement. It made a steady, thumping noise. The house was on fairly low-lying ground not far from the Fraser River, and during the rainy weather the pump had to work most of the time to keep the basement from being flooded. We had a dark rainy January, as is usual in Vancouver, and this was followed by a dark rainy February. Hugo and I felt gloomy. I slept a lot of the time. Hugo couldn't sleep. He claimed it was the pump that kept him awake. He couldn't work because of it in the daytime and he couldn't sleep because of it at night. The pump had replaced Dotty's piano-playing as the thing that most enraged and depressed him in our house. Not only because of its noise, but because of the money it was costing us. Its entire cost went onto our electricity bill, though it was Dotty who lived in the basement and reaped the benefits of

2. American statesman often regarded as extremely right-wing.
3. Characters in D. H. Lawrence's *Lady Chat-*
terley's Lover (1928). The novel was banned for many years, and the first complete edition in English appeared only in 1960.

not being flooded. He said I should speak to Dotty and I said Dotty could not pay the expenses she already had. He said she could turn more tricks. I told him to shut up. As I become more pregnant, slower and heavier and more confined to the house, I got fonder of Dotty, used to her, less likely to store up and repeat what she said. I felt more at home with her than I did sometimes with Hugo and our friends.

All right, Hugo said, I ought to phone the landlady. I said he ought. He said he had far too much to do. The truth was we both shrank from a confrontation with the landlady, knowing in advance how she would confuse and defeat us with shrill evasive prattle.

In the middle of the night in the middle of a rainy week I woke up and wondered what had wakened me. It was the silence.

"Hugo, wake up. The pump's broken, I can't hear the pump."

"I am awake," Hugo said.

"It's still raining and the pump isn't going. It must be broken."

"No, it isn't. It's shut off. I shut it off."

I sat up and turned on the light. He was lying on his back, squinting and trying to give me a hard look at the same time.

"You didn't turn it off."

"All right, I didn't."

"You did."

"I could not stand the goddamn expense any more. I could not stand thinking about it. I could not stand the noise either. I haven't had any sleep in a week."

"The basement will flood."

"I'll turn it on in the morning. A few hours' peace is all I want."

"That'll be too late, it's raining torrents."

"It is not."

"You go to the window."

"It's raining. It's not raining torrents."

I turned out the light and lay down and said in a calm stern voice, "Listen to me, Hugo, you have to go and turn it on, Dotty will be flooded out."

"In the morning."

"You have to go and turn it on *now*."

"Well I'm not."

"If you're not, I am."

"No, you're not."

"I am."

But I didn't move.

"Don't be such an alarmist."

"*Hugo*."

"Don't *cry*."

"Her stuff will be ruined."

"Best thing could happen to it. Anyway, it won't." He lay beside me stiff and wary, waiting, I suppose, for me to get out of bed, go down to the basement and figure out how to turn the pump on. Then what would he have done? He could not have hit me, I was too pregnant. He never did hit me, unless I hit him first. He could have gone and turned it off again, and I could have turned it on, and so on, how long could that last? He could have held me down, but if I struggled he would have been afraid of hurting me. He could have sworn at me and left the house, but we had no car, and it was raining too hard for him to stay out very long. He would probably just have raged and sulked, alternately, and I could have taken a blanket and gone to sleep on the living room couch for the rest of the night. I think that is what a woman of firm character would have done. I think that is what a woman who wanted that marriage to last would have done. But I did not do it. Instead, I said to myself that I did not know how the pump worked, I did not know where to turn it on. I said to myself that I was afraid of Hugo. I entertained the possibility that Hugo might be right, nothing would happen. But I wanted something to happen, I wanted Hugo to crash.

When I woke up, Hugo was gone and the pump was thumping as usual. Dotty was pounding on the door at the top of the basement stairs.

"You won't believe your eyes what's down here. I'm up to my knees in water. I just put my feet out of bed and up to my knees in water. What happened? You hear the pump go off?"

"No," I said.

"I don't know what could've gone wrong, I guess it could've got overworked. I had a couple of beers before I went to bed elst I would've known there was something wrong. I usually sleep light. But I was sleeping like the dead and I put my feet out of bed and Jesus, it's a good thing I didn't pull on the light switch at the same time, I would have been electrocuted. Everything's floating."

Nothing was floating and the water would not have come to any grown person's knees. It was about five inches deep in some places, only one or two in others, the floor being so uneven. It had soaked and stained the bottom of her chesterfield and chairs and got into the bottom drawers and cupboards and warped the bottom of her piano. The floor tiles were loosened, the rugs soggy, the edges of her bedspread dripping, her floor heater ruined.

I got dressed and put on a pair of Hugo's boots and took a broom downstairs. I started sweeping the water towards the drain outside the door. Dotty made herself a cup of coffee in my kitchen and sat for a while on the top step watching me, going over the same monologue about having a couple of beers and sleeping more soundly than usual, not hearing the pump go off, not understanding why it should go off, if it had gone off, not knowing how she was going to explain to her mother who would certainly make it out to be her fault and charge her. We were in luck, I saw. (*We were?*) Dotty's expectation and thrifty relish of misfortune made her less likely than almost anyone else would have been to investigate just what had gone wrong. After the water level went down a bit, she went into her bedroom, put on some clothes and some boots which she had to drain first, got her broom and helped me.

"The things that don't happen to me, eh? I never get my fortune told. I've got these girl friends that are always getting their fortune told and I say, never mind me, there's one thing I know and I know it ain't good."

I went upstairs and phoned the University, trying to get Hugo. I told them it was an emergency and they found him in the library.

"It did flood."

"What?"

"It did flood. Dotty's place is under water."

"I turned the pump on."

"Like hell you did. This morning you turned it on."

"This morning there was a downpour and the pump couldn't handle it. That was after I turned it on."

"The pump couldn't handle it last night because the pump wasn't on last night and don't talk to me about any downpour."

"Well there was one. You were asleep."

"You have no idea what you've done, do you? You don't even stick around to look at it. I have to look. I have to cope. I have to listen to that poor woman."

"Plug your ears."

"Shut up, you filthy moral idiot."

"I'm sorry. I was kidding. I'm sorry."

"Sorry. You're bloody sorry. This is the mess you made and I told you you'd make and you're bloody sorry."

"I have to go to a seminar. I am sorry. I can't talk now, it's no good talking to you now, I don't know what you're trying to get me to say."

"I'm just trying to get you to *realize*."

"All right, I realize. Though I still think it happened this morning."

"You don't realize. You never realize."

"You dramatize."

"*I* dramatize!"

Our luck held. Dotty's mother was not so likely as Dotty to do without explanations and it was, after all, her floor tiles and wallboard that were ruined. But Dotty's mother was sick, the cold wet weather had undermined her too, and she was taken to hospital with pneumonia that very morning. Dotty went to live in her mother's house, to look after the boarders. The basement had a disgusting, moldy smell. We moved out too, a short time later. Just before Clea was born we took over a house in North Vancouver, belonging to some friends who had gone to England. The quarrel between us subsided in the excitement of moving; it was never really resolved. We did not move much from the positions we had taken on the phone. I said you don't realize, you never realize, and he said, what do you want me to say? Why do you make such a fuss over this, he asked reasonably. Anybody might wonder. Long after I was away from him, I wondered too. I could have turned on the pump, as I have said, taking responsibility for both of us, as a patient realistic woman, a really married woman, would have done, as I am sure Mary Frances would have done, did, many times, during the ten years she lasted. Or I could have told Dotty the truth, though she was not a very good choice to receive such information. I could have told somebody, if I thought it was that important, pushed Hugo out into the unpleasant world and let him taste trouble. But I didn't, I was not able fully to protect or expose him, only to flog him with blame, desperate sometimes, feeling I would claw his head open to pour my vision into it, my notion of what had to be understood. What presumptuousness, what cowardice, what bad faith. Unavoidable. "You have a problem of incompatibility," the marriage counselor said to us a while later. We laughed till we cried in the dreary municipal hall of the building in North Vancouver where the marriage counseling was dispensed. That is our problem, we said to each other, what a relief to know it, incompatibility.

I did not read Hugo's story that night. I left it with Clea and she as it turned out did not read it either. I read it the next afternoon. I got home about two o'clock from the girls' private school where I have a part-time job teaching history. I made tea as I usually do and sat down in the kitchen to enjoy the hour before the boys, Gabriel's sons, get home from school. I saw the book still lying on top of the refrigerator and I took it down and read Hugo's story.

The story is about Dotty. Of course, she has been changed in some unimportant ways and the main incident concerning her has been invented, or grafted on from some other reality. But the lamp is there, and the pink chenille dressing gown. And something about Dotty that I had forgotten: When you were talking she would listen with her mouth slightly open, nodding, then she would chime in on the last word of your sentence with you. A touching and irritating habit. She was in such a hurry to agree, she hoped to understand. Hugo has remembered this, and when did Hugo ever talk to Dotty?

That doesn't matter. What matters is that this story of Hugo's is a very good story, as far as I can tell, and I think I can tell. How honest this is and how lovely, I had to say as I read. I had to admit. I was moved by Hugo's story; I was, I am, glad of it, and I am not moved by tricks. Or if I am, they have to be good tricks. Lovely tricks, honest tricks. There is Dotty lifted out of life and held in light, suspended in the marvellous clear jelly that Hugo had spent all his life learning how to make. It is an act of magic, there is no getting around it; it is an act, you might say, of a special, unsparing, unsentimental love. A fine and lucky benevolence. Dotty was a lucky person, people who understand and value this act might say (not everybody, of course, does understand and value this act); she was lucky to live in that basement for a few months and eventually to have this done to her, though she doesn't know what has been done and wouldn't care for it, probably, if she did know. She has passed into Art. It doesn't happen to everybody.

Don't be offended. Ironical objections are a habit with me. I am half-ashamed of them. I respect what has been done. I respect the intention and the effort and the result. Accept my thanks.

I did think that I would write a letter to Hugo. All the time I was preparing dinner, and eating it, and talking to Gabriel and the children, I was thinking of a letter. I was thinking I would tell him how strange it was for me to realize that we shared, still shared, the same bank of memory, and that what was all scraps and oddments, useless baggage, for me, was ripe and usable, a paying investment, for him. Also I wanted to apologize, in some not-outright way, for not having believed he would be a writer. Acknowledgement, not apology; that was what I owed him. A few graceful, a few grateful, phrases.

At the same time, at dinner, looking at my husband Gabriel, I decided that he and Hugo are not really so unalike. Both of them have managed something. Both of them have decided what to do about everything they run across in this world, what attitude to take, how to ignore or use things.

In their limited and precarious ways they both have authority. They are not *at the mercy*. Or think they are not. I can't blame them, for making whatever arrangements they can make.

After the boys had gone to bed and Gabriel and Clea had settled to watch television, I found a pen and got the paper in front of me, to write my letter, and my hand jumped. I began to write short jabbing sentences that I had never planned:

This is not enough, Hugo. You think it is, but it isn't. You are mistaken, Hugo.

That is not an argument to send through the mail.

I do blame them. I envy and despise.

Gabriel came into the kitchen before he went to bed, and saw me sitting with a pile of test papers and my marking pencils. He might have meant to talk to me, to ask me to have coffee, or a drink, with him, but he respected my unhappiness as he always does; he respected the pretense that I was not unhappy but preoccupied, burdened with these test papers; he left me alone to get over it.

AUDREY THOMAS

Initram

Writers are terrible liars. There are nicer names for it, of course, but liars will do. They take a small incident and blow it up, like a balloon—puff puff—and the out-of-work man who comes to ask if he can cut the grass ends up in their story as an out-of-control grey-faced, desperate creature who hurls himself through the garden gate and by his sheer presence wrecks a carefully arranged afternoon between a married woman and her intended lover.

The truth is I was reading an old friend's manuscript. The truth is I thought the man hadn't gone but was lurking in the back lane just beyond the blackberry bushes.

The truth is I only thought I saw him there—flashes of a red-plaid shirt beyond the green. (Writers also lie to themselves.)

The truth is that when the police came and I was asked to describe this man I was overcome with shame and embarrassment to suddenly notice him, half a block away, moving a neighbour's lawn mower up and down in regular and practical stripes.

The truth is I still insisted (to myself, after the grinning policeman had gone) that the man had been sinister, menacing, unpleasant. And of course he is, in my story.

But what do writers do with the big events in life—births and broken hearts and deaths—the great archetypal situations that need no real enhancement or "touching up"? Surely they simply *tell* these, acting as mediums through which the great truths filter. Not at all—or not usually or maybe sometimes when they happen to other people.

That is why I decided to call Lydia when my marriage broke up. I was living on an island—felt I needed a wider audience, an audience that would understand and accept my exaggerations for what they were. It had to be a fellow writer, preferably a woman. I called her up long-distance. One of her daughters answered and said she wasn't there could I leave my number? I put the phone down, already planning the ferry trip, the excitement of the telling of my terrible news. Lydia was perfect. Yes. I couldn't wait for her to call me back.

I didn't, in fact, know her very well. I had done a review of her first published book and then later, when I went to visit her city, had on a sudden whim called from a phone booth and identified myself. She had told me to come right over. I had my husband and three kids with me. That seemed too much of an imposition on anyone we didn't know so I took the littlest and he agreed to take the others to the Wax Museum. We drove up a very classy road, with huge houses—some were really what we used to call mansions—on either side. I began to get cold feet.

I had visions of a patrician face and perfect fingernails—drinking tea from her grandmother's bone china cups. We would talk about Proust and Virginia Woolf with a few casual remarks about *Nightwood* and the diaries of Anaïs Nin.

As we drove up to the front door of a big, imposing, mock-tudor residence I thought of "Our Gal Sunday," a soap-opera I had loved when I was a kid. It always began with a question as to whether a beautiful young girl from a small mining town in the West could find happiness as the wife of England's wealthiest and most titled lord, Lord Henry Brinthrop.

It was her stories, you see. They were about life on the prairies — about farms and poverty (both spiritual and material) and, very often, a young girl's struggle against those things. Yet here was this house, on this road and a statue in the garden.

"Wait for me," I said to my husband, "If a butler or maid answers, I'm not going in."

But Lydia answered — in black slacks and an old black sweater and no shoes. She gave me a hug and I went in with my littlest child and didn't look back.

Through the hall into the sitting-room, then the dining-room (an impression of a piano and lots of books, of a big antique dining table covered with clutter generally, now that I think back on it. Somewhere upstairs a small child was screaming), through another narrow hall and into a big kitchen. She asked if my little girl wanted some orange juice. She wouldn't answer so I answered for her as mothers do on such occasions.

"Yes please."

When Lydia opened the refrigerator a great pile of things fell out on the kitchen floor. Frozen pizzas, a dish of left-over mashed potatoes, the bottle of juice, something unidentifiable in a glass jar. We looked at each other and began to laugh.

"The house," I said, "I was terrified."

"I *hate* this house, she said. "I hate it."

Then talked and talked while our two little girls (we each had three, extraordinary! We each had the same dinner set bought on special at the Hudson's Bay Company years before, "Cherry Thieves" it was called — she used one of the saucers for an ash tray) played something or other upstairs.

She was older than I was (but not much) and very beautiful with dark curly chaotic hair and the kind of white skin that gives off the radiance a candle does when it has burnt down at the core and the sides are still intact. Her book had brought her fame (if not fortune) but she was having trouble with her second one, a novel.

She hated the house and couldn't keep it up. Her husband was a professor — he loved it. It was miserably cold in the winter — sometimes the furnace stopped altogether. What did I think of Doris Lessing, of Joyce Carol Oates, of *The Edible Woman*? Her daughter had made a scene in the supermarket and called her a "fucking bitch." Did that kind of thing happen to me? Her neighbour was a perfect housewife, perfect. She was always sending over cakes and preserves. One day she took one of her neighbour's cheesecakes and stamped all over it with her bare feet, she said. An aging Canadian writer (male) had told her drunkenly, "Well, I might read ya, but I'd never fuck ya." Did I think it was all right to send a kid to day care when she was only three?

And even while I was talking with her, marvelling at her, helping her mop up the floor, I kept wondering why she didn't write about all this, why she had stopped at twenty years ago and written nothing about her marriage or this house or or her child who had been still-born and how the doctor (male) and her husband couldn't understand why it took her so long to get over it. I wondered about her husband but he was off somewhere practicing with a chamber-music group. He liked old instruments, old houses, things with a patina of history and culture. His family accepted her now that she'd won awards.

I only saw her a few times after that — we lived in different cities and there was a boat ride between us. But we wrote (occasionally); she had large round handwriting, like a child's.

Her novel was not going well — it kept turning itself into stories — she was going to Ireland with her husband for a holiday. How was I? Not literary letters: we were both too busy, too involved in our own affairs. Just little notes, like little squeezes or hugs which said, "Sister, I am here."

We read once, at a Women's Week, or rather I read, with two others, while Lydia sat on the blue-carpeted floor with a Spanish cape over her head and let somebody else read for her. She and I were both scared and had gotten drunk before we went — by not reading she had somehow let me down. We four ladies all had dinner together and talked about what it was like to be woman and writer and egged each other on to new witticisms and maybe a few new insights but I did not feel close to Lydia that evening. I was still sore about the way she'd plonked herself down on the carpet and pulled her shawl over her head and let somebody else read for her. It was very clever, I thought to myself, and very dramatic. For there was Lydia's story, unrolling out of the mouth of another woman (whose story it was not), and there was the author herself sitting like an abandoned doll, on the floor beside the reader. The audience loved it and sent out sympathetic vibrations to her. I thought it was a con. And almost said to her, "Lydia, I think that was a very clever con," but didn't because I realized that maybe I wished I had thought of it first and why not store it away for some future date — it was a nice piece of dramatic business.

And once we had lunch in her city — at a medieval place where we swept in in our capes (I had a cape too by then) and ate and drank our way through a rainy West Coast afternoon. I wasn't staying overnight so I still hadn't met her husband. Her novel was out and she was winning more awards. I was a little jealous. My books came out and vanished into the well of oblivion. She just went up and up and up. "I've been writing for twenty years," she said, "don't forget that. Two books in twenty years."

She had pretended she was making the sitting-room curtains when her neighbours invited her over for coffee. She always worked in a basement room. Now her secret was well and truly out.

"How does your husband feel about it all?"

"Oh, I never write about *him*," she said. She lit a cigarette. "He's probably my biggest fan."

Now I waited for her to call me back. My husband (correction, my ex-husband) was coming over to be with his children. I had a whole day and a night off. Whether I wanted to or not, I had to leave this place. And I wanted to, I really wanted to. What was the point in hanging around while he was here, in crying over spilt milk, in locking empty, horseless barn doors, in trying to pick up nine stitches, or in mopping up all the water under the goddamn bridge. I baked bread and cleaned the cabin and got supper for the kids and still she hadn't called. My ex-husband called, however, and said in his new strained, estranged voice, was it all set for tomorrow and I said sure but began to feel sorry for myself because there was really no place I wanted to go except this one place — Lydia's — and I'd got it into my head that if I couldn't go there I couldn't go anywhere and would have to end up going back to the city I had left behind and getting a room in some cheap hotel down near Hastings street, and drinking myself into oblivion with cheap red wine. Or going back and forth all day on the ferry, ending up at midnight on one of the neighbouring islands, getting a room at the inn. A stranger in a brown wool cape. Going into the public room and ordering a drink. Did they have a public room? Would there be local characters sitting around and playing darts — a handsome stranger whose sailing boat was tied up because of the storm? There was not even a small craft warning out but never mind — the weather was almost as fickle as friendship — it was not inconceivable that a sailboat-disabling storm could blow up by tomorrow night —

"I'll always care what happens to you," he said.

We were teasing wool on the floor in front of the potbelly stove, the three of us — the youngest child was asleep. There was only the oil lamp on and the CBC was broadcasting a documentary about Casals. "The quality of a man's life is as important as the quality of his art," the old man said. Our hands were soft and oily from the lanolin in the wool. We touched each other's faces with our new, soft hands. Yes, I thought, yes. And maybe I'll be all right after all. The fleece had been bought by my husband's lover, my ex-best friend. It was from New Zealand, the finest wool in the world. I paid for it, the wool. I had left a cheque on the table the last time I was in town. On the phone my ex-husband mentioned it wasn't enough, she'd mistaken the price or the price had been incorrectly quoted. But it was all right, he'd make up the difference.

"I bet you will," I said.

I was seeing everything symbolically. Lydia phoned and I said, "Just a minute I have to light a candle." The room with the phone in it was in darkness. I stuck the candle in the window and picked up the phone again with my soft lanolin-soaked hands.

"Hello," I said, "Can I come and visit you tomorrow and stay overnight?" Her voice sounded a bit funny but that could be the line, which was notoriously bad.

"Sure," she said, "Of course. But I'll be out until supper-time. Can you find something to do until supper-time?"

"Can I come a little before? I want to talk to you."

"Come around four," she said. She sounded as though she had a cold.

"I'll bring a bottle," I said.

"Fine."

I had to be away on the first ferry — what would I do all day? I rubbed lanolin into my face. Sheep shed their old coats and went on living. Snakes too. I could hear Casals' child laughing in the background. Someone had lent us a spinner and it stood in the corner of the front room. Not a fairytale spinner which would turn straw into gold. Very solid and unromantic — an

Indian spinner without even the big wheel. Nothing for a Sleeping Beauty to prick her finger on. It worked like an old treadle sewing machine but I didn't have the hang of it yet—my wool always broke. Whirr whirr. There was something nice about just pressing down on the treadle.

I took the candle into the kitchen and wrapped my bread in clean tea towels. I put out a jar of blackberry jam and two poems folded underneath the jar. That would have to do.

When I got to Lydia's house she was frying chicken in the kitchen. Same black slacks and old black sweater. Same bare feet and clutter. There were two enormous frying pans full of chicken wings both hissing and spitting away and Lydia had a long two-prong kitchen fork in her hand.

I took off my cape and sat down, unwrapping the bottle.

"Good," she said, "pour us a glass." Her voice didn't sound as if she had a cold any more; it sounded harsh and a little loud, as if she were talking to someone slightly deaf. She was jabbing the chicken wings as if they were sausages in need of pricking. She couldn't leave those chicken wings alone and after my second glass I began.

"Listen," I said, "I've got something I want to tell you."

"I've got something I want to tell you too," she said, and then rather absent-mindedly, "did you buy only one bottle?"

"Sorry. But have some more, it doesn't matter."

"It's all right," she said, "we'll drink the dinner wine. Tony will just have to bring some more."

I was anxious to begin. I wanted to make it funny and witty and brave —to get rid of the pain or to immortalize it and fix it—which? I don't know, I never know. I took another drink of my sherry and wished she'd stop poking at those chicken wings.

"I don't actually live here anymore," she said, waving the long-handled fork. "I only come back to cook the dinners."

"You what?"

Turning all the chicken wings over one more time, she lowered the heat under the pans and came to sit down next to me. She kept her fork with her, however, and laid it on the tablecloth where it left a greasy two-pronged stain.

"I've left him," she said, "the bastard." Her voice was very harsh, very tough. I felt she'd put something over on me, just as I'd felt the day of the reading when she sat on the floor and pulled her cape over her head.

"I wish you'd told me over the phone."

"I couldn't. It's too complicated. Besides, I come back here every day in any case."

It was both moving and bizarre. He had been supposed to move out, she had even found him an apartment only a few minutes away. But at the last minute he panicked, said he couldn't live in an apartment, talked about his piano, his collection of old instruments, the upheaval. He suggested she move out instead.

"But what about the children?"

"That's the trouble. I have to pick Ellen up from school—he can't do it of course and so I just stay on and make the dinners. The other two are all right, it's only the little one who still needs to be looked after."

"But that's crazy."

"Is it? What would you do?"

I admitted that I didn't know.

"But how can you all eat together — how can you stand it?"

"I can't," she admitted, "but he won't move out, and finding a house big enough for me and the girls is going to take time." She got up and rummaged in the pantry. Came back with a bottle of wine.

"I think we'd better start on this," she said. I undid the cork while she got up to turn the chicken wings.

"He brought her right to the house," she said. "When I was on that reading tour. Brought her right here and the children were here too."

The name of the wine was Sangré de Toro.

"At least she wasn't your best friend," I said.

"I knew her, I knew her, she's one of his students. I used to think she was mousey. I encouraged her to do something with herself. Ha. And I think the lady next door too," she said.

"The one who bakes cakes."

"That's the one. The perfect mother."

"Maybe you're just being paranoid."

"Maybe."

We began the Sangré de Toro.

"What's your big news?" she said.

The two older girls were out somewhere for the evening so there was just the youngest child, who must have been six or seven, Lydia, her husband and myself. She and I were pretty drunk by the time we finished the Sangré de Toro but she had insisted I call her husband at the University and ask him to bring home another bottle.

"Tell him specifically what you want," she yelled at me from the kitchen. "Otherwise he'll bring home Calona Red."

I told him. Now he sat opposite me with two huge plates of chicken wings between us. I didn't want to look at his baffled eyes, his embarrassed smile.

"He still wears a handkerchief in his breast pocket," she had said. "Irons them himself."

The vegetable was frozen peas and there was bread on the table because Lydia had forgotten all about potatoes. The child was raucous and unpleasant. I wondered what happened when she woke up in the night with a bad dream and whether he went in to her or whether her teenage sisters did. I wondered if she had been the one to tell about the student. Kids will do things like that and not always out of innocence.

Lydia ate one chicken wing after another. We were all going out as soon as the dishes were done and the babysitter came. My real self didn't want to go but my drunken self thought what the hell it's better than staying here with these three miserable people.

While Tony was doing the dishes Lydia hauled me upstairs, pulled me up after her like an older sister a younger, or a mother a reluctant child. I understood the fierce energy of her anger. It was like someone who is hurt during an exciting game. While the excitement is there the pain is simply not felt. She hurled me into their bedroom.

"Look," she said.

I don't know what I expected to see. Stained sheets piled up in a corner or the student stark naked and manacled to the bed or what. But everything seemed all right. No shattered mirrors or blood-stained bedspreads, just an ordinary pleasant-looking bedroom.

"I don't see."

"Look." She was pointing to the walk-in closet.

"I've left all my shoes here except one pair. Crazy isn't it? I just can't seem to take my shoes away."

"Maybe you don't really want to go."

"Oh no, I want to go. I have to go. Or he does. One of us anyway. It isn't just the girl.

"It never is."

On his side of the closet the tweed jackets and neatly pressed trousers were hung with military precision. On her side there were only empty hangers and a large heap of shoes piled any which way. Was that significant, the order/disorder? Was it an attempt to break through this orderly self that made him bring his student to this bed? Or had he just been lonely? I didn't want to think about that for after all, wasn't he the enemy?

We went back downstairs.

The babysitter came and we went out. Lydia had put on a filthy white crocheted wool poncho. Tony objected mildly. "Are you going out in that? It's dirty."

"That's tough," Lydia said.

They were playing to me, an audience of one. Maybe that's why we were going out—to gain a larger audience. I panicked—what if I had too much to drink and began to cry? Lydia looked witchy and wicked with her uncombed hair and dirty poncho. I felt she was quite capable of doing something terrible to her husband—mocking him or humiliating him in some way, and I was to be her accomplice. He had a heavy projector in his hand.

"We had arranged to show some slides," he said, "before we knew you were coming."

"Slides of our European trip," Lydia said. "One of Tony's colleagues is going this summer—he wanted to see them.

I thought it was strange they didn't invite him over here, but maybe Lydia had refused to actually entertain. I found the whole thing strange—sitting between them in the car, following them up the steps of their friend's house, saying hello and taking off my cape, patting my face to keep the smile in place, the way some women pat their hair before they go into a room. Our host was shy and pale and had a club foot. There didn't seem to be any hostess. But there were two other people in the sitting-room, a tall, lean man in a bright blue shirt, string tie and cowboy boots, and a plump woman in a black crêpe dress, black pointy fifties shoes and a rhinestone brooch. Both the man and the woman had nice faces, expectant faces, as if they expected that whoever walked through the next door was bound to be cheerful and interesting and good. Innocent faces, almost the faces of small children. We were introduced and asked what we would like to drink and Tony began to set up the projector.

Lydia was talking to Tony's colleague in her strange new brassy tough-gal voice, flirting with him, making him smile. "Does he know?" I wondered. He had introduced her as Tony's wife. I sat down next to the man in the blue shirt.

"What do you do?" I asked.

"I'm a bee-keeper," he said.

"You might say he's a bee-baron," said his brother. I could see they were brothers in their smiles and something to do with their ears, a strange extra little fold where the ear joined the head. Other than that they didn't really look alike, the one small and dark and with the pallor of the academic, the other tall and fair and with what we call a "weathered" skin.

"A swarm of bees in May," said Lydia, "is worth a load of hay. I remember hearing farmers say that when I was a kid. I grew up on a farm," she said and flashed a smile at the bee-keeper's wife.

"Do you like it," I asked, "keeping bees?" I had thought of buying one or two hives for the island. I already had hens and a fleece for spinning and would have my nine bean rows in the spring. Lydia had laughed when I told her my real dream was to have a little farm.

"Ha. Only city people yearn to live on a farm. I hated it."

"Why?"

"I'm not even sure why any more. The constant work—the catastrophes—the exhaustion—the women always in the kitchen—something always being butchered, beheaded or skinned or pickled or preserved."

"Maybe it doesn't have to be that way?"

"It has to be that way. If you really live off the land you live off the land. Nothing can be put off or wasted or ignored. I always felt the kitchen smelled of blood or sugar or vinegar or manure or all of these. I felt I went to school stinking of all of it."

"Those are good smells. Honest smells. I worked in an asylum once—I got that smell on me. I used carbolic soap and tried to get it off."

She shook her head and changed the subject, only adding, "They weren't good smells when I was going to school."

Had she been teased, then? Had the boys pulled chicken feathers out of her dark curly hair—had her dresses been too long—were her hands all wrinkled from washwater? I realized how little I actually knew about her except through her stories. I guess this conversation took place before her novel came out.

Tony asked in his apologetic manner if we were ready to see the slides. Lydia and the bee-keeper's wife were sitting in easy chairs on the other side of the room, where the screen had been set up, so they had to move. Lydia came and sat cross-legged on the floor by my feet. The bee-keeper and I were on the couch and we shoved over to make room for the bee-keeper's wife. Tony was next to me, behind the projector and his friend was next to him on a kitchen chair. He got up and after offering us another drink (only Lydia and I accepted) turned out all the lights.

I don't remember much about the slide show. Tony projected and Lydia commented. Ireland, England, Scotland, Wales and then across the Channel into France and down through Spain. They were all "views"— that is to say they told me nothing about the two people who had taken that trip. Alone. Without the children. Was that when they first suspected they had nothing to say to one another? Had they set off with high hopes and become more and more disenchanted? What had finally driven that orderly controlled man to introduce that student into his bedroom? Not secretly but openly, "in front of the children." From where I was sitting I could see that his hands shook every time he put in another slide.

"You've got that one in backwards," Lydia said. We all came to attention and studied the screen—it was a bull fight scene and looked perfectly all right to me.

"I don't think—" Tony began.

"Look for yourself. Look at it. Can't you see it's back to front?"

"I sure don't see anything funny," said the bee-keeper.

"'Initram'," Lydia said in her bold brassy voice. "Look at the advertisements and tell me what kind of a drink is Initram."

"Oh," he said. "Sorry."

"Ha."

His hands shook a little more as he carefully pried out the offending slide and turned it around.

"There," he said. "Is that better?"

"Oh God," said Lydia. "You've done it again." And sure enough he had. There was "Initram" being advertised again.

"I'd like another drink," said Lydia, "Initram on the rocks."

Tony switched the projector off and for a minute we were in a complete and tension-filled darkness before his friend had enough presence of mind to reach up and switch on the lights.

"That's all folks," he said, trying to sound like Woody Woodpecker, trying to be funny.

"Don't you want to show the rest of the slides?" Lydia said.

"No, I think that's enough."

"Well, tell us about bees then," she said, turning around and facing the sofa, backing away a little bit so she could gaze up at the bee-keeper, her pretty head cocked on one side.

"What do you want to know?" he said, smiling. But uncomfortable too for he was not so dumb or naïve that he didn't see what she was doing to her husband.

"Oh. Everything. Everything." She waved her hand. "Their mating habits for instance. Do they really only mate once? The queens, I mean."

"No, they can mate more than once, maybe two, three times. But usually only once. It's funny," he said, "when you stop to think of it. From a human point of view the drone that wins is the loser really."

"I don't follow you," I said. I really knew nothing about bees. Whereas I had a funny feeling about Lydia. Would a kid who had a grandfather who kept bees—? Or maybe she never did have such a grandfather. Maybe her grandfather just said that whenever he saw a swarm—the way my father used to say, "Red sky at night, sailor's delight" when he'd never been near the ocean.

"Fun, frolic and death," he said, "fun, frolic and death. Those drones are the laziest devils you'd like to see. Waited on hand and foot by their sisters—don't have to do nothing except eat and lie around and take the occasional look-see outside. Then one day the queen just zooms up into the

blue with hundreds of those drones dashin' after her. A fantastic sight—
fantastic."

"And the race is to the swift," said Lydia, taking a long sip of her drink
as if it were some strange nectar, then parting her lips and looking up at the
bee-keeper with her new bold look.

"The strongest and swiftest catches her," he said, "Sometimes she
even zooms back toward 'em, because she wants to be caught you know.
That's all part of it."

"She wants to be caught," repeated Lydia. "She has to be caught." She
took another long sip of her drink. The bee-keeper's wife just sat back
against the cushions and smiled.

"She has to be caught."

"So she is caught."

"And then?"

"And then he clasps her to him, face to face—there's a little explosion
as all his male organs pop out and they fly together like that face to face,
while he fertilizes her."

"Then he dies?" I asked.

"Then he dies. You see, they fall to the ground together, outside the
home hive of the queen, and when she tries to pull away, he's stuck so fast
to her she pulls most of his abdomen away."

"Ab-*do*-men," said Lydia, lightly mocking him. But not in the way she
said, "Initram."

"My brother probably knows more about bees than any man in North
America," said the man with the club foot. "He could write a book about
them."

"It's my job," he said simply.

"Oh don't," cried Lydia. "Don't ever write a book about them." She
gave a mock shudder. "I wonder what it feels like," she said. "To fly out like
that after the darkness of the hive into the blue sky and the green trees and
to feel the sunshine on her back. To know that her destiny is about to be
fulfilled." Then she turned toward the bee-keeper's wife. "And you. Is it
your life too? Bees?"

She nodded her head, serene in her black dress and rhinestones. She
had a strong Southern accent.

"It's my life too."

Then the bee-keeper did a beautiful thing. He just reached over and
put his lean brown hand over hers.

"We try to study the bees," he said. "We try to do what they do."

"Fun, frolic and death?" said Lydia, flirting, slyly mocking.

"No," he said, but not angrily. He didn't swat at her any more than he
might swat at a bee who flew a little too close to his ear.

"They are true communists—the bees. No-one works for any profit to
himself. Everything is done only for the good of the colony. If we could live
like that—"

"Ah yes, Utopia." Lydia sighed. "Perhaps if we all ate more honey?"
She was mocking him again, circling back. She smiled at the three men in
the room. All she needed was a yellow sweater.

"Who knows? That's where our word honeymoon comes from, you
know—the old belief in the magical powers of honey. Germany I think it

was, or Austria. The newly-married couple would drink mead for a month after the wedding."

"What was it supposed to do for them?"

"Now that I'm not sure of. Make 'em happy and industrious I guess."

"Is it true," said Lydia, "that the queen can sting over and over—that she doesn't die when she stings? I read that somewhere I think. Tony, do you remember reading that somewhere or somebody telling us that the queen could sting over and over?"

"I don't remember."

"Well, it's true, isn't it?" She appealed to the bee-keeper.

"It's true. She has to defend herself. It's her nature."

"There, you see Tony, I was right. It's her nature."

"There is usually only one queen," said the bee-keeper, "she kills off all the others."

"Why not?" Lydia said, "it's natural."

Then we were all leaving—I can't remember who stood up first. We said goodbye to the bee-keeper and his wife. I wrote down the name of a supply house where I could get supers and bee suits. I wrote down the names of two books. He (the bee-keeper) went out to his van and came back with a little jar of honey for each of us. Alfalfa honey, clear and thick and golden.

"Jim Ritchie and Sons," it said. "Abbotsford, BC," and "Unpasteurized" underneath. "Mary Beth designed the labels," he said proudly.

I slept downstairs in a little parlour with a fireplace. They had coal and started a fire for me. Made up the Hide-A-Bed and went off upstairs together. I lay in the darkness under Lydia's grandmother's Star of Bethlehem quilt and smelled the smell of the coal fire and was back fourteen years under a quilt in a big double bed in Scotland. On my honeymoon. The maid had come in with a stone hot water bottle but we were already warm from drinking a strange mixture in the public bar—something called Atholl Brose and now that I thought of it, I seemed to remember that it was made of porridge and honey. Or maybe I just had honey on the brain.

What had happened to us? What had happened to us all? I began to cry while Lydia made noisy love upstairs. I heard her—she wanted me to hear her. It was the last line in the last paragraph of the story she'd been writing all evening. I wondered if she'd come down the next morning with Tony's abdomen irrevocably stuck to her front.

We don't see each other very much any more. She lives in a distant city. But once a year we meet—at the Writers Union annual general meeting—and compare children and lovers and ideas for stories, usually in that order. We flirt, we get drunk, we congratulate ourselves that somehow miraculously we have survived another year, that we each have money and a room of one's own and are writing fiction. This year I told her (lying) that I was thinking of writing a story about her.

"I'm calling it 'Chicken Wings'," I said.

"Chicken Wings?"

"The night I came to see you, and you and Tony had just split up."

"And you wanted to tell me about your break-up."

"*Sangré de Toro*," I said. We began to laugh.

"Do you remember the bee-keeper and his wife?"

"Of course, they're in the story."

"Fun, frolic and death—oh God."

We laughed until we cried.

"What name d'you want?" I said. "You can choose your own name."

"Lydia," she said. "I always wanted to be called Lydia."

"All right," I said. "You can be Lydia."

"But I don't like your title," she said. "I think you'll have to change it."

ALISTAIR MACLEOD

The Boat

There are times even now, when I awake at four o'clock in the morning with the terrible fear that I have overslept; when I imagine that my father is waiting for me in the room below the darkened stairs or that the shorebound men are tossing pebbles against my window while blowing their hands and stomping their feet impatiently on the frozen steadfast earth. There are times when I am half out of bed and fumbling for socks and mumbling for words before I realize that I am foolishly alone, that no one waits at the base of the stairs and no boat rides restlessly in the waters by the pier.

At such times only the grey corpses on the overflowing ashtray beside my bed bear witness to the extinction of the latest spark and silently await the crushing out of the most recent of their fellows. And then because I am afraid to be alone with death, I dress rapidly, make a great to-do about clearing my throat, turn on both faucets in the sink and proceed to make loud splashing ineffectual noises. Later I go out and walk the mile to the all-night restaurant.

In the winter it is a very cold walk and there are often tears in my eyes when I arrive. The waitress usually gives a sympathetic little shiver and says, "Boy, it must be really cold out there; you got tears in your eyes."

"Yes," I say, "it sure is; it really is."

And then the three or four of us who are always in such places at such times make uninteresting little protective chit-chat until the dawn reluctantly arrives. Then I swallow the coffee which is always bitter and leave with a great busy rush because by that time I have to worry about being late and whether I have a clean shirt and whether my car will start and about all the other countless things one must worry about when he teaches at a great Midwestern university. And I know then that that day will go by as have all the days of the past ten years, for the call and the voices and the shapes and the boat were not really there in the early morning's darkness and I have all kinds of comforting reality to prove it. They are only shadows and echoes, the animals a child's hands make on the wall by lamplight, and the voices from the rain barrel; the cuttings from an old movie made in the black and white of long ago.

I first became conscious of the boat in the same way and at almost the same time that I became aware of the people it supported. My earliest recollection of my father is a view from the floor of gigantic rubber boots and then of being suddenly elevated and having my face pressed against the stubble of his cheek, and of how it tasted of salt and of how he smelled of salt from his red-soled rubber boots to the shaggy whiteness of his hair.

When I was very small, he took me for my first ride in the boat. I rode the half-mile from our house to the wharf on his shoulders and I remember the sound of his rubber boots galumphing along the gravel beach, the tune of the indecent little song he used to sing, and the odour of the salt.

The floor of the boat was permeated with the same odour and in its constancy I was not aware of change. In the harbour we made our little

411

circle and returned. He tied the boat by its painter, fastened the stern to its permanent anchor and lifted me high over his head to the solidity of the wharf. Then he climbed up the little iron ladder that led to the wharf's cap, placed me once more upon his shoulders and galumphed off again.

When we returned to the house everyone made a great fuss over my precocious excursion and asked, "How did you like the boat?" "Were you afraid in the boat?" "Did you cry in the boat?" They repeated "the boat" at the end of all their questions and I knew it must be very important to everyone.

My earliest recollection of my mother is of being alone with her in the mornings while my father was away in the boat. She seemed to be always repairing clothes that were "torn in the boat," preparing food "to be eaten in the boat" or looking for "the boat" through our kitchen window which faced upon the sea. When my father returned about noon, she would ask, "Well, how did things go in the boat today?" It was the first question I remember asking: "Well, how did things go in the boat today?" "Well, how did things go in the boat today?"

The boat in our lives was registered at Port Hawkesbury. She was what Nova Scotians called a Cape Island boat and was designed for the small inshore fishermen who sought the lobsters of the spring and the mackerel of summer and later the cod and haddock and hake. She was thirty-two feet long and nine wide, and was powered by an engine from a Chevrolet truck. She had a marine clutch and a high speed reverse gear and was painted light green with the name *Jenny Lynn* stencilled in black letters on her bow and painted on an oblong plate across her stern. Jenny Lynn had been my mother's maiden name and the boat was called after her as another link in the chain of tradition. Most of the boats that berthed at the wharf bore the names of some female member of their owner's household.

I say this now as if I knew it all then. All at once, all about boat dimensions and engines, and as if on the day of my first childish voyage I noticed the difference between a stencilled name and a painted name. But of course it was not that way at all, for I learned it all very slowly and there was not time enough.

I learned first about our house which was one of about fifty which marched around the horseshoe of our harbour and the wharf which was its heart. Some of them were so close to the water that during a storm the sea spray splashed against their windows while others were built farther along the beach as was the case with ours. The houses and their people, like those of the neighbouring towns and villages, were the result of Ireland's discontent and Scotland's Highland Clearances and America's War of Independence. Impulsive emotional Catholic Celts who could not bear to live with England and shrewd determined Protestant Puritans who, in the years after 1776, could not bear to live without.

The most important room in our house was one of those oblong old-fashioned kitchens heated by a wood- and coal-burning stove. Behind the stove was a box of kindlings and beside it a coal scuttle. A heavy wooden table with leaves that expanded or reduced its dimensions stood in the middle of the floor. There were five wooden home-made chairs which had been chipped and hacked by a variety of knives. Against the east wall, opposite the stove, there was a couch which sagged in the middle and had a cushion for a pillow, and above it a shelf which contained matches, tobacco, pencils, odd fish-hooks, bits of twine, and a tin can filled with bills and receipts. The south wall was dominated by a window which faced the sea and on the north there was a five-foot board which bore a variety of clothes hooks and the burdens of each. Beneath the board there was a jumble of odd footwear, mostly of rubber. There was also, on this wall, a barometer, a map of the marine area and a shelf which held a tiny radio. The kitchen was shared by all of us and was a buffer zone between the immaculate order of ten other rooms and the disruptive chaos of the single room that was my father's.

My mother ran her house as her brothers ran their boats. Everything was clean and spotless and in order. She was tall and dark and powerfully energetic. In later years she reminded me of the women of Thomas Hardy, particularly Eustacia Vye,[1] in a physical way. She fed and clothed a family of seven children, making all of the meals and most of the clothes. She grew miraculous gardens and magnificient flowers and raised broods of hens and ducks. She would walk miles on berry-picking expeditions and hoist her skirts to dig for clams when the tide was low. She was fourteen years younger than my father, whom she had married when she was twenty-six and had been a local beauty for a period of ten years. My mother was of the sea as were all of her people, and her horizons were the very literal ones she scanned with her dark and fearless eyes.

Between the kitchen clothes rack and barometer, a door opened into my father's bedroom. It was a room of disorder and disarray. It was as if the wind which so often clamoured about the house succeeded in entering this single room and after whipping it into turmoil stole quietly away to renew its knowing laughter from without.

My father's bed was against the south wall. It always looked rumpled and unmade because he lay on top of it more than he slept within any folds it might have had. Beside it, there was a little brown table. An archaic goose-necked reading light, a battered table radio, a mound of wooden matches, one or two packages of tobacco, a deck of cigarette papers and an overflowing ashtray cluttered its surface. The brown larvae of tobacco shreds and the grey flecks of ash covered both the table and the floor beneath it. The once-varnished surface of the table was disfigured by numerous black scars and gashes inflicted by the neglected burning cigarettes of many years. They had tumbled from the ashtray unnoticed and branded their statements permanently and quietly into the wood until the odour of their burning caused the snuffing out of their lives. At the bed's foot there was a single window which looked upon the sea.

Against the adjacent wall there was a battered bureau and beside it there was a closet which held his single ill-fitting serge suit, the two or three white shirts that strangled him and the square black shoes that pinched. When he took off his more friendly clothes, the heavy woollen sweaters, mitts and socks which my mother knitted for him and the woollen and doeskin shirts, he dumped them unceremoniously on a single

---

1. A character in Thomas Hardy's *The Return of the Native* (1878).

chair. If a visitor entered the room while he was lying on the bed, he would be told to throw the clothes on the floor and take their place upon the chair.

Magazines and books covered the bureau and competed with the clothes for domination of the chair. They further overburdened the heroic little table and lay on top of the radio. They filled a baffling and unknowable cave beneath the bed, and in the corner by the bureau they spilled from the walls and grew up from the floor.

The magazines were the most conventional: *Time, Newsweek, Life, Maclean's, Family Herald, Reader's Digest*. They were the result of various cut-rate subscriptions or of the gift subscriptions associated with Christmas, "the two whole years for only $3.50."

The books were more varied. There were a few hard-cover magnificents and bygone Book-of-the-Month wonders and some were Christmas or birthday gifts. The majority of them, however, were used paperbacks which came from those second-hand bookstores which advertise in the backs of magazines: "Miscellaneous Used Paperbacks 10¢ Each." At first he sent for them himself, although my mother resented the expense, but in later years they came more and more often from my sisters who had moved to the cities. Especially at first they were very weird and varied. Mickey Spillane and Ernest Haycox vied with Dostoyevsky and Faulkner, and the Penguin Poets edition of Gerard Manley Hopkins arrived in the same box as a litte book on sex technique called *Getting the Most Out of Love*. The former had been assiduously annotated by a very fine hand using a very blue-inked fountain pen while the latter had been studied by someone with very large thumbs, the prints of which were still visible in the margins. At the slightest provocation it would open almost automatically to particularly graphic and well-smudged pages.

When he was not in the boat, my father spent most of his time lying on the bed in his socks, the top two buttons of his trousers undone, his discarded shirt on the ever-ready chair and the sleeves of the woollen Stanfield underwear, which he wore both summer and winter, drawn half way up to his elbows. The pillows propped up the whiteness of his head and the goose-necked lamp illuminated the pages in his hands. The cigarettes smoked and smouldered on the ashtray and on the table and the radio played constantly, sometimes low and sometimes loud. At midnight and at one, two, three and four, one could sometimes hear the radio, his occasional cough, the rustling thud of a completed book being tossed to the corner heap, or the movement necessitated by his sitting on the edge of the bed to roll the thousandth cigarette. He seemed never to sleep, only to doze, and the light shone constantly from his window to the sea.

My mother despised the room and all it stood for and she had stopped sleeping in it after I was born. She despised disorder in rooms and in houses and in hours and in lives, and she had not read a book since high school. There she had read *Ivanhoe* and considered it a colossal waste of time. Still the room remained, like a solid rock of opposition in the sparkling waters of a clear deep harbour, opening off the kitchen where we really lived our lives, with its door always open and its contents visible to all.

The daughters of the room and of the house were very beautiful. They were tall and willowy like my mother and had her fine facial features set off by the reddish copper-coloured hair that had apparently once been my father's before it turned to white. All of them were very clever in school and helped my mother a great deal about the house. When they were young they sang and were very happy and very nice to me because I was the youngest and the family's only boy.

My father never approved of their playing about the wharf like the other children, and they went there only when my mother sent them on an errand. At such times they almost always overstayed, playing screaming games of tag or hide-and-seek in and about the fishing shanties, the piled traps and tubs of trawl, shouting down to the perch that swam languidly about the wharf's algae-covered piles, or jumping in and out of the boats that tugged gently at their lines. My mother was never uneasy about them at such times, and when her husband criticized her she would say, "Nothing will happen to them there," or "They could be doing worse things in worse places."

By about the ninth or tenth grade my sisters one by one discovered my father's bedroom and then the change would begin. Each would go into the room one morning when he was out. She would go with the ideal hope of imposing order or with the more practical objective of emptying the ashtray, and later she would be found spellbound by the volume in her hand. My mother's reaction was always abrupt, bordering on the angry. "Take your nose out of that trash and come and do your work," she would say, and once I saw her slap my youngest sister so hard that the print of her hand was scarletly emblazoned upon her daughter's cheek while the broken-spined paperback fluttered uselessly to the floor.

Thereafter my mother would launch a campaign against what she had discovered but could not understand. At times although she was not overly religious she would bring in God to bolster her arguments, saying, "In the next world God will see to those who waste their lives reading useless books when they should be about their work." Or without theological aid, "I would like to know how books help anyone to live a life." If my father were in, she would repeat the remarks louder than necessary, and her voice would carry into his room where he lay upon his bed. His usual reaction was to turn up the volume of the radio, although that action in itself betrayed the success of the initial thrust.

Shortly after my sisters began to read the books, they grew restless and lost interest in darning socks and baking bread, and all of them eventually went to work as summer waitresses in the Sea Food Restaurant. The restaurant was run by a big American concern from Boston and catered to the tourists that flooded the area during July and August. My mother despised the whole operation. She said the restaurant was not run by "our people," and "our people" did not eat there, and that it was run by outsiders for outsiders.

"Who are these people anyway?" she would ask, tossing back her dark hair, "and what do they, though they go about with their cameras for a hundred years, know about the way it is here, and what do they care about me and mine, and why should I care about them?"

She was angry that my sisters should even conceive of working in such a place and more angry when my father made no move to prevent it, and she was worried about herself and about her family and about her life. Sometimes she would say softly to her sisters, "I don't know what's the matter with my girls. It seems none of them are interested in any of the right things." And sometimes there would be bitter savage arguments. One afternoon I was coming in with three mackerel I'd been given at the wharf when I heard her say, "Well I hope you'll be satisfied when they come home knocked up and you'll have had your way."

It was the most savage thing I'd ever heard my mother say. Not just the words but the way she said them, and I stood there in the porch afraid to breathe for what seemed like the years from ten to fifteen, feeling the damp moist mackerel with their silver glassy eyes growing clammy against my leg.

Through the angle in the screen door I saw my father who had been walking into his room wheel around on one of his rubber-booted heels and look at her with his blue eyes flashing like clearest ice beneath the snow that was his hair. His usually ruddy face was drawn and grey, reflecting the exhaustion of a man of sixty-five who had been working in those rubber boots for eleven hours on an August day, and for a fleeting moment I wondered what I would do if he killed my mother while I stood there in the porch with those three foolish mackerel in my hand. Then he turned and went into his room and the radio blared forth the next day's weather forecast and I retreated under the noise and returned again, stamping my feet and slamming the door too loudly to signal my approach. My mother was busy at the stove when I came in, and did not raise her head when I threw the mackerel in a pan. As I looked into my father's room, I said, "Well, how did things go in the boat today?" and he replied, "Oh not too badly, all things considered." He was lying on his back and lighting the first cigarette and the radio was talking about the Virginia coast.

All of my sisters made good money on tips. They bought my father an electric razor which he tried to use for a while and they took out even more magazine subscriptions. They bought my mother a great many clothes of the type she was very fond of, the wide-brimmed hats and the brocaded dresses, but she locked them all in trunks and refused to wear any of them.

On one August day my sisters prevailed upon my father to take some of their restaurant customers for an afternoon ride in the boat. The tourists with their expensive clothes and cameras and sun glasses awkwardly backed down the iron ladder at the wharf's side to where my father waited below, holding the rocking *Jenny Lynn* in snug against the wharf with one hand on the iron ladder and steadying his descending passengers with the other. They tried to look both prim and wind-blown like the girls in the Pepsi-Cola ads and did the best they could, sitting on the thwarts where the newspapers were spread to cover the splattered blood and fish entrails, crowding to one side so that they were in danger of capsizing the boat, taking the inevitable pictures or merely trailing their fingers through the water of their dreams.

All of them liked my father very much and, after he'd brought them back from their circles in the harbour, they invited him to their rented cabins which were located high on a hill overlooking the village to which they were so alien. He proceeded to get very drunk up there with the beautiful view and the strange company and the abundant liquor, and late in the afternoon he began to sing.

I was just approaching the wharf to deliver my mother's summons when he began, and the familiar yet unfamiliar voice that rolled down from the cabins made me feel as I had never felt before in my young life or perhaps as I had always felt without really knowing it, and I was ashamed yet proud, young yet old and saved yet forever lost, and there was nothing I could do to control my legs which trembled nor my eyes which wept for what they could not tell.

The tourists were equipped with tape recorders and my father sang for more than three hours. His voice boomed down the hill and bounced off the surface of the harbour, which was an unearthly blue on that hot August day, and was then reflected to the wharf and the fishing shanties where it was absorbed amidst the men who were baiting their lines for the next day's haul.

He sang all the old sea chanties which had come across from the old world and by which men like him had pulled ropes for generations, and he sang the East Coast sea songs which celebrated the sealing vessels of Northumberland Strait and the long liners of the Grand Banks, and of Anticosti, Sable Island, Grand Manan, Boston Harbor, Nantucket and Block Island. Gradually he shifted to the seemingly unending Gaelic drinking songs with their twenty or more verses and inevitable refrains, and the men in the shanties smiled at the coarseness of some of the verses and at the thought that the singer's immediate audience did not know what they were applauding nor recording to take back to staid old Boston. Later as the sun was setting he switched to the laments and the wild and haunting Gaelic war songs of those spattered Highland ancestors he had never seen, and when his voice ceased, the savage melancholy of three hundred years seemed to hang over the peaceful harbour and the quiet boats and the men leaning in the doorways of their shanties with their cigarettes glowing in the dusk and the women looking to the sea from their open windows with their children in their arms.

When he came home he threw the money he had earned on the kitchen table as he did with all his earnings but my mother refused to touch it and the next day he went with the rest of the men to bait his trawl in the shanties. The tourists came to the door that evening and my mother met them there and told them that her husband was not in although he was lying on the bed only a few feet away with the radio playing and the cigarette upon his lips. She stood in the doorway until they reluctantly went away.

In the winter they sent him a picture which had been taken on the day of the singing. On the back it said, "To Our Ernest Hemingway" and the "Our" was underlined. There was also an accompanying letter telling how much they had enjoyed themselves, how popular the tape was proving and explaining who Ernest Hemingway was. In a way it almost did look like one of those unshaven, taken-in-Cuba pictures of Hemingway. He looked both massive and incongruous in the setting. His bulky fisherman's clothes were too big for the green and white lawn chair in which he sat, and his rubber boots seemed to take up all of the well-clipped grass square. The beach umbrella jarred with his sunburned face and because he had already been singing for some time, his lips which chapped in the winds of spring and burned in the water glare of summer had already cracked in several places, producing tiny flecks of blood at their corners and on the whiteness of his teeth. The bracelets of brass chain which he wore to protect his wrists from chafing seemed abnormally large and his broad leather belt had been slackened and his heavy shirt and underwear were open at the throat revealing an uncultivated wilderness of white chest hair bordering on the semi-controlled stubble of his neck and chin. His blue eyes had looked directly into the camera and his hair was whiter than the two tiny clouds which hung over his left shoulder. The sea was behind him and its immense blue flatness stretched out to touch the arching blueness of the sky. It seemed very far away from him or else he was so much in the foreground that he seemed too big for it.

Each year another of my sisters would read the books and work in the restaurant. Sometimes they would stay out quite late on the hot summer nights and when they came up the stairs my mother would ask them many long and involved questions which they resented and tried to avoid. Before ascending the stairs they would go into my father's room and those of us who waited above could hear them throwing his clothes off the chair before sitting on it or the squeak of the bed as they sat on its edge. Sometimes they would talk to him a long time, the murmur of their voices blending with the music of the radio into a mysterious vapour-like sound which floated softly up the stairs.

I say this again as if it all happened at once and as if all of my sisters were of identical ages and like so many lemmings going into another sea and, again, it was of course not that way at all. Yet go they did, to Boston, to Montreal, to New York with the young men they met during the summers and later married in those far-away cities. The young men were very articulate and handsome and wore fine clothes and drove expensive cars and my sisters, as I said, were very tall and beautiful with their copper-coloured hair and were tired of darning socks and baking bread.

One by one they went. My mother had each of her daughters for fifteen years, then lost them for two and finally forever. None married a fisherman. My mother never accepted any of the young men, for in her eyes they seemed always a combination of the lazy, the effeminate, the dishonest and the unknown. They never seemed to do any physical work and she could not comprehend their luxurious vacations and she did not know whence they came nor who they were. And in the end she did not really care, for they were not of her people and they were not of her sea.

I say this now with a sense of wonder at my own stupidity in thinking I was somehow free and would go on doing well in school and playing and helping in the boat and passing into my early teens while streaks of grey began to appear in my mother's dark hair and my father's rubber boots dragged sometimes on the pebbles of the beach as he trudged home from the wharf. And there were but three of us in the house that had at one time been so loud.

Then during the winter that I was fifteen he seemed to grow old and ill at once. Most of January he lay upon the bed, smoking and reading and listening to the radio while the wind howled about the house and the needle-like snow blistered off the ice-covered harbour and the doors flew out of people's hands if they did not cling to them like death.

In February when the men began overhauling their lobster traps he still did not move, and my mother and I began to knit lobster trap headings in the evenings. The twine was as always very sharp and harsh, and blisters formed upon our thumbs and little paths of blood snaked quietly down between our fingers while the seals that had drifted down from distant Labrador wept and moaned like human children on the ice-floes of the Gulf.

In the daytime my mother's brother who had been my father's partner as long as I could remember also came to work upon the gear. He was a year older than my mother and was tall and dark and the father of twelve children.

By March we were very far behind and although I began to work very hard in the evenings I knew it was not hard enough and that there were but eight weeks left before the opening of the season on May first. And I knew that my mother worried and my uncle was uneasy and that all of our very lives depended on the boat being ready with her gear and two men, by the date of May the first. And I knew then that *David Copperfield* and *The Tempest* and all of those friends I had dearly come to love must really go forever. So I bade them all good-bye.

The night after my first full day at home and after my mother had gone upstairs he called me into his room where I sat upon the chair beside his bed. "You will go back tomorrow," he said simply.

I refused then, saying I had made my decision and was satisfied.

"That is no way to make a decision," he said, "and if you are satisfied I am not. It is best that you go back." I was almost angry then and told him as all children do that I wished he would leave me alone and stop telling me what to do.

He looked at me a long time then, lying there on the same bed on which he had fathered me those sixteen years before, fathered me his only son, out of who knew what emotions when he was already fifty-six and his hair had turned to snow. Then he swung his legs over the edge of the squeaking bed and sat facing me and looked into my own dark eyes with his of crystal blue and placed his hand upon my knee. "I am not telling you to do anything," he said softly, "only asking you."

The next morning I returned to school. As I left, my mother followed me to the porch and said, "I never thought a son of mine would choose useless books over the parents that gave him life."

In the weeks that followed he got up rather miraculously and the gear was ready and the *Jenny Lynn* was freshly painted by the last two weeks of April when the ice began to break up and the lonely screaming gulls returned to haunt the silver herring as they flashed within the sea.

On the first day of May the boats raced out as they had always done, laden down almost to the gunwales with their heavy cargoes of traps. They were almost like living things as they plunged through the waters of the spring and manoeuvred between the still floating icebergs of crystal white and emerald green on their way to the traditional grounds that they sought out every May. And those of us who sat that day in the high school on the hill, discussing the water imagery of Tennyson, watched them as they passed back and forth beneath us until by afternoon the piles of traps which had been stacked upon the wharf were no longer visible but were spread about the bottoms of the sea. And the *Jenny Lynn* went too, all day, with my uncle tall and dark, like a latter-day Tashtego[2] standing at the tiller with his legs wide apart and guiding her deftly between the floating pans of ice and my father in the stern standing in the same way with his hands upon the ropes that lashed the cargo to the deck. And at night my mother asked, "Well, how did things go in the boat today?"

And the spring wore on and the summer came and school ended in the third week of June and the lobster season on July first and I wished that the two things I loved so dearly did not exclude each other in a manner that was so blunt and too clear.

At the conclusion of the lobster season my uncle said he had been offered a berth on a deep sea dragger and had decided to accept. We all knew that he was leaving the *Jenny Lynn* forever and that before the next lobster season he would buy a boat of his own. He was expecting another child and would be supporting fifteen people by the next spring and could not chance my father against the family that he loved.

I joined my father then for the trawling season, and he made no protest and my mother was quite happy. Through the summer we baited the tubs of trawl in the afternoon and set them at sunset and revisited them in the darkness of the early morning. The men would come tramping by our house at four A.M. and we would join them and walk with them to the wharf and be on our way before the sun rose out of the ocean where it seemed to spend the night. If I was not up they would toss pebbles to my window and I would be very embarrassed and tumble downstairs to where my father lay fully clothed atop his bed, reading his book and listening to his radio and smoking his cigarette. When I appeared he would swing off his bed and put on his boots and be instantly ready and then we would take the lunches my mother had prepared the night before and walk off toward the sea. He would make no attempt to wake me himself.

It was in many ways a good summer. There were few storms and we were out almost every day and we lost a minimum of gear and seemed to land a maximum of fish and I tanned dark and brown after the manner of my uncles.

My father did not tan—he never tanned—because of his reddish complexion, and the salt water irritated his skin as it had for sixty years. He burned and reburned over and over again and his lips still cracked so that they bled when he smiled, and his arms, especially the left, still broke out into the oozing salt-water boils as they had ever since as a child I had first watched him soaking and bathing them in a variety of ineffectual solutions. The chafe-preventing bracelets of brass linked chain that all the men wore about their wrists in early spring were his the full season and he shaved but painfully and only once a week.

And I saw then, that summer, many things that I had seen all my life as if for the first time and I thought that perhaps my father had never been intended for a fisherman either physically or mentally. At least not in the manner of my uncles; he had never really loved it. And I remembered that, one evening in his room when we were talking about *David Copperfield*, he

2. A character in Herman Melville's *Moby Dick* (1851).

had said that he had always wanted to go to the university and I had dismissed it then in the way one dismisses his father's saying he would like to be a tight-rope walker, and we had gone on to talk about the Peggottys and how they loved the sea.

And I thought then to myself that there were many things wrong with all of us and all our lives and I wondered why my father, who was himself an only son, had not married before he was forty and then I wondered why he had. I even thought that perhaps he had had to marry my mother and checked the dates on the flyleaf of the Bible where I learned that my oldest sister had been born a prosaic eleven months after the marriage, and I felt myself then very dirty and debased for my lack of faith and for what I had thought and done.

And then there came into my heart a very great love for my father and I thought it was very much braver to spend a life doing what you really do not want rather than selfishly following forever your own dreams and inclinations. And I knew then that I could never leave him alone to suffer the iron-tipped harpoons which my mother would forever hurl into his soul because he was a failure as a husband and a father who had retained none of his own. And I felt that I had been very small in a little secret place within me and that even the completion of high school was for me a silly shallow selfish dream.

So I told him one night very resolutely and very powerfully that I would remain with him as long as he lived and we would fish the sea together. And he made no protest but only smiled through the cigarette smoke that wreathed his bed and replied, "I hope you will remember what you've said."

The room was now so filled with books as to be almost Dickensian, but he would not allow my mother to move or change them and he continued to read them, sometimes two or three a night. They came with great regularity now, and there were more hard covers, sent by my sisters who had gone so long ago and now seemed so distant and so prosperous, and sent also pictures of small red-haired grandchildren with baseball bats and dolls which he placed upon his bureau and which my mother gazed at wistfully when she thought no one would see. Red-haired grandchildren with baseball bats and dolls who would never know the sea in hatred or in love.

And so we fished through the heat of August and into the cooler days of September when the water was so clear we could almost see the bottom and the white mists rose like delicate ghosts in the early morning dawn. And one day my mother said to me, "You have given added years to his life."

And we fished on into October when it began to roughen and we could no longer risk night sets but took our gear out each morning and returned at the first sign of the squalls; and on into November when we lost three tubs of trawl and the clear blue water turned to a sullen grey and the trochoidal waves rolled rough and high and washed across our bows and decks as we ran within their troughs. We wore heavy sweaters now and the awkward rubber slickers and the heavy woollen mitts which soaked and froze into masses of ice that hung from our wrists like the limbs of gigantic monsters until we thawed them against the exhaust pipe's heat. And almost every day we would leave for home before noon, driven by the blasts of the northwest wind, coating our eyebrows with ice and freezing our eyelids closed as we leaned into a visibility that was hardly there, charting our course from the compass and the sea, running with the waves and between them but never confronting their towering might.

And I stood at the tiller now, on these homeward lunges, stood in the place and in the manner of my uncle, turning to look at my father and to shout over the roar of the engine and the slop of the sea to where he stood in the stern, drenched and dripping with the snow and the salt and the spray and his bushy eyebrows caked in ice. But on November twenty-first, when it seemed we might be making the final run of the season, I turned and he was not there and I knew even in that instant that he would never be again.

On November twenty-first the waves of the grey Atlantic are very very high and the waters are very cold and there are no signposts on the surface of the sea. You cannot tell where you have been five minutes before and in the squalls of snow you cannot see. And it takes longer than you would believe to check a boat that has been running before a gale and turn her ever so carefully in a wide and stupid circle, with timbers creaking and straining, back into the face of the storm. And you know that it is useless and that your voice does not carry the length of the boat and that even if you knew the original spot, the relentless waves would carry such a burden perhaps a mile or so by the time you could return. And you know also, the final irony, that your father like your uncles and all the men that form your past, cannot swim a stroke.

The lobster beds off the Cape Breton coast are still very rich and now, from May to July, their offerings are packed in crates of ice, and thundered by the gigantic transport trucks, day and night, through New Glasgow, Amherst, Saint John and Bangor and Portland and into Boston where they are tossed still living into boiling pots of water, their final home.

And though the prices are higher and the competition tighter, the grounds to which the *Jenny Lynn* once went remain untouched and unfished as they have for the last ten years. For if there are no signposts on the sea in storm there are certain ones in calm and the lobster bottoms were distributed in calm before any of us can remember and the grounds my father fished were those his father fished before him and there were others before and before and before. Twice the big boats have come from forty and fifty miles, lured by the promise of the grounds, and strewn the bottom with their traps and twice they have returned to find their buoys cut adrift and their gear lost and destroyed. Twice the Fisheries Officer and the Mounted Police have come and asked many long and involved questions and twice they have received no answers from the men leaning in the doors of their shanties and the women standing at their windows with their children in their arms. Twice they have gone away saying: "There are no legal boundaries in the Marine area"; "No one can own the sea"; "Those grounds don't wait for anyone."

But the men and the women, with my mother dark among them, do not care for what they say, for to them the grounds are sacred and they think they wait for me.

It is not an easy thing to know that your mother lives alone on an inadequate insurance policy and that she is too proud to accept any other aid. And that she looks through her lonely window onto the ice of winter and the hot flat calm of summer and the rolling waves of fall. And that she lies awake in the early morning's darkness when the rubber boots of the men scrunch upon the gravel as they pass beside her house on their way down to the wharf. And she knows that the footsteps never stop, because no man goes from her house, and she alone of all the Lynns has neither son nor son-in-law that walks toward the boat that will take him to the sea. And it is not an easy thing to know that your mother looks upon the sea with love and on you with bitterness because the one has been so constant and the other so untrue.

But neither is it easy to know that your father was found on November twenty-eighth, ten miles to the north and wedged between two boulders at the base of the rock-strewn cliffs where he had been hurled and slammed so many many times. His hands were shredded ribbons as were his feet which had lost their boots to the suction of the sea, and his shoulders came apart in our hands when we tried to move him from the rocks. And the fish had eaten his testicles and the gulls had pecked out his eyes and the white-green stubble of his whiskers had continued to grow in death, like the grass on graves, upon the purple, bloated mass that was his face. There was not much left of my father, physically, as he lay there with the brass chains on his wrists and the seaweed in his hair.

Acknowledgements

Care has been exercised to trace ownership of copyright material contained in this text. The publishers will gladly receive information that will enable them to rectify any reference or credit in subsequent editions.

Milton Acorn   "I've Tasted My Blood" © Milton Acorn 1969. Reprinted by permission.

Margaret Atwood   "This Is a Photograph of Me" from *The Circle Game*, published by House of Anansi Press. Copyright © Margaret Atwood 1966. Reprinted by permission of the publisher. "The Animals in That Country" from *The Animals in That Country* by Margaret Atwood. © Oxford University Press. Reprinted by permission of the publisher. "Brian the Still-Hunter" from *The Journals of Susanna Moodie* by Margaret Atwood. © Oxford University Press. Reprinted by permission of the publisher.

W. H. Auden   "A Summer Night," "Madrigal," "Seascape," "One Evening," "The Quarry," and "In Memory of W. B. Yeats" from *Collected Shorter Poems* by W. H. Auden, published by Faber and Faber Ltd. Reprinted by permission of the publisher.

Margaret Avison   "A Nameless One" and "In a Season of Unemployment" from *The Dumbfounding, Poems by Margaret Avison*, published by W. W. Norton & Company, Inc. Copyright © 1966 by Margaret Avison. Reprinted by permission of the publisher.

Donald Barthelme   "Report" from "Unspeakable Practices, Unnatural Acts" by Donald Barthelme. Copyright © 1967, 1968 by Donald Barthelme. Published by Farrar, Straus and Giroux, Inc. Reprinted by permission of the publisher.

John Betjeman   "In Westminster Abbey," "The City," and "The Licorice Fields at Pontefract" from *Collected Poems* by John Betjeman, published by John Murray (Publishers) Ltd. Reprinted by permission of the publisher.

Earle Birney   "David," "Way to the West," "The Bear on the Delhi Road," and "Meeting of Strangers" from *Collected Poems of Earle Birney*. Reprinted by permission of The Canadian Publishers, McClelland and Stewart, Limited, Toronto.

Elizabeth Bishop   "First Death in Nova Scotia" from *The Complete Poems* by Elizabeth Bishop. Copyright © 1962, 1969 by Elizabeth Bishop. Published by Farrar, Straus and Giroux, Ltd. Reprinted by permission of the publisher.

Laura Bohannan   "Shakespeare in the Bush" copyright by Laura Bohannan. Reprinted by permission.

George Bowering   "Grandfather" from *Touch: Selected Poems*. Reprinted by permission of The Canadian Publishers, McClelland and Stewart, Limited, Toronto.

John Clare   "I Am" from *The Poems of John Clare*, edited by Tibble. Published by J.M. Dent & Sons Ltd. Reprinted by permission of the publisher.

Fred Cogswell   "Watching These Two" published by Fiddlehead Poetry Books. Reprinted by permission of the author.

e. e. cummings   "my father moved through dooms of love," "anyone lived in a pretty how town," and "next to of course god america i" from *Complete Poems 1913-1962*, published by Harcourt Brace Jovanovich, Inc. Reprinted by permission.

C. Day Lewis   "Song" from *Selected Poems*, published by Harper and Row (Publishers) Inc. Reprinted by permission.

Emily Dickinson   "There's a Certain Slant of Light" and "I Heard a Fly Buzz" from *The Poems of Emily Dickinson*, edited by Thomas H. Johnson. Cambridge, Mass.: The Belknap Press of Harvard University Press. Copyright 1951 © 1955 by The President and Fellows of Harvard College. Reprinted by permission of the publisher and the Trustees of Amherst College.

T. S. Eliot   "The Love Song of J. Alfred Prufrock" and "Journey of the Magi" from *Collected Poems, 1909-1962* by T. S. Eliot, published by Faber and Faber Ltd. Reprinted by permission of the author.

Robert Frost   "Home Burial," "The Oven Bird," "Out, Out—," and "The Road Not Taken" from *The Poetry of Robert Frost*, edited by Edward Connery Lathem. Copyright 1916, 1930, 1939, © 1969 by Holt, Rinehart and Winston. Copyright 1944, © 1958 by Robert Frost. Copyright © 1967 by Lesley Frost Ballantine. Reprinted by permission of Holt, Rinehart and Winston, Publishers.

Northrop Frye "Culture and the National Will": Convocation Address at Carleton University, May 17, 1957. Reprinted by permission.

Bil Gilbert "Fast as an Elephant, Strong as an Ant" from *Sports Illustrated*, April 25, 1966. © 1966 Time Inc. Reprinted courtesy of *Sports Illustrated*.

Robert Graves "Warning to Children," "The Cool Web," and "The Naked and the Nude" from *Robert Graves*, published by William Collins and World. Reprinted by permission.

Graham Greene "The Destructors" from *Collected Stories*, published by The Bodley Head Ltd. and William Heinemann Ltd. Reprinted by permission of Laurence Pollinger Ltd.

Thom Gunn "On the Move" and "Blackie, the Electric Rembrandt" from *My Sad Captains* by Thom Gunn, published by Faber and Faber Ltd. Reprinted by permission of the publisher.

H. D. (Hilda Doolittle) "Heat" from *Collected Poems*, published by Faber and Faber Ltd. Reprinted by permission.

Ernest Hemingway "Soldier's Home" from *In Our Time* by Ernest Hemingway. Copyright 1925 by Charles Scribner's Sons; renewal copyright 1953 by Ernest Hemingway. Reprinted by permission of Charles Scribner's Sons.

Gerard Manley Hopkins "God's Grandeur," "The Windhover," "Spring and Fall," and "Pied Beauty" from *Poems of Gerard Manley Hopkins*, 4th ed. (1967), edited by W. H. Gardner and N. H. MacKenzie. Published by Oxford University Press for the Society of Jesus. Reprinted by permission of the publisher.

A. E. Housman "Terence, This Is Stupid Stuff" from *Collected Poems of A. E. Housman*, published by Jonathan Cape Ltd. Reprinted by permission of the publisher and The Society of Authors, literary representative of the Estate of A. E. Housman.

Ted Hughes "The Horses" and "Wind" from *Selected Poems*, published by Harper & Row, Publishers, Inc. Copyright © 1957 by Ted Hughes. Reprinted by permission of the publishers.

Randall Jarrell "The Death of the Ball-Turret Gunner" from *Complete Poems*, published by Farrar, Straus & Giroux, Inc. Reprinted by permission of the publisher.

James Joyce "The Boarding House" from "Dubliners" in *The Essential James Joyce*, published by Viking Penguin Inc. Copyright © 1967 by the Estate of James Joyce. Reprinted by permission of the publisher.

Patrick Kavanagh "The Great Hunger" excerpted from *The Great Hunger* (1942), published by The Cuala Press. Reprinted by permission.

A. M. Klein "The Rocking Chair" and "Autobiographical" from *The Collected Poems of A. M. Klein*, edited by Miriam Waddington. Copyright © McGraw-Hill Ryerson Limited, 1974. Reprinted by permission.

Philip Larkin "Church Going" from *The Less Deceived*, published by The Marvell Press, England. Reprinted by permission. "High Windows" from *High Windows*, published by Faber and Faber Ltd. Reprinted by permission. "Ambulances" from *The Whitsun Weddings*, published by Faber and Faber Ltd. Reprinted by permission.

D.H. Lawrence "The Horse-Dealer's Daughter" from *The Collected Short Stories of D. H. Lawrence*, published by William Heinemann Ltd. Reprinted by permission of Laurence Pollinger Ltd. and the Estate of the late Mrs. Frieda Lawrence Ravagli.

Irving Layton "Keine Lazarovitch, 1870–1959" and "Song for Naomi" from *Selected Poems*. Reprinted by permission of The Canadian Publishers, McClelland and Stewart, Limited, Toronto.

Kenneth Leslie "Halibut Cove Harvest" from *By Stubborn Stars and Other Poems* by Kenneth Leslie. Published by Ryerson Press.

Sinclair Lewis "How I Wrote a Novel on Trains and beside the Kitchen Sink" from *The Man from Main Street*, edited by H. E. Maule and M. H. Cane. Published by Random House. Reprinted by permission.

Dorothy Livesay "Day and Night" from *Collected Poems: The Two Seasons* by Dorothy Livesay. Copyright Dorothy Livesay, 1972. Reprinted by permission of McGraw-Hill Ryerson Limited.

Douglas Lochhead "Poet Talking" and "Winter Landscape—Halifax" from *Collected Poems: The Full Furnace* by Douglas Lochhead. Copyright © Douglas Lochhead, 1975. Reprinted by permission of McGraw-Hill Ryerson Limited.

Gwendolyn MacEwen "Flight One" from *Armies of the Moon*, published by The Macmillan Co. of Canada Ltd. Reprinted by permission.

Alistair MacLeod "The Boat" from *The Last Salt Gift of Blood*. Reprinted by permission of The Canadian Publishers, McClelland and Stewart, Limited, Toronto.

Louis MacNeice   "Snow" and "Bagpipe" from *The Collected Poems of Louis MacNeice* by Louis MacNeice, published by Faber and Faber Ltd. Reprinted by permission of the publisher.

Jay Macpherson   "The Fisherman" from *The Boatman and Other Poems* by Jay Macpherson, published by Oxford University Press. © Oxford University Press. Reprinted by permission of the publisher.

Bernard Malamud   "Naked Nude" from *Idiots First*, published by Farrar, Straus & Giroux, Inc. Reprinted by permission of the publisher.

Eli Mandel   "Houdini" from *An Idiot Joy*, published by Hurtig Publishers. Reprinted by permission of Eli Mandel.

Katherine Mansfield   "The Garden Party" from *Collected Stories*, published by Alfred A. Knopf, Inc. Reprinted by permission.

Marianne Moore   "Poetry" from *Collected Poems*, published by The Macmillan Co. of Canada Ltd. Reprinted by permission.

Alice Munro   "Material" from *Something I've Been Meaning to Tell You* by Alice Munro. Reprinted by permission of McGraw-Hill Ryerson Ltd. Copyright © Alice Munro, 1974.

Alleen Pace Nilsen   "Sexism in English: A Feminist View" from *Female Studies VI: Closer to the Ground*. Copyright © 1972 by Nancy Hoffman, Cynthia Secor, and Adrian Tinsley. Reprinted by permission of The Feminist Press, Old Westbury, N. Y.

Alden Nowlan   "Warren Pryor" from *Under the Ice*, published by Ryerson Press. Reprinted by permission of the author. "The Bull Moose" and "The Execution" from *Playing the Jesus Game*, published by New Books Ltd. Reprinted by permission of the author.

Tillie Olsen   "I Stand Here Ironing" from *Tell Me a Riddle*, published by Dell Publishing Co. Inc. Reprinted by permission.

George Orwell   "Politics and the English Language" from *Shooting An Elephant and Other Essays*, published by Martin, Secker and Warburg Ltd. Reprinted by permission of Mrs. Sonia Brownell Orwell and the publisher.

Wilfred Owen   "Dulce et Decorum Est," "Miners," "Strange Meeting," and "Anthem for Doomed Youth" from *Collected Poems*, edited by C. Day Lewis. Published by Chatto and Windus Ltd. Reprinted by permission of The Owen Estate and the publisher.

P. K. Page   "The Stenographers" from *Cry Ararat*. Reprinted by permission of The Canadian Publishers, McClelland and Stewart, Limited, Toronto, and the author.

Sylvia Plath   "Black Rook in Rainy Weather" from *The Colossus* by Sylvia Plath, published by Faber and Faber London Ltd. Copyright Ted Hughes 1971. Reprinted by permission of Ted Hughes.

Ezra Pound   "In a Station of the Metro" from *Personae*, copyright 1926 by Ezra Pound; from *The Cantos*, copyright 1934, 1948 by Ezra Pound. Reprinted by permission of New Directions Publishing Corporation.

E. J. Pratt   "The Shark" and "Silences" from *Collected Poems, Second Edition*, edited by Northrop Frye. Published by The Macmillan Co. of Canada Ltd. Reprinted by permission.

Al Purdy   "The Country North of Belleville," "Lament for the Dorsets," and "Wilderness Gothic" from *Selected Poems*. Reprinted by permission of The Canadian Publishers, McClelland and Stewart, Limited, Toronto.

John Crowe Ransom   "Piazza Piece" from *Selected Poems, Third Revised Edition*, published by Alfred A. Knopf, Inc. Reprinted by permission.

James Reaney   "The Katzenjammer Kids" from *Poems*, published by New Press Ltd. Reprinted by permission of Press Porcépic, Victoria, B.C.

Adrienne Rich   "A Valediction Forbidding Mourning" from *The Will to Change, Poems 1968–1970*, by Adrienne Rich. Copyright © 1971 by W. W. Norton & Company, Inc. Reprinted by permission of the publisher.

Mordecai Richler   "Why I Write" from *Canadian Writing Today*, published by Peter Smith. Reprinted by permission.

Charles G. D. Roberts   "The Tantramar Revisited" from *Collected Poems of Sir Charles G. D. Roberts*. Reprinted by permission of McGraw-Hill Ryerson Limited.

Edwin Arlington Robinson   "How Annandale Went Out" and "Karma" from *Collected Poems*, published by The Macmillan Company of Canada Ltd. Reprinted by permission.

Theodore Roethke   "In a Dark Time" from *Collected Poems of Theodore Roethke*. Copyright © 1960 by Beatrice Roethke, Administratrix of the Estate of Theodore Roethke. Reprinted by permission of Doubleday & Company, Inc.

Sinclair Ross   "The Painted Door" from *The Lamp at Noon and Other Stories*. Reprinted by permission of The Canadian Publishers, McClelland and Stewart, Limited, Toronto.

Siegfried Sassoon "Everyone Sang" from *Collected Poems*, published by Viking Penguin Inc. Reprinted by permission of the publisher.

M. H. Scargill "Canadians Speak Canadian" reprinted from *Saturday Night*, December 8, 1956. Reprinted by permission of *Saturday Night* magazine.

Duncan Campbell Scott "The Forsaken" from *The Selected Poetry of Duncan Campbell Scott*, edited by Glenn Clever. Published by Tecumseh Press. Reprinted by permission of John Aylen, Ottawa, Canada.

F. R. Scott "Calamity" from *Events and Signals*, published by Ryerson Press, 1954. Reprinted by permission of the author. "The Canadian Authors Meet" and "W.L.M.K." from *Selected Poems*, published by Oxford University Press. Reprinted by permission.

Anne Sexton "Cinderella" from *Transformations* by Anne Sexton, published by Houghton Mifflin Company. Copyright © 1971 by Anne Sexton. Reprinted by permission of the publisher.

A. J. M. Smith "The Lonely Land" from *The Classic Shade*. Reprinted by permission of The Canadian Publishers, McClelland and Stewart, Limited, Toronto.

Stevie Smith "Not Waving but Drowning" from *Selected Poems of Stevie Smith*, published by New Directions Publishing Corp. Copyright © 1964 by Stevie Smith. Reprinted by permission of James MacGibbon, executor of the Estate of the late Stevie Smith. "The Best Beast of the Fat-Stock Show at Earls Court" from *Best Beast*, published by Alfred A. Knopf, Inc. Reprinted by permission.

Raymond Souster "The Six-Quart Basket" reprinted from *The Colour of the Times: The Collected Poems*, published by Ryerson Press. Reprinted by permission of Oberon Press.

Stephen Spender "The Landscape near an Aerodrome" from *Collected Poems*, published by Faber and Faber Ltd. Reprinted by permission of the publisher.

Wallace Stevens "Thirteen Ways of Looking at a Blackbird" from *The Collected Poems of Wallace Stevens*, published by Alfred A. Knopf, Inc. Reprinted by permission.

Audrey Thomas "Initram" from *Songs My Father Taught Me*, published by Bobbs-Merrill Co. Reprinted by permission.

Dylan Thomas "The Force That through the Green Fuse Drives the Flower," "Fern Hill," and "Do Not Go Gentle into That Good Night" from *Collected Poems*, published by J. M. Dent and Sons Ltd., England. Reprinted by permission of the Trustees for the copyright for the late Dylan Thomas and the publishers.

Edward Thomas "Old Man" from *Collected Poems*, published by Faber and Faber Ltd. Reprinted by permission.

James Thurber "The Bear Who Let It Alone," "The Little Girl and the Wolf," and "The Unicorn in the Garden" from *Fables for Our Time* by James Thurber, published by Harper Brothers. Reprinted by permission of Mrs. Helen Thurber.

W. D. Valgardson "Hunting" from *God Is Not a Fish Inspector*, published by Oberon Press. Reprinted by permission of the publisher.

Miriam Waddington "Advice to the Young" from *Driving Home* by Miriam Waddington, © Oxford University Press. Reprinted by permission of the publishers.

Robert Warshow "The Gangster as Tragic Hero" from *Immediate Experience: Movies, Comics, Theatre and Other Aspects of Popular Culture*, published by Atheneum Publishers. Reprinted by permission.

William Carlos Williams "The Dance" from *Collected Later Poems*, copyright 1944 by William Carlos Williams. Reprinted by permission of New Directions, New York.

William Butler Yeats "The Magi," "Leda and the Swan," "Sailing to Byzantium," "The Choice," and "Lapis Lazuli" from *Collected Poems*, published by Macmillan London Ltd. Reprinted courtesy of M. B. Yeats, Anne Yeats, A. P. Watt Ltd. and the publisher.

Nationality and Date Index

In cases of dual nationality or citizenship (e.g., T. S. Eliot and W. H. Auden), authors are listed according to country of birth.

Canada

British Isles (including Ireland) and Commonwealth (excluding Canada)

Author Index

Title and First Line Index